International Commercial Arbitration in Hong Kong

International Commercial Arbitration in Hong Kong

A Guide

Stephen D. Mau

The research funding for this book was sponsored by
the Hong Kong Institute of Surveyors.

THE HONG KONG INSTITUTE OF
SURVEYORS
香港測量師學會

HKU
PRESS
香港大學出版社

Hong Kong University Press
The University of Hong Kong
Pok Fu Lam Road
Hong Kong
https://hkupress.hku.hk

ISBN 978-988-8528-22-6 (*Hardback*)
ISBN 978-988-8528-23-3 (*Paperback*)

British Library Cataloguing-in-Publication Data
A catalogue record for this book is available from the British Library.

Digitally printed

Contents

Foreword

Historically, the role of Hong Kong in international arbitration was limited. That was the reflection of the state of international arbitration in Asia at the time up to the 1980s. So Professor Julian DM Lew QC, in his key note address entitled 'Increasing Influence of Asia in International Arbitration' at the inaugural Hong Kong Arbitration Week in 2012, observed that "Asia's past contribution to international arbitration has been small" and that "[t]he Asian region was largely a bystander to the development of international arbitration and had little influence and perhaps little interest."[1]

His view fits in with my own recollections. I was first involved in Hong Kong arbitration over 30 years ago. It was of course already an established arbitration centre with a healthy diet of construction and maritime cases but with a strong connection to Hong Kong. There were no especial innovations in the practice or law of arbitration. Within a few years, however, there was an explosion of international cases. Moreover, in common with a limited number of other centres, Hong Kong is now in the forefront of arbitral innovations and has established itself as a firm favourite with the consumers of international arbitration services.

1985 saw two important developments which have greatly contributed to this development of Hong Kong as an international arbitration centre. One was the promulgation of the UNCITRAL Model Law in 1985 and its subsequent success in many countries including just a few years later its adoption by Hong Kong. That coupled with the continuous recognition by Asian governments of the nature and potential benefits of arbitration as a method for resolving private disputes galvanized the development of arbitration in Asia. Hong Kong adopted the Model Law, including the 2006 amendments, in June 2011, by introducing the Arbitration Ordinance (Cap 609).

Another event in 1985 was the establishment of the Hong Kong International Arbitration Centre. Led by successive far-sighted Chairpersons and Secretaries General and assisted by a Council with strong international representation HKIAC

[1] Julian D. M. Lew, 'Increasing Influence of Asia in International Arbitration', *Asian Dispute Review* (Hong Kong International Arbitration Centre (HKIAC); Hong Kong International Arbitration Centre (HKIAC) 2014, Volume 16 Issue 1) pp. 4–9.

has been a great success. The Centre and arbitrations there have not been a pale imitation of other arbitration centres. On the contrary, there have been specifically Hong Kong and Asian innovations in a number of areas being ahead of other institutions. At the heart of this are the HKIAC Rules which have been updated to keep pace with the demands of arbitration in the region. Users need to know how these rules operate.

As for the law in Hong Kong, the Arbitration Ordinance provides a modern and reliable statutory framework for the conduct of arbitration in Hong Kong. Importantly, and consistent with the letter and spirit of the Model Law, the Arbitration Ordinance only permits minimal curial intervention—in cases expressly envisaged by the law, such as granting interim relief in support of arbitration, assisting with taking of evidence and deciding challenges to awards, in the context of set aside and/or enforcement proceedings. So far Hong Kong courts have been careful not to abuse their arbitration-related powers and adhered strictly to the principal of minimal curial intervention, at the heart of the UNCITRAL Model Law.

Hong Kong has also proved a popular choice for international arbitration.

It is accessible. Hong Kong is within a five-hour flight to half of the world's population. Visa and entry requirements are minimised. Visitors may, for example, obtain a visa for a short-term visit on arrival. Anyone who has not been able to secure a witness or expert attendance due to visa issues—and these things happen more often than you think—will no doubt appreciate the potential benefits of this visa regime for the smooth conduct of arbitration proceedings.

Hong Kong also displays an extraordinarily large pool of multilingual professionals who can easily compete with leading arbitral centres. The city is a home to more than 1,300 barristers[2] and 1,299 registered foreign lawyers (from 31 jurisdictions),[3] not to mention an impressive, in size and quality of its members, pool of non-legal professionals, including engineers, accountants, surveyors, and architects (particularly important for construction disputes).

Finally, when it comes to *where* to hold a hearing, Hong Kong has excellent hearing facilities. HKIAC, Hong Kong's flagship arbitral institution, boasts of 20 meeting spaces including seven hearing rooms and 10 conference rooms. (I declare an interest as a past Vice Chairman). In October 2016, the Centre announced that it would offer its hearing and meeting rooms to parties free-of-charge in respect of dispute resolution proceedings administered by HKIAC in which at least one party is a State listed on the OECD DAC List of ODA assistance.[4]

---

2 See the introductory page on the Hong Kong Bar Association website: http://www.hkba.org/the-bar/aboutus/index.html (accessed 28 October 2018).

3 Law Society of Hong Kong, statistics as of 31 December 2015, available at: http://www.hklawsoc.org.hk/pub_e/about/ (accessed 28 October 2018).

4 http://www.hkiac.org/news/free-hearing-space-cases-involving-states.

Adaptiveness/Ability to React to Users' Changing Demands

Hong Kong has also an enviable ability to innovate and to listen and respond—promptly and adequately—to the changing needs and preferences of the users of international arbitration.

Some examples will suffice. Traditionally, Hong Kong law did not permit third party funding for litigation, except in few narrow circumstances. However, as the use and demand for litigation finance in arbitration increased, in 2013 Hong Kong's Law Reform Commission launched a public consultation on whether to permit third party funding for arbitration in Hong Kong. In October 2016, the Commission issued a comprehensive report recommending that third party funding should be expressly permitted for arbitrations seated in Hong Kong, and in June 2017 Hong Kong passed a bill amending the Arbitration Ordinance to allow third party funding in arbitration.[5]

The most recent manifestation of Hong Kong's receptiveness to the changing needs and demands of the users of international arbitration is the revision of the 2013 HKIAC Arbitration Rules. The 2018 HKIAC Arbitration Rules contain a number of notable market-driven innovations. So, the Rules introduce the early determination procedure, which expressly empowers an arbitral tribunal to decide any point of law or fact by way of early determination on the basis that it is "manifestly without merit," "manifestly outside the arbitral tribunal's jurisdiction," or that, even if the point were "assumed to be correct," it would not result in an award in favour of the party that submitted it (Article 43). This mechanism was introduced in recognition of increasing demands for early determinations—a procedure already available under certain other rules but absent from many others. This is potentially a useful tool to narrowing the issues in dispute, increasing the prospects of settlement, or even providing a full answer to claims.

Other notable innovations include:

- an arbitral tribunal's enhanced powers with respect to the conduct of multiple arbitrations where the same tribunal is constituted and where common issues of law or fact are involved (Article 30) (an arbitral tribunal now has a menu of case management options: to run the arbitrations concurrently, consecutively, or even suspend any of the arbitrations pending resolution of the others); and
- provisions clarifying the test for and streamlining the process of emergency arbitration (Schedule 4).

Together with the 2018 Rules, HKIAC has also released a Practice Note on Appointment of Arbitrators, which sets out its general practice of appointing arbitrators, including a non-exhaustive list of the many factors that the Centre considers when selecting arbitrators. The Note provides some useful insights into what has

5 The Arbitration and Mediation Legislation (Third Party Funding) (Amendment) Bill 2016, 14 June 2017.

long been one of the most enigmatic aspects of the arbitral process—appointment of arbitrators—and thus represents an important step towards greater transparency in arbitrations conducted under HKIAC's Rules.

So, all this shows that thus far Hong Kong has proved to be a flexible, reliable, and modern platform for resolution of disputes that values innovation. Indeed, Hong Kong is consistently recognised as one of the leading arbitral seats for resolving international disputes. The 2018 Queen Mary survey, for example, placed Hong Kong among the top five global dispute resolution seats, along with London, Paris, Geneva, and Singapore.[6] Hong Kong also appears to be a popular seat for Russian disputes. While most recent statistics is not available, according to the Russian Arbitration Association Survey conducted in 2016, 22.5% of the users chose Hong Kong as a seat in the contracts drafted in 2014–2015.[7]

This work by Stephen D. Mau is therefore very welcome and very much needed. With its own practices, law, and rules it is no longer possible to get by in a Hong Kong arbitration by reliance purely on knowledge of the law and practices of other jurisdictions. Stephen's excellent work provides therefore an important reference work for those embarking in Hong Kong arbitration. Additionally, in a broader perspective, it also provides an extremely useful introduction to arbitration law and practice in an eminently clear, logical, and readable way.

For the practitioner this book will also provide an important source of theoretical understanding and practical guidance; from the initial choice of arbitration and choice of rules to the appointment of arbitrators and throughout the reference. The important topics of jurisdiction and arbitral duties are dealt with in a thoughtful way with of course ample citation of authority to rules, laws, and cases. Practical guidance is provided on such topics as the preliminary meeting and the difference between a memorials-based and a pleadings-based approach. It also covers some critical practical areas such as the giving and reception of expert evidence and the duties this places on the expert.

The work also rightly deals not only with the contents of the award but also the recognition and enforcement of awards. This is a topic of very great importance in an international arbitration.

Nor does the author ignore the very practical questions of how to improve efficiency and reduce cost in arbitration as he devotes a chapter to this important question.

I am privileged therefore to have been asked to provide this foreword and happy to commend it.

Lord Goldsmith QC, PC
Attorney General for England and Wales (2001–2007)
Vice Chairman of the Hong Kong International Arbitration Centre
London
January 2019

6 http://www.arbitration.qmul.ac.uk/research/2018/ (accessed 16 October 2018).
7 https://shop.americanbar.org/PersonifyImages/ProductFiles/297648970/Roundtable%206.pdf.

Foreword

"Dispute resolution" is now a popular, if not fashionable, term. Included in the concept of dispute resolution are different modes of resolving or settling disputes, and arbitration is certainly one of the key components. Arbitration is no stranger to the Hong Kong community. Indeed, researches reveal that arbitration was used as a means of dispute resolution in Hong Kong more than a century ago. However, the more significant modern development of arbitration in Hong Kong started in the early 1980s, especially in the context of construction disputes and with the setting up of the Hong Kong International Arbitration Centre. Since then, arbitration has become a well-received means of dispute resolution in different areas and Hong Kong has established herself as one of the important international arbitration hubs in the region.

In the past, there were not many arbitration textbooks produced by local authors. The trend, however, has changed, and the change is a positive one. This book, written by a learned author who has many years of experience of dispute resolution both as a practitioner and as an academic, provides a cogent and succinct exposition of the law of arbitration. Apart from the conventional areas which would certainly be covered, the contents of this book illustrate the recent changes we have seen in the development of arbitration in Hong Kong. Emergency relief and third-party funding, for instance, are two of the topics covered in this book. These two topics currently command much attention in the arbitration community in Hong Kong and in the region. In short, this book provides handy and useful assistance to both lawyers and non-lawyers who are in one way or another involved in arbitration or who are interested in the dispute resolution regime of Hong Kong.

I started off by saying that arbitration has a long history in Hong Kong. I would like to conclude by saying that arbitration will have a good prospect in the future. Globalization and development of international trade aside, international arbitration has an important role in the context of the Belt and Road Initiative and that is one of the areas where Hong Kong can and should contribute. Needless to say, much more work would have to be done to promote Hong Kong as an arbitration centre. Publication of books such as this should be encouraged and commended as it would enable more people to understand the arbitration regime in Hong Kong as well as to induce more research and publication in this area.

Last but certainly not least, I congratulate the learned author of this book for the timely publication of this work, which I believe would be a useful addition to the bookshelf of practitioners and students of dispute resolution.

Rimsky Yuen
GBM, SC, JP
Secretary for Justice, Hong Kong SAR (2012–2018)
January 2019

Foreword

The Hong Kong Institute of Surveyors is delighted to sponsor the publication of this reference book, *International Commercial Arbitration in Hong Kong: A Guide*, which is not only written for the HKIS members, but also for global business people and students. Additionally, it is a useful reference for the general public.

The local construction industry continues to grow and evolve. This growth and evolution results in differences and disputes arising from commercial relationships. In response to these disagreements, *International Commercial Arbitration in Hong Kong: A Guide* seeks to offer a sufficiently detailed introduction to methods of resolving disputes other than court litigation, particularly arbitration. This book firstly introduces various alternative dispute resolution solutions before going into detail to review international commercial arbitration. *International Commercial Arbitration in Hong Kong: A Guide* includes a wide range of examples and court cases to illustrate the principles to professionals and non-law students. It is written in accessible language with detailed notes and references expanding upon the principles.

The subjects covered in this book are relevant to both professional and lay readers. It also serves as an excellent reference for undergraduate and postgraduate students who are studying courses related to the field.

Sr Dr Tony Ka Tung Leung
President (2018–2019)
The Hong Kong Institute of Surveyors
28 January 2019

1

Overview of Alternative Dispute Resolution and Arbitration in Hong Kong

I. Introduction

The purpose of this chapter is to provide a cursory overview of some of the Alternative Dispute Resolution [hereinafter "ADR"] choices or processes available in Hong Kong. This overview is to demonstrate the vast array of ADR processes available to parties involved in a dispute[1] and also to compare and contrast ADR with arbitration in particular.

For this chapter, the term *ADR* refers to dispute resolution processes other than court litigation, including arbitration.[2] As this author noted in another publication, ADR evolves in order to satisfy the needs of its users, in substantial part because ADR is flexible and frequently is a process determined by agreement between the parties.[3] This party control of the dispute resolution process is referred to as being *party-driven* or as *party autonomy*.[4] Thus, ADR is unlike court litigation. A listing of some ADR processes follows with a short description of that particular ADR process.[5] This chapter concludes with a discussion of the influence which the two primary and different legal cultures might have upon dispute resolution.

---

[1] Butterworths Hong Kong Arbitration Law Handbook para. [2.09] (Damon YC So, Christopher To *et al.*, eds., 2nd ed. 2018) [hereinafter So & To] defines "dispute" as: "A dispute will exist unless there is a clear and unequivocal admission not only of liability but also of quantum" (citations omitted).

[2] In some jurisdictions, arbitration is distinguished from ADR in that arbitration, like court litigation, results in a final and binding decision known as an *award*. For example, the International Chamber of Commerce distinguishes arbitration from ADR. Donald L Marston, *The Internationalisation of ADR* ICLR 16, 19 [2005].
In other jurisdictions, *e.g.*, the United States and Canada, arbitration comes under the heading of ADR. In the United Kingdom, arbitration is not generally considered to be a form of ADR. Despite this, the UK government includes arbitration within its definition of ADR. Rupert Choat, *ADR*, paper delivered at the IBC Legal's Construction Law Summer School held at Cambridge University, 5–8 Sep. 2016, p. 3 [hereinafter Choat].

[3] Stephen D. Mau, *Arbitration to Mediation to Arbitration with the Same Parties in the Same International Commercial Dispute Before the Same Neutral: Innovative Evolution or Receipt for Disaster?* 31(8) Construction Law Journal 429 (2015).

[4] Arbitration in Hong Kong: A Practical Guide paras. 6.003–6.019 (The Hon Chief Justice Geoffrey Ma and Denis Brock, eds., 4th ed. 2017) [hereinafter Ma & Brock].

[5] *See also id.* at Chapt. 4.

II. Adjudication

The term *adjudication* is defined as the "exercise of a power delegated by contract to a third party to resolve disputes on an interim or final basis as they arise without recourse to formal arbitration or litigation."[6] Adjudication is frequently associated with construction disputes relating to payment.[7] Adjudication is considered to be "rough and ready justice"[8] or a "pay first, argue later"[9] ADR process where the decision is binding upon the disputing parties until the conclusion of the construction works or project whereupon the adjudication decision can be challenged, for example, in an arbitration or in litigation. Adjudication is intended to ensure that cash flow, the life-blood of many small contractors or subcontractors,[10] can be preserved rather than one party withholding payment as a result of a dispute which will not be heard or decided until the completion of the construction works or project. Adjudication is provided for in the UK's *Housing Grants, Construction and*

---

[6] The Academy of Experts, *The Language of ADR* (hereinafter TAE). *See* TAE's website: https://www.academyofexperts.org/alternative-dispute-resolution/language-adr (last visited 11 Jul. 2017).

The Hong Kong International Arbitration Centre [hereinafter HKIAC] provides this definition:

> Adjudications are a simple, effective and quick method of resolving disputes.
>
> Adjudications are conducted by a sole adjudicator in accordance with the Rules and terms of the contract and its applicable law.
>
> Adjudicators make decisions which are binding on the parties; in most cases the decision of an adjudicator can be revised in another forum such as arbitration. Adjudications are common in construction disputes.

Id. at: http://www.hkiac.org/adjudication/what-is-adjudication (last visited 11 Jul. 2017).

Development Bureau, *Proposed 'Security of Payment' Legislation for Construction Industry* (Jun. 2015) translates "adjudication" as 審裁. Available at: http://www.devb.gov.hk/filemanager/en/content_880/SOPL_leaflet.pdf (last visited 10 Aug. 2017).

For a reference source on adjudication in the United Kingdom, *see, e.g.*, Sir Peter Coulson, Coulson on Construction Adjudication (3rd ed. 2013).

[7] Hong Kong's Construction Industry Council explained:

> The specific issue to be resolved will be referred to decision by a third party neutral, the Adjudicator. The Adjudicator produces a decision after the parties present their evidence and made their written and/or oral submissions. The decision is binding in the interim, that is, during the currency of the works. But the Adjudicator's decision is not final and can be challenged in post-completion arbitration. Adjudication has not been commonly used in Hong Kong. It was provided for as a mandatory process in the Airport Core Programme (ACP) in 1990s, in which four construction disputes were resolved in two adjudications with no further steps taken to challenge the adjudicator's decisions. One other adjudication was conducted in 2009 in another context.
>
> . . . voluntary adjudication has been adopted in capital engineering works contracts of the Government with contract value exceeding HK$200 million.

Construction Industry Council, *Reference Materials for Application of Dispute Resolution in Construction Contracts* 24 (Version 2, Aug. 2015) [hereinafter CIC]. This publication may be found at the following website: http://www.cic.hk/cic_data/pdf/about_cic/publications/eng/reference_materials/Reference%20Materials%20Dispute%20Resolution%20(August%202015)_e.pdf (last visited 11 Jul. 2017).

[8] As the court stated in *RSL (South West) Ltd v Stansell Ltd* [2003] EWHC 1390, at para. 31:

> The price, which Parliament, and to a large extent the industry, has considered justified, is that the procedure adopted in the interests of speed is inevitably somewhat rough and ready and carries with it the risk of significant injustice. That risk can be minimised by adjudicators maintaining a firm grasp upon the principles of natural justice and applying them without fear or favour.

[9] *See, e.g.*, International Contractual and Statutory Adjudication 251 (Andrew Burr, ed., 2017); James Pickavance, A Practical Guide to Construction Adjudication 479 (2016).

[10] *See, e.g.*, *Modern Engineering Ltd v Gilbert-Ash* [1974] AC 689.

Regeneration Act 1996; Malaysia's *Construction Industry Payment and Adjudication Act 2012*; and Hong Kong's pending Security of Payment legislation.

III. Arbitration

A long-established ADR process, arbitration is defined as:

> the private judicial resolution by an arbitrator of a civil dispute or difference (which may be legal, technical or commercial, or a combination of these), by the agreement of the parties. The arbitrator is a neutral and independent person, other than a judge in a court of competent jurisdiction, who is selected by or on behalf of the parties on the basis of his expertise, reputation and experience in the legal, professional or economic speciality from which the dispute stems. The normal outcome of the process is an award which is final, legally binding and ultimately enforceable in court in the same manner as a judgement.[11]

The Asian region is amply represented by arbitral institutions in Hong Kong,[12] Kuala Lumpur, mainland China, Seoul, and Singapore.[13] We discuss more about arbitral institutions in the following chapters.

---

[11] Robert Morgan, The Arbitration Ordinance of Hong Kong: A Commentary 1 (1997).
2 Halsbury's Laws of Hong Kong para. [25.001] (2nd ed. 2016) provides this definition:

> Arbitration is the process by which a dispute or difference between two or more parties as to their mutual legal rights and liabilities is referred to and determined in a judicial manner, with binding effect, by the application of law by one or more persons (the arbitral tribunal) instead of by a court of law. The decision of the arbitral tribunal is usually called an award. (citation omitted)

For a discussion on the meaning of the phrase "dispute or difference," *see, e.g.*, So & To, *supra* note 1, at para. [20.09].
The Hong Kong *Arbitration Ordinance* (Cap. 609) § 2 translates "arbitration" as 仲裁.
For a review of the history of arbitration, *see, e.g.*, Redfern and Hunter on International Arbitration Chapt. 1 (Nigel Blackaby *et al.*, eds., 6th ed. 2015) [hereinafter Redfern & Hunter]. *Id.* at para. 1.04 provides this definition:

> Arbitration is essentially a very simple method of resolving disputes. Disputants agree to submit their disputes to an individual whose judgement they are prepared to trust. Each puts its case to this decision maker, this private individual – in a word, this 'arbitrator'. He or she listens to the parties, considers the facts and the arguments, and makes a decision. That decision is final and binding on the parties – and it is final and binding because the parties have agreed that it should be, rather than because of the coercive power of any state. Arbitration, in short, is an effective way of obtaining a final and binding decision on a dispute, or series of disputes, without reference to a court of law (although, because of national laws and international treaties such as the New York Convention, that decision will generally be enforceable by a court of law if the losing party fails to implement voluntarily). (footnote omitted)

[12] The Hong Kong International Arbitration Centre ranked third internationally after the International Chamber of Commerce in Paris and the London Court of International Arbitration according to an international survey. *2015 International Arbitration Survey: Improvements and Innovations in International Arbitration*, Queen Mary University of London 12 (2015). Available at: www.arbitration.qmul.ac.uk/docs/164761.pdf (last visited 11 Jul. 2017).

[13] The Singapore International Arbitration Centre ranked fourth in the same survey. *Id.*

IV. Conciliation

"Conciliation and Mediation are often used interchangeably and indiscriminately."[14] In this book, conciliation[15] is distinguished from mediation.[16] Therefore, we use the following definition of the term *conciliation*:

> a process in which the parties to a dispute, with the assistance of a dispute resolution practitioner (the conciliator), identify the issues in dispute, develop options, consider alternatives and endeavour to reach an agreement. The conciliator may have an advisory role on the content of the dispute or the outcome of its resolution, but not a determinative role. The conciliator may advise on or determine the process of conciliation whereby resolution is attempted, and may make suggestions for terms of settlement, give expert advice on likely settlement terms, and may actively encourage the participants to reach an agreement.
>
> Note: there are wide variations in meanings for 'conciliation', which may be used to refer to a range of processes used to resolve complaints and disputes including:
>
> — Informal discussions held between the parties and an external agency in an endeavour to avoid, resolve or manage a dispute
> — Combined processes in which, for example, an impartial party facilitates discussion between the parties, provides advice on the substance of the dispute,

---

[14] TAE, *supra* note 6.

[15] § 2 of the *Arbitration Ordinance*, *supra* note 11, translates "conciliation" as 調停 and "mediation" as 調解. Hong Kong's *Mediation Ordinance* (Cap. 620) provides the identical Chinese translation for "mediation."

Art. 1(3) of UNCITRAL's *Model Law on International Commercial Conciliation* (2002) provides:

> "conciliation" means a process, whether referred to by the expression conciliation, mediation or an expression of similar import, whereby parties request a third person or persons ("the conciliator") to assist them in their attempt to reach an amicable settlement of their dispute arising out of or relating to a contractual or other legal relationship. The conciliator does not have the authority to impose upon the parties a solution to the dispute.

Id. at Art. 6(4) provides that: "The conciliator may, at any stage of the conciliation proceedings, make proposals for a settlement of the dispute."

See also the *Guide to Enactment and Use of the UNCITRAL Model Law on International Commercial Conciliation* (2002), particularly para. 7.

The text of this *Model Law* is available at: http://www.uncitral.org/pdf/english/texts/arbitration/ml-conc/03-90953_Ebook.pdf (last visited 11 Jul. 2017).

UNCITRAL is the acronym for the United Nations Commission on International Trade Law.

[16] The National Alternative Dispute Resolution Advisory Council of Australia, *Dispute Resolution Terms – The use of terms in (alternative) dispute resolution* (Sept. 2003) [hereinafter NADRAC] notes:

> In NADRAC's view, 'mediation' is a purely facilitative process, whereas 'conciliation' may comprise a mixture of different processes including facilitation and advice. NADRAC considers that the term 'mediation' should be used where the practitioner has no advisory role on the content of the dispute and the term 'conciliation' where the practitioner does have such a role. NADRAC notes, however, that both 'mediation' and 'conciliation' are now used to refer to a wide range of processes and that an overlap in their usage is inevitable.

Id. at 3.

Its website can be found at: https://www.ag.gov.au/LegalSystem/AlternateDisputeResolution/Documents/NADRAC%20Publications/Dispute%20Resolution%20Terms.PDF (last visited 11 Jul. 2017).

See also So & To, *supra* note 1, at para. [2.16].

makes proposals for settlement or actively contributes to the terms of any agreement.[17]

V. Dispute Resolution Advisor/Dispute Resolution Board [DRA/DRB]

At times referred to as a *Dispute Adjudication Board, Dispute Board* or *Dispute Panel*, a DRB is a "panel set up under the terms of a contract to adjudicate, mediae [*sic*], or settle claims, disputes or controversies referred them, either on an interim or a final and binding basis."[18]

---

[17] NADRAC, *supra* note 16, at 5.

The Resolution Institute, based in Australia, provides a similar definition:

> Conciliation is a process in which the parties to a dispute, with the assistance of a dispute resolution practitioner (the conciliator), identify the issues in dispute, develop options, consider alternatives and endeavour to reach an agreement. The conciliator may have an advisory role on the content of the dispute or the outcome of its resolution, but not a determinative role. The conciliator may advise on or determine the process of conciliation whereby resolution is attempted, and may make suggestions for terms of settlement, give expert advice on likely settlement terms, and may actively encourage the participants to reach an agreement.

The Resolution Institute's website is at: http://www.resolution.institute/dispute-resolution/conciliation (last visited 1 Aug. 2017).

Alessandra Sgubini *et al.*, *Arbitration, Mediation and Conciliation: Differences and Similarities from an International and Italian Business Perspective* (Aug. 2004) provides a similar definition:

> Conciliation tries to individualize the optimal solution and direct parties towards a satisfactory common agreement. Although this sounds strikingly similar to mediation, there are important differences between the two methods of dispute resolution. In conciliation, the conciliator plays a relatively direct role in the actual resolution of a dispute and even advises the parties on certain solutions by making proposals for settlement. In conciliation, the neutral is usually seen as an authority figure who is responsible for the figuring out the best solution for the parties. The conciliator, not the parties, often develops and proposes the terms of settlement. The parties come to the conciliator seeking guidance and the parties make decisions about proposals made by conciliators. In this regard, the role of a conciliator is distinct from the role of a mediator. The mediator at all times maintains his or her neutrality and impartiality. A mediator does not focus only on traditional notions of fault and a mediator does not assume sole responsibility for generating solutions. Instead, a mediator works together with the parties as a partner to assist them in finding the best solution to further their interests. A mediator's priority is to facilitate the parties' own discussion and representation of their own interests, and guide them to their own suitable solution- a good common solution that is fair, durable, and workable. The parties play an active role in mediation, identifying interests, suggesting possible solutions, and making decisions concerning proposals made by other parties. The parties come to mediator seeking help in finding their own best solution.

Id. at http://www.mediate.com/articles/sgubinia2.cfm (last visited 11 Jul. 2017).

See also the German Arbitration Institute (*Deutsche Institution für Schiedsgerichtsbarkeit*) [hereinafter DIS] whose Conciliation Rules (2002) § 11 provides in part:

> 1. The conciliators shall support the parties in an impartial and independent manner in their attempt to settle the dispute amicably.
>
> ...
>
> 3. If the parties so wish, the conciliators can make suggestions towards settling the dispute at every stage of the proceedings. Grounds for the suggestions must not be stated.

Similarly, the DIS Mediation Rules (2012) at § 3.4 states: "The mediator shall encourage the settlement of the conflict between the parties in an orderly and efficient manner. He may make proposals for the resolution of the dispute upon consensual wishes of all parties."

Link at: http://www.disarb.org/en/16/rules/overview-id0 (last visited 1 Aug. 2017).

[18] TAE, *supra* note 6.

The Hong Kong Construction Industry Council [hereinafter "CIC"] provides this definition:

> The basic concept of a Dispute Resolution Advisor (DRA) involves the use of a neutral third person who advises the parties to a potential dispute and suggests possible options to avoid the dispute.
>
> The DRA is jointly appointed by the employer and the contractor from contract commencement to contract completion. The DRA's main role is to assist the parties to identify potential disputes and assist in the resolution of disagreements, which if unresolved, may turn into formal disputes.
>
> The DRA has no power to make any decision and his function is to be facilitative, encouraging parties to jointly work towards a common goal of completing the works in accordance with the contract.
>
> If disputes do arise, and where necessary, the DRA can advise on the choice of one of the five means of resolving disputes.
>
> Currently, DRA is engaged in projects involving the Development Bureau and the Housing Authority in Hong Kong.
>
> The DRA is appointed by the employer and the main contractor but is involved in avoiding disputes at main contract and nominated subcontract levels.[19]

Frequently encountered in construction projects, a DRB is intended to address issues as they arise thus providing a "real time" solution. For example, the FIDIC Red Book (1999), Sub-clause 20.4 provides for a Dispute Adjudication Board [hereinafter "DAB"]:

> If a dispute (of any kind whatsoever) arises between the Parties . . . either Party may refer the dispute in writing to the DAB for its decision . . . The decision shall be . . . binding on both Parties . . .
>
> If either Party is dissatisfied with the DAB's decision, then either Party may, within 28 days after receiving the decision, give notice to the other Party . . .

The CIC envisages that a DRA/DRB would operate in the following manner:

> DRA is used in main contract and nominated subcontract only. A DRA should be brought in at the beginning of a contract, continue to participate regularly for the duration of the contract and preferably till the completion of the final account of the contract.
>
> The DRA who [*sic*] meets at regular intervals with representatives of the Employer, Consultant, Main Contractor, Nominated Subcontractors and major Domestic Subcontractors, takes note of potential disagreements between the Employer/Consultant and the Main Contractor as they arise. The DRA will help settle disagreements before they finally turn into disputes which require more formal and timely method to resolve.[20]

---

[19] CIC, *supra* note 7, at 14.

[20] *Id.*

In summary, the DRA/DRB is intended to be a pro-active endeavour by the parties to resolve quickly potential or actual disputes in real time. As noted by the CIC, dispute avoidance "should be introduced through the use of a Dispute Resolution Advisor (DRA), jointly appointed by the Employer and Contractor, who will help the parties to avoid differences crystallising into dispute."[21]

VI. Early Neutral Evaluation

This is:

> a process in which the parties to a dispute present, at an early stage in attempting to resolve the dispute, arguments and evidence to a dispute resolution practitioner. That practitioner makes a determination on the key issues in dispute, and the most effective means of resolving the dispute without determining the facts of the dispute.[22]

An international dispute resolution consultancy explaines this process in greater detail. This ADR process is one in which an independent neutral assesses the merits of the disputing parties' case, and provides a recommendation as to the outcome. Early Neutral Evaluation [hereinafter "ENE"] is different from arbitration. ENE is non-binding and more informal. Unless the parties agree otherwise, ENE is not subject to "due process" and can therefore be more flexible. There is usually no trial-type hearing. Unless the parties agree otherwise, and unlike arbitration, the neutral may conduct investigations independently of the parties and make its recommendation based on those investigations without reference to the parties. Parties may obtain legal advice when undertaking this process, but do not need to be legally represented during the ENE procedure.[23]

VII. Expert Determination

The CIC describes its concept of this ADR process as being:

> a final and binding dispute resolution process. The Expert has to make a determination on the issue before him and is allowed to use his own expertise in coming to his conclusion. Expert Determination can only be challenged in limited circumstances.
>
> The Expert may conduct the determination in such manner as he considers appropriate, taking into account the circumstances of the case, the wishes of the

---

21 *Id.* at 7.

22 NADRAC, *supra* note 16, at 6. For further information on this ADR process, *see, e.g.*, Wayne D. Brazil, Early Neutral Evaluation (2012).

23 Introduction, *Model Early Neutral Evaluation Agreement*, Centre for Effective Dispute Resolution (2016) [hereinafter CEDR].

CEDR states on its website that the organization is "the largest conflict management and resolution consultancy in the world." *Id.* at https://www.cedr.com/about_us/ (last visited 30 Jul. 2017).

> parties and the need for a speedy resolution of the dispute. Expert Determination will be involved if a final decision on the dispute is expected.[24]

Another source provides this definition: "The use of an independent Expert to investigate the referred matters and to give his opinion which becomes binding on the parties. Not strictly an ADR process."[25]

A third source explains that expert determination:

> is a process in which the parties to a dispute present arguments and evidence to a dispute resolution practitioner, who is chosen on the basis of a specialist qualification or experience in the subject matter of the dispute (the expert) and who makes a determination.[26]

From these definitions, it is apparent that the concept of expert determination is similar; however, there is variation as to the methodology which an expert undertakes in coming to a determination. Whether the expert determination is binding or non-binding will be determined by the disputing parties' original agreement or upon any rules to which the disputing parties have subsequently agreed.[27]

One comment notes the difficulty of distinguishing expert determination from ENE:

---

[24] CIC, *supra* note 7, at 30.

[25] TAE, *supra* note 6.

[26] NADRAC, *supra* note 16, at 7.

To these definitions, CEDR, *supra* note 23, would add:

> Expert determination is a private process involving an independent technical expert who makes a binding decision on technical rather than legal issues and who has the power to ask questions of the parties before rendering his or her decision. The decision is binding unless it is agreed by the parties at the outset that the determination will not be. Expert determination is particularly suited to disputes of valuation or a purely technical nature across a range of sectors.

https://www.cedr.com/solve/expert/ (last visited 30 Jul. 2017).

For further information on this ADR process, *see, e.g.*, the website of the Building Disputes Tribunal of New Zealand: http://www.buildingdisputestribunal.co.nz/EXPERT+DETERMINATION.html (last visited 11 Jul. 2017).

[27] For example, Clause 2 of the CEDR *Model Expert Determination Agreement* (2016) provides that the determination "will be final and binding on the parties." CEDR, *supra* note 23.

Rule 5(5) of TAE's Rules for Expert Determination states that "the Expert's determination shall be final and binding on the parties," although under Rule 5(11) and Rule 7(2) the parties can agree otherwise. "The expert's decision is—by prior agreement of the parties—legally binding on the parties." TAE, *supra* note 6. The Academy of Experts' Rules are found at this website: https://www.academyofexperts.org/alternative-dispute-resolution/what-expert-determination (last visited 11 Jul. 2017).

The International Chamber of Commerce [hereinafter ICC] has published its Rules for Expertise, Art. 12(3) of which provides: "Unless otherwise agreed by all of the parties, the findings of the expert shall not be binding upon the parties."

These ICC rules are found at this website: http://library.iccwbo.org/content/dr/RULES/RULE_ALL_Expertise_EN_0034.htm?l1=Bulletins&l2=ICC+International+Court+of+Arbitration+Bulletin+Vol.13%2FNo.2+-+Eng&reqhref=%5Ccontent%5Cdr%5CAWARDS%5CAW_0309.htm?l1=Bulletins (last visited 28 Aug. 2017).

The DIS, *supra* note 17, "advises all parties wishing to obtain an expert determination with preliminary binding effect in order to clarify a dispute" to resort to expert determination. Rules on Expert Determination (2010). Link: http://www.disarb.org/en/16/rules/dis-rules-on-expert-determination-id28 (last visited 17 Aug. 2017).

> differences may be that (1) the type of dispute referable to ENE is not so limited as for expert determination and (2) ENE is carried out with other court or arbitration proceedings under way . . . Expert determination on the other hand is a process in its own right (and tends to envisage the parties making full disclosure).[28]

VIII. Mediation

As used here, *mediation* refers to facilitative mediation which is defined as:[29]

> a process in which the parties to a dispute, with the assistance of a dispute resolution practitioner (the mediator), identify the disputed issues, develop options, consider alternatives and endeavour to reach an agreement. The mediator has no advisory or determinative role in regard to the content of the dispute or the outcome of its resolution, but may advise on or determine the process of mediation whereby resolution is attempted. Mediation may be undertaken voluntarily, under a court order, or subject to an existing contractual agreement.[30]

An alternative definition of mediation is: "a process in which the parties to a dispute, with the assistance of a dispute resolution practitioner (the mediator) negotiate in an endeavour to resolve their dispute."[31]

Facilitative mediation is used in Hong Kong. The Hong Kong Department of Justice states:

> Mediation is a voluntary process in which a trained and impartial third person, the mediator, helps the parties in dispute to reach an amicable settlement that is responsive to their needs and acceptable to all sides.
>
> During the process, each party to the dispute has a chance to put his/her case and to hear what the other side has to say. The mediator's job is not to make a decision for the parties, but to assist the parties to explore the strengths and weaknesses of their own cases and to identify possible solutions, so as to facilitate them to reach a settlement agreement. The mediator does not decide who is right or wrong and

---

[28] CHOAT, *supra* note 2, at 10.

[29] A facilitative mediator does not make recommendations to the parties, give advice or opinions as to the outcome of the case or predict a court's disposition of the dispute. An evaluative mediator would point out weaknesses in the case and could provide an opinion on the merits of the case. *Id.* at 12.

[30] The Australian Disputes Centre. Website at: https://disputescentre.com.au/knowledge-resources/mediation/ (last visited 7 Aug. 2017).

[31] NADRAC, *supra* note 16, at 9. This definition is also the one used by the Hong Kong Department of Justice as its working definition and for the draft of the *Mediation Ordinance*, *supra* note 15.

See also The Accord Group, *Mediation Training Course Notes* (2017) defining "mediation" as:

> a process which is aimed at building consensus and agreement which is voluntarily reached between the parties where the [neutral] does not act as a judge to decide how the parties should resolve their dispute nor give advice or recommendations to tell the parties how to resolve their dispute.
>
> The mediator acts as a catalyst or facilitator for effective communication and negotiation so that the parties themselves are able to reach an agreement.

Compare these definitions to that of § 3(2) of the United States' *Uniform Mediation Act*: "a process in which a mediator facilitates communication and negotiation between parties to assist them in reaching a voluntarily agreement regarding their dispute."

has no authority to impose a settlement on the parties, the decision-making power rests in the hands of them. The mediator is skilled in unlocking negotiations that have become deadlocked and in keeping everyone focused on finding a solution.[32]

The territory's *Mediation Ordinance* (Cap. 620), section 4(1) defines mediation to be:

> 1. For the purposes of this Ordinance, mediation is a structured process comprising one or more sessions in which one or more impartial individuals, without adjudicating a dispute or any aspect of it, assist the parties to the dispute to do any or all of the following—
>   (a) identify the issues in dispute;
>   (b) explore and generate options;
>   (c) communicate with one another;
>   (d) reach an agreement regarding the resolution of the whole, or part, of the dispute.

Another definition and explanation of the mediation process in the territory is provided by the Hong Kong International Arbitration Centre:

> Mediation is a voluntary and private dispute resolution process in which a neutral person, the mediator, helps the parties to reach their own negotiated settlement agreement. The mediator has no power to impose a settlement. His/Her function is to overcome any impasse and encourage the parties to reach an amicable settlement.
>
> In commercial disputes an impasse most often arises from either a lack of trust in the integrity of the other party or a genuine good faith difference of opinion on the facts underlying the dispute or on the probable outcome of the case were it to go to court. The mediator may act as a shuttle diplomat and a channel for communication, by filtering out the emotional elements and allowing the parties to focus on the underlying objectives. The mediator will encourage the parties to reach an agreement themselves as opposed to having it imposed upon them.[33]

The UNCITRAL Working Group II has proposed an update of the UNCITRAL *Model Law on International Commercial Conciliation* (2002). It is expected that the updated version will be known as the UNCITRAL *Model Law on International Commercial Mediation and International Settlement Agreements Resulting from Mediation* (2018).[34] Furthermore, this Working Group has also proposed an

---

[32] *See* the Hong Kong Judiciary's *FAQs on Mediation* at: http://mediation.judiciary.gov.hk/en/mediation_faq.html#01 (last visited 11 Jul. 2017). *See also Mediation Ordinance*, *supra* note 15, at § 4; Hong Kong Mediation Accreditation Association Ltd's website at: www.hkmaal.org (last visited 11 Jul. 2017).
For more information on this ADR process, *see*, *e.g.*, Hong Kong Mediation Handbook (Raymond Hai Ming Leung, gen. ed., 2nd ed. 2014); Mediation in the Construction Industry: An International Review (Penny Brooker, *et al.* eds., 2010). *See* Ma & Brock, *supra* note 4, at para. 4.001 for a flowchart of a Hong Kong International Arbitration Centre mediation.

[33] HKIAC, *supra* note 6, at: http://www.hkiac.org/mediation/what-is-mediation (last visited 30 Jul. 2017).

[34] For further information, *see* http://www.uncitral.org/pdf/english/commissionsessions/51st-session/ACN9-943_advance_copy_website.pdf (last visited 5 May 2018).

international treaty through which signatory states agree to the enforcement of mediated settlements. The name of this international agreement is anticipated to be: *United Nations Convention on International Settlement Agreements Resulting from Mediation.*[35] It is expected that both these instruments will be presented by the Working Group to UNCITRAL for approval in the near future.

IX. Negotiation

As its name implies, with this method the disputing parties meet to negotiate or attempt to negotiate a settlement to their dispute. As explained by one authority:

> Negotiation can be defined as a process through which parties move from their initially divergent positions to a point where agreement can be reached. It is a consensual bargaining process in which parties attempt to reach agreement on a disputed, or potentially disputed, matter. Negotiation allows parties to get something they would not get by acting unilaterally. What sets negotiation apart from the other dispute resolution techniques . . . is that it allows, but does not compel, autonomy without third party intervention, although it can form an important part of certain ADR procedures, *e.g.* mediation or conciliation.[36]

In conclusion, a variety of ADR processes is available to disputing parties, some of which are listed above. Most ADR processes are available before a dispute arises (*e.g.*, an agreement to arbitrate) and most are available after a dispute arises (*e.g.*, an *ad hoc* arbitration). It is possible for these ADR methodologies to overlap in practice and function as well as in name (*e.g.*, conciliation and mediation) as these processes continue to evolve and as these processes frequently are determined by the parties, often resulting in a "hybrid" ADR (*e.g.*, mediation/arbitration). Thus, as noted, a rigid delineation between the different forms of ADR is difficult and

---

As noted in footnote 2 to this instrument:

> In its previously adopted texts and relevant documents, UNCITRAL used the term "conciliation" with the understanding that the terms "conciliation" and "mediation" were interchangeable. In preparing this Model Law, the Commission decided to use the term "mediation" instead in an effort to adapt to the actual and practical use of the terms and with the expectation that this change will facilitate the promotion and heighten the visibility of the Model Law. This change in terminology does not have any substantive or conceptual implications.

This Model Law provides the following definition of "mediation" in Art. 1.3:

> For the purposes of this Law, 'mediation' means a process, whether referred to by the expression mediation, conciliation or an expression of similar import, whereby parties request a third person or persons ('the mediator') to assist them in their attempt to reach an amicable settlement of their dispute arising out of or relating to a contractual or other legal relationship. The mediator does not have the authority to impose upon the parties a solution to the dispute.

[35] A draft of this instrument may be found at: http://undocs.org/A/CN.9/WG.II/WP.205/Add.1 (last visited 5 May 2018). Presently, it is expected that this instrument, after obtaining the requisite approvals within the United Nations organization, will be signed in the second half of 2019 in Singapore and will be referred to informally as the *Singapore Convention* or as the *Singapore Convention on Mediation*.

[36] Ma & Brock, *supra* note 4, at para. 4.007.

See id. at paras. 4.009–4.025 for further discussion, respectively, of: the objective theories of negotiation, problem-solving negotiation, competitive negotiation, subjective factors in negotiation, good faith in negotiation.

that "categorization is incapable of properly capturing the diversity of the ADR landscape."[37]

X. Legal Systems

As mentioned at the beginning of this chapter, this section addresses a matter having the potential to affect all international disputes. A person's background and training forms that person's frame of reference. This influences that individual's thought processes and attitudes. In this section, we focus on the legal system from the places where the parties and/or their legal representatives and/or the neutrals come. An individual's origin might influence the perspective and approach.

Although it is a generalization, for the purposes of this book, we classify legal systems into two categories: the common-law legal system and the civil-law legal system.[38] The former, in simplest terms, is the legal system derived from England and is practiced in that country and its former colonies. The civil-law legal system, again in simplest terms, is derived from continental Europe and its former colonies. The common-law legal system is heavily based upon precedent, *i.e.*, previous court decisions. The common-law system is also adversarial, often portrayed by the entertainment media as lawyers doing battle in the courtroom while the judge remains aloof and neutral. The civil-law legal system is more heavily based upon written law, *i.e.*, codes. The civil-law system is inquisitorial,[39] again often portrayed as active judges directly questioning the lawyers and witnesses as the judges search

---

[37] Choat, *supra* note 2, at 9.

[38] For example, some countries in Saharan Africa have a mixture of civil-law and Sharia-law legal systems. Kim Rosenberg, *Weighing the evidence: documentary evidence v factual/expert witnesses*, presentation delivered at the Chartered Institute of Arbitrators' International Arbitration Conference held in Johannesburg, 19–20 Jul. 2017.

In the country of South Africa, there is a mixed legal system:

- a civil-law system inherited from the Dutch
- a common-law system inherited from the British
- a customary-law system inherited from African customary law

The English influence is mostly in procedural aspects of the legal system and methods of adjudication, and the Roman-Dutch influence is mostly in substantive private law. As a general rule, South Africa follows English law in both criminal and civil procedure, company law, constitutional law and the law of evidence. Roman-Dutch law is followed in South African contract law, law of delict (tort), law of persons, law of things, family law, *etc.* Krinesh Govender, *Arbitration—an in-house perspective*, presentation delivered at the Chartered Institute of Arbitrators' International Arbitration Conference held in Johannesburg, 19–20 Jul. 2017.

One authority states:

> [T]here is just enough uniformity in the general approach to questions concerning the presentation of evidence to justify using the expression 'civil law countries' by way of contrast to the 'common law countries' when discussing the presentation of evidence to international tribunals. Where there are differences between the two systems, they are most noticeable in the area of the procedures that lead to fact-finding.

Redfern & Hunter, *supra* note 11, at para. 6.80. For a more detailed discussion, *see id.* at paras. 6.81–6.88.

[39] The Insider Dealing Tribunal's website translates "inquisitorial" as 訊問式. The Chinese version of the website is at: http://www.idt.gov.hk/chinese/intro.html (last visited 31 Jan. 2018). The English version of this website is at: http://www.idt.gov.hk/english/intro.html (last visited 31 Jan. 2018).

for the truth. How do these different types of legal systems affect ADR, particularly arbitration?

We can take for example, evidence and the conduct of the arbitral process. In Chapter 3, we discuss the International Bar Association's *Rules on the Taking of Evidence in International Arbitration* (2010) in terms of a guideline or good practice in arbitral proceedings. These rules were produced 18 years ago and mainly adopt a common-law legal system approach. Recently, there is a new set of rules which was prepared and was launched on 14 December 2018, the *Inquisitorial Rules on the Taking of Evidence in International Arbitration* (hereinafter "The Prague Rules").[40] The Prague Rules are intended to provide a more civil-law oriented approach to the taking of evidence in an attempt to reduce the time and related costs of an arbitration.[41]

The following table should reveal some additional differences and their impact upon dispute resolution:[42]

---

[40] The final version of the Prague Rules are available in English, Portuguese, Russian and Spanish. Link: https://praguerules.com/upload/medialibrary/9dc/9dc31ba7799e26473d92961d926948c9.pdf (last visited 21 Dec. 2018).

[41] The Working Group for the Prague Rules provided a *Note*:

> It has become almost commonplace these days that users of arbitration are dissatisfied with the time and costs involved in the proceedings. The procedures for taking evidence, particularly document production, and using multiple fact and expert witnesses and their cross-examination at lengthy hearings are, to a large extent, reasons for this dissatisfaction.
>
> The drafters of the IBA Rules on the Taking of Evidence in International Arbitration ("IBA Rules") bridged a gap between the common law and civil law traditions of taking evidence. The IBA Rules were very successful in developing a nearly standardized procedure in international arbitration, at least for proceedings involving parties from different legal traditions and those with significant amounts at stake.
>
> However, from a civil law perspective, the IBA Rules are still closer to the common law traditions, as they follow a more adversarial approach with document production, fact witnesses and party-appointed experts. In addition, the party's entitlement to cross-examine witnesses is almost being taken for granted.
>
> In addition to that many arbitrators are reluctant to actively manage arbitration proceedings, including earlier determination of issues in dispute and the disposal of such issues, to avoid the risk of a challenge.
>
> These factors contribute greatly to the costs of arbitration, while their efficiency is sometimes rather questionable. . . . most commentators admit that it is very rare, if ever, that document production brings a smoking gun to light. . . . many commentators express doubts as to the usefulness of fact witnesses and the impartiality of party-appointed experts. Many of these procedural features are not known or used to the same extent in non-common law jurisdictions, such as continental Europe, Latin America, Middle East and Asia.
>
> In light of all of this, the drafters of the Prague Rules believe that developing the rules on taking evidence, which are based on the inquisitorial model of procedure and would enhance more active role of the tribunals, would contribute to increasing efficiency in international arbitration.
>
> By adopting a more inquisitorial approach, the new rules will help the parties and tribunals to reduce the time and costs of arbitrations.

Link: http://www.praguerules.com/upload/medialibrary/697/697f654d36c0275b310cb3ccc1e0e9f3.pdf (last visited 3 May 2018).

[42] This is a modified version of the table prepared by Grant Herholdt, *The Role of Counsel—Civil v Common Law*, for a presentation delivered at the Chartered Institute of Arbitrators' International Arbitration Conference held in Johannesburg, 19–20 Jul. 2017. Link: http://www.ciarb.org/docs/default-source/ciarbdocuments/events/2017/July/day-2-johannesburg-conference.pdf?sfvrsn=2 (last visited 3 May 2018).
See also So & To, *supra* note 1, at para. [47.09] for a similar table.

Table 1.1

Common Law Legal System	Civil Law Legal System
Adversarial Approach:	**Inquisitorial Approach:**
Counsel pitted against each other to convince tribunal of their respective positions.	Tribunal investigates the case, and counsel aid the tribunal to find answers.
Counsel adopt the dominant role of identifying and interrogating issues.	Tribunal mostly performs the task of identifying and interrogating issues.
Tend to rely more on witnesses and oral evidence. Skillset focuses on preparing witnesses and avoiding attacks on credibility.	Witnesses "belong" to the tribunal. Witness interrogation frowned upon. Requires greater ability to deal with oral evidence on your feet.
Statements of claim usually only an outline of case. Greater ability to maneuver and adapt strategy as the matter progresses.	Statements of claim more detailed and most documentary evidence is attached. More important to understand strategy from the outset.
Approach to Expert Witness:	**Approach to Expert Witness:**
Expert "belongs" to the party. Concern that he/she becomes a client to counsel.	Expert "belongs" to the tribunal. Independent from the parties.
Due to possible eagerness to please instructing counsel, there is a perception of partiality. Exposed to more aggressive cross-examination and attacks on credibility.	Not influenced either way. Less exposed to attacks on credibility.
Must be vigilant to avoid deviation from previous reports, evidence, public statements.	Less likely to deviate from previous positions.
Approach to Mediation—Australia:	**Approach to Mediation—Germany:**
Mediation dates back to 1980s. Mediation more familiar amongst common law jurisdictions.	Mediation established towards mid-1990s. Mediation less familiar in civil law jurisdictions, but gaining momentum.
More focused towards personal interests, fairness and equity.	Processes are more directive, interventionist and rights-based. Less room for equity and fairness.
Perceived as more pragmatic problemsolvers.	Perceived as system-based theoreticians with formalistic focus that inhibits innovation and flexibility within the system.
Historically, meditators were subject to greater regulation/accreditation. Therefore more commonality in styles.	Historically, less regulation and accreditation. Styles and standards vary greatly.

These different approaches of different legal cultures will affect ADR, including arbitration, in the way pleadings, evidence, witnesses of fact and expert witnesses are managed by the parties' lawyers and by the arbitral tribunal. Other differences between common-law and civil-law legal systems will be reviewed in more detail as they arise at the appropriate sections of this work.

2

Considerations for Selecting Arbitration: An Introduction

I. Introduction

In this chapter, we review some of the points that parties anticipating a possible dispute should consider when agreeing to arbitrate. We begin with a reminder of some of the terms which are used in this book. Next, major differences between arbitration and other dispute resolution methods will be reviewed. This will be followed by a short discussion of the two principal types of arbitration on which this book will focus. We then go on to a presentation of the advantages and disadvantages of arbitration in general. Subsequently, we briefly present a section on the concept of party autonomy. Finally, we conclude with a presentation on the arbitration agreement which will serve as an introduction to the subsequent chapters.[1]

This book is about international commercial arbitration.[2] Let us start first with definitions for this phrase. As one authority stated:

> The term 'international' is used to mark the difference between arbitrations that are purely 'national' or 'domestic' and those that in some way transcend national boundaries, hence are 'international' or (in the terminology adopted by Judge Jessup) 'transnational'.
>
> . . .
>
> . . . to the extent that the procedure in any arbitration is regulated by law, that law is normally the law of the place of arbitration – that is, the law of the 'seat' of the

---

[1] For additional information on the features of arbitration, *see, e.g.*, ARBITRATION IN HONG KONG: A PRACTICAL GUIDE paras. 4.127–4.168 (THE HON CHIEF JUSTICE GEOFFREY MA AND DENIS BROCK, eds., 4th ed. 2017) [hereinafter MA & BROCK]; MICHAEL J. MOSER AND TERESA Y.W. CHENG, HONG KONG ARBITRATION: A USER'S GUIDE Chapt. 1 (3rd ed. 2014) [hereinafter MOSER & CHENG].

[2] This book is intended to be an introduction to international commercial arbitration, with the focus on Hong Kong. More specialized or complex areas of international arbitration will not be included. For example, this work will not review multi-party arbitration, energy arbitration or investor-state arbitration. Examples of specialized dispute resolution organizations with rules tailored to their specialty include:

- the International Centre for Settlement of Investment Disputes (ICSID) which administers international investment disputes between investors and nation states
- the World Intellectual Property Organisation (WIPO) Arbitration and Mediation Center which is oriented towards intellectual property and technology disputes
- the Court of Arbitration for Sport (CAS), which administers sport-related disputes
- the Chambre Arbitrale Maritime de Paris (CAMP) which administers and supervises maritime arbitrations

arbitration. In an international arbitration (unlike its 'national' or 'domestic' counterpart), the parties usually have no connection with the seat of the arbitration. Indeed, the seat will generally have been chosen by the parties, or by an arbitral institution, *precisely because* it is a place with which the parties have no connection. It will be a truly *neutral* seat.[3]

The same source provides this definition of *commercial*:

It was once customary to refer to the 'commercial' character of arbitrations . . . This reflects the distinction made in some countries between contracts that are 'commercial' and those that are not. This distinction was important at one time because there were (and still are) countries in which only disputes arising out of 'commercial' contracts may be submitted to arbitration (thus it might be permissible to hold an arbitration between two merchants over a contract made in the course of their business, but not, for example, in respect of a contract for the allocation of property on the marriage of their children).[4]

Next is a reminder of the definition of *arbitration*. Arbitration is a consensual and a private dispute resolution process where the parties agree to have their dispute resolved by a person known as an *arbitrator*[5] or a group of persons known as an *arbitral tribunal* or *arbitration tribunal*.[6] The disputing parties are able to agree on the structure of the arbitral proceedings,[7] including the number and appointment

---

3 Redfern and Hunter on International Arbitration paras. 1.19–1.21 (Nigel Blackaby *et al.*, eds., 6th ed. 2015) [hereinafter Redfern & Hunter] (emphasis in original). For further discussion on what constitutes an *international* arbitration, *see id.* at paras. 1.22–1.34.

4 *Id.* at para. 1.35 (citations omitted).

Id. at para 1.38 makes the following comment:

> The term 'commercial' should be given a wide interpretation so as to cover matters arising from all relationships of a commercial nature, whether contractual or not. Relationships of a commercial nature include, but are not limited to, the following transactions: any trade transaction for the supply or exchange of goods or services; distribution agreement; commercial representation or agency; factoring; leasing; construction of works; consulting; engineering; licensing; investment; financing; banking; insurance; exploitation agreement or concession; joint venture and other forms of industrial or business co-operation; carriage of goods or passengers by air, sea, rail or road. (footnote omitted)

Having said that, it should be noted that another source opines:

> Any dispute or difference in respect of a defined legal relationship may be referred to arbitration. Disputes arising from contract, tort and other forms of legal relationship, such as trusteeship, restitution or pursuant to statutory duties, may be so referred. Disputes falling within the following categories may not, however, be referred to arbitration: criminal charges . . . marriage, divorce, relations between parents and children, personal status, actions in rem against vessels and matters reserved for resolution by state agencies and tribunals (such as taxation, development control, immigration, nationality and social welfare entitlements).

2 Halsbury's Laws of Hong Kong para. [25.003] (2nd ed. 2016) [hereinafter Halsbury's] (citations omitted).

5 § 2 of the *Arbitration Ordinance* (Cap. 609) [hereinafter *Arbitration Ordinance*] translates "arbitrator" as 仲裁員.

6 Note that these terms are interchangeable. The term *arbitrator* might be referred to as the *arbitral tribunal* or as the *tribunal*. The term *arbitral tribunal* also might be referred to as a *panel of arbitrators* or as the *arbitrators*. Likewise, *arbitration* can be substituted for *arbitral* and *vice versa*. For the purposes of this book, the use of the singular term for the decision-maker should also be considered to include the plural term.

§ 2 of the *Arbitration Ordinance*, *supra* note 5, translates "arbitral tribunal" and "arbitration tribunal" as 仲裁庭.

7 Moser & Cheng, *supra* note 1, at para. 1-010 states: "in general, the parties are free to agree on how the arbitration proceedings will be conducted."

See also Ma & Brock, *supra* note 1, at para. 4.132 and paras. 6.015–6.019.

of arbitrators,[8] the location of the arbitration, the applicable substantive law governing the rights and obligations of the parties,[9] the procedural rules,[10] the language of the arbitration[11] and other related matters.[12] Normally, the arbitral tribunal will consider the facts and listen to the arguments of the parties in oral hearings, and make a decision. Parties are also free to agree to have the matter decided by the arbitrator or arbitral tribunal based on documents and written submissions only without any oral hearing.[13] In either event, the arbitral tribunal will consider the facts presented by the parties and make a decision. That decision by the arbitral tribunal is, in theory, final and binding on the parties as per the parties' agreement to arbitrate.[14]

II. Differences between Arbitration and Other Dispute Resolution Methods

Several types of dispute resolution processes are introduced in Chapter 1. In this section, the differences between arbitration and the other dispute resolution processes most commonly found in the territory are briefly summarized.

Arbitration is different from litigation in several respects. First, arbitral proceedings are conducted in a private setting whereas litigation proceedings are generally conducted in a court room which is open to the public and to the media.

> Another choice that parties have is the freedom to select arbitrators. This advantage is so fundamental to international arbitration that it is often categorised as a key feature separate and apart from party autonomy. Parties may choose arbitrators who have appropriate qualifications, experience or expertise to handle a particular dispute. Arbitrators need not be lawyers and can be chosen from any discipline. In fact, choosing an arbitrator with specific technical or expert knowledge may sometimes assist with a more expedient process as such parties would not have to submit evidence that would be considered common knowledge in an industry.

MA & BROCK, *supra* note 1, at para. 6.015 (citations omitted).

8 MOSER & CHENG, *supra* note 1, at para. 5-051: "The parties may agree upon the number of arbitrators, either within the arbitration agreement, or after a dispute has arisen."

9 *Id.* at para. 5-025; MA & BROCK, *supra* note 1, at para. 6.005 [law governing the dispute], and paras. 6.009–6.010 [governing law of the arbitral agreement].

In explaining the importance of the governing law of the arbitral agreement, one authority stated:

> the Court of First Instance was tasked with deciding which law was to govern an arbitration agreement in the absence of the parties' agreement, where the law of the underlying contract and the *lex arbitri* were different. The applicable law of the arbitration agreement was important in the case, as under the *lex arbitri* the arbitration clause was invalid whereas under the substantive law of the dispute the arbitration clause could be invoked to stay court proceedings. . . . This case highlights the position that Hong Kong has taken such that it can no longer be assumed the *lex arbitri* will be applied to an arbitration agreement in the absence of the parties' agreement.

MA & BROCK, *supra* note 1, at para. 6.010 citing to *Klöckner Pentaplast Gmbh & Co Kg v Advance Technology (HK) Company Ltd* [2011] 4 HKLRD 262.

10 MOSER & CHENG, *supra* note 1, at para. 1-031; MA & BROCK, *supra* note 1, at paras. 6.011–6.014.

11 MOSER & CHENG, *supra* note 1, at para. 5-023.

12 BUTTERWORTHS HONG KONG ARBITRATION LAW HANDBOOK para. [26.05] (DAMON YC SO, CHRISTOPHER TO *et al.*, eds., 2nd ed. 2018) [hereinafter SO & TO].

13 MOSER & CHENG, *supra* note 1, at para. 5-141.

14 We discuss in detail this concept of *finality* later in this chapter and in Chapter 9, "Contents of the Award."

Second, parties to an arbitration can choose the arbitral tribunal to decide their dispute, so the parties have input into the expertise and competence of their decision maker. In contrast, parties to a litigation have little or no input on the selection of the judge who will be deciding the case. Third, a decision by the arbitral tribunal, which is known as an *arbitral award* or *award*, depends upon the losing party voluntarily complying with the award.[15] If the losing party does not comply with the award, the winning party can seek enforcement before a national court. A court judgement resulting from litigation is self-enforcing through the coercive powers of the government. Fourth, arbitral awards are final and can only be set aside[16] in exceptional circumstances, *e.g.*, the arbitral tribunal has exceeded its jurisdiction or an arbitrator has been successfully challenged on the grounds of failing to act impartially or of having a conflict of interest.[17] Judgements from court litigation might be appealed by the losing party. Last but not least, arbitration procedures are generally less formal than litigation procedures.

Arbitration is different from mediation. The tribunal in an arbitration serves as the decision-maker with the power to make binding decisions.[18] The mediator in a facilitative mediation does not play the role of decision-maker. Instead, the mediator is an independent third party who facilitates or helps bring the parties to a compromise agreement.

Similarly, arbitration is a different process than conciliation. As previously noted, the term *conciliation* is frequently used interchangeably with the term *mediation*. Although the processes involved in conciliation and mediation are similar and overlap to a certain degree, there seems to be consensus that in the conciliation process, the conciliator may and is permitted to suggest a resolution. The parties are not required to accept the provisions of a settlement proposed in a conciliation.

---

15 Further discussion concerning awards and enforcement will be presented in Chapter 10, "Recognition and Enforcement of the Award."

16 The term "to set aside" simply means "to cancel" or "to invalidate." Hence, to set aside an arbitral award means to make the award ineffective or unenforceable so that the award is no longer binding upon the losing party.

17 Further discussion concerning arbitrators' obligations and challenges to awards will be reviewed in the following chapters of this book.

18 Redfern & Hunter, *supra* note 3, at para. 1.82 states:

> The power (and a duty) of an arbitral tribunal to make binding decisions distinguishes arbitration as a method of resolving disputes from other procedures, such as mediation and conciliation, which aim to arrive at a negotiated settlement. The *procedure* to be followed in order to arrive at a binding decision is flexible, adaptable to the circumstances of each particular case. Nevertheless, it is a *judicial* procedure and a failure by a tribunal to act judicially may be sanctioned by annulment or non-enforcement of that tribunal's award. No similar enforceable requirement governs the procedures to be followed where parties are assisted in arriving at a negotiated settlement by mediation, conciliation, or some other process of this kind. (emphasis in original; citations omitted)

III. Types of Arbitration

There are two forms of arbitration focused upon in this section and in this book, namely *institutional arbitration*[19] and *ad hoc arbitration*.[20] A less frequently used form of arbitration, *submission agreement*, will then be reviewed. *Documents-only* arbitration will conclude this section.

An institutional arbitration is where parties choose to conduct their dispute resolution proceedings under the arbitration rules of a particular institution. The arbitral institution to which a dispute has been referred will administer the proceedings based on its own rules of arbitration. These arbitral institution rules regulate the appointment of the arbitral tribunal and the administration of the arbitration. Hence, this type of arbitration is also known by another name: *administered arbitration*.

Some examples of arbitral institutions are the:

- China International Economic and Trade Arbitration Commission [hereinafter "CIETAC"]
- Hong Kong International Arbitration Centre [hereinafter "HKIAC"]
- International Chamber of Commerce [hereinafter "ICC"]
- London Court of International Arbitration [hereinafter "LCIA"]
- Singapore International Arbitration Centre [hereinafter "SIAC"]
- Swiss Chambers' Arbitration Institution [hereinafter "SCAI"]

The arbitration procedural rules of each of these institutions may be found on the internet.[21]

There are advantages to an institutional arbitration which include:

- the existence of well-known and tested rules to regulate the arbitration procedure[22]

---

[19] For a discussion of the advantages and disadvantages of institutional arbitration, *see, e.g.*, REDFERN & HUNTER, *supra* note 3, at paras. 1.149–1.156.

The Hong Kong International Arbitration Centre [hereinafter HKIAC] has prepared a short publication called *Hong Kong Arbitration 100 Questions and Answers* [hereinafter *100 Q&A*] which translates "institutional arbitration" as 機構仲裁. *See* the *100 Q&A* website at: http://www.hkiac.org/sites/default/files/ck_filebrowser/PDF/arbitration/100%20QnA.pdf (English version, last visited 21 Jun. 2017) and http://hkiac.org/sites/default/files/ck_filebrowser/PDF/arbitration/100_QA_EC.pdf (Chinese version, last visited 21 Jun. 2017).

[20] For a review of the advantages and disadvantages of *ad hoc* arbitration, *see, e.g.*, REDFERN & HUNTER, *supra* note 3, at paras. 1.143–1.145.

100 Q&A, *supra* note 19, translates "*ad hoc* arbitration" as 臨時仲裁.

[21] For a comparison table of some of the major arbitral institutions, *see, e.g.*, *Comparison of the Major Arbitral Institutions*, at: https://www.ashurst.com/en/news-and-insights/legal-updates/qg-international-arbitration-which-institution/ (last visited 12 Aug. 2017).

For a comparison table of some of the major institutional rules, *see, e.g.*, *Comparative Chart of International Arbitration Rules* at: http://www.bakermckenzie.com/-/media/files/insight/publications/2016/11/qrg_dr_intarbitrationrules_nov16.pdf?la=en (last visited 12 Aug. 2017).

[22] The arbitration rules adopted by the arbitral institutions usually undergo periodic revision after consultation with practitioners and after considering recent developments and trends in international arbitration. For example, the recently revised HKIAC Administered Arbitration Rules (2018) provide for online filing of documents,

- the existence of the institution's staff to assist with the management or conduct of the case[23]
- the existence of the institution's staff to assist with administrative matters arising from the arbitration[24]

The major disadvantage for some parties is the cost involved, as these institutions charge a fee for the services provided.[25] Under some institutional rules, parties

---

third-party funding of arbitrations, a single arbitration under multiple contracts, or a single arbitral tribunal to conduct multiple arbitrations consecutively, commensurately or suspend other arbitrations pending the determination of another. The Japan Commercial Arbitration Association's Interactive Arbitration Rules (effective 1 January 2019) will permit a more active arbitral tribunal which "interacts" with the parties by preparing a summary of each party's position, and, by preparing a summary of the facts, legal issues, and other important considerations along with the tribunal's preliminary view of these matters.

Furthermore, arbitral institutions' rules contain mechanisms for the continuation of an arbitration in the event of a default by one of the parties. Additionally, these rules are designed for situations where the arbitral tribunal's appointment is challenged on the grounds of lack of independence or lack of impartiality. REDFERN & HUNTER, *supra* note 3, at para. 1.150.

[23] The institution's staff assisting with the management or conduct of the case is commonly referred to as the *Secretariat*. For example, paragraphs 4 and 5 of the *Note to Parties and Arbitral Tribunals on the Conduct of the Arbitration Under the ICC Rules of Arbitration* (2017) [hereinafter ICC Note] provide that:

> The Secretariat is directed by the Secretary General, the Deputy Secretary General and the Managing Counsel. It is composed of teams headed by a Counsel.
>
> The Secretariat closely monitors the progress of the proceedings and assists the parties and the arbitral tribunals on any questions relating to the conduct of an arbitration. The parties and/or their legal representatives are encouraged to contact the Secretariat with any queries or comments arising from the [arbitration] Rules and/or this Note.

[24] The institution's staff assisting with the administrative matters arising from the arbitration is commonly referred to by the terms *tribunal secretary* or *administrative secretary*. The previous edition of the ICC Note, *supra* note 23, stated at paras. 149–151 that:

> Administrative Secretaries act upon the tribunal's instructions and under its strict supervision. The arbitral tribunal shall, at all times, be responsible for the Administrative Secretary's conduct in relation to the arbitration.
>
> An Administrative Secretary may perform organisational and administrative tasks such as:
>
> - transmitting documents and communications on behalf of the arbitral tribunal;
> - organising and maintaining the arbitral tribunal's file and locating documents;
> - organising hearings and meetings;
> - attending hearings, meetings and deliberations; taking notes or minutes or keeping time;
> - conducting legal or similar research; and
> - proof-reading and checking citations, dates and cross-references in procedural orders and awards, as well as correcting typographical, grammatical or calculation errors.
>
> Under no circumstances may the arbitral tribunal delegate decision-making functions to an Administrative Secretary. Nor should the arbitral tribunal rely on the Administrative Secretary to perform any essential duties of an arbitrator.

The administrative staff of the arbitral institution will also ensure that the arbitral tribunal is appointed, advance payments for the professional fees of arbitrators are made, remind parties of the time limits and thus are important in ensuring the smooth running of the arbitration. REDFERN & HUNTER, *supra* note 3, at para. 1.151.

[25] Most institutions generally use one of two methods of determining fees and sometimes a combination of the two methods. For example, the London Court of International Arbitration [hereinafter LCIA] charges five percent of the fees of the Tribunal (excluding expenses) in respect of the LCIA's general overhead plus the time spent by the Secretariat of the LCIA in the administration of the arbitration. Note that the tribunal's fees are calculated on hourly rates and are capped according to a schedule to the LCIA rules. The LCIA's Secretariat's time is calculated on an hourly basis. *Schedule of LCIA Arbitration Costs*.

Conversely, both the International Chamber of Commerce [hereinafter ICC] and the Singapore International Arbitration Centre [hereinafter SIAC] charge their fees based upon the amount in dispute. This method is known

may be required to pay a fixed fee in advance as the fees and expenses of both the arbitral institution and the arbitral tribunal which are assessed on an *ad valorem* basis. Therefore, it may be less expensive to conduct an arbitration on an *ad hoc* basis if the amount of the dispute is substantial and the parties are represented by experienced advocates.[26]

In contrast, the term *ad hoc arbitration* refers to an arbitration process in which the parties do not choose an institution to administer the arbitral proceedings. *Ad hoc* arbitration is thus not administered by any arbitral institution and requires the parties to make their own arrangements for the appointment of a tribunal. Additionally, the parties either choose the procedural rules to apply to the arbitration or allow the arbitral tribunal to make this decision.[27] Occasionally, parties may choose to create their own procedural rules as long as these rules afford the parties fair and equal treatment, including a reasonable opportunity for each party to present its case. In practice, however, parties to an *ad hoc* arbitration tend to

---

as *ad valorem* which is Latin for "according to value." HKIAC provides an option to the parties of using either method of calculating the institution's fees.

LCIA prepared an analysis in 2015 which concluded that:

> the cases were split into two categories based on the amount in dispute. US$ 1 million was selected for the analysis as it was the smallest amount in dispute that resulted in a statistically significant subset of data. For each category, the actual LCIA's arbitration costs were compared with the costs generated for each case using the costs calculators provided by the other institutions.
>
> This additional comparison shows that for cases of less than US$ 1m the costs of LCIA arbitration are comparable with ICC and SIAC but higher than HKIAC; over US$ 1m, while comparable with HKIAC, LCIA costs are lower than ICC and SIAC.

For additional information on the methodology and on the detailed results, *see* http://www.lcia.org/News/lcia-releases-costs-and-duration-data.aspx (last visited 12 Aug. 2017).

For HKIAC's own data released in 2016, *see* http://www.hkiac.org/content/costs-duration (last visited 12 Aug. 2017).

For SIAC's own data released in 2016, *see* http://www.siac.org.sg/images/stories/press_release/SIAC%20Releases%20Costs%20and%20Duration%20Study_10%20Oct%202016.pdf (last visited 12 Aug. 2017).

26 Redfern & Hunter, *supra* note 3, at para. 1.154.

27 United Nations Commission on International Trade Law, more commonly known by its acronym UNCITRAL, has created a set of procedural rules. Frequently referred to, and hereinafter cited as the UNCITRAL Arbitration Rules, these rules are commonly used in *ad hoc* arbitrations. The UNCITRAL website states:

> The UNCITRAL Arbitration Rules provide a comprehensive set of procedural rules upon which parties may agree for the conduct of arbitral proceedings arising out of their commercial relationship and are widely used in ad hoc arbitrations as well as administered arbitrations. The Rules cover all aspects of the arbitral process, providing a model arbitration clause, setting out procedural rules regarding the appointment of arbitrators and the conduct of arbitral proceedings, and establishing rules in relation to the form, effect and interpretation of the award. At present, there exist three different versions of the Arbitration Rules: (i) the 1976 version; (ii) the 2010 revised version; and (iii) the 2013 version which incorporates the UNCITRAL Rules on Transparency for Treaty-based Investor-State Arbitration.

The 1976 version of the UNCITRAL Arbitration Rules may be found at this website: http://www.uncitral.org/pdf/english/texts/arbitration/arb-rules/arb-rules.pdf (last visited 10 Jul. 2017).

The 2010 version of the UNCITRAL Arbitration Rules may be found at the following website: http://www.uncitral.org/pdf/english/texts/arbitration/arb-rules-revised/arb-rules-revised-2010-e.pdf (last visited 10 Jul. 2017).

The 2013 version of the UNCITRAL Arbitration Rules may be found here: http://www.uncitral.org/pdf/english/texts/arbitration/arb-rules-2013/UNCITRAL-Arbitration-Rules-2013-e.pdf (last visited 10 Jul. 2017).

For further information on UNCITRAL the organization, *see* http://www.uncitral.org/uncitral/en/index.html (last visited 2 Jul. 2017).

agree that the arbitration will be conducted according to a well-established set of rules such as the UNCITRAL Arbitration Rules. Alternatively, the arbitration may be governed by the arbitration law of the place where the arbitration is to be held.[28] Additionally, in *ad hoc* arbitration, the parties themselves attend to the administrative matters relating to the conduct of the arbitration, such as: case management, negotiating and paying the fees of the arbitral tribunal's members, booking hearing rooms, retaining transcription services, etc.

The major advantage of *ad hoc* arbitration over institutional arbitration is that the procedural rules adopted in the arbitration can be tailor-made to suit the parties' needs and the particular type of the dispute.[29] Another advantage of *ad hoc* arbitration might be the potential cost savings compared to institutional arbitration: "This choice usually is made to avoid the cost and procedural complexity perceived as involved when dealing with the institution and the relevant institutional framework."[30]

The principal disadvantage of *ad hoc* arbitration is that the efficient management of the arbitration process depends upon the parties' cooperation. "Where this cooperation is not forthcoming the flexibility, which is the strength of ad hoc arbitration, becomes its Achilles' heel."[31] A related disadvantage is whether the parties have chosen a jurisdiction with a well-established and arbitration-friendly legal system as the seat of arbitration which would have provisions to address deadlock between the parties.[32]

It should be noted that the term *ad hoc arbitration* as used in this book refers to a non-institution or non-administered arbitration. However, there is another meaning to this term. Most arbitration agreements are made *before* a dispute arises between the parties. Thus, the term *ad hoc arbitration* may also refer to an arbitration or an arbitration agreement which is entered into by the parties *after* a dispute has arisen between them. As explained by one authority:

---

28 This is known as the *seat* of the arbitration and will be further discussed in Chapter 3, "Laws and Rules of Arbitration."

29 Redfern & Hunter, *supra* note 3, at para. 1.143.

Alternatively:

> Although the *ad hoc* arbitration agreement may be silent as to relevant procedural rules, this is not the invariable approach, and the HKIAC Domestic Arbitration Rules and the UNCITRAL Arbitration Rules, are, for example, often adopted for use in *ad hoc* arbitration, and can be incorporated by specific reference in the arbitration agreement. The UNCITRAL Rules are the most widely recognized ad hoc [*sic*] arbitration rules that do not involve an arbitration institution. . . . It is not necessary to specify applicable rules in an *ad hoc* arbitration agreement but it remains desirable to do so, since this limits the potential for procedural dispute should arbitration become necessary.

Ma & Brock, *supra* note 1, at para. 10.064.

30 Ma & Brock, *supra* note 1, at para. 10.063.

As noted by another authority: "In comparison to institutional arbitration, ad hoc arbitration offers its user a great deal more flexibility. If the parties and their lawyers can work together then the process can be reasonably cheap and effective." Andrew Tweeddale & Keren Tweeddale, Arbitration of Commercial Disputes – International and English Law and Practice para. 3.77 (2007) [hereinafter Tweeddale & Tweeddale].

31 Tweeddale & Tweeddale, *supra* note 30, at para. 3.77.

32 Redfern & Hunter, *supra* note 3, at para 1.145.

> [This is a] less common, type of agreement to arbitrate, which is made *once* a dispute has arisen. Such an agreement is generally known as a 'submission agreement'. It is generally much more complex than an arbitration clause – because, once a dispute has arisen, it is possible to nominate a tribunal, and to spell out what the dispute is and how the parties propose to deal with it.[33]

This source continues:

> An arbitration agreement that is drawn up to deal with disputes that have *already* arisen between the parties is generally known as a 'submission agreement', a *compromis*, or a *compromiso*. The parties may wish to choose institutional arbitration, or they may prefer to proceed ad hoc, in which case the submission agreement will usually be a fairly detailed document, dealing with the constitution of the arbitral tribunal, the procedure to be followed, the issues to be decided, the substantive law, and other matters. At one time, it was the *only* type of arbitration agreement that the law of many states recognised, since recourse to arbitration was permitted only in respect of *existing* disputes. In some states, this is still the position.[34]

Finally, to conclude this section on types of arbitration, there is a variation which may apply to either an institutional or *ad hoc* arbitration. This variation is known as *documents-only arbitration*. As its name implies, this is an arbitration where there is no oral evidence, *e.g.*, no witness testimony. In a documents-only arbitration process, the parties are limited to written submission and documentary evidence, including written witness statements. Documents-only arbitration might be appropriate for uncomplicated disputes or single-issue disputes.[35]

---

[33] *Id.* at para. 1.42 (emphasis in original).

[34] *Id.* at para. 1.51 (emphasis in original; citations omitted). For further information on submission agreements, *see id.* at paras. 2.119–2.123.

For example, concerning submission agreements, the LCIA provides the following:

> Existing disputes
>
> If a dispute has arisen, but there is no agreement between the parties to arbitrate, or if the parties wish to vary a dispute resolution clause to provide for LCIA arbitration, the following clause is recommended. Words/spaces in square brackets should be deleted/completed as appropriate.
>
> "A dispute having arisen between the parties concerning [ ], the parties hereby agree that the dispute shall be referred to and finally resolved by arbitration under the LCIA Rules.
>
> The number of arbitrators shall be [one/three].
>
> The seat, or legal place, of arbitration shall be [City and/or Country].
>
> The language to be used in the arbitral proceedings shall be [ ].
>
> The governing law of the contract [is/shall be] the substantive law of [ ]. "

http://www.lcia.org/Dispute_Resolution_Services/LCIA_Recommended_Clauses.aspx (last visited 10 Aug. 2017).

[35] Ma & Brock, *supra* note 1, at para. 10.216. *See also id.* at paras. 10.217–10.219.

These authors further explain:

> Where the contemporary documents record the central facts, it is frequently unnecessary for the arbitrator to receive oral testimony of witnesses in a hearing. In these circumstances the parties may agree to conduct a "documents-only" arbitration. . . .
>
> In documents-only arbitration, the arbitrator makes his determination based solely on any statements of case and an agreed bundle of documents provided to him by the parties. It dispenses with Directions, discovery, experts and the hearing. Written statements of claim are usually exchanged, as this is usually the only way for a party to put forward its case, since no oral evidence will be received.

Id. at paras. 4.138–4.139.

IV. Advantages of Arbitration

Arbitration, particularly international commercial arbitration, has started to prevail around the globe.[36] The reasons for this type of dispute resolution gaining popularity are several. Some of the perceived reasons are discussed in this section.

First, arbitration gives the parties an opportunity to choose a neutral venue for resolving their dispute and to choose a neutral tribunal.[37] This avoids one party having to make a claim or defend a claim in a court outside of that party's home territory. Thus, with a neutral location for a dispute's resolution, neither party can be seen to have any advantage over the other. A similar perspective applies to a neutral tribunal: neither party has an advantage with an arbitral tribunal compared to a local judicial tribunal in some jurisdictions.[38]

The second reason is that arbitral proceedings are supposedly more private and confidential than litigation.[39] Arbitration proceedings are not open to the public whereas most court proceedings are open to the public.[40] This feature is important to parties who want to keep confidential the details of their commercial dispute to avoid their business reputation from being tarnished, or to protect their trade secrets or other sensitive information.[41] For example, pursuant to the *Arbitration Ordinance* (Cap. 609), arbitrations conducted in Hong Kong are confidential.[42]

---

[36] In a recent international survey, "90% of respondents said that international arbitration is their preferred dispute resolution mechanism." *2015 International Arbitration Survey: Improvements and Innovations in International Arbitration*, Queen Mary University of London 5 (2015) [hereinafter Queen Mary]. Available at: http://www.arbitration.qmul.ac.uk/media/arbitration/docs/2015_International_Arbitration_Survey.pdf (last visited 1 Aug. 2017).

[37] For further discussion, *see* MA & BROCK, *supra* note 1, at paras. 6.020–6.021.

[38] Queen Mary, *supra* note 36, at 6 reports that 64% of respondents selected "Avoiding specific legal systems/national courts" as the second most valuable characteristic of arbitration.

[39] For further discussion, *see* MA & BROCK, *supra* note 1, at paras. 6.026–6.033, and paras. 10.202–10.207; SO & TO, *supra* note 12, at para. [18.01].

[40] SO & TO, *supra* note 12, at para. [16.01].

[41] Queen Mary, *supra* note 36, at 6 indicates that "Confidentiality and privacy" ranked fifth overall in the category of "What are the three most valuable characteristics of international arbitration?" However, "Confidentiality and privacy" was the second most frequently listed valuable characteristic by in-house legal counsels. *Id.*
This goal of confidentiality and privacy is not always achievable:

> One of the prime advantages of arbitration is that it is a private process. That is true in the sense that it is a "closed" hearing and members of the public or press are excluded from the hearing. The press are not able to report. But there is a larger question of whether matters discussed may then find their way into the newspapers. That question is one as to the implied obligations on the parties, their representatives and witnesses to keep matters confidential. Any bold assumption that all proceedings should be kept confidential by all parties is not supported by the law in all countries however.

MA & BROCK, *supra* note 1, at para. 10.202 (citations omitted). This source continues at para. 10.207:

> Under the Arbitration Ordinance in Hong Kong, there are provisions on the protection of confidentiality in arbitration proceedings as well as court hearing related to those proceedings. To enhance confidentiality for international arbitration, s.16 of the Ordinance provides . . . court proceedings relating to arbitration are not to be heard in open court. Such proceedings will be heard in open court only if any party so applying can satisfy the court that for good reasons the proceedings ought to be heard in open court. Section 18 of the Ordinance also provides that unless otherwise agreed by the parties or under any exceptions as provided for in the Ordinance, no party may publish, disclose or communicate any information relating to arbitral proceedings and awards. . . .

[42] § 18(1) of the *Arbitration Ordinance*, *supra* note 5, states:

The third reason is that the parties enjoy flexible arbitration procedures. As long as the parties are treated fairly, an arbitration may be tailored to meet the specific requirements of the dispute, rather than conducted in accordance with the fixed procedural rules of a court. For instance, an arbitral tribunal is not bound by the strict rules of the courts in respect of the taking of evidence.[43] This procedural freedom also provides the parties the opportunity to choose a tribunal that is sufficiently experienced in the subject matter of their dispute rather than a judge who handles all disputes.[44] As mentioned above, in some instances, judges are randomly assigned to cases without any involvement by the parties. The parties are not given the opportunity to specify or to assess this judge's technical competence to decide the parties' dispute.[45]

Another reason is the almost-worldwide enforceability of a tribunal's decision made in international arbitration.[46] The tribunal's decision, known as an *arbitral award* or simply as an *award*, made in an international arbitration is enforceable against the losing party in the place where the award is made. More importantly, the arbitral award is also enforceable nearly worldwide under an international treaty signed in New York in 1958, the *Convention on the Recognition and Enforcement of Foreign Arbitral Awards* [hereinafter "*New York Convention*"]. Under this treaty, if the award was made in a member state of the treaty and the country where enforcement is sought by the winning party is also a member state, enforcement would be greatly simplified. Pursuant to the terms of this international treaty, an arbitral award made in one Convention state can be enforced in any other Convention state upon the production of the arbitration agreement and the award.[47]

> (1) Unless otherwise agreed by the parties, no party may publish, disclose or communicate any information relating to—
> (a) the arbitral proceedings under the arbitration agreement; or
> (b) an award made in those arbitral proceedings.

See also id. at § 16 "Proceedings to be heard otherwise than in open court" and § 17 "Restrictions on reporting of proceedings heard otherwise than in open court."

For an analysis of these three sections, *see* John Choong and Romesh Weeramantry, The Hong Kong Arbitration Ordinance: Commentary and Annotations paras. 16.00–18.32 (2nd ed. 2015) [hereinafter Choong & Weeramantry].

43 Queen Mary, *supra* note 36, at 6; Moser & Cheng, *supra* note 1, at para. 1-031.

44 One authority states that:

> [T]he cost of court proceedings is made even greater by the need to explain technical matters involved in a dispute to a judge who will probably have little or no familiarity with such issues . . . This problem may be resolved . . . by choosing arbitrators who have a background in the relevant industry . . . and who therefore have an understanding . . . of the technical issues . . . involved.

Mosher & Cheng, *supra* note 1, at para. 1-031.

See also Ma & Brock, *supra* note 1, at paras. 6.015–6.019 concerning the selection of arbitrators.

45 Queen Mary, *supra* note 36, at 6 states that 38% of respondents indicated "Selection of arbitrators" as being amongst the three most valuable characteristics of arbitration. This characteristic tied for third place with "Flexibility."

46 *Id.* revealed that 65% of respondents ranked "Enforceability of award" as the most valuable characteristic of arbitration.

47 This topic will be reviewed in detail in Chapter 3, "Laws and Rules of Arbitration" and Chapter 10, "Recognition and Enforcement of Award."

See, e.g., discussion in Ma & Brock, *supra* note 1, at paras. 6.022–6.025.

V. Disadvantages of Arbitration

One disadvantage of arbitration is its potential cost. With a scratch-sniff type of commodities arbitration, costs may be relatively low. Also known as a *look-sniff* arbitration, this type of dispute resolution frequently involves two merchants disagreeing as to the quality of a product rather than sophisticated legal or technical issues. For example, a shipment of rice arrives at the buyer's location. The buyer claims that the rice has turned mouldy. Because the rice is perishable, the disputing merchants need to resolve their dispute quickly in order to prevent further deterioration. The disputing merchants can appoint another rice merchant to examine the shipment and determine its quality: whether the rice is fit for human consumption, fit for use as animal feed, or unfit for any use. This neutral third party can visually inspect and perhaps sniff the product in order to come to an assessment.

At the opposite end of the cost spectrum, with an administered arbitration adopting courtroom-style procedures, costs may be as expensive as or even more expensive than litigation.[48] The principal reason is that arbitration is privately funded whereas litigation is substantially publicly funded.[49] Consequently, the parties in an arbitration need to pay for one or three arbitrators, their travel and accommodation expenses, arbitral institution's fees, transcription services, hearing rooms, *et cetera*.

---

[48] For example, one authority notes:

> International arbitration was once a relatively inexpensive method of dispute resolution. It is no longer so. There are several reasons for this. First, the fees and expenses of the arbitrators (unlike the salary of a judge) must be paid by the parties – and in international arbitrations of any significance, these charges are substantial. Secondly, it may be necessary to pay the administrative fees and expenses of an arbitral institution – and these too may be substantial. It may also be thought necessary to appoint a secretary or 'administrative assistant' to administer the proceedings. Once again, a fee must be paid. Finally, it will be necessary to hire rooms for meetings and hearings, rather than make use of the public facilities of the courts of law.
>
> But the fees of the arbitrators and of the arbitral institutions, the charges for room hire, the costs of court reporters, and other such expenses are usually a drop in the ocean compared with the fees and expenses of the parties' legal advisers and expert witnesses. In a major arbitration, these will run into many millions, and even tens of millions, of dollars. This means that international arbitration is not likely to be cheaper than proceedings in a court of first instance unless there is a very conscious effort to make it so.
>
> However, one point that should not be forgotten in considering the cost of arbitration is that it is a form of 'one-stop shopping'. Although the initial cost is not likely to be less than that of proceedings in court, the award of the arbitrators is unlikely to be followed by a series of costly appeals to superior local courts.

REDFERN & HUNTER, *supra* note 3, at paras. 1.123–1.125 (footnotes omitted).

Another authority notes:

> An arbitrator normally takes a passive role in the proceedings and relies on the parties to raise those matters which are considered to be relevant, and to solicit the truth by means of examination and cross-examination of witnesses in order to reach a decision. To this end, the same system of pleadings as in the court system is often adopted whereby the parties set out their cases in writing. The issues are usually complicated, involving painstaking examination and analysis of documents and other evidence by the staff of both parties and the need to give evidence at the hearing. As a result an arbitration can be as time consuming and expensive as litigation.

MA & BROCK, *supra* note 1, at para. 4.164.

[49] *See, e.g.*, MA & BROCK, *supra* note 1, at para. 4.165.

Litigation in a public court comes with the provision of a judge, a court room and usually meeting rooms for the parties and their lawyers.[50]

A second disadvantage is that a legal dispute may be decided by non-lawyers. Arbitration seems to be more suitable when the nature of the dispute is one of fact, especially of a technical character. If the dispute mainly centres on a legal issue, litigation might be more suitable unless the parties agree to appoint a legally-trained professional as arbitrator.

Another disadvantage is that arbitration is based on the parties' agreement to arbitrate. This results in a tribunal having jurisdiction over only the parties to the arbitration agreement. Other parties who are not bound by this agreement are not subject to the arbitral tribunal's jurisdiction. This results in the arbitrators having no power to make any order affecting an individual who is not a party to the arbitration agreement. For example, arbitrators have no power to order witnesses either to testify or to produce documents, to require third parties to participate in arbitration proceedings,[51] or to make awards requiring a third party to do or not to do something, including injunction and any form of interim relief binding on third parties.[52] A court, however, is able to make orders concerning all of these procedures. Therefore, sometimes, it may be necessary for an arbitral tribunal to request a court to order one or more of the interim relief measures.[53]

A further disadvantage arises with an administered arbitration where the rules of an arbitral institution may require the parties to follow deadlines which might not be suited for that type of dispute between the parties. Similarly, the institutional requirements might lead to delays and thus additional costs. For example, in an ICC arbitration, the duration of the proceedings might be extended both at the beginning and near the end of the arbitration. At the beginning of the process, a *Terms of Reference* is required.[54] Both the drafting and the potential contentiousness of the *Terms of Reference* might increase the duration and cost of the proceedings. At the conclusion of the proceedings, the arbitral tribunal's award is required to be submitted to the ICC Court of Arbitration for scrutiny which might increase the

---

[50] Queen Mary, *supra* note 36, at 7 listed the following top five ranked items by respondents to the question "What are the three worst characteristics of international arbitration?" These were:

- cost: 68%
- lack of effective sanctions during the arbitral process: 46%
- lack of insight into arbitrators' efficiency: 39%
- lack of speed: 36%
- national court intervention: 25%

See also Ma & Brock, *supra* note 1, at paras. 4.164–4.165.

[51] Moser & Cheng, *supra* note 1, at para. 1-032.

[52] *Id.* For example, an arbitral tribunal cannot order a bank to freeze the assets of one of the parties pending the outcome of the arbitration.

[53] This topic will be further discussed in Chapter 3, "Laws and Rules of Arbitration."

[54] ICC Rules of Arbitration (2017), Art. 23. These rules are available at: https://iccwbo.org/dispute-resolution-services/arbitration/rules-of-arbitration/ (last visited 21 June 2017).

time frame for concluding the arbitration process as "[n]o award shall be rendered by the arbitral tribunal until it has been approved by the Court as to its form."[55]

VI. Party Autonomy

International commercial arbitration is based on the concept or principle of party autonomy. What does this principle mean? *Party autonomy* indicates that the parties to an international commercial agreement are free to choose for themselves how to conduct much of the arbitration process.[56] The parties can select, amongst others, the following items:

- the law or the legal principles to be applied in deciding the dispute
- the procedural rules to be applied in conducting the arbitration
- the language to be used in the arbitration
- the location where the arbitration will be conducted

Party autonomy has been described in the following terms:

> Probably the most important principle on which the model law should be based is the freedom of the parties in order to facilitate the proper functioning of international commercial arbitration according to their expectations. This would allow them to freely submit their disputes to arbitration and to tailor the "rules of the game" to their specific needs.[57]

This principle can be found in UNCITRAL's *Model Law on International Commercial Arbitration* [hereinafter "*Model Law*"] which stipulates that: "Subject to the provisions of this Law, the parties are free to agree on the procedure to be followed by the arbitral tribunal in conducting the proceedings."[58] As mentioned previously, party autonomy would allow the parties the freedom mutually to select such particular items as:

- the place of arbitration
- the time where arbitral proceedings will be deemed to have commenced
- the language to be used in the arbitral proceedings
- the submission of statements of claim and defence, oral hearings and written proceedings[59]
- the powers of the tribunal in the event of a party's default

---

[55] *Id.* at Art. 34. Singapore International Arbitration Centre's Arbitration Rules (6th ed. 2016), Rule 32.3 contains a similar provision for vetting of the proposed award for form.

[56] For further discussion on this topic, *see, e.g.*, Ma & Brock, *supra* note 1, at paras. 6.003–6.019.

[57] United Nations Commission on International Trade Law (UNCITRAL), Report of the Secretary-General: Possible Features of a Model Law on International Commercial Arbitration, UN Doc. A/CN.9/207 (UN, 1981), para. 17.

[58] *See* § 47(1) of the *Arbitration Ordinance*, incorporating *Model Law* Art 19(1), *supra* note 5.

[59] So & To, *supra* note 12, at para. [52.03].

- experts appointed by the arbitral tribunal, as distinct from experts appointed by the parties
- general powers exercisable by the arbitral tribunal when conducting proceedings[60]

Further confirmation of the principle is found in the *New York Convention*, as well as another provision of the *Model Law*, which include deviation of arbitral procedures from parties' agreement as one of the grounds for refusing the recognition and enforcement of an arbitral award.[61]

Party autonomy does not mean total freedom for the parties. There remain restrictions on party autonomy. These restrictions are intended to preserve fairness which is often referred to by the term *natural justice*. Additionally, these restrictions are to maintain a country's public order and safety. These are two major restrictions on party autonomy: equal treatment of each party, and, public policy. We now discuss each of these in turn.

The *Model Law* provides that: "The parties shall be treated with equality and each party shall be given a full opportunity of presenting his case."[62] This requirement of equal treatment limits party autonomy. For example, a provision in an agreement which stipulates that only one party be permitted to present its case verbally to the arbitral tribunal might be invalid despite both parties having agreed to this procedure. This absence of the opportunity for a party to present its case to the tribunal is also a ground for setting aside an award as stated in the *New York Convention* as well as of the *Model Law*.[63] This subject is presented in greater detail in Chapter 10, "Recognition and Enforcement of the Award."

---

60 CHOONG & WEERAMANTRY, *supra* note 42, at para. 47.01.

61 *See* the *Convention on the Recognition and Enforcement of Foreign Arbitral Awards* [hereinafter *New York Convention*] Art. V(1)(d); UNCITRAL's *Model Law on International Commercial Arbitration* (2006) [hereinafter *Model Law*] Art. 36(1)(a)(iv).

62 § 46 of the *Arbitration Ordinance*, *supra* note 5, provides in part:

(1) Subsections (2) and (3) have effect in substitution for article 18 of the UNCITRAL Model Law.
(2) The parties must be treated with equality.
(3) When conducting arbitral proceedings or exercising any of the powers conferred on an arbitral tribunal by this Ordinance or by the parties to any of those arbitral proceedings, the arbitral tribunal is required—
   (a) to be independent;
   (b) to act fairly and impartially as between the parties, giving them a reasonable opportunity to present their cases and to deal with the cases of their opponents; and
   (c) to use procedures that are appropriate to the particular case, avoiding unnecessary delay or expense, so as to provide a fair means for resolving the dispute to which the arbitral proceedings relate.

63 *New York Convention*, *supra* note 61, at Art. V(1)(b); *Model Law*, *supra* note 61, at Art. 36(1)(a)(ii).
For example, § 86 of the *Arbitration Ordinance*, *supra* note 5, provides in part:

(1) Enforcement of an award referred to in section 85 may be refused if the person against whom it is invoked proves—
   . . .
   (c) that the person—
      (i) was not given proper notice of the appointment of the arbitrator or of the arbitral proceedings; or

Another restriction on party autonomy is public policy. This is a difficult term to define, being "one of the most elusive and divergent notions in the world of juridical science."[64] Nonetheless, the term *public policy* is defined by a source as:

> The collective rules, principles, or approaches to problems that affect the commonwealth or promote the general good . . . principles and standards regarded by the legislature or by the courts as being of fundamental concern to the state and the whole of society.[65]

For example, an application for enforcement of an arbitral award against a city-forming enterprise may be refused since such enforcement may result in bankruptcy and unemployment of the whole city.[66] Different countries and places have different application of public policy. For instance, in mainland China, public policy refers to "social and public interest."[67] In Hong Kong, the enforcement of an arbitral award made in circumstances where a respondent was unable to present its case would be regarded as a violation of public policy.[68] In Russia, public policy refers to the fundamental constitutional principles of the country and the imperative norms of that country's legislation, including international treaties ratified by Russia which constitute part of its domestic legislation.[69] In the United States, public policy is interpreted as "the most basic understanding by courts of morals and justice."[70] In Canada, public policy means the basic principles of public morals.[71] Public policy in England, for example, would not allow the enforcement of an illegal contract.[72]

The parties cannot confer powers on an arbitral tribunal that would cause the arbitration to be conducted in a manner contrary to the public policy of the country where the arbitration is held or cause the arbitration award to be contrary

---

(ii) was otherwise unable to present the person's case;

. . .

(2) Enforcement of an award referred to in section 85 may also be refused if—
(a) the award is in respect of a matter which is not capable of settlement by arbitration under the law of Hong Kong;
(b) it would be contrary to public policy to enforce the award; or
(c) for any other reason the court considers it just to do so.

64 Guy Horsmans, *L'arbitrage et l'Order Public Interne Belge*, 2 Rev Arb 79, 80 (1978).

65 Black's Law Dictionary 1426 (10th ed. 2014).

66 Diana V. Tapola, *Enforcement of Foreign Arbitral Awards: Application of the Public Policy Rule in Russia*, 22(1) Arbitration International 151, 156 (2006) (citations omitted) [hereinafter Tapola].

67 Art. 260 of the *Civil Procedure Law of the People's Republic of China* provides that: "If the people's court determines that the enforcement of the award goes against the social and public interest of the country, the people's court shall make a written order not to allow enforcement of the arbitral award."
Available at: http://www.npc.gov.cn/englishnpc/Law/2007-12/12/content_1383880.htm (last visited 9 Aug. 2017).

68 In *Sun Tian Gang v Hong Kong & China Gas (Jilin) Ltd* [2016] 5 HKLRD 221, the court, at para. 60, stated that: "to enforce an award made in circumstances when Sun [the losing party] was in fact unable to present his case in the Arbitration . . . would itself be contrary to the public policy of Hong Kong."

69 Tapola, *supra* note 66, at 160–161.

70 *Id.* at 151 (citations omitted).

71 *Id.* at 151–152 (citations omitted).

72 In *Soleimany (Abner) v Soleimany (Sion)* [1999] QB 785, the Court of Appeal refused to enforce an arbitral award that was rendered under Jewish law which recognized a party's contractual right even though the contract was for smuggling.

to public policy of the country where that award is sought to be enforced. Any such agreement would be unenforceable in that country.[73] For example, parties cannot contravene a mandatory provision in the *lex arbitri*.

> Although the modern philosophy is generally that parties should be at liberty to frame and regulate an arbitration as they see fit, this is only permitted and achievable to the extent that their choices do not conflict with provisions of the law of the seat which are expressly or impliedly of mandatory application. The freedom to derogate from the *lex arbitri* is only achievable to the extent that the *lex arbitri* itself permits it.[74]

As one commentator stated concerning the case of *Union of India v McDonnell Douglas*:

> English procedural law governed the proceedings, with the addition of the sections of Indian Statute that were not inconsistent with English procedure, because Indian procedural law cannot override the mandatory provisions of the English Arbitration Act 1996.[75]

VII. The Arbitration Agreement

In modern arbitration practice, it is critical to have an arbitration agreement in writing.[76] As noted by one authority:

> As arbitration is fundamentally consensual, it follows that the arbitration agreement is pivotal to the success of the process. Although this seems blindingly obvious, it is surprising that, in general, insufficient attention is given to the specific drawing up of the arbitration clause. Whilst in principle discussion of divorce is not a desirable topic on the night before the wedding, nevertheless businessmen should avoid acting as "star-crossed" lovers; indeed, they should be as rigorous about the provision relating to the resolution of potential disputes as they are about the other, more substantive, terms of the agreement.
>
> The arbitration clause essentially should be seen as an empowering provision: it enables the parties, whilst still friendly, to agree upon a number of matters which are likely to make any future disputes easier and cheaper to manage. Given the

---

[73] *New York Convention*, *supra* note 61, at Art. V(2)(b); *Model Law*, *supra* note 61, at Art. 36(1)(b)(ii).
More details on this subject of public policy will be found in Chapter 10, "Recognition and Enforcement of the Award."

[74] ALASTAIR HENDERSON, *Lex Arbitri, Procedural Law and the Seat of Arbitration*, 26 SACLJ 886, 898 (2014) [hereinafter HENDERSON]. *See also* REDFERN & HUNTER, *supra* note 3, at Chapt. 3.

[75] RAMAZAN ZORLU, *International Arbitration and Lex Arbitri* 2 (undated). Available at: http://www.akellawfirm.com/yayinlar/INTERNATIONAL_ARBITRATION_AND_LEX_ARBITRI.pdf (last visited 21 Jun. 2017).
This case is reported at [1993] 2 Lloyd's Rep 48. The parties' arbitration clause provided:

> In the event of a dispute . . . the arbitration shall be conducted in accordance with the procedure provided in the Indian Arbitration Act of 1940 or any . . . modification thereof. The arbitration shall be conducted in the English language . . . The seat of the arbitration proceedings shall be London, United Kingdom . . . *Id.* at 49.

[76] For an extensive discussion of this topic, *see, e.g.*, HALSBURY'S, *supra* note 4, at para. [25.012].

vagaries of human nature, once a dispute exists, it is usually next to impossible to achieve agreement on any objectively sensible arbitration agreement.[77]

Furthermore, a written arbitration agreement is a requirement under one option of the *Model Law*,[78] the *New York Convention*[79] and Hong Kong's *Arbitration*

---

[77] Ma & Brock, *supra* note 1, at paras. 10.001–10.002. For a detailed discussion of arbitration clauses, *see id.* at Chapt. 10. *See also* Choong & Weeramantry, *supra* note 42, at Chapt. 5.

[78] The *Model Law, supra* note 61, provides two versions of its Art. 7 for nation states to adopt into their national arbitration law. Option I requires the arbitration agreement to be in writing although the term *in writing* is liberally interpreted. Option II does not require a written arbitration agreement.

Option I

Article 7. Definition and form of arbitration agreement
(As adopted by the Commission at its thirty-ninth session, in 2006)

(1) "Arbitration agreement" is an agreement by the parties to submit to arbitration all or certain disputes which have arisen or which may arise between them in respect of a defined legal relationship, whether contractual or not. An arbitration agreement may be in the form of an arbitration clause in a contract or in the form of a separate agreement.
(2) The arbitration agreement shall be in writing.
(3) An arbitration agreement is in writing if its content is recorded in any form, whether or not the arbitration agreement or contract has been concluded orally, by conduct, or by other means.
(4) The requirement that an arbitration agreement be in writing is met by an electronic communication if the information contained therein is accessible so as to be useable for subsequent reference; "electronic communication" means any communication that the parties make by means of data messages; "data message" means information generated, sent, received or stored by electronic, magnetic, optical or similar means, including, but not limited to, electronic data interchange (EDI), electronic mail, telegram, telex or telecopy.
(5) Furthermore, an arbitration agreement is in writing if it is contained in an exchange of statements of claim and defence in which the existence of an agreement is alleged by one party and not denied by the other.
(6) The reference in a contract to any document containing an arbitration clause constitutes an arbitration agreement in writing, provided that the reference is such as to make that clause part of the contract.

Option II

Article 7. Definition of arbitration agreement
(As adopted by the Commission at its thirty-ninth session, in 2006)

"Arbitration agreement" is an agreement by the parties to submit to arbitration all or certain disputes which have arisen or which may arise between them in respect of a defined legal relationship, whether contractual or not.

The original 1985 version of the *Model Law* is more akin to Option I; there was no Option II. Art. 7(2) states:

The arbitration agreement shall be in writing. An agreement is in writing if it is contained in a document signed by the parties or in an exchange of letters, telex, telegrams or other means of telecommunication which provide a record of the agreement, or in an exchange of statements of claim and defence in which the existence of an agreement is alleged by one party and not denied by another. The reference in a contract to a document containing an arbitration clause constitutes an arbitration agreement provided that the contract is in writing and the reference is such as to make that clause part of the contract.

[79] The *New York Convention, supra* note 61, will be discussed in more detail in the following chapters. For the present, note that this *Convention's* Art. II mandates:

1. Each Contracting State shall recognize an agreement in writing under which the parties undertake to submit to arbitration all or any differences which have arisen or which may arise between them in respect of a defined legal relationship, whether contractual or not, concerning a subject matter capable of settlement by arbitration.
2. The term "agreement in writing" shall include an arbitral clause in a contract or an arbitration

Ordinance.[80] Due to the requirement in the *New York Convention* that the arbitration agreement be in writing in order for an arbitral award to be recognized and enforced, most countries have followed the *Model Law* Art. 7's Option I. This is true in Hong Kong where the *Arbitration Ordinance* requires an arbitration agreement to be in writing, however wide and liberal the interpretation may be of that term. Consequently, there may arise two preliminary issues: whether there was an arbitration agreement between the parties; and, whether this agreement was in writing.[81]

Several cases demonstrate the difficulties which may arise with this term. The first case is from Ireland which has incorporated the *Model Law* into its *Arbitration Act 2010*. In *Maguire v Motor Services Ltd t/a MSL Park Motors*,[82] Mr. and Mrs.

---

agreement, signed by the parties or contained in an exchange of letters or telegrams.

3. . . .

[80] § 19 of the *Arbitration Ordinance*, *supra* note 5, contains a more expansive provision of its requirements that an arbitration agreement be *in writing* in order to accommodate current communications technology:

(1) Option I of Article 7 of the UNCITRAL Model Law, the text of which is set out below, has effect—
"*Option I*

Article 7. Definition and form of arbitration agreement

(1) "Arbitration agreement" is an agreement by the parties to submit to arbitration all or certain disputes which have arisen or which may arise between them in respect of a defined legal relationship, whether contractual or not. An arbitration agreement may be in the form of an arbitration clause in a contract or in the form of a separate agreement.
(2) The arbitration agreement shall be in writing.
(3) An arbitration agreement is in writing if its content is recorded in any form, whether or not the arbitration agreement or contract has been concluded orally, by conduct, or by other means.
(4) The requirement that an arbitration agreement be in writing is met by an electronic communication if the information contained therein is accessible so as to be useable for subsequent reference; "electronic communication" means any communication that the parties make by means of data messages; "data message" means information generated, sent, received or stored by electronic, magnetic, optical or similar means, including, but not limited to, electronic data interchange (EDI), electronic mail, telegram, telex or telecopy.
(5) Furthermore, an arbitration agreement is in writing if it is contained in an exchange of statements of claim and defence in which the existence of an agreement is alleged by one party and not denied by the other.
(6) The reference in a contract to any document containing an arbitration clause constitutes an arbitration agreement in writing, provided that the reference is such as to make that clause part of the contract."

(2) Without affecting subsection (1), an arbitration agreement is in writing if—
(a) the agreement is in a document, whether or not the document is signed by the parties to the agreement; or
(b) the agreement, although made otherwise than in writing, is recorded by one of the parties to the agreement, or by a third party, with the authority of each of the parties to the agreement.

(3) A reference in an agreement to a written form of arbitration clause constitutes an arbitration agreement if the reference is such as to make that clause part of the agreement.

[81] The reader should be aware that in mainland China, *ad hoc* arbitration is not allowed in principle where the disputants are mainland parties. There are exceptions for business entities situated in areas designated as *Free Trade Zones* or in instances where a foreign-related civil relationship exists. Therefore, in these cases, additional preliminary issues often arise.

[82] [2017] IEHC 532 (unreported, High Court, 7 Sep. 2017).

Maguire purchased a vehicle from the respondents. Only Mrs. Maguire signed the purchase contract which contained an arbitration clause. When mechanical difficulties arose with the vehicle, the claimants began court proceedings for breach of contract, misrepresentation and negligence against Motor Services as the seller and Mazda Motor Ireland as the manufacturer. The respondents attempted to stop the court proceedings and force the parties to arbitration pursuant to *Model Law* Art. 8(1).[83] The issue before the court was whether Mr. Maguire could continue with the court proceedings despite the commonalities between the litigation and the arbitration. The court decided:

> Art. 8(1) only operates where "an action is brought in a matter which is the subject of an arbitration agreement". Though it is possible for an arbitration agreement to apply to a non-party where sufficient connection presents, and though the court understands Mazda Motor Ireland to have charge of the within proceedings on the defendants' side, there is not between MSL Park Motors and Mazda Motor Ireland

---

For a further discussion of persons bound by an arbitration agreement, *see, e.g.*, HALSBURY'S, *supra* note 4, at para. [25.013].

[83] *Model Law*, *supra* note 61, at Art. 8(1) provides:

> A court before which an action is brought in a matter which is the subject of an arbitration agreement shall, if a party so requests not later than when submitting his first statement on the substance of the dispute, refer the parties to arbitration unless it finds that the agreement is null and void, inoperative or incapable of being performed.

One source has provided a definition of the terms "null and void," "inoperative" and "incapable of being performed" as follows:

- "Null and void" does not encompass a merely voidable agreement. The court will refuse a stay where, for example:
  - There is initial or supervening illegality which impeaches not only the substantive contract but also the arbitration clause
  - The subject matter of the arbitration agreement is not arbitrable or the arbitration agreement is otherwise invalid for any reason
  - Where there is no arbitration agreement within the meaning of this provision. This includes the situation where no agreement came into being because there was no offer and acceptance and where the agreement is void for uncertainty. The use of permissive word 'may' rather than 'shall' in arbitration agreement is not, however, necessarily fatal to its validity
  - Where a party did not have legal capacity to enter into an arbitration agreement
  - Where an arbitration agreement in a superior or parallel contract has not be properly incorporated by reference
  - Where the subject-matter of the arbitration may not be arbitrated for reasons of Hong Kong public policy
- "Inoperative" encompasses the following situations:
  - Where a limitation period has expired, by virtue either of statue [*sic*] or of contract
  - Where a particular matter does not fall within the terms of the arbitration agreement
  - Where a person nominated by the arbitration agreement to arbitrate any dispute arising between the parties to the arbitration proceedings is a party to the underlying contract, though not a party to the proceedings, and is for that reasons [*sic*] incapable of acting impartially
- "Incapable of being performed" means where the arbitration cannot effectively be set in motion, for example, because the terms of the arbitration agreement are rather too vague, or because there are contradictory terms in the contract which affect the parties' intention to arbitrate. These words refer only to the arbitration agreement itself, and the circumstance of the party is rather irrelevant.

SO & TO, *supra* note 12, at paras. [20.11]–[20.13].

See also REDFERN & HUNTER, *supra* note 3, at para. 2.202 and TWEEDDALE & TWEEDDALE, *supra* note 30, at paras. 4.33–4.54 for similar definitions.

> that "more than . . . bare commercial or legal connection between two entities" which MacEochaidh J. considered should [be] present before an arbitration agreement would be so applied.... So there is only an arbitration agreement between Ms Maguire and MSL Park Motors; and hence it is only to that dimension of the within proceedings that the stay granted by the court below could have been granted.[84]
>
> Two questions then arise:
>
> (1) should (a) Mr. Maguire's claims against MSL Park Motors and Mazda . . . which claims are not based on the [contract] (to which he is not party) be stayed because (b) his wife's claim against MSL Park Motors has been stayed pending the outcome of contractually-mandated arbitration pursuant to the standard terms and conditions (to which she is party)?
>
> (2) should (a) Ms. Maguire's claim against Mazda . . . as producer of the Mazda M6 motor-car, be stayed because (b) her claim against the vendor of that motor-car has been the subject of . . . [a] stay pending the outcome of contractually-mandated arbitration?[85]
>
> The court's answer to each of the questions just posed is 'no'. If parties have validly agreed that a legal dispute should go to arbitration, then to arbitration that dispute must go. But if parties have not agreed that a legal dispute should go to arbitration, then to the courts that dispute should go. And despite the factually related nature of the disputes that will fall to the arbitrator/court respectively to arbitrate/adjudicate upon in the context of the above-described claims, there does not seem to this Court to be any reason why those factually related but substantively different claims cannot separately be arbitrated/adjudicated upon.[86]

In another case, an Indian court refused to enforce an arbitral award in a case similar to the above, *i.e.*, whether an entity not a party to an arbitration agreement was bound by that agreement. *Virgoz Oils and Fats Pte Ltd v National Agricultural Marketing Federation of India*[87] involved three parties: Virgoz, a broker and National Agricultural. Only the broker and Virgoz signed the contracts. The court referred to the *New York Convention*'s requirement for an arbitration agreement in writing and signed or contained in an exchange of letters or telegrams. The court decided that National Agriculture had not signed any contract containing an arbitration clause. Moreover, Virgoz and National Agriculture communications did not indicate any agreement to submit disputes to arbitration. Consequently, the court concluded that National Agriculture was not a party to the contracts containing an arbitration agreement between the broker and Virgoz.

It should be noted that courts could determine that the conduct of a party implied its agreement to participate in arbitration proceedings in the event of a dispute. In the case of *Jiangsu Overseas Group Co Ltd v Concord Energy Pte Ltd*,[88] Jiangsu alleged that it did not enter into any contract with Concord as there were

---

84 [2017] IEHC at para. 5.
85 *Id.* at para. 6.
86 *Id.* at para. 7.
87 EX.P. 149/2015 and EA(OS) No. 66/2016.
88 [2016] SGHC 153.

no signed contracts between the parties. Hence, the agreement for arbitration was invalid, in part as there was no arbitration agreement in writing. The court decided otherwise, finding that there was at least one written contract incorporating an arbitration agreement and that the contract was validly and impliedly created by the parties' conduct. The Singapore High Court stated:

> 30 Jiangsu was repeatedly invited to participate in the arbitrations but failed to do so. It did not attend any procedural hearings or file any pleadings, witness statements, or submissions. Initially, it even refused to accept delivery of the statement of claim and supporting documents via courier. This prompted the tribunal to issue a procedural order directing Concord to serve the statement of claim and supporting documents on Jiangsu through Concord's Chinese lawyers. On 22 October 2014, Jiangsu's Chinese lawyers confirmed receipt of the documents, but added that due to Jiangsu's "network server's problem", Jiangsu had been unable to obtain the attachments sent to it "during the whole arbitration procedure". . . . Jiangsu instructed Singapore lawyers, who informed the tribunal of their appointment on 28 October 2014. When Jiangsu was unable to obtain an immediate adjournment of the arbitration hearing, it informed the tribunal . . . on 29 October 2014 that it would not be able to attend the hearing on 31 October 2014 because it had little time "for preparing to travel to Singapore". Jiangsu discharged its Singapore lawyers that same day. The hearing before the tribunal therefore proceeded in its absence. (footnotes omitted)
>
> . . .
>
> 79 I should first dispose of Jiangsu's initial defence to the claim, *ie*, that Jiangsu did not formally indicate its assent by signing the Spot and Term contacts [*sic*]. The non-signing of the contracts cannot in itself be a bar to the formation of contract, for "the sterile formality of a signature is not always necessary in law to breathe life into contractual undertakings" . . . In *R1 International*, the Court of Appeal found that the fact that a party did not counter-sign and return the contract note did not mean that the unsigned contract note was not contractually binding . . . Jiangsu's allegation that it would not consider itself bound until its company seal had been applied fails for the same reason. . . . Jiangsu cannot have it both ways. If it shows objectively by its conduct vis-a-vis Concord that it was intending to perform the contracts, it cannot then rely on the unsigned contracts to evade the consequences of the contracts when it suits them. (citations omitted)

In the following paragraphs of its decision, the Singapore court detailed the actions taken by Jiangsu which the court interpreted to be activities pursuant to an agreement between the two parties. The court concluded its decision by stating:

> 93 I find that the . . . contracts were validly concluded between Jiangsu and Concord. Consequently, the arbitration agreements . . . in both contracts were valid and the tribunal had jurisdiction to hear the disputes in respect of Jiangsu's breaches of the . . . contracts.

In a similar case in Switzerland,[89] the parties exchanged a series of contract drafts. None of these drafts were signed by either party. Each draft contained an identical arbitration clause for Swiss Chamber of Commerce arbitration in Lugano under the Swiss rules. The sole arbitrator in the case determined that he had jurisdiction as the arbitration clause was binding. On appeal, the Swiss court decided that:

- the arbitration clause is a separate agreement from the contract; hence, the status of the contract does not affect the validity of the arbitration clause
- Swiss law requires an arbitration agreement to be in writing but this agreement need not be signed by the parties

On similar facts in another case, a Singapore court decided that there was no arbitration agreement.[90] In this instance, the parties had agreed upon the dispute resolution clause during their overall contract negotiations. The negotiations ultimately failed and subsequently a dispute arose. The arbitral tribunal ruled that it had jurisdiction as the parties had agreed to arbitrate all disputes during the course negotiations prior to signing the contract. The court decided that:

> 71 In my judgment, the arbitration agreement here was clearly intended to be part of the [Sale & Purchase Agreement]. It was at all times negotiated as part of the SPA. The question . . . is whether the parties agreed to be bound by the arbitration clause first, with agreement on the rest of the terms of the SPA to follow later when it was executed.[91]
>
> . . .
>
> 90 . . . agreeing to the wording of the arbitration clause does not *per se* equate to an intention to be contractually bound to arbitrate absent the conclusion of the contract under which the arbitration clause was negotiated.[92]

Likewise, a party's actual participation in the arbitration indicates a party's intent to be bound to this dispute resolution process.[93]

The next chapter discusses in more detail the law of the seat of the arbitration. Here, we briefly consider the difficulty caused by an arbitration agreement

---

[89] *X Co v Z Ltd*, 4A_84/2015, English summary available at: http://www.swissarbitrationdecisions.com/unsigned-arbitration-clause-upheld?search=4A_84%2F2015 (last visited 30 Jun. 2017).
English translation of the court decision available at: http://www.swissarbitrationdecisions.com/sites/default/files/18%20f%C3%A9vrier%202016%204A%2084%202016.pdf (last visited 30 Jun. 2017).

[90] *BCY v BCZ* [2016] SGHC 249.

[91] *Id.* at para. 70.

[92] *Id.* at para. 90.

[93] *See, e.g.*, Bernard Hanotiau, *Consent to Arbitration: Do We Share a Common Vision?*, 27(4) Arbitration International 539 (2011); Andrea Marco Steingruber, Consent in International Arbitration (2012); Mohamed S. Abdel Wahab, *Extension of Arbitration Agreements to Third Parties* in Conflict of Laws in Arbitration (Franco Ferrari and Stefan Kröll, eds., 2011); *Jiangsu Overseas Group, supra* note 88. In *Chloro Controls India Pvt Ltd v Severn Trent Water Purification* (2013) 1 SCC 641, the court decided that related subsidiaries in a business group, under certain circumstances, can be bound by the arbitration agreement entered into by another subsidiary member of the business group.

specifying a seat in one jurisdiction but applying the law of another jurisdiction.[94] *Braes of Doune Wind Farm v Alfred McAlpine Business Services Ltd*[95] involved a claim by Braes against McAlpine for damages arising from contractual delay. The governing law provision of the contract stipulated:

> The Contract shall be governed by and construed in accordance with the laws of England and Wales and, subject to Clause 20.2 [Dispute Resolution], the Parties agree that the courts of England and Wales have exclusive jurisdiction to settle any dispute arising out of or in connection with the Contract.

The dispute resolution clause stated:

> This arbitration agreement is subject to English Law and the seat of the arbitration shall be Glasgow, Scotland. Any such reference to arbitration shall be deemed to be a reference to arbitration within the meaning of the Arbitration Act 1996 or any statutory re-enactment.

The court ultimately decided:

> the parties' express agreement that the "seat" of arbitration was to be Glasgow, Scotland must relate to the place in which the parties agreed that the hearings should take place. However, by all the other references the parties were agreeing that the curial law or law which governed the arbitral proceedings was that of England and Wales. Although authorities establish that, prima facie and in the absence of agreement otherwise, the selection of a place or seat for an arbitration will determine what the curial law or "lex fori" or "lex arbitri" will be, I consider that, where in substance the parties agree that the laws of one country will govern and control a given arbitration, the place where the arbitration is to be heard will not dictate what the governing or controlling law will be.[96]

In essence, the United Kingdom's High Court decided that it is possible to have one law apply to an arbitration being seated in a jurisdiction whose law is different. The court also interpreted the arbitration agreement to mean that the United

---

[94] As noted by Henderson, *supra* note 74, at 890:

> The basic approach of the Model Law (and all national laws derived from it) is thus that the law applicable to each arbitration (the *lex arbitri*) will be the law of the place where that arbitration takes place (the *lex loci arbitri*), and the selection of a particular place (seat) of arbitration ordinarily results in the arbitration being conducted in accordance with that jurisdiction's legal framework. (citations omitted) *Id.* at 890.
>
> . . .
>
> . . . there is a technical distinction between the *lex loci arbitri* (the law of the place of the arbitration) and the *lex arbitri* (the law of the arbitration). It was noted earlier that in most cases these two concepts will be entirely congruent: the *lex arbitrai* will be the *lex loci arbitri* and it is unnecessary to maintain a distinction between them. Strictly speaking, however, they are separate concepts which allow for the possibility that parties will choose to modify the *lex loci arbitri* by the adoption of a foreign procedural law . . . *Id.* at 906–907.

[95] [2008] EWHC 426 (TCC).

[96] *Id.* at para. 17(e).

Kingdom's *Arbitration Act* would apply as the arbitration was seated in England while the hearings would be conducted in Scotland.

In relation to the above items, a potential major disadvantage to arbitration is the parties' poorly drafted agreement to arbitrate. While each institution has its own model arbitration clause for adoption by interested parties, there are those parties who attempt to write their own arbitration agreements resulting in what are commonly referred to as *midnight clauses*.[97] The resulting agreements to arbitrate become what are also termed *pathological clauses* either due to misunderstanding the purpose and function of arbitration, and/or making compromises with the other party in order to meet the midnight deadline.[98]

In an older Hong Kong case, *Lucky-Goldstar International v Ng Moo Kee Engineering Ltd*,[99] the parties' arbitration clause stated in part:

> Any dispute or difference arising out of or relating to this contract or the breach thereof which cannot be settled amicably without undue delay by the interested parties shall be arbitrated in the third country under the rules of the third country and in accordance with the rules of procedure of the International Commercial Arbitration Association.

Ignoring the obvious error of using the word *rules* rather than the word *laws*, the court had to deal with the interpretation to be applied to *third country* along with the issue that the International Commercial Arbitration Association was a non-existent organization. The court made the following comments:

> This is not the first case with which I have had to deal where the arbitration clause has left something to be desired. Many contract drafters seem to have difficulty in the fairly simple task of drafting an arbitration clause or even replicating a standard form clause. Arbitral institutions and associations go to the trouble of drafting standard form arbitration clauses and disseminating them . . . yet in far too high a percentage of cases something goes wrong. The former Secretary General of the

---

[97] *Midnight clauses* refers to those clauses left amongst the last to be considered by the parties. Frequently, the scenario involving midnight clauses is where the parties have been negotiating contract terms for a full day. As the time approaches the midnight deadline, the parties are exhausted and most likely only interested in concluding the task of producing a contract. Those items left to this time, generally the dispute resolution clause, receive short shrift in part because, like engaged couples or newlyweds, the parties also refuse to contemplate the possibility of a separation or contentious divorce arising from their relationship. As a Singapore court noted:

> It is not uncommon that commercial parties omit to include in their contracts an express choice of law governing their international arbitration agreements. These "midnight clauses" may be included in the main contract very late in the day along with other standard terms just before the contract is signed, understandably so as most parties would be enthusiastic about concluding the negotiations on the contractual obligations, while failing to direct their minds to a possible breakdown of the commercial relationship and the attendant specifics of the dispute resolution process.

FirstLink Investments Corp Ltd v GT Payment Pte Ltd [2014] SGHCR 12 para. 1.

[98] For an explanation of the origins of this term and for examples of other pathological clauses and their results, *see* Shaun Lee, *Pathological Arbitration Clauses*, Singapore International Arbitration Blog (8 Mar. 2013). Link at https://singaporeinternationalarbitration.com/2013/03/08/pathological-arbitration-clauses/ (last visited 11 Aug. 2017); Redfern & Hunter, *supra* note 3, at paras. 2.197–2.203.

[99] [1993] 1 HKC 404.

> ICC told an audience . . . that only in a very small number of cases which came to the ICC, did the parties manage to replicate accurately in their contract the standard ICC Clause. A badly drafted clause leads to disputes and wasted costs, both of which are anathema to the arbitral process.[100]

Two recent Singapore cases have demonstrated that pathological, or at least poorly drafted, arbitration clauses continue to exist. In the first case, *TMT v The Royal Bank of Scotland*,[101] the arbitration clause provided:

> Any dispute arising from or relating to these terms or any Contract made hereunder shall, unless resolved between us, be referred to arbitration under the arbitration rules of the *relevant exchange* or any other organisation as the *relevant exchange* may direct and both parties agree to, such agreement not to be unreasonable [*sic*] withheld, before either of us resort to the jurisdiction of the Court. (emphasis added)

The Singapore court concluded that the parties' arbitration clause to be inoperative or to be incapable of being performed, concluding that Singapore courts would not:

> readily rewrite the agreements entered into between parties, especially in a commercial agreement between commercial entities, which presumably would have been scrutinised by legal advisors. If there were any slips despite such scrutiny, the parties would have to live with the consequences.[102]

In the second Singapore case, *KVC Rice Intertrade Co Ltd v Asian Mineral Resources Pte Ltd*,[103] the parties' arbitration clause contained an ambiguity:

> The Seller and the Buyer agree that all disputes arising out of or in connection with this agreement that cannot be settled by discussion and mutual agreement shall be referred to and finally resolved by arbitration as per *Indian Contract Rules*. (emphasis added)

The intended meaning of the emphasized phrase is unclear. The court concluded that the wording *Indian Contract Rules* lacked any intelligible meaning and should be disregarded in interpreting the arbitration clause.[104]

---

100 *Id.* at 408.
101 [2017] SGHC 21.
102 *Id.* at para. 68.
103 [2017] SGHC 32.
104 *Id.* at paras. 50–56. The court's dilemma is explained in the beginning of its decision:

1. This case concerns two . . . appeals . . . in two separate suits . . . that were heard together before me. The Suits each concern an international contract containing a bare arbitration clause, ie, an arbitration clause which specifies neither the place of arbitration nor the means of appointing arbitrators. As a result, the plaintiffs faced difficulties getting an arbitration underway in the absence of cooperation from the defendant. . . .
2. Since the relevant provisions of the International Arbitration Act . . . ("IAA") apply only when the place of arbitration is Singapore, a bare arbitration clause which fails to designate the place of arbitration raises questions regarding the extent to which the Singapore courts and the Singapore

A final example involved the Hong Kong case of *Bio-Chem Technology (HK) Ltd v Rich Leaf International (HK) Ltd.*[105] Here, the parties disputed, amongst other issues, whether the claim fell outside the scope of application of the arbitration clause which stated:

> All disputes in connection with this *contract of the execution* thereof shall be settled by negotiation. In case no settlement can be reached the case in dispute shall then be submitted for arbitration in accordance with the Hong Kong Arbitration ordinance [*sic*] and with arbitration to take place in Hong Kong.[106]

As the court noted in its judgement:

> 15. The plaintiff submits that the Arbitration clause [*sic*] is limited to disputes in connection with the execution of the contract and that . . . the plaintiff's claim is a debt, which only becomes due and payable after the execution of the contract by delivery of the product to the defendant.
>
> 16. This submission relies on a restricted reading of the Arbitration Clause and in particular the use of the word "of" in line 1 to narrow the scope of disputes covered to those connected to execution only.
>
> 17. The defendant on the other hand submits that the word "of" is a typographical error and should read "or" which would be the more usual formulation in a standard arbitration clause. . . .
>
> . . .
>
> 19. I accept the defendant's submissions and am satisfied that the disputes . . . are within the ambit of the Arbitration Clause. It seems to me to be clear that the parties intended the Arbitration Clause to apply to disputes between them arising out of their relationship under the contracts in question, and the contrary interpretation flies in the face of commercial sense: *Klöckner Pentaplast GmbH v Advance Technology (HK) Co Ltd* [2011] HKCFI 458; [2011] 4 HKLRD 262 at § 10.

International Arbitration Centre ("SIAC"), in its capacity as the default appointing authority under the IAA, are able to support and facilitate an arbitration pursuant to such a clause. This in turn raises the question of whether a clause of this nature should be considered "null and void, inoperative or incapable of being performed" for the purposes of s 6(2) of the IAA. The principal issue presented in this case is neatly summarised in the following observation from Nigel Blackaby *et al*, *Redfern and Hunter on International Arbitration* (Oxford University Press, 5th Ed, 2009) ("*Redfern and Hunter*"), at para 4.43:

> A clause that fails to provide either for an effective method of constituting the arbitral tribunal, or for the place of arbitration, may turn out to be inoperable. It is likely to lead to the claimant being unable to enforce the arbitration agreement. If a claimant takes its case to a national court, it may be met by an application for a stay of the proceedings on the grounds of the existence of an arbitration clause. At best there is considerable potential for delay. *At worst, there is the possibility that the claimant may find there is no effective remedy at all, since the courts will refuse to entertain an action and the arbitration clause is defective.* (emphasis added)

[105] [2017] HKCFI 2048.

For further discussion concerning the form of words used in an arbitration agreement, *see, e.g.*, HALSBURY'S, *supra* note 4, at para. [25.022].

[106] [2017] HKCFI 2048 at para. 14 (emphasis added).

VIII. Summary

We began this chapter with an overview of the definition of the phrase international commercial arbitration and its differences with other dispute resolution methods. We then discussed the types of arbitration along with the advantages and disadvantages of this dispute resolution process including party autonomy. We concluded this chapter with an examination of the arbitration clause, its requirements and good practices relating to the same in order to avoid disputes over the clause and wasted costs, both of which are an anathema to the arbitral process.[107]

[107] *Lucky-Goldstar v Ng*, *supra* note 99, at para. 21.

3

Laws and Rules of Arbitration

I. Introduction

In this chapter, we review two items which affect the manner in which arbitration is conducted. The first of these items is the laws, such as statutes or ordinances, which create the framework for the management of arbitration at the venue where those laws apply. The second of these items is the procedural rules which primarily regulate how arbitration will be conducted. Related to an arbitral institution's rules, there are also rules or guidelines commonly used in arbitration which have no binding effect unless agreed by the parties. These rules or guidelines are discussed at the end of the chapter.

II. Laws

In this section, we examine three main laws that apply to international commercial arbitration. These three laws are commonly referred to as the:

A. UNCITRAL *Model Law*
B. law of the seat of arbitration
C. *New York Convention*

Each of these is reviewed. Thereafter, discussed in more detail is the Hong Kong *Arbitration Ordinance* in the event Hong Kong is chosen as the seat.

While reviewing the effect of laws on an arbitration proceeding, the reader should keep the following in mind: At times, a law, or an ordinance in the case of Hong Kong, may have some overlap with the procedural rules. It may be helpful to consider laws as being more general than procedural rules and the laws as having precedence over these procedural rules in the event of conflict between the two.

A. UNCITRAL *Model Law on International Commercial Arbitration*[1]

The United Nations Commission on International Trade Law [hereinafter "UNCITRAL"][2] issued in 1985 the Commission's *Model Law on International Commercial Arbitration* [hereinafter "*Model Law*"]. Commonly known as the UNCITRAL *Model Law*, this work was updated in 2006.[3] As its name implies, this *Model Law* is intended to serve as a model or a template for nations to use in creating their own laws on international commercial arbitration.[4] An underlying purpose of the *Model Law* is to provide for universal consistency or harmonization of the arbitration laws of nations.[5]

Numerous jurisdictions have adopted the *Model Law*. Hong Kong adopted the *Model Law* for only international arbitrations in 1990, under the former *Arbitration Ordinance* (Cap. 341) which also provided for a different and separate regime for domestic arbitrations. In 2010, Hong Kong unified its international arbitration regime and its domestic arbitration regime in its current *Arbitration Ordinance* (Cap. 609) which incorporates nearly all the *Model Law* provisions.[6]

---

1 The United Nations Commission on International Trade Law's website translates "*Model Law on International Commercial Arbitration*" as 貿易法委員會國際商事仲裁示範法. *See* the Chinese version of the website at: http://www.uncitral.org/uncitral/zh/uncitral_texts/ar bitration/1985Model_arbitration.html (last visited 7 Jul. 2017). The English version of this website may be found at: http://www.uncitral.org/pdf/english/texts/arbitration/ml-arb/07-86998_Ebook.pdf (last visited 7 Jul. 2017).

For the purposes of this book, the term *Model Law* refers to the 2006 version of the *Model Law on International Commercial Arbitration*.

2 UNCITRAL's website, *supra* note 1, translates "UNCITRAL" as 聯合國國際貿易法委員會.

The Hong Kong International Arbitration Centre [hereinafter HKIAC] provides an identical translation. *See* the HKIAC's website at: http://www.hkiac.org/zh-hant/arbitration/rules-practice-notes/uncitral-arbitration-rules (last visited 7 Jul. 2017).

3 *See* http://www.uncitral.org/pdf/english/texts/arbitration/ml-arb/07-86998_Ebook.pdf (last visited 7 Jul. 2017).

4 BUTTERWORTHS HONG KONG ARBITRATION LAW HANDBOOK para. [4.01] (DAMON YC SO, CHRISTOPHER TO *et al.*, eds., 2nd ed. 2018) [hereinafter SO & TO] notes: "The Model Law is a 'model' that States are free to adopt in a method appropriate to their domestic legal system. Thus, the Model Law itself has no binding legal effect on UN Member States."

Certain provisions of the *Model Law* are mandatory; the parties cannot derogate or deviate from these provisions. Other provisions of the *Model Law* are default provisions in the event the parties have not made or specified other arrangements, *e.g.*, the number of arbitrators; parties are permitted to derogate or deviate from these provisions. *Id.* at para. [11.04] provides a list of the mandatory; the non-mandatory; and the mixed provisions. With the non-mandatory provisions and with the appropriate sub-parts of the mixed provisions, there is party autonomy.

5 The *Model Law* website, *supra* note 1, provides:

> The Model Law is designed to assist States in reforming and modernizing their laws on arbitral procedure so as to take into account the particular features and needs of international commercial arbitration. It covers all stages of the arbitral process from the arbitration agreement, the composition and jurisdiction of the arbitral tribunal and the extent of court intervention through to the recognition and enforcement of the arbitral award. It reflects worldwide consensus on key aspects of international arbitration practice having been accepted by States of all regions and the different legal or economic systems of the world.

6 The full text of the *Model Law* is set out in Schedule 1 of the *Arbitration Ordinance* (Cap. 609) [hereinafter *Arbitration Ordinance*].

For review of the sections of the Model Law, *see* 2 HALSBURY'S LAWS OF HONG KONG para. [25.008] (2nd ed. 2016) [hereinafter HALSBURY'S].

B. Law of the Seat

As mentioned in the previous chapter, *law of the seat* refers to the forum or the venue where the arbitration is deemed to be held.[7] Thus, the seat of the arbitration simply refers to the place of the arbitration which is usually agreed by the parties in an arbitration agreement.[8] The seat determines the applicable procedural law for the arbitration, unless the parties have agreed otherwise.[9] The applicable procedural law for the arbitration might include default provisions which apply in instances where the parties have not made any provisions or if the parties' chosen arbitration rules do not address a particular issue. The applicable procedural law may, for example, contain provisions to assist the parties or the arbitral tribunal in such matters as:[10]

- appointment of the arbitral tribunal, including how and by whom[11]
- a party challenging the appointment of an arbitrator[12]

---

[7] Sometimes also known as *lex arbitri*, *curial law*, or *lex loci arbitri*. There can be as many as six applicable national laws in an arbitration:

1. Law applicable to each party's capacity to enter into a contract or arbitration agreement
2. Law governing the arbitration agreement (governing law)
3. Law of the seat of the arbitration (*lex arbitri*)
4. Law governing the procedure of the arbitration (curial law, procedural law, *lex loci arbitri* or *lex fori*)
5. Law governing the contract giving rise to the main dispute (*lex causae* or substantive law)
6. Law of the place where the award will be enforced

Ordinarily, the laws listed in items 2–4 above would coincide so that there would be no issue. However, if the parties seek to apply laws of different jurisdictions to each of these, there would be complications and confusion. Essentially, this complexity would be centred upon which court will decide which law applies.

See ARBITRATION IN HONG KONG: A PRACTICAL GUIDE paras. 9.091–9.092 (THE HON CHIEF JUSTICE GEOFFREY MA AND DENIS BROCK, eds., 4th ed. 2017) [hereinafter MA & BROCK] for slightly differently worded list of nine; REDFERN AND HUNTER ON INTERNATIONAL ARBITRATION para. 3.07 (NIGEL BLACKABY *et al.*, eds., 6th ed. 2015) [hereinafter REDFERN & HUNTER] for a slightly differently worded list of five.

For more information on competing laws from different jurisdictions, *see* THE CONFLICT OF LAWS IN HONG KONG (GRAEME JOHNSTON *et al.*, eds., 3rd ed. 2017) and DICEY, MORRIS & COLLINS ON THE CONFLICT OF LAWS (LORD COLLINS *et al.*, eds., 15th ed. 2016).

See also ALAN TSANG, *Determining the Law Applicable to Arbitration Agreements: The Common Law Approach*, 29(5) MEALEY'S INTERNATIONAL ARBITRATION REPORT (2014).

[8] MICHAEL J. MOSER AND TERESA Y. W. CHENG, HONG KONG ARBITRATION: A USER'S GUIDE para. 5-021 (3rd ed. 2014) [hereinafter MOSER & CHENG].

[9] As noted in REDFERN & HUNTER, *supra* note 7, at para. 3.56 concerning the seat of the arbitration: "It is the territorial link between the arbitration itself and the law of the place in which that arbitration is legally situated." The authors continue:

> When one says that London, Paris or Geneva is the place of arbitration, one does not refer solely to a geographical location. One means that the arbitration is conducted within the framework of the law of arbitration of England, France or Switzerland or, to use an English expression, under the curial law of the relevant country. The geographical place of arbitration is the factual connecting factor between that arbitration law and the arbitration proper.

Id., quoting CLAUDE REYMOND, *Where is an arbitral award made?*, 108 LQR 1, 3 (1992).

[10] REDFERN & HUNTER, *supra* note 7, at para. 3.46 provides "examples of the matters with which the *lex arbitri* might be expected to deal."

[11] *See, e.g.*, § 24 of the *Arbitration Ordinance*, incorporating *Model Law* Art. 11, *supra* note 6. For a discussion of this section of the Ordinance, *see, e.g.*, JOHN CHOONG and ROMESH WEERAMANTRY, THE HONG KONG ARBITRATION ORDINANCE: COMMENTARY AND ANNOTATIONS paras. 24.00–24.38. (2nd ed. 2015) [hereinafter CHOONG & WEERAMANTRY].

[12] *See, e.g.*, § 25 of the *Arbitration Ordinance*, incorporating *Model Law* Art. 12 and § 26 of the *Arbitration*

- a court order to terminate an arbitrator's mandate[13]
- a court order to prevent relocation of assets out of the jurisdiction[14]
- a court order to prevent the disposal of assets
- a court order for the production of evidence[15]
- a court order for a witness to attend the arbitration hearing
- a court order to stay the legal proceedings in favour of arbitration where the matter in dispute is subject to an arbitration agreement[16]
- deciding any challenge to the arbitral award[17]

Thus, the seat of the arbitration is considered to be the legal connection between the forum or venue and the arbitration. The seat of the arbitration provides the legal framework for an arbitration and the seat determines which courts may assist the parties or the tribunal in the arbitration and may exercise supervisory powers over the arbitration.[18]

The location of the seat of the arbitration, however, is not necessarily the place where the arbitration hearings and other related activities are to take place. Consider a scenario involving an American seller and an Australian buyer for a product to be delivered to Papua New Guinea where payment will be made. In this scenario, the parties could select, for example, Hong Kong as the seat of the arbitration. The parties and the tribunal may hold hearings in the United States and Australia because the witnesses and the documents are located in those countries. The parties and the tribunal may also conduct arbitration-related activities in Papua New Guinea because the product has been delivered to that location. Nonetheless, it is the courts in Hong Kong which will exercise jurisdiction over this arbitration because Hong Kong is the arbitral forum, *i.e.*, the seat of the arbitration.

The seat of the arbitration may also determine the place where the award is made.[19] The place where an arbitration award is made is important when it comes to enforcing that award. We come to this point later in the chapter when we discuss the international treaty commonly known as the *New York Convention*. In Chapter 10 on the recognition and enforcement of arbitral awards, these points are analysed in greater detail.

In an international commercial contract, it is possible for two, if not more, national laws to apply to that arbitration. For example, the previous scenario

---

Ordinance, incorporating *Model Law* Art. 13, *supra* note 6. For an analysis of these sections of the Ordinance, *see, e.g.*, CHOONG & WEERAMANTRY, *supra* note 11, at paras. 25.00–25.30 and paras. 26.00–26.23 respectively.

13 *See, e.g.*, § 27 of the *Arbitration Ordinance*, incorporating *Model Law* Art. 14, *supra* note 6. For a review of this section of the Ordinance, *see, e.g.*, CHOONG & WEERAMANTRY, *supra* note 11, at paras. 27.00–27.12.

14 *See, e.g.*, § 21 of the *Arbitration Ordinance*, incorporating *Model Law* Art. 9, *supra* note 6. For an analysis of this section of the Ordinance, *see, e.g.*, CHOONG & WEERAMANTRY, *supra* note 11, at paras. 21.00–21.16.

15 *See, e.g.*, § 24 of the *Arbitration Ordinance*, incorporating *Model Law* Art. 11, *supra* note 6. For a discussion of this section of the Ordinance, *see* CHOONG & WEERAMANTRY, *supra* note 11, at paras. 24.00–24.38.

16 *See, e.g.*, § 20 of the *Arbitration Ordinance*, incorporating *Model Law* Art. 8, *supra* note 6.

17 *See, e.g.*, § 81 of the *Arbitration Ordinance*, incorporating *Model Law* Art. 34, *supra* note 6.

18 Hence, the importance of determining the *lex arbitri* as reviewed in Chapter 2.

19 MOSER & CHENG, *supra* note 8, at para. 5-021.

involved a party in the United States which sells a product to a buyer in Australia and the product is to be delivered to Papua New Guinea. If a dispute arises, and the parties did not specify a seat or forum for their arbitration, which country's arbitration law should be applied? Should the arbitration law be that of the United States, Australia or Papua New Guinea?

In this scenario, if the parties made no selection, but agreed to arbitrate the dispute in a particular forum or venue, *e.g.*, Hong Kong, it will be assumed that Hong Kong's *Arbitration Ordinance* will apply to the parties' arbitration procedure. This assumption is expressed in the Latin maxim: *qui indicem forum elegit jus*. This translates as: "a choice of venue is a choice of law" for the arbitration.[20]

> The basic approach of the Model Law (and all national laws derived from it) is thus that the law applicable to each arbitration (the *lex arbitri*) will be the law of the place where that arbitration takes place (the *lex loci arbitri*), and the selection of a particular place (seat) of arbitration ordinarily results in the arbitration being conducted in accordance with that jurisdiction's legal framework . . . (citations omitted)[21]
>
> . . . there is a technical distinction between the *lex loci arbitri* (the law of the place of the arbitration) and the *lex arbitri* (the law of the arbitration). It was noted earlier that in most cases these two concepts will be entirely congruent: the *lex arbitri* will be the *lex loci arbitri* and it is unnecessary to maintain a distinction between them. Strictly speaking, however, they are separate concepts which allow for the possibility that parties will choose to modify the *lex loci arbitri* by the adoption of a foreign procedural law.[22]

---

[20] BLACK'S LAW DICTIONARY 294 (10th ed. 2014) [hereinafter BLACK'S] defines "choice of law" as "the question of which jurisdiction's law should apply in a given case."
The parties are entitled to choose for themselves the law applicable to the dispute, subject to the qualifications of good faith, legality and no public policy objection. REDFERN & HUNTER, *supra* note 7, at para. 3.107.
The court's decision in the case of *Shagang South-Asia (Hong Kong) Trading Co Ltd v Daewoo Logistics* [2015] EWHC 194 (Comm), suggested that there is a strong presumption that selection of a seat of arbitration will also select the law of arbitration:

> The close link which exists between the place of arbitration and the procedure which governs the arbitration is the reason why choice of place generally carries with it an implied choice of governing procedure. . . . *Id.* at para. 28.
>
> . . .
>
> An agreement that the arbitration is "to be held in Hong Kong" would ordinarily carry with it an implied choice of Hong Kong as the seat of the arbitration and of the application of Hong Kong law as the curial law. Clear words or "significant contrary indicia" are necessary to establish that some other seat or curial law has been agreed. *Id.* at para. 38.
>
> For reasons already given I do not consider that "English law to be applied" provides clear wording to that effect. Indeed, it is most naturally to be read as referring to the substantive law applicable. *Id.* at para. 39.

[21] ALASTAIR HENDERSON, *Lex Arbitri, Procedural Law and the Seat of Arbitration*, 26 SAcLJ 886, 890 (2014) [hereinafter HENDERSON]. *See also* ROY GOODE, *The Role of the* Lex Loci Arbitri *in International Commercial Arbitration*, 17(1) ARBITRATION INTERNATIONAL 19 (2014); ANDREW TWEEDDALE & KEREN TWEEDDALE, ARBITRATION OF COMMERCIAL DISPUTES—INTERNATIONAL AND ENGLISH LAW AND PRACTICE paras. 7.38–7.44 (2007) [hereinafter TWEEDDALE & TWEEDDALE].
[22] HENDERSON, *supra* note 21, at 906–907.
As mentioned in Chapter 2, there is:

Much has been written concerning this complex and confusing area known as *choice of law*.[23] In essence, the issue is what law did the parties choose to apply to their

- arbitration clause
- arbitration procedure
- contract dispute[24]

Ordinarily, the first two items would be considered to be identical and hence will not present any issues or disputes. Where, however,

> the parties expressly choose particular rules to be applicable to the procedural aspect of an arbitration (law governing the arbitration agreement) and specifically chooses the substantive law governing the arbitration (law of the seat of arbitration), then a difference between the law governing the arbitration agreement and law of the seat of the arbitration is clearly established. (For example - the parties choose ICC rules to be applicable to an international commercial arbitration held in India. In this case, the curial law or lex fori or procedural law or law governing the arbitration agreement would be ICC Rules but as the seat of arbitration is India, the substantive law or lex arbitri would be [the] Indian Arbitration Act 1996, for the purpose of challenge of award, interim measures, enforcement etc.).[25]

This issue was addressed in the United Kingdom Court of Appeal case of *Sulamérica Cia Nacional de Seguros SA v Enesa Engenharia SA*.[26] The dispute involved two sets of parties, the insurance companies [hereinafter the "insurers"] against the companies to whom the insurers issued policies [hereinafter the "insured"]. These insurance policies contained substantially the same terms, particularly the dispute resolution clauses which state:

> the conceptual possibility of parties agreeing that an arbitration seated in country A should be made subject to the arbitration laws of country B, to the exclusion (as far as possible) of the arbitration laws of country A. It is difficult to imagine why parties would wish to complicate their affairs in this way; such a proposal would be likely to inspire the greatest scepticism if anyone were to propose it during contract negotiations.

HENDERSON, *supra* note 21, at 903.

"This is not surprising when one considers the complexities and inconveniences which such an agreement would involve." *Naviera Amazonica Peruana SA v Compania International de Seguros del Peru* [1988] 1 Lloyd's Rep 116, 120. *See also Braes of Doune Wind Farm v Alfred McAlpine Business Services Ltd* [2008] EWHC 426 (TCC), discussed in Chapter 2, "Considerations for Selecting Arbitration—An Introduction."

[23] *See, e.g.*, SAM LUTTRELL, *An Introduction to Conflict of Laws in International Commercial Arbitration*, 14 INT'L TRADE & BUS. L. REV. 404 (2011).

[24] This is also known by the terms *proper law of the contract*, *substantive law*, or *applicable law*, meaning the law applicable to the contract. This choice of law will not be reviewed here for several reasons. Firstly, most parties are now sufficiently sophisticated to include a choice of law clause in their contract. Secondly, this issue concerning the applicable law can be presented to and decided by the arbitral tribunal. Hence, it is more important to establish the arbitral tribunal and establish its jurisdiction. *See also* TWEEDDALE & TWEEDDALE, *supra* note 21, at Chapt. 6.

[25] R. V. Prabhat, *'Lex Arbitri v. Lex Arbitri'- Choice of Law Conundrum* (May 22, 2015). Available at: https://www.linkedin.com/pulse/lex-arbitri-v-arbitri-supreme-court-india-rv-prabhat (last visited 12 Aug. 2017). For further discussion of this topic, *see, e.g.*, TWEEDDALE & TWEEDDALE, *supra* note 21, at Chapt. 6 and Chapt. 7.

[26] [2012] EWCA Civ 638.

> 7. Law and Jurisdiction
> It is agreed that this policy will be governed exclusively by the laws of Brazil.
> Any disputes arising under, out of or in connection with this policy shall be subject to the exclusive jurisdiction of the courts of Brazil.
> . . .
> 11. Mediation
> If any dispute or difference of whatsoever nature arises out of or in connection with this policy including any question regarding its existence, validity or termination, hereafter termed as Dispute, the parties undertake that, prior to a reference to arbitration, they will seek to have the dispute resolved amicably by mediation.
> . . .
> If the Dispute has not been resolved to the satisfaction of either party within 90 days of service of the notice initiating mediation . . . then either party may refer to [*sic*] the Dispute to arbitration. . . .
> 12. Arbitration
> In case the Insured and the Insurer(s) shall fail to agree as to the amount to be paid under this policy through mediation as above, such *dispute shall then be referred to arbitration* . . . (emphasis added)
> . . .
> The Tribunal shall have the widest discretion permitted under the law governing the arbitral procedure . . .
> The seat of the arbitration shall be London, England.

The court was hearing an appeal of the imposition of an anti-suit injunction preventing the insured from pursuing court proceedings against the insurers in Brazil.[27] The insured contended that under Brazilian law, the arbitration agreement was not enforceable against them without their consent. If the insured's argument were correct, the reference to arbitration would be ineffective and the entire anti-suit injunction would have to be dismissed.[28] The court decided that the arbitration agreement was to be governed by English law by concluding:

> No doubt the arbitration agreement has a close and real connection with the contract of which . . . [the arbitration agreement] forms part, but its nature and purpose are very different. . . . an agreement to resolve disputes by arbitration in London, and therefore in accordance with English arbitral law, does not have a close juridical connection with the system of law governing the policy of insurance, whose purpose is unrelated to that of dispute resolution; rather, it has its closest and most real connection with the law of the place where the arbitration is to be held and which will exercise the supporting and supervisory jurisdiction necessary to ensure that the procedure is effective. Its closest and most real connection is with English law.[29]

---

[27] In essence, an anti-suit injunction stops court proceedings in order to allow arbitration of the parties' dispute, *i.e.*, to stay legal proceedings in favour of arbitration.

[28] [2012] EWCA at para. 7.

[29] *Id.* at para. 32.

Part of the court's reasoning follows:

As discussed further in the series of footnotes below, parties contemplating arbitration should adhere to the model arbitration clause of an institution or, if an *ad hoc* arbitration, the UNCITRAL Arbitration Rules model clause rather than attempt to be clever at midnight, as discussed in Chapter 2.

It has long been recognised that . . . the proper law of an arbitration agreement which itself forms part of a substantive contract may differ from that of the contract as a whole, but . . . in the absence of any indication to the contrary, the parties intended . . . their relationship to be governed by the same system of law. It is common for parties to make an express choice of law to govern their contract, but unusual for them to make an express choice of the law to govern any arbitration agreement contained within it; and where they have not done so, the natural inference is that they intended the proper law chosen to govern the substantive contract also to govern the agreement to arbitrate. *Id.* at para. 11 (citation omitted).

. . .

In the absence of any indication to the contrary, an express choice of law governing the substantive contract is a strong indication of the parties' intention in relation to the agreement to arbitrate. A search for an implied choice of proper law to govern the arbitration agreement is therefore likely . . . to lead to the conclusion that the parties intended the arbitration agreement to be governed by the same . . . law as the substantive contract, unless there are other factors present which point to a different conclusion. These may include the terms of the arbitration agreement itself or the consequences for its effectiveness of choosing the proper law of the substantive contract . . . *Id.* at para. 26 (citation omitted).

. . .

Although there are powerful factors in favour of an implied choice of Brazilian law as the governing law of the arbitration agreement, two important factors point the other way. . . . the choice of another country as the seat of the arbitration inevitably imports an acceptance that the law of that country relating to the conduct and supervision of arbitrations will apply to the proceedings. . . . even though the arbitration agreement in this case does not specifically refer to the provisions of the *Arbitration Act* 1996, the parties must have foreseen and intended that its provisions should apply to any arbitration commenced pursuant to . . . [the parties' contract clause] 12 . . . This tends to suggest that the parties intended English law to govern all aspects of the arbitration agreement, including matters touching on the formal validity of the agreement and the jurisdiction of the arbitrators. *Id.* at para. 29 (citation omitted)

The second factor is the consequence . . . [of Brazilian] law governing the arbitration agreement. . . . the insured say that it renders the agreement enforceable only with their consent. If correct, that is a powerful factor and one which the court must take into account when considering an implied choice of Brazilian law. Although most arbitration agreements permit either party to refer disputes to arbitration, some provide for arbitration only at the option of one or other party. . . . In the present case, however, there is nothing to indicate that the parties intended to enter into a one-sided arrangement of that kind; indeed, [the parties' contract clause] 11, which provides the immediate context for [the parties' contract clause] 12, expressly provides that either party may refer to arbitration a dispute that has not been satisfactorily resolved by mediation. The possible existence of a . . . Brazilian law which would undermine that position tends to suggest that the parties did not intend the arbitration agreement to be governed by that . . . law. *Id.* at para 30.

In the light of these conflicting indications . . . [I] return to the two critical questions raised earlier: have the parties impliedly chosen the law of Brazil to govern the arbitration agreement; and if not, with which system of law does that agreement have the closest and most real connection? . . . I do not think that . . . the parties' express choice of Brazilian law to govern the substantive contract is sufficient evidence of an implied choice of Brazilian law to govern the arbitration agreement, because . . . there is at least a serious risk that a choice of Brazilian law would significantly undermine that [arbitration] agreement. . . . I do not think that the parties can have intended to choose a system of law that . . . would . . . have that effect. . . . although one may start from the assumption that the parties intended the same law to govern the whole of the contract, including the arbitration agreement, specific factors may lead to the conclusion that that cannot in fact have been their intention. . . . I am unable to accept that the parties made an implied choice of Brazilian law to govern the arbitration agreement. *Id.* at para. 31.

Returning to our scenario, we now focus on which law should apply to the arbitration procedure. Recall that the American seller and the Australian buyer did not choose an arbitration law to apply to their dispute. Thus, because the parties did not make an express choice of law but did agree to have their dispute arbitrated in a particular country or forum, it is generally assumed that these parties intend the law of that country to govern the arbitration of their disputes.[30]

There are court cases supporting this assumption. In the case of *Raguz (Angela) v Sullivan (Rebecca)*,[31] the Court of Appeal in New South Wales adopted what is known as the *close connection* test.[32] The court said that:

---

[30] "Forum" refers to the place where the arbitration is held. REDFERN & HUNTER, *supra* note 7, at para. 3.53.

[31] [2000] NSWCA 240.

[32] As an example of the confusion that this complex topic engenders, readers should note that there are different applications of this test and that some uncertainties remain. ADRIAN BRIGGS, PRIVATE INTERNATIONAL LAW IN ENGLISH COURTS para. 14.39 (2014) and DAVID JOSEPH, JURISDICTION AND ARBITRATION AGREEMENTS para. 6.36 (3rd ed. 2015) both cited in *BCY v BCZ* [2016] SGHC 249, para. 58.

In the case of *Arsanovia Ltd v Cruz City 1 Mauritius Holdings* [2012] EWHC 3702 (Comm), the parties had expressly chosen Indian law to govern the underlying contract and London as the seat of arbitration. This dispute involved several parties dealing in several interrelated contracts. There were three separate awards, one in each separate arbitration. In the first arbitration, the parties were Cruz City claiming against Asanovia and Burly. In the second arbitration, Cruz City claimed against Burley and Unitech. In the third arbitration, Arsanovia and Burley were the claimants against Cruz City.

The issue before the court focused upon the significance of the Indian governing law clause compared to the law of the seat of arbitration in London when determining the law of an arbitration agreement. Under Indian law:

i) The law applicable to the arbitration agreement in the [parties' contract] is Indian law and therefore Indian law determines whether Burley is a party to it.

ii) Under Indian law, Burley did not agree to be bound by the arbitration agreement in the [parties' contract]; and even if the arbitration agreement is governed by English law it did not do so.

iii) Under Indian law, where an arbitration is brought against two respondents only one of whom is party to the arbitration agreement, the arbitration cannot be maintained against either; and so, because the Tribunal did not have jurisdiction over Burley, it did not have jurisdiction to decide the claims against Arsanovia either.

iv) The law governing the arbitration agreement in [the parties' other related contract] is Indian law and therefore Indian law determines its scope.

v) Under Indian law and on the proper construction of the [the parties' other related contract] the claims against Unitech and Burley could be brought only after Burley's liability under the [parties' contract] had been adjudicated (if not admitted); and they were therefore premature and beyond the Tribunal's jurisdiction.

vi) In any case, under Indian law the question whether Burley was liable under the [parties' contract] in the arbitration leading to Award 2 was not within the scope of the arbitration agreement in [the parties' other related contract], and, since Award 1 was invalid, therefore Burley had not been validly found to be liable under the [the parties' contract] and so the Tribunal in Arbitration 2 had no jurisdiction to make an award against Burley or Unitech under the [the parties' other related contract].

Arsanovia Ltd v Cruz City 1 Mauritius Holdings at para. 6.

The court found that on the facts the parties had intended that Indian law should apply:

> Although, as Lord Mustill pointed out in *Channel Tunnel Group Ltd v Balfour Beatty Construction Ltd*, [1993] AC 334, 357F, more than one national system of law can bear upon an international arbitration, the parties would not be expected to have chosen pointlessly to resort to numerous different systems to govern their affairs, and so an express choice of a law to govern them in one respect is a strong indication that they might have understood or intended that it should apply to others. The difficulty that arises here . . . is that the parties have chosen as the lex causae the law of one country, but by agreeing to resolve disputes through arbitrations with a seat elsewhere they have clearly indicated the choice of a different lex fori. . . . which law is . . . applicable to the arbitration agreement and determines the jurisdiction of a tribunal appointed under it? . . . here the lex causae of the [parties' contract]

> where the parties have failed to choose the law governing the conduct of arbitration, it will prima facie be the law of the country in which the arbitration is held because that is the country most closely connected with the proceedings.[33]

Another example is the case of *Chalbury McCouat International Ltd v PG Foils Ltd*,[34] where the close connection test was also used to explain that a choice of forum should be a choice of law. In this case, Chalbury McCouat was an English company. PG Foils was an Indian company. These parties' contract was for the dismantling of PG Foils' factory in the Netherlands. The parties' arbitration agreement provided that "arbitration as per prevailing laws of European Union in the [*sic*] Europe." A dispute arose. The English company sought to have the arbitration conducted in England under UK law. The Indian company argued that their contract was signed in India and the factory was to be re-assembled in India. The Indian party further argued that either an "Arbitral Tribunal in India" or the Indian arbitration law should apply to the dispute. Therefore, the Indian party refused to consent to the appointment of the sole arbitrator as provided under the UK law.[35]

The court decided the venue of arbitration must be somewhere in Europe because of the parties' agreement for arbitration in Europe. Furthermore, the dismantling of the factory was to be done by the English company and payment was "by way of payment in England." Based upon these factors, the court decided the close connection test was satisfied and concluded that the venue of the arbitration should be the UK.

A final example is the case of *Taizhou Haopu Investment Co, Ltd v Wicor Holding AG*.[36] In this dispute, the parties' arbitration clause provided that the "arbitration will be conducted under the Conciliation and Arbitration Rules of the ICC. If one

---

> is . . . the law of India whereas the seat of the arbitration is . . . London and so the curial law of the arbitration is English. Which of these two . . . is applicable to the arbitration agreement? *Id.* at para. 10.
>
> . . . parties . . . are to be taken to have evinced an intention that the arbitration agreement in it be governed by Indian law for the reasons that Moore-Bick LJ explained [in Sulamérica]. The governing law clause is, at the least, a strong pointer to their intention about the law governing the arbitration agreement and there is no contrary indication other than choice of a London seat for arbitrations. The wording of the arbitration agreement itself reinforces the conclusion that the parties intended Indian law to govern it. *Id.* at para 21.
>
> Had I had to decide which system of law has the closest and most real connection with the arbitration agreement, I would have concluded that it is English law for the reasons . . . that the English law had the closest and most real connection with the arbitration agreement . . . But in view of my decision about the parties' choice of applicable law, that question does not arise. *Id.* at para. 24.

In order to avoid such complexities and uncertainties which could cause preliminary disputes over jurisdiction before the main substantive contractual dispute, parties should consider specifying the law to apply to the arbitration agreement to be the same as the law of the seat of arbitration. For example, the HKIAC, *supra* note 2, provides these two optional clauses in its model arbitration agreement:

- The law of this arbitration clause shall be [Hong Kong law].
- The seat of arbitration shall be [Hong Kong].

33 *Raguz (Angela) v Sullivan (Rebecca)*, *supra* note 31, at para. 93 quoting *American Diagnostica Inc v Gradipore Ltd* (1998) 44 NSWLR 312, 324 (citations omitted).

34 [2010] EWHC 2050.

35 *See* the United Kingdom's *Arbitration Act 1996*, § 15(3).

36 [2015] Tai Zhong Shang Zhong Shen Zi, No. 00004 (2 Jun. 2016).

party commences arbitration, the seat of arbitration shall be chosen by the other party." The court applied PRC law because the parties did not specify a law to govern the arbitration clause or an arbitral seat which would have permitted the application of a different law. Applying PRC law, the court determined that the arbitration clause was invalid. If a seat had been designated by the parties, it is possible that the court would have applied the law of the seat to determine the validity of the parties' arbitration agreement.

C. *New York Convention*

The *New York Convention*[37] is the commonly used name for the *Convention on the Recognition and Enforcement of Foreign Arbitral Awards* (done in New York, 1958).[38] This is an international treaty. Nations which have signed this treaty are referenced by various names, such as: contracting states, member states, state parties, signatory states or signatories. The *New York Convention* is one of the key agreements in the field of international arbitration with more than 157 countries having signed this treaty. The purpose of the *New York Convention* is to regulate the recognition and enforcement of foreign arbitral awards and the referral by a court to arbitration.[39]

---

[37] The *New York Convention*'s website translates this treaty's title as 紐約公約. The website is at: http://www.uncitral.org/uncitral/en/uncitral_texts/arbitration/NYConvention.html (last visited 12 Jul. 2017).

[38] The *New York Convention*'s website, *id.*, translates "*Convention on the Recognition and Enforcement of Foreign Arbitral Awards*" as 承認及執行外國仲裁裁決公約.

[39] *Id.* provides the objectives of the *New York Convention* as follows:

> Recognizing the growing importance of international arbitration as a means of settling international commercial disputes, the Convention on the Recognition and Enforcement of Foreign Arbitral Awards (the Convention) seeks to provide common legislative standards for the recognition of arbitration agreements and court recognition and enforcement of foreign and non-domestic arbitral awards. The term "non-domestic" appears to embrace awards which, although made in the state of enforcement, are treated as "foreign" under its law because of some foreign element in the proceedings, *e.g.* another State's procedural laws are applied.
>
> The Convention's principal aim is that foreign and non-domestic arbitral awards will not be discriminated against and it obliges Parties to ensure such awards are recognized and generally capable of enforcement in their jurisdiction in the same way as domestic awards. An ancillary aim of the Convention is to require courts of Parties to give full effect to arbitration agreements by requiring courts to deny the parties access to court in contravention of their agreement to refer the matter to an arbitral tribunal.

New York Convention Art. II(3) which provides that:

> The court of a Contracting State, when seized of an action in a matter in respect of which the parties have made an agreement within the meaning of this article, shall, at the request of one of the parties, refer the parties to arbitration, unless it finds that the said agreement is null and void, inoperative or incapable of being performed.

One source has provided an explanation of the terms "null and void," "inoperative" and "incapable of being performed":

> An arbitration agreement is 'null and void' if it is 'devoid of legal effect', for example owing to mistake, duress, or fraud. At first sight, it is difficult to see a distinction between the terms 'inoperative' and 'incapable of being performed'. However, an arbitration clause is inoperative where it has 'ceased to have legal effect' as a result, for example, of a failure by the parties to comply with a time limit, or where the parties have repudiated, or by their conduct impliedly revoked, the arbitration agreement. By contrast, the expression 'incapable of being performed' appears to refer to more practical aspects

The term *recognition* refers to a signatory recognizing all arbitral awards within the treaty's scheme as binding.[40] The term *enforcement* simply means to carry out the directions contained in the award.[41] Again, this is further discussed in Chapter 10 on the topics of recognition and enforcement.

Arbitration awards made in countries which are members of the *New York Convention* are recognized and enforced by the courts of the other member states to the *New York Convention*. Because this treaty refers to foreign awards, even a domestic award may be enforced under the *New York Convention* when enforcement is sought in another signatory state. For example, Hong Kong is a member of the *New York Convention* via China. Germany is also a member state. An arbitration has Hong Kong as its seat. The arbitral award which is made in Hong Kong, even between two Hong Kong entities, can be enforced in Germany as a foreign award as the award was not made in Germany, the member state where the award is sought to be enforced.

The procedure to enforce an arbitration award under the *New York Convention* requires the party seeking to enforce the award to do the following:

- produce the original authenticated arbitration award or a certified copy
- the original arbitration agreement or a certified copy
- where applicable, certified translations of these documents

The only reasons upon which a party can seek to invalidate an arbitral award are provided in this treaty. These grounds for a party to apply to set aside or invalidate a foreign award are listed in Article V of the *New York Convention*:

- lack of capacity by one party to enter into the arbitration agreement
- invalidity of the arbitration agreement
- lack of proper notice of the appointment of the tribunal or of the arbitration proceedings, such that a party was unable to present its case

---

of the prospective arbitration proceedings. It applies, for example, if it is for some reason impossible to establish the arbitral tribunal. Courts intend to construe these provisions narrowly, to avoid offering a 'back door' for a party wishing to escape the arbitration agreement.

Redfern & Hunter, *supra* note 7, at para. 2.202 (citations omitted).

See also So & To, *supra* note 4, at paras. [20.11]–[20.13].

[40] "Recognition" is defined as a defensive process where a court is requested to grant a remedy in a dispute which has been the subject of previous arbitral proceedings and the winning party asks the court to confirm that the arbitral award is valid and binding on the parties to the arbitration. Redfern & Hunter, *supra* note 7, at para. 11.20.
§ 43 of the *Arbitration Ordinance*, *supra* note 6, translates "recognition" as 承認.
The identical translation is also provided by the Hong Kong government's e-legislation English-Chinese Glossary [hereinafter *e-legislation glossary*].
See the *e-legislation glossary* website at: https://www.elegislation.gov.hk/glossary/en (last visited 26 Aug. 2017).

[41] § 43 of the *Arbitration Ordinance*, *supra* note 6, and the *e-legislation glossary*, *supra* note 40, all translate "enforcement" as 執行.
Black's, *supra* note 20, at 1580, defines "enforcement of foreign judgment" as "a court's enforcement of a judgment by a court outside the court's territory after determining that the judgment should be recognised."
Enforcement means the court is being asked to ensure that the award is carried out by using any legal sanctions where appropriate after it has recognized the legal force of that award. Redfern & Hunter, *supra* note 7, at para. 11.22.

- the tribunal's award exceeds the tribunal's jurisdiction by purporting to determine matters not falling within the submission to arbitration
- improper constitution of the arbitral tribunal
- the award has not yet become binding upon the parties
- the subject matter of the dispute is not capable of settlement by arbitration under the law of the state where enforcement of the award is sought
- the award contravenes the public policy of the state where its enforcement is sought

Should a party be successful in challenging the enforcement of an arbitral award on one of these grounds, the court may nonetheless decide to enforce the award.[42]

D. *Arbitration Ordinance*

The current Hong Kong *Arbitration Ordinance* (Cap. 609) came into force on 1 June 2011. The new Ordinance is based on the UNCITRAL *Model Law*, and incorporates elements of the 2006 amendments to the *Model Law*. The Ordinance unified the former domestic arbitration and international arbitration regimes of Hong Kong into one regime.[43]

Compared to the former *Arbitration Ordinance* (Cap. 341), there are some major changes under the new Ordinance:

- unification of the domestic and the international arbitration regimes[44]
- the opt-in provisions to proceed under the former domestic arbitration regime[45]
- clarification of the definitions of interim measures[46]
- higher efficiency in arbitration proceedings[47]
- more stringent confidentiality requirements[48]

Each of these changes is reviewed below.[49]

i. Unification of domestic and international arbitration regimes

As mentioned above, the former *Arbitration Ordinance* adopted separate regimes or procedures for domestic and international arbitrations. A domestic arbitration's procedures were governed by the former Ordinance which was based on the

42 *New York Convention*, *supra* note 37, at Art. V(1) is phrased permissively, using the word *may* rather than *must* or *shall*: "Recognition and enforcement of the award *may* be refused" (emphasis added).

43 For review of the different sections of the *Arbitration Ordinance*, *see* HALSBURY'S, *supra* note 6, at para. [25.005].

44 *See, e.g.*, MA & BROCK, *supra* note 7, at paras.1.004, 1.012–1.013.

45 *See, e.g.*, *id.* at paras. 1.016–1.019.

46 *See, e.g.*, *id.* at paras. 1.024–1.028.

47 *See, e.g.*, *id.* at para. 1.015.

48 *See, e.g.*, *id.* at paras. 1.020–1.023 but *see* paras. 10.202–10.207.

49 For a more detailed review of the history of this Ordinance, *see, e.g.*, *id.* at paras. 1.002–1.011.

English *Arbitration Act 1996*. An international arbitration's procedures were governed by the *Model Law*. This separation of regimes led to disputes between parties over the appropriate regime to govern their arbitration.[50] Moreover, the domestic regime gave additional powers to the Hong Kong courts to intervene in the arbitral process, whereas the international regime did not. For example, the former Ordinance provided parties with the right of appeal against an arbitral award if all parties consented to such appeal or the court granted leave for such appeal.[51] The new Ordinance unifies the domestic and international arbitration regime under the single framework of the *Model Law*.

ii. Opt-in provisions

Under the new Ordinance, an opt-in system allows parties to agree to apply certain provisions which governed domestic arbitrations under the former Ordinance. These provisions are found in Schedule 2 of the current Ordinance. The opt-in system was included following a construction industry request to retain features of the domestic regime.[52] Hence, generally it is parties from the construction sector who usually make use of the opt-in provisions which provide, in part, opportunities for more court intervention. Additionally, if an arbitration agreement, which was entered into before or within six years of the commencement of the present Ordinance, provides for domestic arbitration, the opt-in provisions will apply automatically.[53]

---

[50] In *Fung Sang Trading Ltd v Kai Sun Sea Products & Food Co Ltd* [1992] 1 HKLR 40, a dispute arising from a sale of goods contract was being submitted to arbitration and the parties disagreed as to whether the arbitration was international or domestic. The Plaintiff (the seller) submitted that it was an international arbitration and therefore the arbitration should be governed by the *Model Law* on the basis that the place of delivery of goods, which constituted a "substantial part" of the contractual obligations, was mainland China. On the other hand, the Defendant (the buyer) claimed that it was a domestic arbitration and thus governing law was the former Ordinance on the grounds that the contract was made in Hong Kong between parties from Hong Kong and that payment was to be made in Hong Kong under the contract. The court held that the fact that "delivery was to take place in mainland China" was a "substantial" part of the contractual obligation. Accordingly, the arbitration was an international arbitration governed by the *Model Law*.

[51] § 23(3) of the former *Arbitration Ordinance* (Cap. 341) [hereinafter former Ordinance].
The parties' right of appeal against the arbitral award under § 23(3) of the former Ordinance can be excluded by agreement in writing under section 23B of the same Ordinance.

[52] JAMES KWAN AND CHRISTOPHER TO, CONSTRUCTION ARBITRATION IN HONG KONG: A PRACTICAL GUIDE paras. 2-033 and 12-080 (2015).
However, the opt-in provisions shall not apply to "non-local sub-contractors." *Id.* at para. 12-080.
See also MA & BROCK, *supra* note 7, at paras. 1.016–1.019.
See HALSBURY'S, *supra* note 6, at para. [25.142] and paras. [25.160]–[25.175] for a detailed review of the opt-in provisions and their application.

[53] § 100 of the *Arbitration Ordinance*, *supra* note 6, provides:

> All the [opt-in] provisions in Schedule 2 apply, subject to section 102, to—
> (a) an arbitration agreement entered into before the commencement of this Ordinance which has provided that arbitration under the agreement is a domestic arbitration; or
> (b) an arbitration agreement entered into at any time within a period of 6 years after the commencement of this Ordinance which provides that arbitration under the agreement is a domestic arbitration.

§ 102(1) of the *Arbitration Ordinance*, *supra* note 6, provides:

Schedule 2 includes these provisions:

§ 1: a sole arbitrator absent any agreement by the parties[54]

§ 2: court consolidation of arbitrations[55]

§ 3: court determination of a preliminary question of law[56]

§ 4: challenging an arbitral award on the grounds of serious irregularity[57]

§ 5: right to appeal against an arbitral award on a question of law[58]

§ 6: application for leave to appeal against an arbitral award on a question of law[59]

§ 7: supplementary provisions on challenge to or appeal against an arbitral award[60]

After six years of automatic application of the opt-in provisions as per § 100 of the Ordinance, parties now must expressly opt into the Schedule 2 provisions pursuant to § 99. Thus, parties wishing any or all of the Schedule 2 provisions to apply to their arbitration must expressly so state in their arbitration agreement, as per § 99 of the Ordinance.

iii. Interim measures[61]

During the arbitration process but before the final outcome, it may be necessary for parties to apply to the arbitral tribunal or court for orders to preserve evidence, to

---

> Sections 100 . . . do[es] not apply if—
> (a) the parties to the arbitration agreement concerned so agree in writing; or
> (b) the arbitration agreement concerned has provided expressly that—
> (1) section 100 . . . does not apply . . .

54 For further discussion, *see, e.g.*, MA & BROCK, *supra* note 7, at para. 14.067; HALSBURY'S, *supra* note 6, at para. [25.160].

55 For further discussion, *see, e.g.*, MA & BROCK, *supra* note 7, at paras. 14.068–14.080; HALSBURY'S, *supra* note 6, at para. [25.161].

56 For further discussion, *see, e.g.*, MA & BROCK, *supra* note 7, at para. 14.081; HALSBURY'S, *supra* note 6, at para. [25.162].

57 For further discussion, *see, e.g.*, MA & BROCK, *supra* note 7, at para. 14.082–14.099; HALSBURY'S, *supra* note 6, at para. [25.164].

58 For further discussion, *see, e.g.*, MA & BROCK, *supra* note 7, at para. 14.100–14.112; HALSBURY'S, *supra* note 6, at para. [25.169].

59 For further discussion, *see, e.g.*, MA & BROCK, *supra* note 7, at para. 14.100–14.112; HALSBURY'S, *supra* note 6, at para. [25.169].

60 For further discussion, *see, e.g.*, HALSBURY'S, *supra* note 6, at paras. [25.172]–[25.175].

61 "Interim measure" is sometimes referred to as "preliminary order," and is defined by § 35(1) of the *Arbitration Ordinance*, incorporating *Model Law* Art. 17(2), *supra* note 6, as:

> (2) An interim measure is any temporary measure, whether in the form of an award or in another form, by which, at any time prior to the issuance of the award by which the dispute is finally decided, the arbitral tribunal orders a party to:
> (a) Maintain or restore the status quo pending determination of the dispute;
> (b) Take action that would prevent, or refrain from taking action that is likely to cause, current or imminent harm or prejudice to the arbitral process itself;
> (c) Provide a means of preserving assets out of which a subsequent award may be satisfied; or
> (d) Preserve evidence that may be relevant and material to the resolution of the dispute.

Interim measures include an injunction. § 45(9) of the *Arbitration Ordinance*, *supra* note 6.

protect assets or to maintain the *status quo*.[62] Such orders which take different forms are known by the term *interim measures* or *preliminary orders*.[63] An arbitral tribunal only has the power to grant interim measures against a party to the arbitration.[64] Therefore, court assistance is required if a party wishes to obtain a third-party order, such as an order that a bank shall hold the deposits of the opposing party.[65]

Under the former Ordinance, interim measures or preliminary orders were not sufficiently addressed.[66] Under the current Ordinance, there is a specific and detailed process, which includes preliminary orders made on an *ex parte* basis.[67] A new procedure for the enforcement of interim measures separate from the recognition and enforcement of awards has been created. This means that orders and directions for interim measures can be enforced by the court as a judgement, whether the interim measure order was made within or outside Hong Kong.[68]

So & To, *supra* note 4, at para. [37.01] comments:

> Although preliminary orders might be regarded as a subset of interim measures, it could be distinguished from an interim measure: (i) by its narrower purpose, which was limited to preventing the frustration of the specific interim measure being applied for; (ii) by its function, which was limited to directing a party to preserving the status quo until the tribunal had heard from the other party and ruled on the application for the interim measure; and (iii) by its legal regime, which was subject to stricter time limits than other interim measures. It was limited to providing a bridging device until an inter partes hearing could take place in respect of a requested interim measure. (citation omitted)

§ 2(1) of the *Arbitration Ordinance*, *supra* note 6, translates "interim measure" as 臨時措施 and § 22B translates "injunction" as 強制令.

[62] Redfern & Hunter, *supra* note 7, at para. 7.45 provides these two examples:

> For example, a manufacturer may refuse to continue supplies under a distribution agreement, alleging breach of contract. If the distributor does not receive the supplies for which it has contracted, it may not be able to fulfil the contracts that it, in turn, has made. This may damage the distributor's reputation. . . . the distributor would . . . argue that the status quo should be maintained and that the manufacturer should continue to supply, pending resolution of the dispute . . . Similarly, a pharmaceutical company may produce a particular drug under licence, then decide to manufacture and market a competing product under its own name, claiming that there is nothing in the licence agreement to prevent it doing so. In such a case, the licensor probably wishes to argue that, until the dispute is resolved . . . the licensee should be restrained from manufacturing and marketing the competing product.

[63] Redfern & Hunter, *supra* note 7, at para. 7.14.

[64] For further discussion, *see, e.g.*, Halsbury's, *supra* note 6, at paras. [25.104]–[25.106].

[65] Redfern & Hunter, *supra* note 7, at para. 7.18.

[66] For example, although § 2GB(1)(f) (applicable to domestic arbitrations only) and Schedule 5 (which has incorporated the opt-in provision of *Model Law* Art. 17 and applicable to international arbitrations only) of the former Ordinance, *supra* note 51, provide the arbitral tribunal with the power to grant interim measures when conducting arbitral proceedings, the former Ordinance does not provide for the procedure of applying for interim measures or preliminary orders.

[67] Black's, *supra* note 20, at 697, defines "*ex parte*" as "done or made at the instance and for the benefit of one party only, and without notice to, or argument by, anyone having an adverse interest . . . usu[ally] for temporary or emergency relief."

The *e-legislation glossary*, *supra* note 40, translate "*ex parte*" as 單方面.

§ 37(1) of the *Arbitration Ordinance*, incorporating *Model Law* Art. 17B(1), *supra* note 6, stipulates the procedure of "applications for preliminary orders on an *ex parte* basis" being: "a party may, without notice to any other party, make a request for an interim measure together with an application for a preliminary order directing a party not to frustrate the purpose of the interim measure requested."

See § 37 of the *Arbitration Ordinance*, *supra* note 6. For an analysis of this section of the Ordinance, *see, e.g.*, Choong & Weeramantry, *supra* note 11, at paras. 37.00–37.13.

[68] Art. 17H(1) of the *Model Law*, *supra* note 1, states: "An interim measure issued by an arbitral tribunal shall be

The current *Arbitration Ordinance* provides that a preliminary order made by an arbitral tribunal shall be binding on the parties though it does not constitute an award and is not subject to enforcement by a court.[69] Nevertheless, § 45 of the Ordinance also authorises the court to grant an interim measure upon the application of any party while subsection (4) sets out the grounds upon which the court may refuse to grant an interim measure.[70] Specifically, § 45 of the Ordinance provides in part:

> (1) Article 17J of the UNCITRAL Model Law does not have effect.
> (2) On the application of any party, the Court may, in relation to any arbitral proceedings which have been or are to be commenced in or outside Hong Kong, grant an interim measure.
> (3) The powers conferred by this section may be exercised by the Court irrespective of whether or not similar powers may be exercised by an arbitral tribunal under section 35 in relation to the same dispute.
> (4) The Court may decline to grant an interim measure under subsection (2) on the grounds that—
> (a) the interim measure sought is currently the subject of arbitral proceedings; and
> (b) the Court considers it more appropriate for the interim measure sought to be dealt with by the arbitral tribunal.[71]

iv. Greater efficiency in arbitration proceedings

Under the current Ordinance, the parties are given a *reasonable* opportunity to present their case and to deal with the cases of their opponents rather than a *full*

---

recognized as binding and, unless otherwise provided by the arbitral tribunal, enforced upon application to the competent court, irrespective of the country in which it was issued."

§ 43 of the *Arbitration Ordinance, supra* note 6, provides: "Section 61 has effect in substitution for article 17H of the UNCITRAL Model Law."

§ 61 of the *Arbitration Ordinance, supra* note 6, provides:

> (1) An order or direction made, whether in or outside Hong Kong, in relation to arbitral proceedings by an arbitral tribunal is enforceable in the same manner as an order or direction of the Court that has the same effect, but only with the leave of the Court.
> (2) Leave to enforce an order or direction made outside Hong Kong is not to be granted, unless the party seeking to enforce it can demonstrate that it belongs to a type or description of order or direction that may be made in Hong Kong in relation to arbitral proceedings by an arbitral tribunal.
>
> . . .
>
> (5) An order or direction referred to in this section includes an interim measure.

For an analysis of § 43 and § 61 of the Ordinance, *see, e.g.*, CHOONG & WEERAMANTRY, *supra* note 11, at paras. 43.00–43.14 and paras. 61.00–61.13 respectively.

[69] § 38 of the *Arbitration Ordinance*, incorporating *Model Law* Art. 17C, *supra* note 6. This section of the Ordinance is entitled "Specific regime for preliminary orders."
See also Ma & Brock, *supra* note 7, at para.10.153; CHOONG & WEERAMANTRY, *supra* note 11, at paras. 38.00–38.13.

[70] Ma & Brock, *supra* note 7, at para. 10.154. *See generally* CHOONG & WEERAMANTRY, *supra* note 11, at paras. 45.00–45.19.

[71] § 45(1)–§ 45(4) of the *Arbitration Ordinance, supra* note 6.

opportunity.[72] Under the domestic regime of the former Ordinance, parties could apply to the court:

- for determination of a preliminary point of law
- for consolidation of proceedings
- to appeal an arbitral award based on a question of law

Parties now have limited scope to make these applications to the court. According to the current Ordinance, the court should not interfere except for circumstances expressly provided in the Ordinance.[73] These circumstances include:

- challenging an arbitrator[74]
- ending the authority, which is also known by the term *mandate*, of an arbitrator[75]

---

[72] *Id.* at § 46(3) provides in part:

(1) When conducting arbitral proceedings or exercising any of the powers conferred on an arbitral tribunal by this Ordinance or by the parties to any of those arbitral proceedings, the arbitral tribunal is required—

. . .

(c) to act fairly and impartially as between the parties, *giving them a reasonable opportunity to present their cases* and to deal with the cases of their opponents . . . (emphasis added)

[73] *Id.* at § 12 stipulates:

Article 5 of the UNCITRAL Model Law, the text of which is set out below, has effect—

"*Article 5. Extent of court intervention*

In matters governed by this Law, no court shall intervene except where so provided in this Law."

[74] *Id.* at § 25, incorporating *Model Law* Art. 12(2), states:

An arbitrator may be challenged only if circumstances exist that give rise to justifiable doubts as to his impartiality or independence, or if he does not possess qualifications agreed to by the parties. A party may challenge an arbitrator appointed by him, or in whose appointment he has participated, only for reasons of which he becomes aware after the appointment has been made.

For a review of this provision, *see* Choong & Weeramantry, *supra* note 11, at paras. 25.13–25.30.

§ 26(1) of the *Arbitration Ordinance*, incorporating *Model Law* Art. 13, *supra* note 6, provides:

(1) The parties are free to agree on a procedure for challenging an arbitrator, subject to the provisions of paragraph (3) of this article.

(2) Failing such agreement, a party who intends to challenge an arbitrator shall, within fifteen days after becoming aware of the constitution of the arbitral tribunal or after becoming aware of any circumstance referred to in article 12(2), send a written statement of the reasons for the challenge to the arbitral tribunal. Unless the challenged arbitrator withdraws from his office or the other party agrees to the challenge, the arbitral tribunal shall decide on the challenge.

(3) If a challenge under any procedure agreed upon by the parties or under the procedure of paragraph (2) of this article is not successful, the challenging party may request, within thirty days after having received notice of the decision rejecting the challenge, the court or other authority specified in article 6 to decide on the challenge, which decision shall be subject to no appeal.

[75] So & To, *supra* note 4, at para. [27.07] defines "mandate" as: "generally equivalent to 'authority to act'." § 26(4) of the *Arbitration Ordinance*, *supra* note 6, states in part:

The mandate of a challenged arbitrator terminates under article 13 of the UNCITRAL Model Law . . . if—

(a) the arbitrator withdraws from office;

(b) the parties agree to the challenge;

(c) the arbitral tribunal upholds the challenge and no request is made for the Court to decide on the challenge; or

(d) the Court, upon request to decide on the challenge, upholds the challenge.

- setting aside an arbitral award[76]
- assisting in taking evidence[77]

These changes are intended to contribute to increased efficiency in arbitral proceedings by limiting court intervention.

v. More stringent confidentiality requirements

The former *Arbitration Ordinance* did not sufficiently address the issue of confidentiality in arbitral proceedings.[78] Thus, previously the matter of confidentiality was governed by court decisions. The present Ordinance sets stricter requirements on confidentiality.[79]

See Choong & Weeramantry, *supra* note 11, at paras. 26.00–26.23 for a discussion of this section of the Ordinance. *See also* Halsbury's, *supra* note 6, at para. [25.087].

§ 27 of the *Arbitration Ordinance*, incorporating *Model Law* Art. 14, *supra* note 6, states as follows:

> Article 14 of the UNCITRAL Model Law, the text of which is set out below, has effect subject to section 13(4)—
>
> "*Article 14. Failure or impossibility to act*
>
> (1) If an arbitrator becomes *de jure* or *de facto* unable to perform his functions or for other reasons fails to act without undue delay, his mandate terminates if he withdraws from his office or if the parties agree on the termination. Otherwise, if a controversy remains concerning any of these grounds, any party may request the court or other authority specified in article 6 to decide on the termination of the mandate, which decision shall be subject to no appeal.
>
> (2) If, under this article or article 13(2), an arbitrator withdraws from his office or a party agrees to the termination of the mandate of an arbitrator, this does not imply acceptance of the validity of any ground referred to in this article or article 12(2)."

So & To, *supra* note 4, at para. [27.04] defines "*de jure*" by applying it in two situations:

> *De jure* inability to perform would arise where, for example, a party has obtained an injunction to prevent the arbitrator or arbitration from proceeding or a declaration that the arbitrator has been invalidly appointed . . .
>
> *De jure* inability to perform functions may also arise where, for any reason, the arbitration proceedings purport to deal with illegal subject-matter, or if the arbitrator is imprisoned.

So & To, *supra* note 4, at para. [27.05] explains "*de facto*" as:

> [the] inability to perform encompasses unavailability, illness or physical or mental incapacity.
>
> The wording of this provision envisages long-term incapacity or shorter-term incapacity, which will nevertheless seriously inconvenience the arbitration process.
>
> A disability must be serious enough to put the arbitrator out of action altogether for the duration and the purposes of the arbitration. (citations omitted)

[76] *See* § 81 of the *Arbitration Ordinance*, *supra* note 6.

[77] *Id.* at § 55(2) provides: "The Court may order a person to attend proceedings before an arbitral tribunal to give evidence or to produce documents or other evidence."

[78] § 2B(2)(a) of the former Ordinance, *supra* note 51, expressly provides that an arbitrator at the time of acting as a conciliator shall treat information obtained by him from the parties as confidential. § 2E(3) of the same statute stipulates that the court shall not permit information relating to court proceedings concerning the arbitration not being heard in open court to be published if the court is satisfied that parties to the arbitration would reasonably wish such information to remain confidential. Despite these two sections touching upon confidentiality, no further elaboration on the issue of confidentiality is found in the former Ordinance.

[79] § 18 of the *Arbitration Ordinance*, *supra* note 6, states:

> (1) Unless otherwise agreed by the parties, no party may publish, disclose or communicate any information relating to—
>
> (a) the arbitral proceedings under the arbitration agreement; or
>
> (b) an award made in those arbitral proceedings.

III. Rules

Rules regulate the conduct of an arbitration. Laws govern how the arbitration process will function by providing a framework. Rules or regulations implement the laws and thus govern how the parties will implement those laws in the conduct of their arbitration case. We now proceed to review some of these arbitration rules.

A. UNCITRAL Arbitration Rules[80]

The United Nations Commission on International Trade Law [hereinafter "UNCITRAL"] is:

> The core legal body of the United Nations system in the field of international trade law. A legal body with universal membership specializing in commercial law reform worldwide for over 50 years, UNCITRAL's business is the modernization and harmonization of rules on international business.[81]

---

(2) Nothing in subsection (1) prevents the publication, disclosure or communication of information referred to in that subsection by a party—
  (a) if the publication, disclosure or communication is made—
    (i) to protect or pursue a legal right or interest of the party; or
    (ii) to enforce or challenge the award referred to in that subsection, in legal proceedings before a court or other judicial authority in or outside Hong Kong;
  (b) if the publication, disclosure or communication is made to any government body, regulatory body, court or tribunal and the party is obliged by law to make the publication, disclosure or communication; or
  (c) if the publication, disclosure or communication is made to a professional or any other adviser of any of the parties.

The duty to maintain confidentiality under § 18 of the *Arbitration Ordinance*, *supra* note 6, applies only to the parties, but not to the arbitral tribunal or any other participants in the arbitration proceedings. Choong & Weeramantry, *supra* note 11, at para. 18.13.

§ 18(1) of the *Arbitration Ordinance*, *supra* note 6, extends the duty to maintain confidentiality to any awards rendered during the arbitral proceedings. Choong & Weeramantry, *supra* note 11, at para. 18.17.

§ 18(2)(a) of the *Arbitration Ordinance*, *supra* note 6, provides another exception to the general duty to maintain confidentiality: in instances where a party needs to raise *res judicata* in subsequent proceedings through the disclosure of an award obtained in a previous arbitration. Choong & Weeramantry, *supra* note 11, at para. 18.21.

§ 18(2)(b) of the *Arbitration Ordinance*, *supra* note 6, provides another exception to the general duty to maintain confidentiality: where a person who knows or suspects that a particular property represents proceeds of drug trafficking is required to disclose that knowledge or suspicion to an authorized officer under § 25A of the *Drug Trafficking (Recovery of Proceeds) Ordinance* (Cap. 405). Choong & Weeramantry, *supra* note 11, at para. 18.26.

§ 18(2)(c) of the *Arbitration Ordinance*, *supra* note 6, provides a third exception to the general duty to maintain confidentiality: where the parties disclose information to their respective lawyers for the purpose of obtaining legal advice. Such an exception will also be invoked when the parties disclose information to a potential expert. Choong & Weeramantry, *supra* note 11, at paras. 18.27 and 18.28.

See also Ma & Brock, *supra* note 7, at paras. 1.020–1.023 for a discussion of the confidentiality requirements, particularly § 17 and § 18 of this Ordinance.

[80] The UNCITRAL Arbitration Rules translates "Arbitration Rules" as 貿易法委員會仲裁規則 on its website at: http://www.uncitral.org/uncitral/zh/uncitral_texts/arbitration/2010Arbitration_rules.html (last visited 13 Jul. 2017).

HKIAC, *supra* note 2, translates "Arbitration Rules" as 聯合國國際貿易法委員會仲裁規則. The HKIAC's website on its rules is available at: http://www.hkiac.org/zh-hant/arbitration/rules-practice-notes/uncitral-arbitration-rules (last visited 13 Jul. 2017).

[81] UNCITRAL website at: http://www.uncitral.org/uncitral/en/about_us.html (lasted visited 9 Aug. 2017).

As part of its remit, UNCITRAL has created a set of arbitration rules. There is some overlap between this organization's *Model Law* and its Arbitration Rules, although these are separate and distinct documents. UNCITRAL explains the difference between its *Model Law* and its Arbitration Rules as follows:

> The UNCITRAL Model Law provides a pattern that law-makers in national governments can adopt as part of their domestic legislation on arbitration. The UNCITRAL Arbitration Rules (hereinafter "Arbitration Rules"), on the other hand, are selected by parties either as part of their contract, or after a dispute arises, to govern the conduct of an arbitration intended to resolve a dispute or disputes between themselves. Put simply, the Model Law is directed at States, while the Arbitration Rules are directed at potential (or actual) parties to a dispute.[82]

UNCITRAL adopted the Arbitration Rules in 1976 for use in the resolution of international commercial disputes by arbitration. The latest version of this set of rules dates from 2013.[83]

The Arbitration Rules provide a set of procedures on which parties may agree for regulating their arbitral proceedings. The Arbitration Rules may be used in both *ad hoc* arbitration as well as institution arbitration. The Arbitration Rules cover all aspects of the arbitral process:

- providing a model arbitration clause [Annex]
- setting out procedural rules regarding the appointment of arbitrator(s) [Section II]
- conduct of arbitral proceedings [Section III]
- establishing rules in relation to the form, effect and interpretation of the award [Section IV]

B. Institutional Rules

Institutional rules are the arbitration rules under which various arbitration institutions manage arbitral proceedings. Similar to the UNCITRAL Arbitration Rules, institutional rules regulate the parties' conduct of their arbitration. Some examples of institutional rules include the following:

- International Chamber of Commerce—Rules of Arbitration (2017)
- London Court of International Arbitration—Arbitration Rules (2014)
- Swiss Chambers' Arbitration Institution—Swiss Rules of International Arbitration (2012)

---

[82] *See* UNCITRAL's *FAQ – UNCITRAL and Private Disputes/Litigation.* Available at: http://www.uncitral.org/uncitral/en/uncitral_texts/arbitration_faq.html (last visited 13 Jul. 2017).

[83] The 2013 version of these rules is available at: http://www.uncitral.org/pdf/english/texts/arbitration/arb-rules-2013/UNCITRAL-Arbitration-Rules-2013-e.pdf (last visited 13 Jul. 2017).

- China International Economic and Trade Arbitration Commission—Arbitration Rules (2015)
- Hong Kong International Arbitration Centre—Administered Arbitration Rules (2018)

Although there are quite a few similarities between these different sets of institutional rules, there are differences such that any user should consult the applicable rules. These differences are particularly problematic in hybrid clauses where one institution's rules are to be administered by another institution.[84]

[84] Having one arbitral institution administer the rules of another institution would be inadvisable as demonstrated in the discussion in the main text of the *Insigma* case and the following discussion in this note. It is possible for an institution, such as the Hong Kong International Arbitration Centre, to administer, manage or supervise an arbitration using the rules of another arbitral institution rather than its own arbitration rules. Difficulties may arise in some jurisdictions whose national laws do not permit such a hybrid. Difficulties may also arise where an arbitral institution is not as familiar with the other institution's rules as it is with its own procedural rules.

Several cases other than *Insigma* have addressed these so-called "hybrid" arbitrations. A similar case occurred in mainland China which involved a hybrid arbitration clause providing for arbitration at CIETAC according to UNCITRAL Arbitration Rules. *Zhejiang Yisheng Petrochemical Co v INVISTA Technologies S.á.r.l* involved an arbitration clause providing for arbitration "at China International Economic Trade Arbitration Centre [*sic*] according to UNCITRAL Arbitration Rules." Yisheng contended that the arbitration clause failed to state an arbitration commission as required by the PRC's *Arbitration Law* and the selection of the UNITRAL Arbitration Rules indicated *ad hoc* arbitration which was contrary to the *Arbitration Law*. The court recognized the parties' intention to arbitrate by determinining the reference to *Centre* rather than *Commission* as unimportant by deciding that the English acronym CIETAC referred to *Commission*. The court interpreted the phrase *take place at* to refer to selecting CIETAC as the administering arbitral institution, hence the arbitration was not *ad hoc*.

In the case of *Top Gains Minerals Macao Commercial Offshore Ltd v TL Resources Pte Ltd* [2015] HKEC 2439, the Hong Kong Court of First Instance upheld an injunction in support of prospective arbitral proceedings in Singapore under an SIAC/ICC hybrid arbitration clause which stated: "such dispute or claim shall be referred to Singapore International Arbitration Centre (SIAC) for arbitration in accordance with the Rules of Conciliation and Arbitration of the International Chamber of Commerce." The court decided:

> 44. At first blush, it may seem clear that the plaintiff has departed from the arbitration clause by initiating arbitration in Singapore by referring the dispute to the ICC, instead of SIAC. However, this is a question of or challenge to the jurisdiction of the arbitral tribunal, which should be determined by the tribunal itself. Neither the Hong Kong Court nor the Singapore Court should interfere by deciding the jurisdiction of the tribunal at this stage. Even if the tribunal constituted by ICC should decide that it has jurisdiction over the Arbitration, and makes an award in the arbitral proceedings, it is still possible for the award to be recognized and enforced by the Hong Kong Court at the enforcement and recognition stage, either by exercise of its discretion on the facts of the case (as in *China Nanhai* [*sic*] *Joint Service Corporation Shenzhen Branch v Gee Tai Holdings* [1995] 2 HKLR 215), or because the award has not been set aside by the Singapore Court as the supervisory court (on jurisdiction, or any other ground).
>
> 45. I am therefore not persuaded by the defendant's argument, that there is no good arguable case that the Arbitration which has now been commenced by the plaintiff in Singapore is capable of giving rise to an award that may be enforced in Hong Kong.

In a similar case, there was a challenge to the competency of one arbitral institution to administer the rules of another institution. *The Government of the Russian Federation v I M Badprim S.R.L.*, Case No. T 2454-14, Svea Court of Appeal, 23 January 2015 is a Swedish case which can be found at this unofficial link: https://www.arbitration.sccinstitute.com/Views/Pages/GetFile.ashx?portalId=89&cat=95791&docId=2281406&propId=1578 (last visited 26 Aug. 2017). In this court case, the Stockholm Chamber of Commerce administered an arbitration under the ICC rules. The losing party (Russia) challenged the arbitral tribunal's award in part on the basis that:

> [the award] is in any event unenforceable and thus invalid . . . because the parties have agreed that the arbitration should be administered by the Arbitration Institute of the Stockholm Chamber of Commerce (SCC), but under the rules of arbitration of the International Chamber of Commerce (ICC), which is not doable in practice. The SCC lacks both the required organizational structure as

One example is the case of *Insigma Technology Co Ltd v Alstom Technology Ltd*.[85] In this case, the parties had agreed that "any and all such disputes shall be finally resolved by arbitration before the Singapore International Arbitration Centre in accordance with the Rules of Arbitration of the International Chamber of Commerce." When a dispute arose, Alstom made a request for arbitration before the ICC. Insigma challenged the validity of the arbitration agreement and the appointment of the tribunal by the ICC, stating that the SIAC should administer the arbitration using the ICC Rules of Arbitration.

The arbitral tribunal ruled that it had jurisdiction and that the arbitration clause was valid. The tribunal determined that "the rules of an arbitral institution can be legally divorced from the administration of an arbitration by that institution."[86] The adoption of ICC Rules for administration by other institutions was also not unheard of in practice.[87] The arbitral tribunal stated that the parties' arbitration agreement was not inoperable:

> due to a lack of capacity on the part of the SIAC to administer an arbitration conducted in accordance with the ICC Rules. Having obtained SIAC's confirmation that it would be prepared to administer the arbitration in accordance with the ICC Rules, as well as a proposal that the SIAC Secretariat, Registrar and Board of Directors perform the roles of the ICC Secretariat, Security-General [*sic*] and Court respectively, the tribunal was satisfied that the SIAC was capable of administering the arbitration . . . performing *mutatis mutandis* the functions assigned by the ICC Rules to the ICC.[88]

Dissatisfied, Insigma brought an appeal before the Singapore High Court raising four issues. The three most relevant to this chapter are set out below:

- whether there is a valid arbitration agreement
- whether the tribunal was validly constituted by the SIAC in accordance with the ICC Rules
- whether the defendant Alstom breached the arbitration agreement by first commencing the arbitration before the ICC Court of Arbitration[89]

The High Court addressed these issues by stating:

---

well as experience to carry out the most vital tasks under the arbitration rules of the ICC. Among these are the appointment of arbitrators based on ICC's national committees, the confirmation of arbitrators based on the experience of their performance in other ICC arbitrations, confirmation of "Terms of Reference" and scrutiny of arbitral awards. *Id.* at 4–5.

Although the challenge to the validity of the arbitral award was rejected, this case is an example of additional time and cost being spent on a dispute resolution process that is considered final, fast and less expensive than litigation. The novelty of the innovation seems to outweigh the resources involved for all involved, except for the losing party seeking to avoid paying the award.

85 [2008] SGHC 134.

86 *Id.* at para. 14 (citations omitted).

87 *Id.*

88 *Id.* at para. 15.

89 *Id.* at para. 20.

> Thus, the administering or supervising authority and the procedural rules adopted for the arbitration do not have to be of the same institution as long as the choices made do not result in significant inconsistency. . . . the present case is not one where reference to two different sets of *arbitration rules* may lead to inconsistencies rendering the arbitration inoperative. Here, only the ICC Rules have been designated, and the SIAC as administering body has confirmed that it would be able to follow the ICC Rules, substituting the appropriate corresponding actors to perform the functions of the ICC Secretariat, Secretary-General, and Court. This adaptation would be within the degree of flexibility allowed by the ICC Rules since the ICC Rules recognise the autonomy of the parties as a guiding principle. . . .[90]
>
> . . . [Concerning] whether the tribunal was constituted in accordance with the arbitration agreement . . . the court must decide what the substantive appointment procedure was. As shown by the analysis of the ICC Rules and the SIAC Rules, it is possible for a procedure for the appointment of an arbitral tribunal to be simultaneously "in accordance" with more than one set of rules, simply by virtue of the fact that the two sets of rules are to the same effect on that issue, and irrespective of whether the procedure is carried out by reference to only one set of rules.[91]
>
> Since the appointment procedures under the ICC Rules . . . and under the SIAC Rules (2nd Ed) are the same, I agree . . . that the tribunal was correct in stating that the "process by which the Tribunal was appointed was in accord with the agreement of the Parties, and whether the confirmation of the appointments by the SIAC was made with reference to the SIAC Rules or the ICC Rules would have made no difference at all to the outcome" . . . Thus, the tribunal was actually constituted by the SIAC in accordance with (albeit without express reference to) the ICC Rules, and it was validly constituted under [the parties' arbitration agreement].[92]
>
> . . . [The tribunal] accepted that technically the defendant's initial referral of the dispute to the ICC was not in compliance with the arbitration agreement. It held however that there was no basis for taking the matter further as the ICC arbitration had been terminated and the breach had thereby been cured. Further, the plaintiff has adduced no evidence to show that it suffered any prejudice as a result of the commencement of the ICC arbitration.[93]
>
> I see no reason to come to a different conclusion. The plaintiff's arguments on appeal are not convincing.[94]

Insigma, still being dissatisfied, brought its case to the Singapore Court of Appeal.[95] The Court of Appeal stated:

> This was an appeal against the decision of the High Court . . . on the novel and important legal issue of whether an arbitration agreement may validly provide

---

90 *Id.* at para. 28.

91 *Id.* at para. 42.

92 *Id.* at para. 43 (citations omitted).

93 *Id.* at para. 44.

94 *Id.* at para. 45.

95 *Insigma Technology Co Ltd v Alstom Technology Ltd* [2009] SGCA 24.

> for *one* arbitral institution to administer an arbitration under the rules of *another* arbitral institution . . .[96]
>
> In those proceedings, Insigma . . . had applied to set aside the decision of the arbitral tribunal ("the Tribunal") constituted by the Singapore International Arbitration Centre . . . that it had jurisdiction to hear the arbitration between . . . [Alstom] and Insigma, on the grounds that the Tribunal lacked such jurisdiction and that the arbitration agreement between the parties was inoperative for uncertainty. The High Court dismissed Insigma's application, leading to this appeal. . . . At the end of the hearing before us, we dismissed the appeal and awarded indemnity costs against Insigma.[97]
>
> . . .
>
> . . . As for costs, we decided to award indemnity costs against Insigma for the following reasons:
>
> (a) it approbated the Arbitration Agreement when it objected to the ICC Arbitration initiated by Alstom, but subsequently (and unreasonably) reprobated the arbitration agreement when it objected to Alstom initiating the SIAC-administered arbitration; and
>
> (b) having already lost two rounds on arguments which both the Tribunal and the High Court had demonstrated to be unmeritorious, it nevertheless persisted with an appeal to this court, and thereby wasted judicial time and made Alstom incur unnecessary costs in this appeal.[98]

C. Others

There are other rules which serve as guidelines or serve as commonly accepted good practice. We briefly set out below some frequently used guidelines.

i. UNCITRAL *Notes on Organizing Arbitral Proceedings* (2016)

These Notes are another product by UNCITRAL and are intended to serve as a check-list for participants in an arbitration. As the organization explains:

> Initially adopted by UNCITRAL in 1996 and up-dated in 2016, the Notes are designed to assist arbitration practitioners by providing an annotated list of matters on which an arbitral tribunal may wish to formulate decisions during the course of arbitral proceedings, including deciding on a set of arbitration rules, the language and place of an arbitration and questions relating to confidentiality, as well as other matters such as conduct of hearings and the taking of evidence and possible requirements for the filing or delivering of an award. The text may be used in both ad hoc and institutional arbitrations.[99]

---

96 *Id.* at para. 1.

97 *Id.* at para. 2.

98 *Id.* at para. 44. *Costs* will be discussed in Chapter 9, "Contents of the Award."

99 http://www.uncitral.org/uncitral/en/uncitral_texts/arbitration/2016Notes_proceedings.html (last visited 26 Aug. 2017).

ii. International Bar Association

The International Bar Association, commonly known as the IBA, was created in 1947, with a present membership of more than 80,000 individual lawyers in approximately 160 countries. The IBA is the world's leading organization of international legal practitioners, bar associations and law societies.[100]

Amongst the work produced by the IBA are its arbitration-related publications which have frequently been used as guidelines or as indicators of best practices. Some of these publications include the following, which are commonly used in arbitrations.

a. *Guidelines on Conflict of Interest in International Arbitration* (2014)

The Guidelines serve as a standard by which any potential conflict of interest by a prospective arbitrator or serving arbitrator can be determined. This set of guidelines:

> represents the most comprehensive work to date defining the framework by which the impartiality of arbitration in the international arena can be most effectively assured. The publication sets out a series of seven general standards of independence and disclosure to govern the selection, appointment and continuing role of an arbitrator.[101]

b. *Rules on the Taking of Evidence in International Arbitration* (2010)

The title is descriptive of the use and the purpose of this publication. As further described by the IBA's website:

> The IBA issued these Rules as a resource to parties and to arbitrators to provide an efficient, economical and fair process for the taking of evidence in international arbitration. The Rules provide mechanisms for the presentation of documents, witnesses of fact and expert witnesses, inspections, as well as the conduct of evidentiary hearings. The Rules are designed to be used in conjunction with, and adopted together with, institutional, ad hoc or other rules or procedures governing international arbitrations. The IBA Rules of Evidence reflect procedures in use in many different legal systems, and they may be particularly useful when the parties come from different legal cultures.[102]
>
> The IBA Rules of Evidence contain procedures initially developed in civil law systems, in common law systems and even in international arbitration processes themselves. Designed to assist parties in determining what procedures to use in their particular case, they present some (but not all) of the methods for conducting international arbitration proceedings. Parties and arbitral tribunals may adopt the IBA Rules of Evidence in whole or in part—at the time of drafting the arbitration

---

[100] The IBA website. Link is at: http://www.ibanet.org/About_the_IBA/About_the_IBA.aspx (last visited 13 Jul. 2017).

[101] The *Guidelines on Conflicts of Interest in International Arbitration* (2014). Available at: http://www.ibanet.org/Publications/publications_IBA_guides_and_free_materials.aspx# (last visited 26 Aug. 2017).

[102] *Foreword* to *Rules on the Taking of Evidence in International Arbitration* (2010) [hereinafter Rules], at 2.

clause in a contract or once an arbitration commences—or they may use them as guidelines. Parties are free to adapt them to the particular circumstances of each matter.[103]

c. *Guidelines on Party Representation in International Arbitration* (2013)

The Guidelines are published with the intention of providing assistance to those representing parties to an arbitration, generally the legal professionals. This publication also provides guidance to the arbitration tribunal.

> By virtue of these Guidelines, Arbitral Tribunals need not, in dealing with such issues, and subject to applicable mandatory laws, be limited by a choice-of-law rule or private international law analysis to choosing among national or domestic professional conduct rules. Instead, these Guidelines offer an approach designed to account for the multi-faceted nature of international arbitral proceedings. These Guidelines shall apply where and to the extent that the Parties have so agreed. Parties may adopt these Guidelines, in whole or in part, in their arbitration agreement or at any time subsequently. An Arbitral Tribunal may also apply, or draw inspiration from, the Guidelines, after having determined that it has the authority to rule on matters of Party representation in order to ensure the integrity and fairness of the arbitral proceedings.[104]

This publication is comprised of 27 sections:

---

[103] *Commentary* on the revised text of the Rules, at 3. Available at: https://www.ibanet.org/Publications/publications_IBA_guides_and_free_materials.aspx# (last visited 26 Aug. 2017).
One authority stated:

> International arbitrations often refer to the "IBA Rules on the Taking of Evidence in International Arbitration" ("2010 IBA Rules") as a guideline or some procedural orders direct that it be adopted. The 2010 IBA Rules are intended to provide an efficient, economical and fair process for the taking of evidence in international arbitrations, particularly those between parties from different legal cultures. They are designed to supplement the legal provisions and the institutional, or other rules that apply to the conduct of the arbitration. Article 3 of the IBA Rules lays down the test for production of documents being one of "relevant and material" and the steps to be adopted for the request to produce documents (specific discovery). In the request to produce, the documents requested need to be sufficiently identified together with a statement as to how the documents are relevant to the case and material to its outcome. There needs also to be a statement as to the possession, custody or control of the documents in support of the request. Objection to the request may be raised. Grounds for opposing production of documents are provided in art. 9.2 of the IBA Rules, which include legal privilege; lack of sufficient relevance to the case or materiality to its outcome; unreasonable burden to produce the requested documents; loss or destruction of the documents; commercial or technical confidentiality; special political or institutional sensitivity; or considerations of procedural economy, proportionality, fairness or equality of parties.
>
> Frequently, the basis for request to produce and the grounds of opposition are set out in the form of a table for ease of reference, often called the Redfern Schedule, to aid the tribunal in making determinations.

Ma & Brock, *supra* note 7, at paras. 15.047–15.048 (citations omitted).

[104] *Guidelines on Party Representation in International Arbitration* (2013), at 5. The *Guidelines* is available at: https://www.ibanet.org/Publications/publications_IBA_guides_and_free_materials.aspx#Practice Rules and Guidelines (last visited 26 Aug. 2017).

- §§ 1–3 (and accompanying Comments to Guidelines): Application of the Guidelines
- §§ 4–6 (and accompanying Comments to Guidelines): Party Representation
- §§ 7–9 Communications with Arbitrators
- §§ 8–10 Submissions to the Arbitral Tribunal
- §§ 11–17 (and accompanying Comments to Guidelines): Evidence
- §§ 18–25 (and accompanying Comments to Guidelines): Witnesses and Experts
- §§ 26–27 (and accompanying Comments to Guidelines): Remedies for Misconduct

iii. Chartered Institute of Arbitrators

The Chartered Institute of Arbitrators is commonly known by its acronym: CIArb. The organization is a not-for-profit, United Kingdom registered charity with an approximate membership of 15,000 based across 133 countries and supported by an international network of 38 branches. For over 100 years, the CIArb has provided support for the global promotion, facilitation and development of all ADR methods through a range of resources including guidance, support, advice, networking and promotional opportunities.[105]

Amongst the range of resources is a publication entitled *Protocol for the Use of Party Appointed Expert Witnesses in International Arbitration* (2007). As explained in this publication's *Foreword*:

> Chartered Institute of Arbitrators Protocol for the Use of Party-Appointed Expert Witnesses in International Arbitration (the "CIArb Protocol") has been prepared by the Practice and Standards Committee of the CIArb.
>
> The CIArb has issued this Protocol so that parties and arbitrators can use it when party-appointed experts are needed to give evidence in arbitration proceedings.
>
> It provides a complete regime for the giving of such evidence and provides a procedure for identifying the issues to be dealt with by way of expert evidence, the number of experts, their identity, what tests or analyses are required, the independence of the experts, the contents of the experts' opinions, privilege, meetings of experts and the manner of expert testimony.
>
> The CIArb Protocol applies only to party-appointed experts. It is not intended to cover tribunal-appointed experts or single-joint experts.
>
> It has been structured along similar lines to the IBA Rules of Evidence (which are gaining increasingly wide acceptance internationally) and has been aligned with those parts of the IBA Rules which deal with party-appointed experts.
>
> The CIArb Protocol expands upon the IBA Rules in that, amongst other things, it caters for tests and analyses to be conducted, it gives more detailed guidance as to what should (and should not) be in an expert's written opinion and it deals with

[105] http://www.ciarb.org/about (last visited 19 Aug. 2017).

> independence and privilege. It only differs from the IBA Rules in providing for an experts' meeting before reports are produced.
>
> The CIArb Protocol can be used in its entirety by the arbitral tribunal directing (or the parties agreeing) . . .
>
> Alternatively, the CIArb Protocol can be used in part or as a guideline for developing the procedures to be adopted.[106]

IV. Summary

In this chapter, we introduced some of the various laws, rules, and guides which have application to arbitration, either on a mandatory basis or an optional basis. In relation to laws, we primarily reviewed three: the *Model Law*, law of the seat, and the *New York Convention*. As well, we presented Hong Kong's *Arbitration Ordinance*, which incorporates most of the Model Law, as an example of the application of the concept of the law of the seat should the territory be designated as the arbitral venue. This was followed by an introduction to arbitral institutions' rules, their purpose, and their application. The topic of guidelines issued by various organizations concluded this chapter.

[106] *Foreword* to Chartered Institute of Arbitrators Protocol for the Use of Party-Appointed Expert Witnesses in International Arbitration. Available at: http://www.ciarb.org/docs/default-source/ciarbdocuments/international-arbitration-protocols/partyappointedexpertsinternationalarbitration.pdf?sfvrsn=8 (last visited 19 Aug. 2017).

4

Appointment of the Arbitrator/Tribunal

I. Introduction

In this chapter, the process involved in selecting an individual to serve as the arbitrator is reviewed. This frequently is referred to as *appointing an arbitrator(s)* to sit as the tribunal. Remember that the term *tribunal* can refer to a single arbitrator or a panel of arbitrators, usually a panel of three.[1] Also remember that the terms

[1] Theoretically, it is possible to appoint a panel of two arbitrators but the obvious difficulties which would arise in the event of a split decision render this possibility impractical. Nevertheless, Hong Kong's *Arbitration Ordinance* (Cap. 609) [hereinafter *Arbitration Ordinance*] provides for such situations in § 30 with the appointment of a person known as an *umpire*. In the event of deadlock amongst the two appointed arbitrators, § 31 of the Ordinance sets out the umpire's function in determining the dispute. These two sections provide:

> 30. Appointment of umpire
>
> In an arbitration with an even number of arbitrators, the arbitrators may, unless otherwise agreed by the parties, appoint an umpire at any time after they are themselves appointed.
>
> 31. Functions of umpire in arbitral proceedings
>
> (1) The parties are free to agree what the functions of an umpire are to be and, in particular—
> a. whether the umpire is to attend the arbitral proceedings; and
> b. when, and the extent to which, the umpire is to replace the arbitrators as the arbitral tribunal with the power to make orders, directions and awards.
>
> (2) If or to the extent that there is no such agreement of the parties, the arbitrators are free to agree on the functions of the umpire.
>
> (3) Subsections (4) to (11) apply subject to any agreement of the parties or the arbitrators.
>
> (4) After an umpire is appointed, the umpire must attend the arbitral proceedings.
>
> (5) The umpire must be supplied with the same documents and other materials as are supplied to the arbitrators.
>
> (6) Orders, directions and awards are to be made by the arbitrators unless, subject to subsection (9), the arbitrators cannot agree on a matter relating to the dispute submitted to arbitration.
>
> (7) If the arbitrators cannot agree on a matter relating to the dispute submitted to arbitration . . . in which case the umpire is to replace the arbitrators as the arbitral tribunal with the power to make orders, directions and awards, in respect of that matter only, subject to subsection (9) (b), as if the umpire were the sole arbitrator.
>
> (8) If the arbitrators cannot agree on a matter relating to the dispute submitted to arbitration but—
> a. they fail to give notice of that fact; or
> b. any of them fails to join in the giving of notice,
> c. any party may apply to the Court which may decide that the umpire is to replace the arbitrators as the arbitral tribunal with the power to make orders, directions and awards, in respect of that matter only, as if the umpire were the sole arbitrator.
>
> (9) Despite the replacement by the umpire as the arbitral tribunal in respect of a matter, on which the arbitrators cannot agree, relating to the dispute submitted to arbitration, the arbitrators

arbitration tribunal, *arbitral tribunal*, and *tribunal* can be used interchangeably. Equally, the term *panel* can be interchanged with *tribunal*.

Appointing the tribunal is one of the critical stages in the arbitral process, as the actual resolution of the dispute between the parties cannot begin until the tribunal is constituted.[2] While this chapter concerns the selection of an individual to serve as arbitrator, it should be kept in mind that the nominated individual has the choice of declining the appointment. Generally, the reasons for rejecting the appointment may include: conflict of interest; lack of impartiality; lack of experience or qualification in the subject matter of the dispute; or, lack of availability or time. Some of these reasons are discussed briefly below in the context of the qualifications of an arbitrator.[3]

In the following chapter, the jurisdiction or authority of the tribunal over the parties and their dispute is analysed. We also review the obligations, the responsibilities and the powers of the arbitral tribunal.

> may—
> a. still make orders, directions and awards in respect of the other matters relating to the dispute if they consider that it would save costs by doing so; or
> b. refer the entirety of the dispute to the umpire for arbitration.

For review of the purpose and role of an umpire, *see* 2 HALSBURY'S LAWS OF HONG KONG para. [25.074] (2nd ed. 2016) [hereinafter HALSBURY'S] which states as follows:

> Where the reference is to an even number of arbitrators, the arbitrators may at any time after their own appointment appoint an umpire, unless a contrary intention is expressed in the arbitration agreement. There is no requirement . . . that they may only do so upon disagreement. The parties are free to agree what the functions of an umpire are to be and, in particular (1) whether the umpire is to attend the arbitral proceedings and (2) when, and the extent to which, the umpire is to replace the arbitrators as the arbitral tribunal with the power to make orders, directions and awards. If or to the extent that there is no such agreement of the parties, the arbitrators are free to agree on the functions of the umpire. Failing such agreement, the Arbitration Ordinance (Cap 609) provides for the functions of the umpires in relation to the foregoing.
>
> The umpire can acquire powers to decide issues as if he was the sole arbitrator. If the arbitrators cannot agree on a matter relating to the dispute submitted to arbitration, they must forthwith give notice of that fact in writing to the parties and the umpire, in which case the umpire is to replace the arbitrators as the arbitral tribunal with the power to make orders, directions and awards, in respect of that matter only, as if the umpire were the sole arbitrator. . . . (citations omitted)

For information on the appointment of umpires, *see* HALSBURY'S, *supra* note 1, at para. [25.117].

For details on the function of an umpire, *see* HALSBURY'S, *supra* note 1, at para. [25.118].

Other countries, *e.g.* Brazil, avoid this scenario by requiring an odd number of arbitrators. *See* Arbitration Act (Law 9.307/96 as amended by Law 13.129/2015).

[2] BUTTERWORTHS HONG KONG ARBITRATION LAW HANDBOOK para. [26.05] (DAMON YC SO, CHRISTOPHER TO *et al.*, eds., 2nd ed. 2018) [hereinafter SO & TO] states:

> The tribunal is constituted when, in the case of a sole arbitrator, his appointment becomes effective, or, in the case of a tribunal of two, three or more arbitrators, when the appointment of the last arbitrator in time becomes effective.

[3] For a more detailed discussion on this topic, *see*, *e.g.*, ARBITRATION IN HONG KONG: A PRACTICAL GUIDE paras. 13.052–13.078 (THE HON CHIEF JUSTICE GEOFFREY MA AND DENIS BROCK, eds., 4th ed. 2017) [hereinafter MA & BROCK].

II. Appointment of the Arbitrator

Until the members of the arbitration tribunal are appointed, the arbitral proceedings cannot begin.[4] Therefore, the parties firstly need to appoint the arbitral tribunal which will decide the dispute.[5] Under the concept of party autonomy, the parties are to decide the number of arbitrators to be appointed to decide the dispute.[6] If the parties cannot or refuse to agree on the composition of the tribunal, the arbitrator may be appointed by the designated institution or by the appropriate court under the law where the arbitration is seated.[7]

The usual number of arbitrators to be appointed is either one or three for an international commercial dispute.[8] Generally, the monetary amount or the complexity of the dispute will determine the number of arbitrators. While it is possible to have more than three arbitrators, this is usually not done because of the increased costs and the increased complexity concerning coordination of schedules.[9] Furthermore, with each increase in the number of arbitrators, there is a possibility

---

[4] In relation to appointment of arbitrators, many of the major arbitral institutions now have provisions for the appointment of emergency arbitrators who would handle urgent matters which might arise before the arbitral tribunal is appointed. Emergency arbitrator provisions would allow the parties to seek interim relief from the emergency arbitrator rather than from national courts prior to the appointment of the arbitral tribunal. *See, e.g.*, REDFERN AND HUNTER ON INTERNATIONAL ARBITRATION paras. 4.17–4.21 (NIGEL BLACKABY *et al.*, eds., 6th ed. 2015) [hereinafter REDFERN & HUNTER].
More information on emergency arbitrators can be found in Chapter 11, "Cost-saving Techniques in Arbitration."

[5] As noted by one source:

> It is not usually necessary to include much in the arbitration agreement to deal with the appointment of arbitrators in the absence of agreement. Most arbitration rules, be they "institutional" or *ad hoc*, contain provisions for the default appointment of arbitrator(s). Incorporation of those rules means that further provisions for default appointment are unnecessary, provided that the parties to not wish to specify a "default appointment organisation" that may be more able in selecting an appropriate arbitrator; for example, an engineering contract may lead the parties to choose a professional body of engineers to select the arbitrator.
>
> . . .
>
> The "default appointment" mechanism usually is that the court makes the appointment. Hong Kong has a default provision for arbitrations so that the HKIAC makes the appointment from a designated and approved panel which is in existence for that purpose. The HKIAC also decides disputes as to whether there should be one or three arbitrators.

MA & BROCK, *supra* note 3, at paras. 10.077–10.079 (citations omitted).

[6] *See id.* at para. 13.065.

[7] As one authority noted:

> If the parties fail to make any choice at all in this regard, including a failure to incorporate rules that address the issue, the Arbitration Ordinance provides as a final default that the number of arbitrators is to be either one or three, as decided by the HKIAC. However, this is the case only where s. 1 of Sch.2 of the Arbitration Ordinance does not apply. . . . If s. 1 of Sch. 2 applies, then any dispute between the parties to an arbitration agreement is to be submitted to a sole arbitrator for arbitration.

Id. at para. 13.068 (citations omitted).
Section 1 of Schedule 2 of the *Arbitration Ordinance, supra* note 1, pertains to domestic arbitrations, which are discussed in Chapter 3, "Laws and Rules of Arbitration."
See also HALSBURY'S, *supra* note 1, at paras. [25.075]–[25.081] in relation to the default appointment of arbitrators.

[8] For a discussion on the advantages and disadvantages of having one or three arbitrators, *see, e.g.*, MA & BROCK, *supra* note 3, at paras. 10.088–10.096.

[9] As noted in *id.* at para. 10.088: "Five arbitrators, or some other larger number being appointed, are not unheard of, but remain rare in practice given the additional expense and lack of obvious immediate advantage."

of a greater delay in reaching an award. If the parties had failed to designate the number of arbitrators and when a dispute arises the parties cannot agree, the default provisions would apply.[10] If the seat of the arbitration is in Hong Kong and if there is no administering institution, the *Arbitration Ordinance* (Cap. 609) [hereinafter "*Arbitration Ordinance*"] will apply. Pursuant to this Ordinance, the Hong Kong International Arbitration Centre [hereinafter "HKIAC"] will serve as the appointing authority and will appoint either one or three arbitrators.[11] If the parties had agreed on an arbitration administered by an institution, that institution's arbitration rules would apply.[12]

---

[10] *See id.* at paras. 13.067–13.069.

[11] § 23 of the *Arbitration Ordinance*, incorporating *Model Law* Art. 10, *supra* note 1, provides:

(1) Article 10(1) of the UNCITRAL Model Law, the text of which is set out below, has effect—

"*Article 10. Number of arbitrators*

(1) The parties are free to determine the number of arbitrators.

(2) [Not applicable.]"

(2) For the purposes of subsection (1), the freedom of the parties to determine the number of arbitrators includes the right of the parties to authorize a third party, including an institution, to make that determination.

(3) The number of arbitrators in an arbitration is to be either 1 or 3 as decided by the HKIAC in the particular case if—

(a) the parties fail to agree on the number of arbitrators; and

(b) section 1 of Schedule 2 does not apply.

[12] For example, the Hong Kong International Arbitration Centre's Administered Arbitration Rules (2018) [hereinafter HKIAC Arbitration Rules], state:

Article 6–Number of Arbitrators

6.1 If the parties have not agreed upon the number of arbitrators before the arbitration commences or within 30 days from the date the Notice of Arbitration is received by the Respondent, HKIAC shall decide whether the case shall be referred to a sole arbitrator or to three arbitrators, taking into account the circumstances of the case.

. . .

Article 7–Appointment of a Sole Arbitrator

7.1 Unless the parties have agreed otherwise:

(a) where the parties have agreed before the arbitration commences that the dispute shall be referred to a sole arbitrator, they shall jointly designate the sole arbitrator within 30 days from the date the Notice of Arbitration was received by the Respondent.

(b) where the parties have agreed after the arbitration commences to refer the dispute to a sole arbitrator, they shall jointly designate the sole arbitrator within 15 days from the date of that agreement.

(c) where the parties have not agreed upon the number of arbitrators and HKIAC has decided that the dispute shall be referred to a sole arbitrator, the parties shall jointly designate the sole arbitrator within 15 days from the date HKIAC's decision was received by the last of them.

. . .

Article 8–Appointment of Three Arbitrators

8.1 Where a dispute between two parties is referred to three arbitrators, the arbitral tribunal shall be constituted as follows, unless the parties have agreed otherwise:

a. where the parties have agreed before the arbitration commences that the dispute shall be referred to three arbitrators, each party shall designate in the Notice of Arbitration and the Answer to the Notice of Arbitration, respectively, one arbitrator. If either party fails to designate an arbitrator, HKIAC shall appoint the arbitrator.

b. where the parties have agreed after the arbitration commences to refer the dispute to three arbitrators, the Claimant shall designate an arbitrator within 15 days from the date of that agreement, and the Respondent shall designate an arbitrator within 15 days from receiving notice of the Claimant's designation. If a party fails to designate an arbitrator, HKIAC shall appoint the arbitrator.

A. Procedure for the Appointment

There are several ways in which an arbitrator can be appointed.[13] As mentioned above, party autonomy permits the parties to the arbitration agreement to specify:

- a particular individual who will be nominated in the arbitration agreement
- the expertise which an arbitrator should possess, *e.g.*, a geotechnical engineer with 20 years' experience in tunneling works
- the language in which the arbitrator should be conversant, *e.g.*, a person fluent in the language of the contract or the language of the dispute[14]
- the nationality of the sole or a presiding arbitrator in the context of an international arbitration, *e.g.*, a person who is not of the same nationality as either of the parties[15]
- the professional qualification of the arbitrator, *e.g.*, a solicitor with a practising certificate
- a professional organization in which an arbitrator should hold a membership, *e.g.*, a Fellow of the Chartered Institute of Arbitrators or a Fellow of the Hong Kong Institution of Engineers
- a particular institution to make the appointment on behalf of the parties, *e.g.*, the president of the Hong Kong Institute of Surveyors

---

c. where the parties have not agreed upon the number of arbitrators and HKIAC has decided that the dispute shall be referred to three arbitrators, the Claimant shall designate an arbitrator within 15 days from receipt of HKIAC's decision, and the Respondent shall designate an arbitrator within 15 days from receiving notice of the Claimant's designation. If a party fails to designate an arbitrator, HKIAC shall appoint the arbitrator.

d. the two arbitrators so appointed shall designate a third arbitrator, who shall act as the presiding arbitrator. Failing such designation within 30 days from the confirmation or appointment of the second arbitrator, HKIAC shall appoint the presiding arbitrator.

. . .

See also the HKIAC's Practice Note on the Appointment of Arbitrators (2018). A copy of this Practice Note may be found here: http://hkiac.org/sites/default/files/ck_filebrowser/PDF/arbitration/Practice%20Note%20on%20Appointment%20of%20Arbitrators%20-%2018%20Oct%202018.pdf

Another example is the London Court of International Arbitration's Arbitration Rules (2014) [hereinafter LCIA Rules] which provide:

5.7 No party or third person may appoint any arbitrator under the Arbitration Agreement: the LCIA Court alone is empowered to appoint arbitrators (albeit taking into account any written agreement or joint nomination by the parties).

5.8 A sole arbitrator shall be appointed unless the parties have agreed in writing otherwise or if the LCIA Court determines that in the circumstances a three-member tribunal is appropriate (or, exceptionally, more than three).

5.9 The LCIA Court shall appoint arbitrators with due regard for any particular method or criteria of selection agreed in writing by the parties. The LCIA Court shall also take into account the transaction(s) at issue, the nature and circumstances of the dispute, its monetary amount or value, the location and languages of the parties, the number of parties and all other factors which it may consider relevant in the circumstances.

The LCIA Rules may be found here: http://www.lcia.org/Dispute_Resolution_Services/lcia-arbitration-rules-2014.aspx (last visited 12 July 2017).

13 *See, e.g.*, Ma & Brock, *supra* note 3, at paras. 13.065–13.078.

14 Redfern & Hunter, *supra* note 4, at para. 4.50 and para. 4.61.

15 *Id.* at paras. 4.61–4.67.

Note that sometimes future problems are caused by specifying too-exacting qualifications for the arbitrator before a dispute develops. We present two examples. In the first example, the parties in their contract specify a particular person to serve as arbitrator. In one relatively recent case, an arbitration agreement named a specific individual to serve as arbitrator. The Supreme Court of India in *ACC Limited v Global Cements* (2012) 7 SCC 71 needed to decide whether the arbitration clause would remain valid if the arbitrator named in the arbitration clause was no more. The court came to the conclusion that the arbitration clause remained in effect even if the arbitrator did not.

In the second example, the contract gives rise to disputes of an entirely different nature than that anticipated by the parties. For example, in negotiating the contract for a tunneling project, the parties may anticipate disputes concerning ground conditions and progress of the Works and thus require the appointment of a geotechnical engineer with 20-years' experience in tunneling work. Subsequently, if a dispute arises concerning fraud in the inducement of the contract, an arbitrator with a legal background might be more suitable. Therefore, the parties should consider whether there is the need to over-specify the arbitral tribunal's qualifications before a dispute has arisen in order to maintain flexibility to choose the most suitable person to be the arbitrator.[16]

Proceeding on the presumption that the parties already know the characteristics or type of arbitrator that they desire to decide their dispute, we address the topic of appointment of the tribunal. We start first with the appointment procedure for a single arbitrator before discussing the appointment procedure for a tribunal of three arbitrators.[17] Later in the chapter some of the criteria for deciding the composition of the arbitral tribunal are reviewed, that is, the suitability of an individual to serve as arbitrator.

The simplest way to appoint a single arbitrator is for the parties to agree on a suitably qualified individual and for that individual to accept the appointment to

---

[16] *Id.*

As noted:

> It is possible, and indeed sometimes desirable, to set out additional pre-requisites in the arbitration agreement itself. A typical example might be that "the arbitrator shall be a commercial barrister practising in London and have been appointed as Queen's Counsel for not less than 10 years" . . . Different contracts require discrete consideration at the drafting stage, but this tool for "targeted appointment" is not much used in practice. It can be difficult to predict the nature of all disputes which will arise, and it is not always possible to have set out in advance in the arbitration agreement the desirable qualities of the relevant arbitrator.
>
> A risk also can be created by express qualifications being required of an arbitrator. It is possible that the individual(s) appointed will not satisfy the requirements, and also entirely feasible that the parties may not know this until the arbitration is underway . . . The problem is not peculiarly a drafting one however, but more the subject of proper administration of the process if such expertise specification specifically is required.

MA & BROCK, *supra* note 3, at paras. 10.085–10.086.

[17] For further details, *see, e.g.*, MA & BROCK, *supra* note 3, at paras. 13.069–13.078.

serve. This individual can be based on the recommendation of the parties' advisors or selected from a panel of arbitrators maintained by an arbitral institution.

If the parties cannot agree, another method of constituting the tribunal is known as a *list* or *list procedure*. With this procedure, the parties exchange lists containing names of potential arbitrators. In one variation of this procedure, if a single name appears on both lists, that individual is usually selected to serve as arbitrator. In another variation, if more than one name appears on the two lists, the two individuals would be ranked in order of preference as indicated on each list.

Should the parties fail to agree on the appointment of an arbitrator, or should one party refuse to participate in the appointment process, a default appointment might be made. In a default situation, if the arbitration is one administered by an institution, the institution's arbitration rules will apply to the appointment of an arbitrator.[18] If there is no institution, the parties will have to rely upon the law of the seat where the arbitration is to be held. Generally, if the seat is an established arbitration location, the venue's national law will contain provisions for the default appointment by a court or similar institution.[19]

If the parties in the dispute cannot agree on the joint appointment of the sole arbitrator, the default provision in their arbitration agreement should specify an

---

[18] For example, the HKIAC Arbitration Rules, *supra* note 12.

[19] For example, § 24(1) of the *Arbitration Ordinance*, incorporating *Model Law* Art. 11, *supra* note 1 provides in part:

> (1) Article 11 of the UNCITRAL Model Law, the text of which is set out below, has effect subject to section 13(2) and (3)—
>
> "*Article 11. Appointment of arbitrators*
>
> (1) No person shall be precluded by reason of his nationality from acting as an arbitrator, unless otherwise agreed by the parties.
> (2) The parties are free to agree on a procedure of appointing the arbitrator or arbitrators, subject to the provisions of paragraphs (4) and (5) of this article.
> (3) Failing such agreement,
> (a) in an arbitration with three arbitrators, each party shall appoint one arbitrator, and the two arbitrators thus appointed shall appoint the third arbitrator; if a party fails to appoint the arbitrator within thirty days of receipt of a request to do so from the other party, or if the two arbitrators fail to agree on the third arbitrator within thirty days of their appointment, the appointment shall be made, upon request of a party, by the court or other authority specified in article 6;
> (b) in an arbitration with a sole arbitrator, if the parties are unable to agree on the arbitrator, he shall be appointed, upon request of a party, by the court or other authority specified in article 6.
> (4) Where, under an appointment procedure agreed upon by the parties,
> (a) a party fails to act as required under such procedure, or
> (b) the parties, or two arbitrators, are unable to reach an agreement expected of them under such procedure, or
> (c) a third party, including an institution, fails to perform any function entrusted to it under such procedure,
> (d) any party may request the court or other authority specified in article 6 to take the necessary measure, unless the agreement on the appointment procedure provides other means for securing the appointment.
> (5) . . ."

authority to make the appointment.[20] This authority is commonly referred to by the term *appointing authority*. If there is no such provision in the parties' arbitration agreement, the law of the seat will specify the appointing authority. In Hong Kong, the *Arbitration Ordinance* provides: "in an arbitration with a sole arbitrator, if the parties are unable to agree on the arbitrator, he shall be appointed . . . by the court or other authority specified in article 6."[21] Where an arbitration is seated in a venue other than Hong Kong, that jurisdiction's arbitration law should designate which institution or which court will serve as the appointing authority.

We now turn to discuss the appointment of multiple arbitrators to serve on a tribunal. The general procedure for the appointment of a tribunal consisting of three arbitrators is that each party appoints its arbitrator. This individual is referred to as the *party-appointed arbitrator*. The two party-appointed arbitrators will then appoint the third arbitrator to serve as the presiding arbitrator, sometimes referred to as the *chair* or *president* of the tribunal. Should one of the parties refuse to appoint its arbitrator in an attempt to thwart or to delay the arbitration, or should the two party-appointed arbitrators fail to agree on the third arbitrator, the appointing authority will appoint the third member of the tribunal.[22]

---

[20] As stated by one source:

> Where a sole arbitrator is to be appointed, the parties must obviously agree on the identity of that person if they wish to avoid the application of the default arrangements for appointment. Where a tribunal of three is to be appointed, each party will typically nominate one arbitrator but then the parties or their nominated arbitrators must agree on the identity of the third arbitrator if they wish to avoid the application of the default arrangements. In both cases the parties (or their nominated arbitrators) will nominate and evaluate candidates by reference to many factors.

MA & BROCK, *supra* note 3, at para. 13.070. This authority further stated:

> Where the UNCITRAL Arbitration Rules apply, if a sole arbitrator is to be appointed, but the parties cannot agree on the choice of the sole arbitrator, the sole arbitrator shall be appointed by the appointing authority (typically, the HKIAC in Hong Kong) using the list procedure under which the appointing authority will communicate to the parties a list of possible arbitrators which the parties will then rank in order of preference, having deleted any name(s) which they object to. The appointing authority will then appoint a sole arbitrator based on the approved list. If the appointment cannot be made according to this procedure, then the appointing authority may exercise its own discretion in appointing the sole arbitrator. If three arbitrators are to be appointed, each party shall appoint one arbitrator with the two party-appointed arbitrators appointing the third, presiding arbitrator. Again, the appointing authority may be asked to appoint the second and/or third arbitrators if they are not appointed within the prescribed time limits.

Id. at para. 13.077.

[21] § 24(1) of the *Arbitration Ordinance*, incorporating *Model Law* Art. 11, *supra* note 1. Under this section of the Ordinance, the "court or other authority specified in article 6" is the Hong Kong International Arbitration Centre as designated in § 13(2).

See also MA & BROCK, *supra* note 3, at paras. 13.075–13.076.

[22] § 24 of the *Arbitration Ordinance*, incorporating *Model Law* Art. 11, *supra* note 1 provides in relevant part:

> (3) Failing such agreement,
> (a) in an arbitration with three arbitrators, each party shall appoint one arbitrator, and the two arbitrators thus appointed shall appoint the third arbitrator; if a party fails to appoint the arbitrator within thirty days of receipt of a request to do so from the other party, or if the two arbitrators fail to agree on the third arbitrator within thirty days of their appointment, the appointment shall be made, upon request of a party, by the court or other authority specified in article 6;
> (b) in an arbitration with a sole arbitrator, if the parties are unable to agree on the arbitrator, he

B. Qualifications and Qualities Expected of the Tribunal

In Hong Kong under its *Arbitration Ordinance*, there are certain requirements which the arbitral tribunal must meet and maintain throughout the arbitration. Failure to meet these requirements may result in an arbitrator being challenged as unsuitable or unqualified for the arbitration. Failure to meet these requirements and maintain them throughout the arbitration may further subject the tribunal's award to a challenge for being in violation of the Ordinance.

One of these requirements relates to the arbitrator's qualifications.[23] As the parties may specify the professional qualifications of the individual, the person appointed as arbitrator must possess these professional qualifications.[24] For

---

shall be appointed, upon request of a party, by the court or other authority specified in article 6.

(4) Where, under an appointment procedure agreed upon by the parties,
  (a) a party fails to act as required under such procedure, or
  (b) the parties, or two arbitrators, are unable to reach an agreement expected of them under such procedure, or
  (c) a third party, including an institution, fails to perform any function entrusted to it under such procedure,

any party may request the court or other authority specified in article 6 to take the necessary measure, unless the agreement on the appointment procedure provides other means for securing the appointment.

23 For additional information on this topic, *see, e.g.*, MA & BROCK, *supra* note 3, at paras. 11.075–11.077; 13.059.

24 Along with the expressed qualifications of a tribunal, there are other characteristics which might not be expressed but are nonetheless desirable. For example, this excerpt:

It is not possible to formulate general rules as to who should be appointed as arbitrators. Commercial disputes cover an infinite range of issues whereas the choice of tribunal will depend completely on the nature and circumstances of the particular dispute under consideration. Nevertheless, certain factors are commonly found to be relevant to the decision:

(1) *Professional experience and qualifications.* This is a critical consideration. It is vital to select arbitrators whose experience and skills suit the subject matter of the claim. . . .
(2) *A mix of skills.* The principal advantage of having a three-person tribunal is that the parties can procure a mix of skills that are all relevant to the matters in issue. Particularly in large and complex cases, there may well be a range of different issues arising for decision, some legal, some factual and some technical, possibly involving a number of different technical disciplines. In construction disputes, for example, it may well be desirable for the tribunal to possess both technical knowledge of the relevant construction issues and legal knowledge relevant to the contested issues of law. . . . the ultimate goal is to procure a tribunal whose collective skills allow it to deal effectively with all the issues arising for determination.
(3) *Language and cultural factors.* It is plainly sensible to appoint arbitrators who will be able to understand the majority of witnesses without the need for interpretation and who can read the majority of relevant documents. . . . More subtly, it may also be necessary to consider any cultural issues that are likely to arise during the course of the proceedings, and to ensure as far as possible that the tribunal possesses the cultural understanding necessary to ensure that such issues are properly understood.
(4) *Integrity.* Arbitration is an independent process. The avoidance of any perception of local bias or favouritism is often seen as one of the major advantages of arbitration over litigation. . . . it will be important to ensure that appointed arbitrators are people of undoubted integrity who will decide the dispute on its merits without reference to external factors.
(5) *Familiarity with law.* . . . it is generally desirable for arbitrators to be familiar with the law and practice of arbitration. Arbitration is . . . a formal process for determining legal rights, and it is obviously important that the determination should be made in a way that complies with the law. Further, whilst technical skills and experience may be crucial in relation to the final

example, if the parties are involved in a shipping contract, most likely the parties would require their arbitral tribunal to possess knowledge of commercial shipping law and maritime law. To appoint an arbitrator for this dispute who is knowledgeable about construction works would not be suitable. Thus, this individual could be challenged under UNCITRAL's *Model Law on International Commercial Arbitration* [hereinafter "*Model Law*"] on the grounds that this individual does not possess the qualifications upon which the parties agreed.[25] In this situation, the *Convention on the Recognition and Enforcement of Foreign Arbitral Awards* (done in New York, 1958) [hereinafter "*New York Convention*"] provides similar grounds on which to challenge the arbitral award: the arbitral tribunal's composition was not in accordance with the parties' agreement.[26]

i. Qualifications required by the *Arbitration Ordinance*

The Ordinance sets out certain standards required of an arbitrator. Amongst these standards, the two most obvious prohibitions are conflict of interest resulting in bias, and a lack of independence.[27] There are several forms of bias which will be reviewed below.

First, one requirement of an arbitrator is impartiality or a lack of bias. An arbitrator should keep an open mind and render an award based on the evidence presented. The arbitrator should not have any preconceptions or any connections

---

> determination, prior procedural experience and legal knowledge will be invaluable in ensuring that the tribunal guides the arbitration effectively through its preparatory phases and into the final hearing. . . . In the worst case, inadequate procedures may even give rise to later grounds on which to set aside or oppose enforcement of the resulting award, for example, on the basis that the losing party was effectively unable to present its case.
>
> (6) *Additional attributes.* Where there are three arbitrators on the tribunal . . . the presiding arbitrator should ordinarily have certain additional attributes, in addition to what has been set out above. The presiding arbitrator should typically have strong personal qualities enabling him to work with the two party-appointed arbitrators; he should have sufficient experience and be of sufficient seniority, compared to the other two arbitrators; he should be procedurally robust and able to drive the arbitration process; be culturally sensitive; and ideally, to know both the party-appointed arbitrators.

MA & BROCK, *supra* note 3, at para. 13.059.

[25] UNCITRAL *Model Law on International Commercial Arbitration* [hereinafter "*Model Law*"] Art. 12(2) provides in part: "An arbitrator may be challenged only if circumstances exist that give rise to justifiable doubts as to his impartiality or independence, or if he does not possess qualifications agreed to by the parties."

[26] *Convention on the Recognition and Enforcement of Foreign Arbitral Awards* (done in New York 1958) [hereinafter "*New York Convention*"] Art. V(1)(d) provides in relevant part: "The composition of the arbitral authority or the arbitral procedure was not in accordance with the agreement of the parties."

[27] As noted in HALSBURY'S, *supra* note 1, at para. [25.084]:

> Section 25 of the Arbitration Ordinance (Cap 609) provides that a prospective arbitrator . . . must disclose any circumstances that could give rise to justifiable doubts as to his impartiality or independence. After the appointment has been accepted, he is under a continuing obligation to inform the parties without delay of any such circumstances or further circumstances which may arise. . . . In international cases justifiable doubts as to an arbitrator's impartiality or independence forms a ground of challenge in its own right. Satisfaction of the requirement of independence may be demonstrated by compliance with any applicable professional or institutional ethical guidance, [for] example, the International Bar Association Guidelines on Conflicts of Interest in International Arbitration (2004). (citations omitted)

with the disputing parties or with witnesses. If circumstances exist which may cause doubts as to the arbitrator's impartiality, the arbitrator should disclose the details to the parties and to the other arbitrators, if any, immediately.[28]

One definition of the term *impartiality* provides:

> *impartiality* means complete receptivity to the parties' arguments: the concurrent absence of both *party* and *outcome* preference. *Party preference* relates to identity – the identity of the decision maker and identities of the disputants; *outcome preference* means pre-judgment of one or more of the legal issues in dispute.[29]

Reviewing the evidence needed to prove impartiality or bias, the court in *Jung Science Information Technology Co Ltd v ZTE Corp*[30] stated that the test for apparent bias is whether an objective fair-minded and informed observer, having considered the relevant facts, would conclude that there was a real possibility that the tribunal was biased.

In court, Jung Science Information Technology claimed that the arbitrator was biased due to his professional and social relationship with ZTE Corp's lawyer. Where the claim of bias arises from an association between the arbitrator and the lawyer for the opposing party, there must be a cogent and rational link between the association and its capacity to influence the decision to be made in the particular case, before it can be concluded that the arbitrator might not bring an impartial and unprejudiced mind to the resolution of the dispute.[31]

The court in *Regina v Robert Gough*[32] decided that the general test for establishing bias is *real danger*. This test has been summarized by the Hong Kong courts as follows:

> Whether, having regard to [the] circumstances, there was a real danger of bias on the part of the relevant member of the tribunal in question, in the sense that he might unfairly regard (or have unfairly regarded) with favour, or disfavour, the case of a party or the issue under consideration by him.[33]

In summary, impartiality is concerned with the bias of an arbitrator either in favour of one of the parties or in regards to the matter in dispute.[34]

---

[28] § 25 of the *Arbitration Ordinance*, incorporating *Model Law* Art. 12 and § 46(3)(b) of the *Arbitration Ordinance*, *supra* note 1.

[29] Sam Luttrell, Bias Challenges in International Commercial Arbitration—the Need for a "Real Danger" Test 15 (2009) (emphasis in original) (citations omitted).

[30] [2008] 4 HKLRD 776, 794 (citations omitted).

[31] John Choong and Romesh Weeramantry, The Hong Kong Arbitration Ordinance: Commentary and Annotations para. 25.17 (2nd ed. 2015) [hereinafter Choong & Weeramantry].

[32] [1993] AC 646.

[33] Ma & Brock, *supra* note 3, at para. 11.032 (citations omitted).
See also So & To, *supra* note 2, at para. [25.05].

[34] Redfern & Hunter, *supra* note 4, at para. 4.78. *See also* Choong & Weeramantry, *supra* note 31, at paras. 25.21–25.30.
Halsbury's *supra* note 1, at para. [25.084] n. 5 states in part:

> The test now is whether there is a real danger rather than a real likelihood, in order to ensure that the court is thinking in terms of the possibility rather than the probability of bias: see *R v Gough* . . . In that

Another requirement concerns an arbitrator's independence. Here the term *independence* relates to any possible relationship between an arbitrator and one of the parties.

> independence raises questions relating to the existence of a relationship between the arbitrators and one of the parties. This might relate to past professional, commercial or even social links. Independence should be a concept which is capable of objective qualification, e.g. whether or not a particular relationship does or does not conform to the requirement of independence.[35]
>
> "Independence" connotes an absence of connection with either of the parties in the sense of an absence of any interest in, or of any present or prospective business or other connection with, one of the parties which might lead the arbitrator to favour the party concerned.[36]

For example, if a law firm consistently appoints one individual to serve as its party-appointed arbitrator such that these appointments comprise a substantial portion of this individual's income, this financial relationship may raise questions concerning this individual's independence.[37] Whether an individual is independent is an objective test, unlike impartiality which relates to the arbitrator's subjective state of mind.[38] In the case of *Panel on Takeovers and Mergers v Cheng Kai-man*,[39] the court interpreted bias to include instances where the individual had a proprietary or pecuniary interest in the subject-matter of the parties' dispute.

A third statutory requirement pertains to judicial temperament or capacity. This is the duty in all cases to observe natural justice.[40] Natural justice is the requirement that every party be treated fairly, *e.g.*, be notified timeously of the claim; be afforded the opportunity to be involved in the appointment of the arbitral tribunal; and, be given an equal opportunity to present its case and to challenge the opponent's case.

An arbitrator is also required to disclose any conflict of interest.[41] Where an arbitrator has a prior interest which may give rise to doubts concerning his impartiality, the arbitrator should disclose this interest at the earliest opportunity to ensure

---

case, Lord Goff of Chieveley said this principle was applicable to all courts and tribunals, including arbitration tribunals. In *Jung Science Information Technology Co Ltd v ZTE Corp* . . . the Court held that the same test applied in determining the an [*sic*] issue of apparent bias on the part of arbitrators as it did to judges, that is whether a hypothetical, objective, fair-minded and impartial observer, having considered the relevant facts, would conclude that there was a real possibility that the tribunal was biased. Where an objection arose from a link between an adjudicator and a representative of a litigant, a cogent and rational link must be made between that association and its capacity to influence the decision to be made in the particular case before it could be concluded that the adjudicator might be biased.

[35] Ma & Brock, *supra* note 3, at para. 11.016.

[36] *AT&T Corp & Lucent Technologies Inc v Saudi Cable Co* [2000] 2 All ER (Comm) 625, para. 67.

[37] *See* Ma & Brock, *supra* note 3, at paras. 11.052–11.061.

[38] *Id.* at para. 4.77. *See also*, § 25 of the *Arbitration Ordinance*, incorporating *Model Law* Art. 12, *supra* note 1 and § 46(3)(b) of the *Arbitration Ordinance*, *supra* note 1.

[39] [1995] 2 HKLR 302.

[40] *See* § 25 of the *Arbitration Ordinance*, incorporating *Model Law* Art. 12, and § 46(3)(b) of the *Arbitration Ordinance*, *supra* note 1.

[41] *See* Ma & Brock, *supra* note 3, at para. 11.062–11.074.

that costs are not wasted should the arbitrator need to be replaced.[42] This obligation of disclosure is a continuing one. In other words, if new circumstances arise causing doubt as to the arbitrator's independence and/or impartiality, the arbitrator immediately should disclose such circumstances to the parties and to the other arbitrators, if any.[43] In the case of *S.té Spadem v S.té ADAGP*, the court determined that the arbitrator's appointment is considered to be proper once the arbitrator has disclosed the potential grounds of challenge to his appointment and the parties do not object to his appointment.[44]

The final statutory standard which we discuss concerns diligence. This duty is apparent from language of the *Arbitration Ordinance* pertaining to an arbitrator's failure or impossibility to act: "fails to act without undue delay."[45] An application for the removal of an arbitrator can thus be brought if the arbitrator's conduct amounts to undue and unreasonable delay but not misconduct.[46] For example, if the arbitral tribunal delays in making its award, the court has the power to terminate the tribunal's mandate.[47] Parties also have the right to request a court to terminate the arbitrator's mandate if the arbitrator becomes *de jure* or *de facto* unable to perform his obligations.[48]

> *De jure* inability to perform would arise where, for example, a party has obtained an injunction to prevent the arbitrator or arbitration from proceeding or a declaration that the arbitrator has been invalidly appointed . . .
>
> *De jure* inability to perform functions may also arise where, for any reason, the arbitration proceedings purport to deal with illegal subject-matter, or if the arbitrator is imprisoned.[49]

Concerning *de facto* inability, one authority notes:

---

42 Choong & Weeramantry, *supra* note 31, at para. 25.09.
Section 25 of the *Arbitration Ordinance*, incorporating *Model Law* Art. 12, and § 46(3)(b) of the *Arbitration Ordinance*, *supra* note 1 require prospective or appointed arbitrators to make prompt disclosure of any circumstances which may create doubts concerning his impartiality and/or independence. Choong & Weeramantry, *supra* note 31, at para. 25.08.
One court defined *personal interest* as follows:

> (1) any personal interest, pecuniary or otherwise, the arbitrator has in the proceeding; (2) the directness of the relationship between the arbitrator and the party he is alleged to favor; (3) the connection of the relationship to the arbitration; and (4) the proximity in time between the relationship and the arbitration proceeding.

Consolidation Coal Co v Local 1643, United Mine Workers of America, 48 F.3d 125, 130 (4th Cir. 1995).

43 Choong & Weeramantry, *supra* note 31, at para. 25.11.

44 *Cour d'appel de Paris* (Court of Appeal, Paris), March 22, 1990, Rev Arb 123 (1991), cited in Mauro Rubino-Sammartano, International Arbitration Law and Practice 501 (3rd ed. 2014).

45 § 27 of the *Arbitration Ordinance*, incorporating *Model Law* Art. 14, *supra* note 1, states in part: "fails to act without undue delay." For a discussion concerning this section of the Ordinance, *see* Choong & Weeramantry, *supra* note 31, at paras. 27.00–27.12.

46 Ma & Brock, *supra* note 3, at para. 14.096.

47 *Id.* at para. 17.012.

48 § 27 of the *Arbitration Ordinance*, incorporating *Model Law* Art. 14, *supra* note 1.

49 So & To, *supra* note 2, at para. [27.04].

> *De facto* inability to perform encompasses unavailability, illness or physical or mental incapacity.
>
> The wording of this provision envisages long-term incapacity or shorter-term incapacity, which will nevertheless seriously inconvenience the arbitration process.
>
> A disability must be serious enough to put the arbitrator out of action altogether for the duration and the purposes of the arbitration.[50]

The consequences in situations where these statutory requirements are not met can be found in the Ordinance.[51] If a challenge is successful, the arbitrator's mandate

---

[50] *Id.* at para. [27.05] (citations omitted).

[51] § 25 of the *Arbitration Ordinance*, incorporating *Model Law* Art. 12, *supra* note 1, provides the grounds for challenging an arbitrator's appointment:

> Article 12 of the UNCITRAL Model Law, the text of which is set out below, has effect—
>
> "*Article 12. Grounds for challenge*
>
> . . .
>
> (2) An arbitrator may be challenged only if circumstances exist that give rise to justifiable doubts as to his impartiality or independence, or if he does not possess qualifications agreed to by the parties. A party may challenge an arbitrator appointed by him, or in whose appointment he has participated, only for reasons of which he becomes aware after the appointment has been made."

§ 26(1) of the *Arbitration Ordinance*, incorporating *Model Law* Art. 13, *supra* note 1, provides the procedures involved in challenging an arbitrator's appointment:

> (1) Article 13 of the UNCITRAL Model Law, the text of which is set out below, has effect subject to section 13(4)—
>
> "*Article 13. Challenge procedure*
>
> (1) The parties are free to agree on a procedure for challenging an arbitrator, subject to the provisions of paragraph (3) of this article.
>
> (2) Failing such agreement, a party who intends to challenge an arbitrator shall, within fifteen days after becoming aware of the constitution of the arbitral tribunal or after becoming aware of any circumstance referred to in article 12(2), send a written statement of the reasons for the challenge to the arbitral tribunal. Unless the challenged arbitrator withdraws from his office or the other party agrees to the challenge, the arbitral tribunal shall decide on the challenge.
>
> (3) If a challenge under any procedure agreed upon by the parties or under the procedure of paragraph (2) of this article is not successful, the challenging party may request, within thirty days after having received notice of the decision rejecting the challenge, the court or other authority specified in article 6 to decide on the challenge, which decision shall be subject to no appeal; while such a request is pending, the arbitral tribunal, including the challenged arbitrator, may continue the arbitral proceedings and make an award."

So & To, *supra* note 2, at para. [26.11] comments in relation to *Model Law* Art. 13(3) that the arbitral proceedings may continue during the challenge:

> The arbitral tribunal is . . . left free to decide whether to make an award if it is in no doubt about the propriety of allowing the challenged arbitrator to continue sitting or to adjourn the arbitration, await the court's decision and thus save costs if doubts persist.
>
> In the absence of case law on this point, it is submitted that a party who has reservations about an arbitrator may, alternatively, await the outcome of the arbitration and challenge the award in proceedings to set it aside under s 81 (Article 34 of the Model Law).
>
> That party must, however, voice his objection and reserve his position as to the award in order that his right to object should not be deemed to have been waived: see s 11 (Article 4 of the Model Law).

§ 27 of the *Arbitration Ordinance*, incorporating *Model Law* Art. 14, *supra* note 1, provides that the failure to act or the impossibility of acting on the arbitrator's part is also a ground for terminating the arbitrator's mandate:

> Article 14 of the UNCITRAL Model Law, the text of which is set out below, has effect subject to section 13(4)—

will be terminated. A replacement arbitrator will be appointed using the same procedure which appointed the replaced arbitrator.[52]

ii. Qualifications required by the Arbitration Agreement

As this has been discussed in other sections of this book, only a brief overview will be provided in this section. Recall that under the principle of party autonomy, the parties to an arbitration agreement may specify certain requirements to be possessed by the arbitral tribunal. Such attributes may include certain skills or certain experience such as:

- trade experience
- professional qualifications
- nationality
- other[53]

These requirements may be positive or negative. For example, a positive requirement might be that the arbitrator be an architect; a negative requirement might be that the arbitrator cannot be a medical doctor.

In Hong Kong, the HKIAC must, in making an appointment in an international arbitration, take into consideration any qualifications specified in the parties' arbitration agreement and to the advisability of appointing an arbitrator of a nationality other than those of the parties.[54]

"*Article 14. Failure or impossibility to act*

> (1) If an arbitrator becomes *de jure* or *de facto* unable to perform his functions or for other reasons fails to act without undue delay, his mandate terminates if he withdraws from his office or if the parties agree on the termination. Otherwise, if a controversy remains concerning any of these grounds, any party may request the court or other authority specified in article 6 to decide on the termination of the mandate, which decision shall be subject to no appeal.
>
> (2) . . ."

The *Arbitration Ordinance*, *supra* note 1, translates "*de jure*" as 法律行為 and "*de facto*" as 事實行為. Black's Law Dictionary 518 (10th ed. 2014) defines "*de jure*" as "existing by right or according to law" and "*de facto*" as "actual; existing in fact; having effect even though not formally or legally recognized."

52 *See* Halsbury's, *supra* note 1, at paras. [25.087]–[25.088].

53 *See* the case of *Jivraj (Nurdin) v Hashwani (Sadruddin)* discussed below in section III, "Challenge to the Arbitrator." In this United Kingdom case, the parties stipulated that the arbitrator be a member of the Iswali religious community, which the court determined was a "genuine occupational requirement on the basis that it was not only genuine but both legitimate and justified." [2011] UKSC 40, para. 68.

54 § 24(1) of the *Arbitration Ordinance*, incorporating *Model Law* Art. 11(5), *supra* note 1, states in relation to the HKIAC being the appointing authority:

> in appointing an arbitrator, shall have due regard to any qualifications required of the arbitrator by the agreement of the parties and to such considerations as are likely to secure the appointment of an independent and impartial arbitrator and, in the case of a sole or third arbitrator, shall take into account as well the advisability of appointing an arbitrator of a nationality other than those of the parties.

III. Challenge to the Arbitrator

Is it possible for a party to object to the appointment of an arbitrator? In principle, the answer is *yes*. If the individual nominated to serve as an arbitrator does not possess the qualifications or expertise upon which the disputing parties had agreed in their arbitration agreement, a party may raise an objection, or *challenge*, to the individual.[55]

In an international arbitration, it is common for each party to appoint an arbitrator from its own jurisdiction or who has the same nationality as the appointing party. Frequently this is intended to minimise any cultural misunderstandings or legal miscommunications. The party-appointed arbitrator, without losing its impartiality, is intended to be able to understand its appointing party's presentation and perhaps to serve as a resource to explain to the other members of the tribunal. Let us assume that each party-appointed arbitrator possesses the same nationality as the party which appointed the individual. What nationality should be possessed by the presiding arbitrator or the chair of the tribunal? Very frequently the presiding arbitrator will be of a different nationality. Indeed, it is the practice of most arbitration institutions to appoint a sole arbitrator or a presiding arbitrator who is of a different nationality from either party in order to avoid bias.[56] There are some conflicts with this practice as it may contravene the *Model Law* which provides that an arbitrator cannot be disqualified solely on the basis of nationality.

The case of *Jivraj (Nurdin) v Hashwani (Sadruddin)* involved the appointment of an arbitrator who did not meet the stipulations set out in the parties' arbitration agreement.[57] Although there was no restriction in the parties' arbitration agreement concerning nationality, the parties had agreed that the arbitrators would all be from the Ismaili religious community. Jivraj challenged Hashwani's appointment of an individual who was from outside of this community. This challenge was finally decided by the United Kingdom's Supreme Court which opined that there was no employment discrimination resulting from this stipulation as the arbitrators were not employees. The Supreme Court stated that:

> the arbitrators' role is not one of employment under a contract personally to do work. Although an arbitrator may be providing services . . . and he of course receives fees for his work, and although he renders personal services which he

---

[55] The relevant sections of the Ordinance have been set out in *supra* note 51.
For further information on this topic, *see, e.g.*, Ma & Brock, *supra* note 3, at paras. 11.019–11.084; Choong & Weeramantry, *supra* note 31, at paras. 26.00–26.23.

[56] Art. 13(5) of the International Chamber of Commerce's Rules of Arbitration (2017) [hereinafter ICC Rules] provides that the "sole arbitrator or the chairman of an arbitral tribunal shall be of a nationality other than those of the parties."
Similarly, the LCIA Rules, *supra* note 12, at Art. 6.1 states:

> Where the parties are of different nationalities, a sole arbitrator or the presiding arbitrator shall not have the same nationality as any party unless the parties who are not of the same nationality as the arbitral candidate all agree in writing otherwise.

[57] [2011] UKSC 40.

> cannot delegate, he does not perform those services or earn his fees for and under the direction of the parties.[58]

The objective of the relevant European Community legislation was to give protection against inequality and discrimination to those who might be vulnerable to exploitation. On the contrary, arbitrators are not subordinate to the appointing parties and hence do not need this protection.

Hong Kong has adopted the *Model Law* provisions concerning the grounds for challenge and the challenge procedure. Section 25 of the *Arbitration Ordinance* sets out the *Model Law* Art. 12 grounds upon which an arbitrator may be challenged.[59] Section 26 of the Ordinance sets forth the *Model Law* Art. 13 procedure for challenging an arbitrator.[60] Section 27 of the Ordinance incorporates the *Model Law* Art. 14 provision that the failure or impossibility to act is a ground for terminating an arbitrator's mandate.[61]

From the foregoing, we can see that parties have the right to challenge the appointment of an arbitrator and to seek a replacement for that individual. The provisions regulating challenges as well as the replacement of arbitrators are found in the institutional arbitration rules and the national laws.[62] The grounds for a challenge are usually mandatory provisions from which the parties cannot deviate or ignore. These rules and laws provide for the grounds and the procedure to challenge the appointment of an individual as arbitrator.[63] These rules and laws also provide for the competent authority to decide the challenge, which depending upon the circumstances, might be one of the following:

- the arbitral tribunal itself (without the challenged arbitrator)
- the appointing authority
- the arbitration institution
- the national courts

---

[58] *Id.* at para. 40.

Id. at para. 70 the court addressed the legitimacy of the stipulation:

> The question is whether, in all the circumstances the provision that all the arbitrators should be respected members of the Ismaili community was legitimate and justified. In my opinion it was. . . . The parties could properly regard arbitration before three Ismailis as likely to involve a procedure in which the parties could have confidence and as likely to lead to conclusions of fact in which they could have particular confidence.

[59] The relevant text of § 25 is set out in *supra* note 51.

[60] The relevant text of § 26 is set out in *supra* note 51.

Ma & Brock, *supra* note 3, at para. 11.001 has a flowchart of the challenge procedure under § 26 of the Ordinance.

[61] The relevant text of § 27 is set out in *supra* note 51.

[62] *See, e.g.*, Articles 12–14 of the United Nations Commission on International Trade Law's Arbitration Rules (2013) [hereinafter Arbitration Rules].

The 2013 version of the Arbitration Rules may be found here:
http://www.uncitral.org/pdf/english/texts/arbitration/arb-rules-2013/UNCITRAL-Arbitration-Rules-2013-e.pdf (last visited 10 Jul. 2017).

[63] Most of the established arbitration institutions' rules provide a common ground to challenge an arbitrator: justifiable doubts as to the arbitrator's impartiality or independence. *See, e.g.*, HKIAC Arbitration Rules, *supra* note 12, at Art. 11.4; ICC Rules, *supra* note 56, at Art. 14(1).

The procedure to challenge an arbitrator is quite similar amongst the arbitral institutions, the UNCITRAL Arbitration Rules Art. 13 and the *Model Law* Art. 13. In essence, the basic procedure is for the challenging party to send a notice of its challenge. The notice should be in writing and contain the reasons for the challenge. The difference amongst the various arbitral institution rules usually relates to the timeframe in which the notice must be sent as well as to whom. For example, the HKIAC Administered Arbitration Rules (2018) provide for a 15-day time limit and the challenging party is to send its notice to all parties, all arbitrators and the HKIAC.[64] In contrast, the ICC rules provide for a 30-day time limit and the notice should be sent to the ICC Secretariat which will then notify the arbitrator(s) and the other party.[65]

A vacancy occurs if a challenge is successful or if an individual is no longer able to perform the duties of an arbitrator. One source states:

> Article 15 provides a mechanism for appointing substitute arbitrators. It covers the appointment of a substitute arbitrator in the following circumstances, where the mandate of an arbitrator terminates:
> (a) Under Articles 13 and 14 of the UNCITRAL Model Law;
> (b) By the arbitrator's withdrawal from office for any other reasons;
> (c) By agreement of the parties; or
> (d) In any other case.[66]

This vacancy will usually be filled using the same procedure used to appoint the removed arbitrator.[67]

In instances where an arbitrator is replaced, there is no clear guideline whether the arbitration hearing needs to be repeated.[68] The deciding factor will be the time at which the arbitrator is replaced. For example, if the challenge arose at the time of appointment of the challenged arbitrator, the arbitration hearings most likely have not begun. If the vacancy occurs during the hearing stage, it would seem that the hearing stage should be repeated for the benefit of the replacement arbitrator and for fairness to the parties. Depending upon the circumstances of each case, some institutional rules permit the arbitration to continue in progress. Again, this

---

64 HKIAC Arbitration Rules, *supra* note 12, at Art. 11.7 and 11.8.

65 ICC Rules, *supra* note 56, at Art. 14.

66 Choong & Weeramantry, *supra* note 31, at para. 28.06.

67 § 28 of the *Arbitration Ordinance*, incorporating *Model Law* Art. 15, *supra* note 1, provides:

> Article 15 of the UNCITRAL Model Law, the text of which is set out below, has effect—
>
> "Article 15. *Appointment of substitute arbitrator*
>
> Where the mandate of an arbitrator terminates under article 13 or 14 or because of his withdrawal from office for any other reason or because of the revocation of his mandate by agreement of the parties or in any other case of termination of his mandate, a substitute arbitrator shall be appointed according to the rules that were applicable to the appointment of the arbitrator being replaced."

For an analysis of this section of the Ordinance, *see* Choong & Weeramantry, *supra* note 31, at paras. 28.00–28.10.

68 For a discussion of some considerations pertinent to such situations, *see* Choong & Weeramantry, *supra* note 31, at paras. 28.08–28.10.

decision should be made after consultation with the parties and review of the appropriate institutional rules or national law.[69]

IV. Summary

In this chapter, we set out the appointment process for an arbitrator. The methods available to the parties in appointing a single arbitrator or a panel of arbitrators were reviewed. Also addressed were the qualifications required of one being appointed as an arbitrator. This was followed by a discussion of the grounds for challenging the appointment of an arbitrator. In the next chapter, we analyze the authority and powers of a person appointed as arbitrator.

---

69 *See, e.g.*, HKIAC Arbitration Rules, *supra* note 12, at Art. 12.2 and 12.3 which provides:

> 12.2 If . . . to designate a substitute arbitrator, HKIAC may, after giving an opportunity to the parties and the remaining arbitrators to express their views:
>
> (a) . . .
>
> (b) authorise the other arbitrators to proceed with the arbitration and make any decision or award.
>
> 12.3 If an arbitrator is replaced, the arbitration shall resume at the stage where the arbitrator was replaced or ceased to perform his or her functions, unless the arbitral tribunal decides otherwise.

Similarly, ICC Rules, *supra* note 56, at Art. 15(4) and 15(5) provide:

> 4)
>
> When an arbitrator is to be replaced . . . Once reconstituted, and after having invited the parties to comment, the arbitral tribunal shall determine if and to what extent prior proceedings shall be repeated before the reconstituted arbitral tribunal.
>
> 5)
>
> Subsequent to the closing of the proceedings, instead of replacing an arbitrator who has died or been removed . . . pursuant to Articles 15(1) or 15(2), the [ICC International] Court [of Arbitration] may decide, when it considers it appropriate, that the remaining arbitrators shall continue the arbitration. In making such determination, the Court shall take into account the views of the remaining arbitrators and of the parties and such other matters that it considers appropriate in the circumstances.

5

Jurisdiction, Duties, and Powers

I. Introduction

In this chapter, we discuss the next phase of the arbitration process following the appointment of the arbitral tribunal. This phase addresses a tribunal's authority, the exercise of that authority, and, the obligations of the tribunal. As usual, we begin with a definition of the terms before proceeding to examine each of these terms.

The first term to be defined is *jurisdiction* which sometimes is also referred to as *mandate*. This term refers to the overall authority given to the arbitrator to resolve or determine the dispute. Jurisdiction is the arbitral tribunal's scope of authority in deciding a dispute.[1] As noted by one source:

> It is the parties who give a . . . tribunal the authority to decide disputes between them, and the arbitral tribunal must take care to stay within the terms of its mandate. The rule to this effect is expressed in several different ways. Sometimes, it is said that an arbitral tribunal must conform to the mission entrusted to it, or that it must not exceed its mandate, or that it must stay within its terms of reference, competence, or authority. Another way of expressing the rule . . . is to state that an arbitral tribunal must not exceed its jurisdiction (this term being used in the sense of mandate, competence, or authority).[2]

The next term to be defined is *duties*. This term indicates the mandatory requirements which regulate the arbitrator's exercise of powers, *i.e.*, what the appointed individuals must observe or undertake as members of an arbitral tribunal.

The final term relates to the word *powers*. This refers to the mechanisms conferred on the arbitrator by the arbitration agreement and by, *e.g.*, the *Arbitration*

---

[1] As noted by one source:

> arbitrators must conduct proceedings in accordance with the requirements of the parties. The parties vest the arbitrator with procedural powers and, to the extent that requirements are laid down in any arbitration agreement such as notice, rules or terms of reference, the arbitrator is obliged to observe these. This is subject to overriding considerations of public policy.

Arbitration in Hong Kong: A Practical Guide para. 14.002 (The Hon Chief Justice Geoffrey Ma and Denis Brock, eds., 4th ed. 2017) [hereinafter Ma & Brock].

[2] Redfern and Hunter on International Arbitration para. 5.91 (Nigel Blackaby *et al.*, eds., 6th ed. 2015) [hereinafter Redfern & Hunter] (citations omitted).

Ordinance (Cap. 609) [hereinafter "*Arbitration Ordinance*"]. These conferred mechanisms allow the exercise of the arbitral tribunal's authority, *i.e.*, the actions which the tribunal may take.[3] "The powers of the arbitral tribunal are the tools of the arbitral tribunal for the conduct of the arbitration."[4] Arbitral tribunals exercise powers in order to perform their mandate to resolve the parties' dispute.[5]

II. Jurisdiction

From where does the tribunal's authority to resolve the dispute come? The usual sources of a tribunal's authority are:

- the arbitration agreement which states the particular dispute or types of disputes which the parties may refer to arbitration proceedings before a tribunal[6]
- the *notice of arbitration*, also known as the *submission to arbitration*, which would specify the particular dispute or disputes which are being referred to arbitration[7]

---

[3] *Id.* at para. 5.06 states:

> The powers of an arbitral tribunal are those conferred upon it by the parties within the limits allowed by the applicable law, together with any additional powers that may be conferred automatically by operation of law. These powers are established to enable the arbitral tribunal to carry out its task properly and effectively. (citations omitted)

[4] Andrew Tweeddale & Keren Tweeddale, Arbitration of Commercial Disputes—International and English Law and Practice para. 9.01 (2007).

[5] Redfern & Hunter, *supra* note 2, at para. 5.06.

For example, § 46 of the *Arbitration Ordinance* (Cap. 609) [hereinafter *Arbitration Ordinance*] provides in part:

> (2) The parties must be treated with equality.
> (3) When conducting arbitral proceedings or exercising any of the powers conferred on an arbitral tribunal by this Ordinance or by the parties to any of those arbitral proceedings, the arbitral tribunal is required—
> (a) to be independent;
> (b) to act fairly and impartially as between the parties, giving them a reasonable opportunity to present their cases and to deal with the cases of their opponents; and
> (c) to use procedures that are appropriate to the particular case, avoiding unnecessary delay or expense, so as to provide a fair means for resolving the dispute to which the arbitral proceedings relate.

See also 2 Halsbury's Laws of Hong Kong paras. [25.101]–[25.1088] (2nd ed. 2016) which discuss the powers of the tribunal.

[6] Redfern and Hunter, *supra* note 2, at para. 1.59 states:

> The 'agreement to arbitrate' also establishes the jurisdiction of the arbitral tribunal. In the ordinary legal process whereby disputes are resolved through the public courts, the jurisdiction of the relevant court may come from several sources. An agreement by the parties to submit to the jurisdiction will be only one of those sources. Indeed, a defendant will often find itself in court against its will. In the arbitral process, the jurisdiction of the arbitral tribunal is derived simply and solely from the express or implied consent of the parties. (footnote omitted)

[7] Not to be confused with *submission agreement* which is the document whereby parties agree to arbitrate an existing dispute, *i.e.*, the dispute arose before the parties' agreement to arbitrate. Confusingly, a submission agreement is also known as an *arbitration deed* or *terms of reference*. A *notice of arbitration* is sometimes also referred to as *terms of reference*. In the past, some jurisdictions such as Argentina, Brazil and possibly the United Arab Emirates required a submission agreement to be entered into between the disputing parties, despite the existence of an arbitration agreement.

The distinction between the submission agreement and the arbitration clause is generally founded on whether or not the arbitration agreement precedes the disputes.

- the document appointing the tribunal[8]
- the arbitration rules which the parties have selected, if any
- the relevant arbitration law. For arbitrations seated in Hong Kong, the relevant law is the *Arbitration Ordinance*. For example, this law gives the tribunal the authority to award interest in a dispute.[9] The Ordinance also authorises a tribunal to award costs of the arbitration proceedings.[10]

> The arbitration clause has in practice become a synonym of a clause preceding the dispute, while the submission agreement is a synonym of an agreement entered into subsequent to a dispute.
>
> . . .
>
> Therefore, it is suggested that the most acceptable distinction between a submission agreement and an arbitration clause is the one that, rather than being based on the form . . . is based on the timing of the agreement, i.e. whether it was made before or after the dispute arises.

MAURO RUBINO-SAMMARTANO, INTERNATIONAL ARBITRATION—LAW AND PRACTICE 256 (3d ed. 2014).

For example, Art. 23(1) of the International Chamber of Commerce's Rules of Arbitration (2017) [hereinafter ICC Rules] uses *terms of reference* to designate the document which sets out the following information:

> 1)
> As soon as it has received the file from the Secretariat, the arbitral tribunal shall draw up, on the basis of documents or in the presence of the parties and in the light of their most recent submissions, a document defining its Terms of Reference. This document shall include the following particulars:
> a) the names in full, description, address and other contact details of each of the parties and of any person(s) representing a party in the arbitration;
> b) the addresses to which notifications and communications arising in the course of the arbitration may be made;
> c) a summary of the parties' respective claims and of the relief sought by each party, together with the amounts of any quantified claims and, to the extent possible, an estimate of the monetary value of any other claims;
> d) unless the arbitral tribunal considers it inappropriate, a list of issues to be determined;
> e) the names in full, address and other contact details of each of the arbitrators;
> f) the place of the arbitration; and
> g) particulars of the applicable procedural rules and, if such is the case, reference to the power conferred upon the arbitral tribunal to act as amiable compositeur or to decide ex aequo et bono.

The Hong Kong Mediation and Arbitration Centre uses *terms of reference* to refer to the notice of arbitration:

> The party who wishes to refer the dispute to arbitration should give a written notice to the other party that the dispute shall be referred to arbitration. The notice of the dispute will become the terms of reference of the arbitration. Care must be taken to make sure that the dispute is described in a sufficiently wide manner in the notice to enable the arbitrator to deal with all issues in dispute between the parties.

The Hong Kong Mediation and Arbitration Centre's website is at: https://www.hkmaac.org/arbitration/arbitration_services.php (last visited 11 Jul. 2017).

[8] MA & BROCK, *supra* note 1, at paras. 15.030–15.037; REDFERN AND HUNTER, *supra* note 2, at para. 1.59 and para. 5.91.

[9] § 79(1) of the *Arbitration Ordinance*, *supra* note 5, provides:

> (1) Unless otherwise agreed by the parties, an arbitral tribunal may, in the arbitral proceedings before it, award simple or compound interest from the dates, at the rates, and with the rests that the tribunal considers appropriate, subject to section 80, for any period ending not later than the date of payment—
> (a) on money awarded by the tribunal in the arbitral proceedings;
> (b) on money claimed in, and outstanding at the commencement of, the arbitral proceedings but paid before the award is made; or
> (c) on costs awarded or ordered by the tribunal in the arbitral proceedings.

The purpose of awarding interest is to compensate the innocent party, rather than to punish the defaulting party. JOHN CHOONG AND ROMESH WEERAMANTRY, THE HONG KONG ARBITRATION ORDINANCE: COMMENTARY AND ANNOTATIONS para. 79.09 (2nd ed. 2015) [hereinafter CHOONG & WEERAMANTRY]. Discussion of awards of interest or costs is found in Chapter 9, "Contents of the Award."

[10] § 74(1) of the *Arbitration Ordinance*, *supra* note 5, stipulates: "An arbitral tribunal may include in an award

There are two types of challenge to an arbitral tribunal's jurisdiction. The first type is a *partial challenge* which contends that some, but not all, of the claims or matters being submitted to arbitration are beyond the tribunal's jurisdiction under the arbitration agreement. This type of challenge does not fundamentally attack the tribunal's jurisdiction. The second type of challenge, in contrast, is a *total challenge* which questions the whole basis of the tribunal's jurisdiction. An example of a total challenge is the instance of one party contesting the validity of the arbitration agreement which would thus challenge the tribunal's overall jurisdiction to decide the parties' dispute.[11]

A party may object to a tribunal's substantive jurisdiction.[12] What happens in this situation? Let us review as an example the relevant provision of the *Arbitration Ordinance* governing jurisdiction. This provision would be § 34 of the Ordinance which incorporates Art. 16 of the UNCITRAL *Model Law on International Commercial Arbitration* [hereinafter "*Model Law*"].[13] Referring to § 34(1)(1) of

---

directions with respect to the costs of arbitral proceedings (including the fees and expenses of the tribunal)."

[11] REDFERN & HUNTER, *supra* note 2, at para. 5.92.

[12] *Id.*

"A partial challenge is usually dependent on whether the particular matters referred to arbitration fall within the scope of the arbitration agreement. A total challenge usually questions whether there is a valid arbitration agreements at all." *Id.*

While on the topic of challenges, note this authority's comment upon submission agreements arising from *ad hoc* arbitrations where the dispute arose before the parties' agreement to arbitrate:

> An arbitral tribunal that derives its authority from a submission agreement is unlikely to face a total challenge to its jurisdiction. The purpose of a submission agreement is to give the arbitral tribunal jurisdiction to determine specific disputes between specific parties. Total challenges to jurisdiction are therefore likely to arise in practice only where the authority (or purported authority) of the arbitral tribunal is derived from an arbitration clause.

Id. at para. 5.98.

For further analysis of these two types of challenge, *see id.* at paras. 5.93–5.99.

[13] UNCITRAL is the acronym for the United Nations Commission on International Trade Law. It is responsible for the creation of the *Model Law on International Commercial Arbitration* [hereinafter *Model Law*].

§ 34 of the *Arbitration Ordinance*, incorporating *Model Law* Art. 16, *supra* note 5, provides in full:

> (1) Article 16 of the UNCITRAL Model Law, the text of which is set out below, has effect subject to section 13(5)—
>
> "*Article 16. Competence of arbitral tribunal to rule on its jurisdiction*
>
> (1) The arbitral tribunal may rule on its own jurisdiction, including any objections with respect to the existence or validity of the arbitration agreement. For that purpose, an arbitration clause which forms part of a contract shall be treated as an agreement independent of the other terms of the contract. A decision by the arbitral tribunal that the contract is null and void shall not entail *ipso jure* the invalidity of the arbitration clause.
>
> (2) A plea that the arbitral tribunal does not have jurisdiction shall be raised not later than the submission of the statement of defence. A party is not precluded from raising such a plea by the fact that he has appointed, or participated in the appointment of, an arbitrator. A plea that the arbitral tribunal is exceeding the scope of its authority shall be raised as soon as the matter alleged to be beyond the scope of its authority is raised during the arbitral proceedings. The arbitral tribunal may, in either case, admit a later plea if it considers the delay justified.
>
> (3) The arbitral tribunal may rule on a plea referred to in paragraph (2) of this article either as a preliminary question or in an award on the merits. If the arbitral tribunal rules as a preliminary question that it has jurisdiction, any party may request, within thirty days after having received notice of that ruling, the court specified in article 6 to

the Ordinance which is the equivalent of Art. 16(1) of the *Model Law*, the provision states: "The arbitral tribunal may rule on its own jurisdiction." This ability of the tribunal to decide its own jurisdiction is commonly known as the doctrine of *Kompetenz-Kompetenz*. This doctrine is also known as the *Principle of Competence-Competence*. Essentially, this concept states that a tribunal is competent to determine its own competence to settle a dispute. In other words, the arbitral tribunal has the power to determine its own jurisdiction over a particular arbitration.[14] As one source noted:

> An arbitral tribunal may rule on its own substantive jurisdiction, including the question of whether there is a valid arbitration agreement. Some other matters that an arbitral tribunal may decide on when it rules on its own jurisdiction . . . include:
> (1) whether the tribunal is properly constituted; or
> (2) what matters have been submitted to arbitration in accordance with [the] arbitration agreement[15]

Section 34(1)(2) of the Ordinance, which is the equivalent of Art. 16(2) of the *Model Law*, provides the procedure for objecting to a tribunal's jurisdiction:

> that the arbitral tribunal does not have jurisdiction shall be raised not later than the submission of the statement of defence.[16] A party is not precluded from raising

---

decide the matter, which decision shall be subject to no appeal; while such a request is pending, the arbitral tribunal may continue the arbitral proceedings and make an award."

(2) The power of the arbitral tribunal to rule on its own jurisdiction under subsection (1) includes the power to decide as to—
   (a) whether the tribunal is properly constituted; or
   (b) what matters have been submitted to arbitration in accordance with the arbitration agreement.
(3) If a dispute is submitted to arbitration in accordance with an arbitration agreement and a party—
   (a) makes a counter-claim arising out of the same dispute; or
   (b) relies on a claim arising out of that dispute for the purposes of a set-off, the arbitral tribunal has jurisdiction to decide on the counter-claim or the claim so relied on only to the extent that the subject matter of that counter-claim or that claim falls within the scope of the same arbitration agreement.
(4) A ruling of the arbitral tribunal that it does not have jurisdiction to decide a dispute is not subject to appeal.
(5) Despite section 20, if the arbitral tribunal rules that it does not have jurisdiction to decide a dispute, the court must, if it has jurisdiction, decide that dispute.

14 CHOONG & WEERAMANTRY, *supra* note 9, at para. 34.06 states:
Thus, by applying the twin concepts of competence-competence and separability, even though a tribunal's competence is challenged by one of the parties, it is nonetheless empowered to rule on whether that challenge is valid. This is the case even where the challenge relates to the existence or validity of the arbitration agreement itself, or to the validity of the contract containing the arbitration agreement. . . . this competence extends to the tribunal's power to rule on the "foundation, content and extent of its mandate and power." (citations omitted)

15 MA & BROCK, *supra* note 1, at para. 14.016 (citation omitted).
This position seems to have been confirmed once again in the United States by it Supreme Court decision in *Henry Schein, Inc. v Archer & White Sales, Inc.*, 2019 WL 122164, 586 US ____ (2019). The Court decided that the arbitrability of a dispute is to be decided by the arbitral tribunal as the parties had contracted to do so. The Court held that contracts are to be enforced.

16 This requirement that objections to the arbitral tribunal's jurisdiction be raised at an early stage is sensible

> such a plea by the fact that he has appointed, or participated in the appointment of, an arbitrator.[17] A plea that the arbitral tribunal is exceeding the scope of its authority shall be raised as soon as the matter alleged to be beyond the scope of its authority is raised during the arbitral proceedings. The arbitral tribunal may, in either case, admit a later plea if it considers the delay justified.

Section 34(1)(3) of the Ordinance, which is the equivalent of Article 16(3) of the *Model Law*, allows an arbitral tribunal to rule on a challenge to its jurisdiction. The tribunal may make such a ruling either as a point of the preliminary questions[18] or as part of the award on the merits of the dispute.[19]

In most countries, a tribunal's decision concerning its jurisdiction can be appealed to the national court which has the power to review an arbitral tribunal's decision. In Hong Kong, this initial determination by an arbitral tribunal may be subject to review by the Court of First Instance.[20]

> Where the tribunal rules as a preliminary question that it has jurisdiction, the party may then request the Court of First Instance to decide the matter. In effect, this amounts to a challenge of the tribunal's preliminary decision on jurisdiction.[21]

---

and practical. It is undesirable to allow a party to object to the tribunal's jurisdiction at a late stage of the arbitral proceedings, when that party might begin to find that its case is not going well. Redfern & Hunter, *supra* note 2, at para. 5.118.

[17] Choong & Weeramantry, *supra* note 9, at para. 34.22 states: "This is sensible, since a party should not lose its fundamental right to appoint, or to participate in the appointment of the arbitrators, simply because it intends to make a jurisdictional objection."

[18] Butterworths Hong Kong Arbitration Law Handbook para. [34.14] (Damon YC So, Christopher To *et al.*, eds., 2nd ed. 2018) [hereinafter So & To] provides this definition of "preliminary question":

> it means a ruling expressed by the tribunal in a document other than an award, e.g. an order for directions. This is significant in terms of the forms of recourse that is available . . . Meanwhile, if the tribunal is not sure whether it shall issue an award or order for direction, the Court expressed that the tribunal shall issue an award.

[19] Ma & Brock, *supra* note 1, at para. 20.14 elaborates:

> In respect of an arbitral tribunal's ruling on its own jurisdiction as a preliminary question, within thirty days after having received notice of that ruling, the matter may be referred to the Court for decision under s.34(1)(3)/art.16(3) of the UNCITRAL Model Law. On the other hand, if the decision on jurisdiction is made as part of an award on the merits, an application for setting aside may be made under s.81/art.34 of the UNCITRAL Model Law. (citation omitted)

[20] § 34 of the *Arbitration Ordinance*, incorporating *Model Law* Art. 16, *supra* note 5. *See supra* note 13 which sets out in full this section of the Ordinance.

§ 81 of the *Arbitration Ordinance*, incorporating *Model Law* Art. 34, *supra* note 5, stipulates in part:

> (2) An arbitral award may be set aside by the court specified in article 6 only if:
> (a) the party making the application furnishes proof that:
> (i) a party to the arbitration agreement referred to in article 7 was under some incapacity; or the said agreement is not valid under the law to which the parties have subjected it or, failing any indication thereon, under the law of this State; or
> . . .
> (iii) the award deals with a dispute not contemplated by or not falling within the terms of the submission to arbitration, or contains decisions on matters beyond the scope of the submission to arbitration, provided that, if the decisions on matters submitted to arbitration can be separated from those not so submitted, only that part of the award which contains decisions on matters not submitted to arbitration may be set aside

[21] Choong & Weeramantry, *supra* note 9, at para. 34.26 (citation omitted).

If the Court of First Instance is presented with such a request, the court will decide the matter, and its decision is not subject to appeal. The court will be "substituting its decision, i.e. by way of rehearing, for that of the arbitral tribunal."[22] In other words, the court is entitled to re-open the issues and to re-hear them anew and in full.[23] In doing so, however, the court is to confine its review only to the subject of the tribunal's jurisdiction and the court should not broaden its review to effectively decide the case on its merits thereby usurping the jurisdiction of the arbitral tribunal.[24]

Model Law Art. 16(3) provides for court review of an arbitral tribunal's decision that the tribunal does have jurisdiction. This provision is little used in practice, "because if a challenge is unsuccessful, the parties will be obliged to continue the arbitration before the tribunal whose decision they challenged."[25] Section 34(4) of the *Arbitration Ordinance* specifically provides that in the event the arbitral tribunal rules that it does not have jurisdiction to decide a dispute, this decision is not subject to appeal.[26]

Where an arbitral tribunal rules that it does not have jurisdiction as part of its award on the merits of the dispute, there is no similar appeal to the Court of First Instance.[27] The UNCITRAL Report 2008 states that judicial review on the question of jurisdiction is available in setting aside proceedings pursuant to *Model Law* Art. 34 or in enforcement proceedings pursuant to *Model Law* Art. 35 and Art. 36.[28]

---

[22] *Id.* at para. 34.30 (citation omitted).

[23] *Id.*

[24] *Id.*

[25] *Id.* at para. 34.29.

[26] *Id.* at para. 34.31 states:

> It is notable that the party's right to ask the Court of First Instance to decide the jurisdictional objection only applies where the tribunal rules that it has jurisdiction. Where the tribunal rules that it lacks jurisdiction, no similar right exists . . . and section 34(4) of the Arbitration Ordinance expressly states that this is the case. The reason for this is suggested by the UNCITRAL Report 1985, that "a ruling by the arbitral tribunal that it lacked jurisdiction was final as regards its proceedings since it was inappropriate to compel arbitrators who had made such a ruling to continue the proceedings." (citation omitted)

[27] Ma & Brock, *supra* note 1, at para. 20.17 explains:

> As regards a tribunal's negative ruling on its own jurisdiction as a preliminary question, it appears that there is no recourse under art.16(3)/s.34(1)(3) in such a case. The Hong Kong court in *Brunswick Bowling & Billiards Corp v Shanghai Zhonglu Industrial Co Ltd* held that with the negative ruling on jurisdiction, no award had been made and there was nothing to set aside under art. 34. This has also been confirmed at least in a Singapore case, the stated rationale being that it would be inappropriate to compel arbitrators who have made such a ruling to continue with the arbitration proceedings. The Singapore court further held that a negative ruling on jurisdiction cannot constitute an award either because it is not a decision on the substance of the dispute. On the contrary, it is a decision not to determine the substance of the dispute. As such, even if a negative ruling is actually wrong in law, it cannot be set aside under art.34 or the UNCITRAL Model Law (given effect by s.81 in Hong Kong) either. (citations omitted)

[28] *See* Choong & Weeramantry, *supra* note 9, at para. 34.32.

Model Law, *supra* note 13, Art. 34, "Application for setting aside as exclusive recourse against arbitral award" is incorporated into § 81 of the *Arbitration Ordinance*, *supra* note 5. *Model Law*, *supra* note 13, Art. 35 "Recognition and enforcement" and Art. 36 "Grounds for refusing recognition or enforcement" have not been incorporated into the Ordinance. Rather, the Ordinance opted for the comparable provisions of the *Convention on the Recognition*

Another concept affecting jurisdiction is the *Doctrine of Separability*, which is sometimes also known as the *Doctrine of Severability*. Under this concept, an arbitration agreement, or an arbitration clause in a contract, is considered to be a separate contract from the main contract. Thus, for example, *Model Law* Art. 16(1) recognises the total separability of the arbitration agreement, *i.e.*, the arbitration agreement can be severed or cut out from the underlying contract and can remain valid even if the main contract was illegal, invalid, invalidly entered into or for some other reason vitiated from the start.

The Doctrine of Separability gives to a tribunal the jurisdiction to decide on the effects of an invalid contract or a terminated contract upon the arbitration clause. Again, under the Doctrine of Separability, an arbitration clause in a contract is regarded as an independent agreement separated from the contract. Therefore, should the main contract be declared invalid or a terminated, the arbitration clause remains valid and enforceable. This allows the parties to appoint an arbitral tribunal to decide disputes which arose before the main contract was invalidated or terminated.[29] This is to prevent a recalcitrant respondent alleging invalidity in order to bring the dispute before the courts thereby placing the parties in the very situation they agreed to avoid by arbitration.[30]

The case of *Fiona Trust and Holding Corporation v Yuri Privalov*,[31] involved a contract dispute where the validity of the whole agreement, including the arbitration clause, was challenged on the basis of bribery. The court stated:

> it is not enough to say that the contract as a whole is impeachable. There must be something more than that to impeach the arbitration clause [within that contract]. That extra element is missing in the present case.[32]
>
> . . .
>
> It is not enough to say that the bribery impeaches the whole contract unless there is some special reason for saying that the bribery impeaches the arbitration clause in particular.[33]

This decision was upheld by the House of Lords where the court stated:

> The appellants' argument was not that there was no contract at all, but that they were entitled to rescind the contract including the arbitration agreement because the contract was induced by bribery. Allegations of that kind, if sound, may affect the validity of the main agreement. But they do not undermine the validity of the

and Enforcement of Foreign Arbitral Awards (done in New York, 1958) [hereinafter *New York Convention*] whose provisions are essentially identical to those of Art. 35 and Art. 36.

29 Redfern & Hunter, *supra* note 2, at para. 5.101.

30 *Id.* at para. 5.100.

31 [2007] EWCA Civ 20.

32 *Id.* at para. 25.

33 *Id.* at para. 29.

See also the cases of *Fung Sang Trading Ltd v Kai Sun Products & Food Company Ltd* [1992] HKLR 40 and *Ling Ming v Chen Shu Quan* [2012] 2 HKLRD 547.

> arbitration agreement as a distinct agreement. The doctrine of separability requires direct impeachment of the arbitration agreement before it can be set aside.[34]

In conclusion, separability and *Kompetenz-Kompetenz* are complementary to each other. A ruling by the arbitral tribunal that the underlying contract is invalid does not automatically lead to the conclusion that the arbitration agreement is also invalid.[35] If the arbitration agreement remains valid, the tribunal has jurisdiction to determine its ability to decide the dispute. Generally, in international commercial arbitrations, once a dispute is submitted to arbitration, a national court will not intervene by exercising jurisdiction over the parties and their dispute.[36] In part, these two doctrines prevent a reluctant or recalcitrant party from delaying or totally thwarting the arbitration by bringing the dispute to the national courts. As one source has noted:

> Challenging the existence or validity of an arbitration will not prevent the arbitrators from proceeding with the arbitration, ruling on their own jurisdiction and, if they retain jurisdiction, rendering a decision on the merits of their disputes notwithstanding any court action aimed at setting aside the decision on jurisdiction[37] ... Accepting this positive effect of the principle of competence-competence ... The court should limit, at this stage, their review to a *prima facie* determination that the agreement is not "null and void, inoperative and incapable of being performed."[38]

---

34 *Premium Nafta Products Limited v Fili Shipping Company Limited* [2007] UKHL 40, para. 35.

35 As noted by one authority:

> Under the separability doctrine, the validity of the arbitration clause is independent of the validity of the other terms of the contract. Thus, even where the tribunal rules that the contract is null and void, this will not entail ipso jure the invalidity of the arbitration clause itself.

Choong & Weeramantry, *supra* note 9, at para. 34.07 (citations omitted).

36 *See, e.g.*, Art. II(3) of the *New York Convention*, *supra* note 28, which provides:

> 3. The court of a Contracting State, when seized of an action in a matter in respect of which the parties have made an agreement within the meaning of this article, shall, at the request of one of the parties, refer the parties to arbitration, unless it finds that the said agreement is null and void, inoperative or incapable of being performed.

37 Choong & Weeramantry, *supra* note 9, at para. 34.28 states:

> When Article 16(3) was drafted, there was concern that a party might seek to delay or obstruct the arbitration proceedings, by making unmeritorious objections to jurisdiction, followed by a court challenge if the tribunal were to rule against it. . . . Article 16(3) as finally adopted provides three safeguards against this. First, a party intending to challenge the tribunal's decision has to do so within 30 days; secondly, the court's decision is not subject to appeal; and thirdly, while such a request is pending, the tribunal may continue the arbitral proceedings and make an award. (citations omitted)

Ma & Brock, *supra* note 1, at para. 20.15 reiterates essentially the same points as the above quotation.

See, e.g., § 26(1) of the *Arbitration Ordinance*, incorporating *Model Law* Art. 13(3), *supra* note 5, empowers an arbitrator whose appointment is being challenged to continue with the arbitral proceedings and render an award despite that there is a pending challenge. This is effective in preventing a party from using "challenging the arbitral tribunal's appointment" as a delaying tactic. Ma & Brock, *supra* note 1, at para. 11.022.

38 Emmanuel Galliard and Yas Banifatemi, *Negative Effect of Competence-Competence: The Rule of Priority in Favour of the Arbitrators*, *in* Enforcement Of Arbitration Agreements and International Arbitral Awards: The New York Convention in Practice 257, 259 (E. Gaillard *et al.*, eds. 2008).

See also the analysis in Choong & Weeramantry, *supra* note 9, at paras. 34.12–34.17 leading these authors to conclude at para. 34.18:

> it appears clear that Article 16(1) does not give the tribunal exclusive authority to decide its own jurisdiction; neither does it always grant the tribunal the primary power to do so. Instead, in some

III. Duties

The requirements regulating an arbitrator's exercise of powers come from several sources. The first source is the arbitration law of the venue where the arbitration is seated. For example, in Hong Kong, the *Arbitration Ordinance* sets out several overriding duties imposed on the tribunal. Under this law, the arbitral tribunal is required to observe natural justice. The concept of *natural justice* requires the tribunal to treat the disputing parties equally and fairly.[39] As stated in the *Arbitration Ordinance*:

---

situations, the court is empowered to decide such questions before the tribunal does, and its decision may also take precedence over that of the tribunal.

An authority defined the terms "null and void," "inoperative" and "incapable of being performed" as follows:

> An arbitration agreement is 'null and void' if it is 'devoid of legal effect', for example owing to mistake, duress, or fraud. At first sight, it is difficult to see a distinction between the terms 'inoperative' and 'incapable of being performed'. However, an arbitration clause is inoperative where it has 'ceased to have legal effect' as a result, for example, of a failure by the parties to comply with a time limit, or where the parties have repudiated, or by their conduct impliedly revoked, the arbitration agreement. By contrast, the expression 'incapable of being performed' appears to refer to more practical aspects of the prospective arbitration proceedings. It applies, for example, if it is for some reason impossible to establish the arbitral tribunal. Courts tend to construe these provisions narrowly, to avoid offering a 'back door' for a party wishing to escape the arbitration agreement.

REDFERN & HUNTER, *supra* note 2, at para. 2.202 (citations omitted).

39 The duties of an arbitral tribunal are to act fairly and to manage the arbitration. *See* §§ 3, 46, and 47 of the *Arbitration Ordinance*, *supra* note 5. To act fairly includes following the rules of natural justice which require an arbitral tribunal:

- to give each party an equal and reasonable opportunity of presenting its case and dealing with that of its opponent
- to act impartially

Several court decisions and the Ordinance may be summarized into the following statements of this principle of natural justice:

- each party must be timely notified of any meeting, hearing or determination of a matter in the arbitration
- each party must have a reasonable opportunity to be present throughout such a meeting, hearing or determination in order to present evidence and argument in support of its own case
- each party must have a reasonable opportunity to challenge its opponent's case by cross-examining the opposing party's witnesses, presenting rebutting evidence and addressing oral argument
- the hearing must, unless the contrary is expressly agreed, be the occasion on which the parties present the whole of the evidence and argument
- the arbitrator may only decide the case on the evidence and submissions placed before the arbitral tribunal by the parties. (Where a tribunal or arbitrator is empowered to act inquisitorially, the arbitrator must not take the parties by surprise by making an award without presenting the results of the arbitrator's independent investigations to the parties for comment.)
- where one party requests an oral hearing, it is no longer the law that an arbitrator must accede to such a request. The arbitrator must, rather, adopt a procedure which is appropriate to the circumstances of the case, avoiding unnecessary delay and expense, so as to provide for a fair means of resolving the dispute

A failure by an arbitral tribunal to follow these requirements may lead to termination of the arbitrator's mandate or the setting aside of the arbitral tribunal's award. In Hong Kong, this would be by order of the Court of First Instance. The termination of mandate would be under § 25 and § 26 of the *Arbitration Ordinance*, *supra* note 5. The setting aside of an arbitral award would be pursuant to *id.* at § 81.

So & To, *supra* note 18, at para. [46.14] notes that for breach of the duty of impartiality:

> the Ordinance deals with bias in two ways: (a) by termination of the mandate of an arbitrator by agreement or, failing such agreement, by order of the High Court . . . and (b) by the setting aside of an award . . . The wording of Article 34(2)(b)(ii) . . . embraces not only conflict of the substance of the award with public policy but also the manner in which it was arrived at . . .

> (2) The parties must be treated with equality.
> (3) When conducting arbitral proceedings or exercising any of the powers conferred on an arbitral tribunal by this Ordinance or by the parties to any of those arbitral proceedings, the arbitral tribunal is required—
> (a) to be independent;
> (b) to act fairly and impartially as between the parties, giving them a reasonable opportunity to present their cases and to deal with the cases of their opponents; and
> (c) to use procedures that are appropriate to the particular case, avoiding unnecessary delay or expense, so as to provide a fair means for resolving the dispute to which the arbitral proceedings relate.[40]

This duty applies to all actions taken and decisions made by a tribunal in the exercise of its powers under the arbitration agreement and under the Ordinance.[41] As one authority notes:

> It is important that an arbitral tribunal should act, and should be seen to act, judicially (that is, respecting the rules of due process). This is more than a mere moral obligation; it is also one that, to some extent at least, may be enforced under international or institutional rules, or under the applicable law. The duty to act judicially is a duty that extends to all aspects of the proceedings.[42]

Another duty imposed by law upon the tribunal is to adopt appropriate procedures for that particular dispute. This requires the tribunal to implement the appropriate case management procedures: the arbitral tribunal is required to use procedures appropriate to the case, avoiding unnecessary delay or expense.[43] Note, however, the possible tension with party autonomy as provided in the Ordinance:

---

40 § 46(2) and § 46(3) of the *Arbitration Ordinance*, *supra* note 5.

41 *See id.* at § 81, incorporating *Model Law* Art. 34(2), *supra* note 5, as to sanctions for non-observance of this duty. This section of the Ordinance is titled: *Application for setting aside as exclusive recourse against arbitral award.*

42 REDFERN & HUNTER, *supra* note 2, at para. 5.70. These authors further expound on this requirement:

> What does this mean in practice? Neither the arbitral tribunal as a whole nor any of its individual members should . . . discuss the case with one party in the absence of the other . . . At the hearing, the duty to act judicially means that each party must be accorded equality of treatment and given a fair opportunity to present its case. It would be wrong . . . to allow one party to call witnesses and to deny the other party a similar opportunity. . . . it would be improper to allow one party to address the arbitral tribunal orally and to deny the same to the other party. International and institutional rules, which are usually silent as to the duties of the arbitral tribunal, also find common ground on this point.

Id. at para. 5.71.

> The duty to act judicially is not simply a matter of ensuring equality between the parties and giving each the right to respond to the other party's position; it also arises where the arbitral tribunal decides to base its decision on an issue not specifically raised by the parties. . . .

Id. at para. 5.73.

43 § 46(3)(c) of the *Arbitration Ordinance*, *supra* note 5. In essence, this provision requires the tribunal to exercise case management.

"the parties to a dispute should be free to agree on how the dispute should be resolved."[44]

Another source of a tribunal's duty may come from the arbitration agreement or from the parties. "Specific duties may be imposed upon an arbitral tribunal by the parties. This may be done before the arbitrators are appointed, or during the course of the arbitration, or both."[45]

> Duties may also be imposed on the arbitral tribunal during the course of the proceedings by the parties, but usually only after consultation with the arbitral tribunal. For example, in a dispute arising out of a construction project in a warzone, the parties may decide in the course of the arbitration that they wish the arbitral tribunal to inspect the construction site. The proposal for such a site inspection would usually be discussed with, and agreed by, the arbitral tribunal — but if a particular arbitrator were unwilling to accept the proposal and the parties were to insist upon it, that arbitrator would have to resign.[46]

The arbitration rules adopted by the parties may be another source of the arbitral tribunal's duty. For example, Rule 6(2) of the ICSID Arbitration Rules requires arbitrators to sign a declaration of independence and readiness to judge fairly as between the parties no later than the end of the first session, failing which these arbitrators "shall be deemed to have resigned."[47] Rule 13(1) of the same set of rules further imposes a duty upon the arbitral tribunal to commence its first session within 60 days of its constitution, or such other period as the parties may agree. Another example of institutional rules is Art. 11(2) of the ICC Rules of Arbitration requiring the arbitral tribunal members to confirm their acceptance, availability, impartiality and independence. Art. 30 of the same rules requires the tribunal to render an award within six months while Art. 33 requires the arbitral tribunal to submit its draft award for scrutiny to the ICC's International Court of Arbitration.[48]

As previously mentioned, an arbitrator's duty may derive from the law. Thus, an arbitrator's duty may be imposed by statute. For example, Hong Kong's *Arbitration Ordinance* imposes certain duties upon an arbitrator:

- to treat the parties with equality
- to be independent
- to act fairly and impartially as between the parties, giving them a reasonable opportunity to present their cases and to deal with the cases of their opponents

---

44 *Id.* at § 3(2)(a).

45 Redfern & Hunter, *supra* note 2, at para. 5.44.

46 *Id.* at para. 5.45.

47 ICSID is the acronym for the International Centre for the Settlement of Investment Disputes. This organization's Rules of Procedure for Arbitration Proceedings (2006) may be found at this web site: https://icsid.worldbank.org/en/Pages/icsiddocs/ICSID-Convention-Arbitration-Rules.aspx (last visited 21 June 2017).

48 Redfern & Hunter, *supra* note 2, at para. 5.46.
The ICC Rules, *supra* note 7, may be found at: https://iccwbo.org/dispute-resolution-services/arbitration/rules-of-arbitration/ (last visited 21 June 2017).

- to use procedures that are appropriate to the particular case, avoiding unnecessary delay or expense, so as to provide a fair means for resolving the dispute to which the arbitral proceedings relate[49]

A tribunal's obligations or duties may be imposed by case law, that is, previous court decisions, which may serve as precedent or examples. Four such precedents are discussed in the following paragraphs.

The first example is the case of *OAO Northern Shipping Co v Remocadores De Marin SL (Remmar)*,[50] where the United Kingdom's High Court confirmed the principal rule that an arbitral tribunal must give each party a fair opportunity to address all issues which the tribunal considered in rendering its award. "The tribunal must give the parties a fair opportunity to address its arguments on all of the essential building blocks in the tribunal's conclusion."[51] One source states in relation to this case:

> On the facts of the case, the claimant had been deprived of the opportunity to advance submissions on an issue that had formed part of the tribunal's reasoning in the award, but had not been debated by the parties. The court held that such action amounted to a serious irregularity capable of causing substantial injustice, thus meeting the criteria for the setting aside of an award . . . The court set aside the award and remitted the issue to the arbitral tribunal for further consideration.[52]

A similar issue arose in the case of *Apex Tech Investment Ltd v Chuang's Development (China) Ltd*[53] where the tribunal conducted its own investigation as it was allowed to do under the applicable arbitration rules. The arbitral tribunal, however, failed to notify the results of its own investigation to the parties. The tribunal did not afford the parties an opportunity to address the results by making submissions before rendering the arbitral award.[54]

In *Annie Fox v P G Wellfair Ltd*[55] the arbitrator independently sought evidence on his own without the knowledge of the parties. Lord Denning stated:

---

[49] § 46 of the *Arbitration Ordinance*, *supra* note 5.
For an analysis of the duties imposed by law upon an arbitral tribunal, *see* Redfern & Hunter, *supra* note 2, at paras. 5.47–5.78. See also the two Australian cases where an international arbitration award was set aside and the arbitrator removed by the Federal Court under the *International Arbitration Act 1974* which incorporated the UNCITAL *Model Law* Articles 12, 18 and 34: *Hui v Esposito Holdings Pty Ltd* [2017] FCA 648 and *Hui v Esposito Holdings Pty Ltd* [2017] FCA 728.

[50] [2007] EWHC 1821, [2007] 2 Lloyd's Rep 302.

[51] [2007] EWHC at para. 22 citing to *ABB Ag v Hochtief Airport GmbH* [2006] 2 Lloyd's Rep 1, para. 70.
Redfern & Hunter, *supra* note 2, at para. 1.121 reinforces this point by stating that:

> the arbitrator is required to make a decision in accordance with the law. In reaching that decision, the arbitrator must proceed judicially – giving each party a proper opportunity to present its case and treating each party equally, on pain of having the arbitral award set aside for procedural irregularity. (citations omitted)

[52] Redfern & Hunter, *supra* note 2, at para. 5.74.

[53] [1996] 2 HKLR 155.

[54] Ma & Brock, *supra* note 1, at para. 19.030.

[55] [1981] 2 Lloyd's Rep 514.
For other examples, *see Checkpoint Ltd. v Strathclyde Pension Fund* [2003] EWCA Civ 84; *Top Shop Estates Ltd v*

> His [the arbitrator's] function is not to supply evidence for the defendants but to adjudicate upon the evidence given before him. He can and should use the special knowledge so as to understand the evidence that is given – the letters that have passed – the usage of the trade – the dealings in the market – and to appreciate the worth of all that he sees upon a view. But he cannot use his special knowledge – or at any rate he should not use it – so as to provide evidence on behalf of the defendants which they have not chosen to provide for themselves. For then he would be discarding the role of an impartial arbitrator and assuming the role of advocate for the defaulting side. At any rate he should not use his own knowledge to derogate from the evidence of the plaintiff's experts – without putting his own knowledge to them and giving them a chance of answering it and showing that his view is wrong.[56]

The final example is the case of *Chilton v Saga Holidays plc*,[57] where the arbitrator took the questioning of witnesses out of the hands of a party. In this case, the claimant sued in person whereas the respondent was represented by a lawyer. The arbitrator forbade the respondent's lawyer from cross-examining the claimant on the basis that it would give the respondent an unfair advantage. The respondent appealed the arbitrator's decision to the Chelmsford County Court where the arbitrator's decision was upheld. On a further appeal to the Court of Appeal, it decided that an arbitrator is not allowed to deprive the respondent of its lawyer's services through whom the respondent would confront a witness/opposing party. The Court of Appeal stated:

> both courts and arbitrators . . . operate on an adversarial system of achieving justice. It is a system which can be modified by rules of court; it is a system which can be modified by contract between the parties; but . . . it is basically an adversarial system, and it is fundamental to that that each party shall be entitled to tender their own evidence and that the other party shall be entitled to ask questions designed to probe the accuracy or otherwise, or the completeness of [*sic*] otherwise, of the evidence which has been given.
>
> . . .
>
> The problem which arises where you have one represented party and one unrepresented party is very well known to all judges and in particular to judges who deal with small claims in the county court. It becomes the duty of the judge so far as he can, without entering the arena to a point where he is no longer able to act judicially, to make good any deficiencies in the advantages available to the unrepresented party. . . . That is the proper course to be adopted. The informality which is stressed by the rule and the requirement that the arbitrator may adopt any method of procedure which he considers to be convenient . . . covers the situation where . . . a litigant in person is quite incapable of cross-examining but is perfectly capable in the time available for cross-examination of putting his own case. The

Danino [1985] 1 EGLR 9.

56 [1981] 2 Lloyd's Rep at 522. *See also* Redfern & Hunter, *supra* note 2, at para. 5.73.

57 [1986] 1 All ER 841.

judge or the registrar then picks up the unrepresented party's complaints and puts them to the other side.

In summation, we can discern the main duties imposed on an arbitral tribunal to include the following:

- to act judicially, including the exercise of discretion on proper grounds according to all relevant circumstances[58]
- to decide only the dispute(s) submitted by the parties, *i.e.*, not exceeding its mandate or failing to fulfil its mandate[59]
- to conduct the dispute resolution procedure according to the parties' agreement[60]
- to demonstrate the elementary skills of an arbitrator[61]
- to proceed expeditiously[62]

IV. Powers

Similar to the duties of an arbitral tribunal, the powers of the tribunal are derived from several sources.[63] The first source is the law of the seat or venue of the arbitration. For example, the *Arbitration Ordinance* in Hong Kong provides for the general powers which an arbitrator can exercise in an arbitration which is seated in the territory. Some of these statutory powers are listed below in the order in which they might be used in an arbitration proceeding:

---

[58] § 46(2) and § 46(3) of the *Arbitration Ordinance*, *supra* note 5.

[59] *Id.* at § 81, incorporating *Model Law* Art. 34. In particular, *see Model Law* Art. 34(2)(a)(iii), *supra* note 13.

[60] § 3(2)(a) and § 46(3)(c) of the *Arbitration Ordinance*, *supra* note 5.

[61] *See* the case of *Pratt v Swanmore Builders Ltd and Baker* [1980] 2 Lloyd's Rep 504 where the court removed the arbitrator for misconduct. The reasons for the arbitrator's removal included:

- the misconduct resulting in delay
- failing to show the elementary skills of an arbitrator
- imposing regulations contrary to the wishes of a party in the absence of an agreement as to procedure
- reducing the arbitration to such a state that there was no prospect of justice being done

[62] *See* § 27 of the *Arbitration Ordinance*, incorporating *Model Law* Art. 14, *supra* note 5, concerning an arbitral tribunal's failure "to act without undue delay."

[63] Ma & Brock, *supra* note 1, at para. 14.011 states: "The tribunal needs these powers to control the progress of the arbitration and to fulfil its duties. Without these powers the arbitral process could not work."
Id. at para. 14.010 notes that an arbitral tribunal is vested with powers from four main sources:

- Express terms agreed upon by the parties to the arbitration agreement
- Implied terms (particularly terms implied by the custom of a particular trade)
- Terms of some trade or professional institution (e.g., Hong Kong International Arbitration Centre) incorporated into the agreement
- *Arbitration Ordinance*

- to order interim injunctions[64] or other interim measures.[65] (An exception is where a third party is involved. In this circumstance, the Court of First

[64] The pertinent sections of the Ordinance are set out as follows:

35. Article 17 of UNCITRAL Model Law (Power of arbitral tribunal to order interim measures)

(1) Article 17 of the UNCITRAL Model Law, the text of which is set out below, has effect—

"*Article 17. Power of arbitral tribunal to order interim measures*

(1) Unless otherwise agreed by the parties, the arbitral tribunal may, at the request of a party, grant interim measures.

(2) An interim measure is any temporary measure, whether in the form of an award or in another form, by which, at any time prior to the issuance of the award by which the dispute is finally decided, the arbitral tribunal orders a party to:

(a) Maintain or restore the status quo pending determination of the dispute;

(b) Take action that would prevent, or refrain from taking action that is likely to cause, current or imminent harm or prejudice to the arbitral process itself;

(c) Provide a means of preserving assets out of which a subsequent award may be satisfied; or

(d) Preserve evidence that may be relevant and material to the resolution of the dispute."

(2) An interim measure referred to in article 17 of the UNCITRAL Model Law, given effect to by subsection (1), is to be construed as including an injunction but not including an order under section 56.

(3) If an arbitral tribunal has granted an interim measure, the tribunal may, on the application of any party, make an award to the same effect as the interim measure.

36. Article 17A of UNCITRAL Model Law (Conditions for granting interim measures)

Article 17A of the UNCITRAL Model Law, the text of which is set out below, has effect—

"*Article 17A. Conditions for granting interim measures*

(1) The party requesting an interim measure under article 17(2)(a), (b) and (c) shall satisfy the arbitral tribunal that:

(a) Harm not adequately reparable by an award of damages is likely to result if the measure is not ordered, and such harm substantially outweighs the harm that is likely to result to the party against whom the measure is directed if the measure is granted; and

(b) There is a reasonable possibility that the requesting party will succeed on the merits of the claim. The determination on this possibility shall not affect the discretion of the arbitral tribunal in making any subsequent determination.

(2) With regard to a request for an interim measure under article 17(2)(d), the requirements in paragraphs (1)(a) and (b) of this article shall apply only to the extent the arbitral tribunal considers appropriate."

For further discussion concerning this section of the Ordinance, *see, e.g.*, MA & BROCK, *supra* note 1, at paras. 14.035–14.039.

[65] § 37 of the *Arbitration Ordinance*, incorporating *Model Law* Art. 17B, *supra* note 5, provides:

Article 17B of the UNCITRAL Model Law, the text of which is set out below, has effect—

"*Article 17B. Applications for preliminary orders and conditions for granting preliminary orders*

(1) Unless otherwise agreed by the parties, a party may, without notice to any other party, make a request for an interim measure together with an application for a preliminary order directing a party not to frustrate the purpose of the interim measure requested.

(2) The arbitral tribunal may grant a preliminary order provided it considers that prior disclosure of the request for the interim measure to the party against whom it is directed risks frustrating the purpose of the measure.

(3) The conditions defined under article 17A apply to any preliminary order, provided that the harm to be assessed under article 17A(1)*(a)*, is the harm likely to result from the order being granted or not."

For further discussion concerning this section of the Ordinance, *see, e.g.*, MA & BROCK, *supra* note 1, at paras. 14.040–14.042.

Instance should exercise this power.)[66]

- to proceed without regard to the strict rules of evidence[67]
- unless otherwise agreed by the parties to the arbitration, to order security for costs. (There is a limitation on this power. This restriction is on the making of this order solely on the grounds of a party's residence.[68])

---

[66] § 45(2) and § 45(3) of the *Arbitration Ordinance*, incorporating *Model Law* Art. 17J, *supra* note 5, stipulates:

(2) On the application of any party, the Court may, in relation to any arbitral proceedings which have been or are to be commenced in or outside Hong Kong, grant an interim measure.

(3) The powers conferred by this section may be exercised by the Court irrespective of whether or not similar powers may be exercised by an arbitral tribunal under section 35 in relation to the same dispute.

[67] *Id.* at § 47(3), incorporating *Model Law* Art. 19, states:

(3) When conducting arbitral proceedings, an arbitral tribunal is not bound by the rules of evidence and may receive any evidence that it considers relevant to the arbitral proceedings, but it must give the weight that it considers appropriate to the evidence adduced in the arbitral proceedings.

[68] *See id.* at § 56(1)(a) and § 56(2).

As the main text refers to § 56, this section is set out below in full for convenience:

(1) Unless otherwise agreed by the parties, when conducting arbitral proceedings, an arbitral tribunal may make an order—
  (a) requiring a claimant to give security for the costs of the arbitration;
  (b) directing the discovery of documents or the delivery of interrogatories;
  (c) directing evidence to be given by affidavit; or
  (d) in relation to any relevant property—
    (i) directing the inspection, photographing, preservation, custody, detention or sale of the relevant property by the arbitral tribunal, a party to the arbitral proceedings or an expert; or
    (ii) directing samples to be taken from, observations to be made of, or experiments to be conducted on the relevant property.

(2) An arbitral tribunal must not make an order under subsection (1)(a) only on the ground that the claimant is—
  (a) a natural person who is ordinarily resident outside Hong Kong;
  (b) a body corporate—
    (i) incorporated under the law of a place outside Hong Kong; or
    (ii) the central management and control of which is exercised outside Hong Kong; or
  (c) an association—
    (i) formed under the law of a place outside Hong Kong; or
    (ii) the central management and control of which is exercised outside Hong Kong.

(3) An arbitral tribunal—
  (a) must, when making an order under subsection (1)(a), specify the period within which the order has to be complied with; and
  (b) may extend that period or an extended period.

(4) An arbitral tribunal may make an award dismissing a claim or stay a claim if it has made an order under subsection (1)(a) but the order has not been complied with within the period specified under subsection (3)(a) or extended under subsection (3)(b).

(5) Despite section 35(2), sections 39 to 42 apply, if appropriate, to an order under subsection (1)(d) as if a reference to an interim measure in those sections were an order under that subsection.

(6) Property is a relevant property for the purposes of subsection (1)(d) if—
  (a) the property is owned by or is in the possession of a party to the arbitral proceedings; and
  (b) the property is the subject of the arbitral proceedings, or any question relating to the property has arisen in the arbitral proceedings.

(7) Unless otherwise agreed by the parties, an arbitral tribunal may, when conducting arbitral proceedings, decide whether and to what extent it should itself take the initiative in ascertaining the facts and the law relevant to those arbitral proceedings.

(8) Unless otherwise agreed by the parties, an arbitral tribunal may—
  (a) administer oaths to, or take the affirmations of, witnesses and parties;

- unless otherwise agreed by the parties to the arbitration, to order security for the monetary amount in dispute.[69] (Again, as an arbitral tribunal does not have any jurisdiction over an individual or party not involved in the arbitration, the Court of First Instance should exercise this power in situations where such a third party is involved.[70])
- to order discovery of documents or delivery of interrogatories[71]
- to order evidence to be given by affidavit[72]
- to order the inspection, preservation, etc. of the subject-matter.[73] (Where a third party is involved, the Court of First Instance may exercise this power.[74])
- to decide whether and to what extent the tribunal should itself take the initiative in ascertaining the facts and the law, unless the parties otherwise agree.[75] (In any event, the arbitrator must not take the parties by surprise in the award.[76])
- to administer oaths and take affirmations, unless the parties otherwise agree[77]
- to take evidence on oath or affirmation, unless the parties otherwise agree[78]
- to direct the attendance of witnesses, unless the parties otherwise agree.[79] (If court assistance is required in the taking of evidence, it is for the Court of First Instance to apply this power.[80])

(b) examine witnesses and parties on oath or affirmation; or
(c) direct the attendance before the arbitral tribunal of witnesses in order to give evidence or to produce documents or other evidence.

(9) A person is not required to produce in arbitral proceedings any document or other evidence that the person could not be required to produce in civil proceedings before a court.

For an analysis of the application of these provisions, *see* Choong & Weeramantry, *supra* note 9, at paras. 56.00–56.29.

[69] *See, e.g.*, § 56(1)(d)(i) and § 40 of the *Arbitration Ordinance, supra* note 5.

[70] *Id.* at § 60(1)(a), provides:

(1) On the application of any party, the Court may, in relation to any arbitral proceedings which have been or are to be commenced in or outside Hong Kong, make an order—
(a) directing the inspection, photographing, preservation, custody, detention or sale of any relevant property by the arbitral tribunal, a party to the arbitral proceedings or an expert . . .

[71] *Id.* at § 56(1)(b).

[72] *Id.* at § 56(1)(c).

[73] *Id.* at § 56(1)(d).

[74] *Id.* at § 60(1)(a).

[75] *Id.* at § 56(7). *See also* § 47(2) of the Ordinance which permits the arbitral tribunal, unless the parties agree otherwise, to "conduct the proceedings in the manner that it considers appropriate."
For further discussion on the inquisitorial procedure, *see, e.g.*, Ma & Brock, *supra* note 1, at para. 14.033.

[76] *See, e.g., Fox v Wellfair, supra* note 55; *Apex Tech Investment v Chuang's Development, supra* note 53; *OAO Northern Shipping v Remocardores, supra* note 50.

[77] § 56(8)(a) of the *Arbitration Ordinance, supra* note 5.

[78] *Id.* at § 56(8)(b).

[79] *Id.* at § 56(8)(c).

[80] *Id.* at § 55(1) and § 55(2) provide:

(1) Article 27 of the UNCITRAL Model Law, the text of which is set out below, has effect—

"*Article 27. Court assistance in taking evidence*

The arbitral tribunal or a party with the approval of the arbitral tribunal may request from a competent court of this State assistance in taking evidence. The court may execute the request within its competence and according to its rules on taking evidence."

- to extend the time for commencing arbitral proceedings.[81] (The Court of First Instance may use this power where no tribunal is in existence at the relevant time.[82])
- to dismiss a claim or counterclaim for want of prosecution.[83] (If no arbitral tribunal is in existence at the relevant time, the parties may seek the assistance of the Court of First Instance to use this power.)[84]
- to make interim or partial awards[85]
- to award simple or compound interest on sums awarded and on sums claimed in the arbitration and paid late but prior to the award[86]
- to award costs[87]

---

(2) The Court may order a person to attend proceedings before an arbitral tribunal to give evidence or to produce documents or other evidence.
(3) The powers conferred by this section may be exercised by the Court irrespective of whether or not similar powers may be exercised by an arbitral tribunal under section 56 in relation to the same dispute.

[81] *Id.* at § 58 is titled, *Power to extend time for arbitral proceedings.*

[82] *Id.* at § 58(7) states: "The power conferred on an arbitral tribunal by this section is exercisable by the Court if at the relevant time there is not in existence an arbitral tribunal that is capable of exercising that power."

[83] *Id.* at § 59 is titled, *Order to be made in case of delay in pursuing claims in arbitral proceedings.* For a more detailed review of § 59, *see, e.g.*, MA & BROCK, *supra* note 1, at paras. 14.025 - 14.028; SO & TO, *supra* note 18, at paras. [59.06] and [59.07].

[84] § 59(5) of the *Arbitration Ordinance*, *supra* note 5, provides: "The power conferred on an arbitral tribunal by this section is exercisable by the Court if there is not in existence an arbitral tribunal that is capable of exercising that power."

[85] For a discussion of the different terminology concerning awards, such as *interim, interlocutory, partial, see* CHOONG & WEERAMANTRY, *supra* note 9, at paras 71.06 - 71.14.

[86] § 79(1) of the *Arbitration Ordinance*, *supra* note 5, stipulates:

(1) Unless otherwise agreed by the parties, an arbitral tribunal may, in the arbitral proceedings before it, award simple or compound interest from the dates, at the rates, and with the rests that the tribunal considers appropriate, subject to section 80, for any period ending not later than the date of payment—
  (a) on money awarded by the tribunal in the arbitral proceedings;
  (b) on money claimed in, and outstanding at the commencement of, the arbitral proceedings but paid before the award is made; or
  (c) on costs awarded or ordered by the tribunal in the arbitral proceedings.

[87] *Id.* at § 74 states in full:

(1) An arbitral tribunal may include in an award directions with respect to the costs of arbitral proceedings (including the fees and expenses of the tribunal).
(2) The arbitral tribunal may, having regard to all relevant circumstances (including the fact, if appropriate, that a written offer of settlement of the dispute concerned has been made), direct in the award under subsection (1) to whom and by whom and in what manner the costs are to be paid.
(3) The arbitral tribunal may also, in its discretion, order costs (including the fees and expenses of the tribunal) to be paid by a party in respect of a request made by any of the parties for an order or direction (including an interim measure).
(4) The arbitral tribunal may direct that the costs ordered under subsection (3) are to be paid forthwith or at the time that the tribunal may otherwise specify.
(5) Subject to section 75, the arbitral tribunal must—
  (a) assess the amount of costs to be awarded or ordered to be paid under this section (other than the fees and expenses of the tribunal); and
  (b) award or order those costs (including the fees and expenses of the tribunal).

. . .

(7) The arbitral tribunal—
  (a) must only allow costs that are reasonable having regard to all the circumstances; and

- to limit recoverable costs[88]
- to correct awards[89]

(b) unless otherwise agreed by the parties, may allow costs incurred in the preparation of the arbitral proceedings prior to the commencement of the arbitration.

(8) A provision of an arbitration agreement to the effect that the parties, or any of the parties, must pay their own costs in respect of arbitral proceedings arising under the agreement is void.

(9) A provision referred to in subsection (8) is not void if it is part of an agreement to submit to arbitration a dispute that had arisen before the agreement was made.

[88] *Id.* at § 57(1) provides: "Unless otherwise agreed by the parties, an arbitral tribunal may direct that the recoverable costs of arbitral proceedings before it are limited to a specified amount."

[89] *Id.* at § 69 states in full:

(1) Article 33 of the UNCITRAL Model Law, the text of which is set out below, has effect—

"*Article 33. Correction and interpretation of award; additional award*

(1) Within thirty days of receipt of the award, unless another period of time has been agreed upon by the parties:

(a) a party, with notice to the other party, may request the arbitral tribunal to correct in the award any errors in computation, any clerical or typographical errors or any errors of similar nature;

(b) if so agreed by the parties, a party, with notice to the other party, may request the arbitral tribunal to give an interpretation of a specific point or part of the award. If the arbitral tribunal considers the request to be justified, it shall make the correction or give the interpretation within thirty days of receipt of the request. The interpretation shall form part of the award.

(2) The arbitral tribunal may correct any error of the type referred to in paragraph (1)*(a)* of this article on its own initiative within thirty days of the date of the award.

(3) Unless otherwise agreed by the parties, a party, with notice to the other party, may request, within thirty days of receipt of the award, the arbitral tribunal to make an additional award as to claims presented in the arbitral proceedings but omitted from the award. If the arbitral tribunal considers the request to be justified, it shall make the additional award within sixty days.

(4) The arbitral tribunal may extend, if necessary, the period of time within which it shall make a correction, interpretation or an additional award under paragraph (1) or (3) of this article.

(5) The provisions of article 31 shall apply to a correction or interpretation of the award or to an additional award."

(2) The arbitral tribunal has the power to make other changes to an arbitral award which are necessitated by or consequential on—

(a) the correction of any error in the award; or

(b) the interpretation of any point or part of the award,

under article 33 of the UNCITRAL Model Law, given effect to by subsection (1).

(3) The arbitral tribunal may review an award of costs within 30 days of the date of the award if, when making the award, the tribunal was not aware of any information relating to costs (including any offer for settlement) which it should have taken into account.

(4) On a review under subsection (3), the arbitral tribunal may confirm, vary or correct the award of costs.

See also the discussion in Chapter 9, "Contents of the Award." The general principle is that an arbitral tribunal, with the issuance of a Final Award, becomes *functus officio*. There are some exceptions to this general principle. So & To, *supra* note 18, at para. [69.04] provides some details:

> This article [*Model Law* Art. 33] preserves or extends the mandate of the arbitral tribunal beyond the termination of the proceedings . . . for the limited purposes of (i) acting upon requests by the parties for correction or interpretation of awards or the making of additional awards, and (ii) acting on its own initiative to correct awards.
>
> Correction of an award may (a) be sought by a party, with the agreement of the [other] party . . . or . . . (b) be implemented by the tribunal on its own initiative . . . A party may also seek interpretation of a specific point or part of an award . . . the tribunal cannot take the initiative on this matter. A party may request the tribunal to make an additional award (which is a matter for the tribunal's discretion)

- to give an interpretation of a specific point or part of an award, if so agreed by the parties[90]
- to make an additional award, unless otherwise agreed by the parties[91]

The powers of the arbitral tribunal can also be derived from the parties' arbitration agreement.[92] That is, the parties expressly agree on the powers to be exercised by the arbitral tribunal by setting out those powers in the arbitration agreement. Examples of powers exercisable by the tribunal include the powers to order discovery, to appoint experts, to hold oral hearings, to take evidence, *et cetera*. The conferment of certain powers on the tribunal through an express agreement is also known by the phrase *direct conferment*.[93] Powers conferred on the arbitral tribunal by the parties' arbitration agreement, however, are subject to the limits of the applicable law. If the powers granted by the arbitration agreement exceed that which is permitted under the applicable law, such powers will be invalid, *i.e.*, the arbitral tribunal has no right to exercise such powers, even if the tribunal is permitted to do so by the applicable arbitration rules.[94]

The tribunal's powers can also derive from the applicable arbitration rules. This is also known by the term *indirect conferment* of powers where the parties have agreed in their arbitration agreement upon the applicable arbitration rules without specifying the powers to be exercised by the tribunal. For instance, if the parties have agreed to apply the ICC Rules of Arbitration to their dispute, some of the powers are automatically conferred on the ICC's International Court of Arbitration in addition to the arbitral tribunal. Article 18(1) of the ICC Rules stipulates that, subject to the parties' contrary agreement, the ICC International Court of Arbitration determines the place of arbitration.

Operation of law is another source of power for the arbitral tribunal. One example is the power to act on an *ex parte* basis in the event of a reluctant respondent.[95] Proceeding *ex parte* simply means "without notice to the party against whom the measure is directed"[96] in the event of a defaulting party.

. . . the tribunal cannot take the initiative on this matter. . . .

[90] This ability is found in § 69(1) of the *Arbitration Ordinance*, incorporating *Model Law* Art. 33(1)(b), *supra* note 5.

[91] *Id.* at § 69(1), incorporating *Model Law* Art. 33(3).

[92] Redfern & Hunter, *supra* note 2, at para. 1.58 states:

> An arbitration agreement does not merely serve to establish the obligation to arbitrate, but is also a basic source of the powers of the arbitral tribunal. In principle, and within the limits of public policy, an arbitral tribunal may exercise such powers as the parties are entitled to confer and do confer upon it, whether expressly or by implication, together with any additional or supplementary powers that may be conferred by the law governing the arbitration. Parties to an arbitration are masters of the arbitral process to an extent impossible in proceedings in a court of law. Thus, for example . . . the parties may determine the number of arbitrators on the arbitral tribunal, how this tribunal is to be appointed, in what country it should sit, what powers it should possess, and what procedure it should follow. (footnote omitted)

[93] *Id.* at para. 5.09.

[94] *Id.* at para. 5.08.

[95] *See* § 53 of the *Arbitration Ordinance*, incorporating *Model Law* Art. 25, *supra* note 5.

[96] Redfern & Hunter, *supra* note 2, at para. 7.21.

As the above discussion demonstrates, the powers of the Court of First Instance to support arbitration are minimal. The court should only so act where all interim relief sought by a party cannot be given within a single order, *e.g.*, where third parties are involved, no tribunal is yet in existence, or the powers conferred on the tribunal are inadequate.[97]

Generally, an arbitral tribunal may exercise the following powers in relation to a default by a party:

- power to act *ex parte* where a party refuses to obey an order or attend a hearing[98]
- power to draw adverse inferences from non-compliance[99]
- to determine the costs and to impose penalties[100]
- power of the Court of First Instance to enforce an arbitral tribunal's orders and directions[101]

For specific defaults by a party, such as the following, an arbitral tribunal may exercise its powers as provided in the *Arbitration Ordinance*:

- non-compliance with an order to give security for costs[102]
- failure by a party to prosecute its claim or counterclaim[103]
- failure by a party to submit a statement of claim[104]
- failure by a party to submit a statement of defence[105]

Order 70, rule 2(1) of the High Court Rules (Cap. 4A) translates "*ex parte*" as 單方面提出.

97 *See* § 3(2)(b) of the *Arbitration Ordinance*, *supra* note 5, for the general principle concerning court involvement in arbitrations. *See also* the case of *Leviathan Shipping Co Ltd v Sky Sailing Overseas Co Ltd* [1998] 4 HKC 347 with the court stating the following principle: the court's jurisdiction to intervene in an arbitration should be used sparingly and only where a special reason is existed, such as where the arbitral tribunal does not have the power to grant all the interim relief sought in a single application.

98 § 56(4) of the *Arbitration Ordinance*, *supra* note 5.

99 This refers to the right of the arbitral tribunal under *Model Law* Art. 25(b) which will be further discussed later. Although the respondent's failure to submit the defence will not amount to an admission of liability, this does not prevent the tribunal from forming adverse inferences from that party's failure to participate or to observe an order of the tribunal. Choong & Weeramantry, *supra* note 9, at para. 53.18.

100 § 74 of the *Arbitration Ordinance*, *supra* note 5.

101 *Id.* at § 61.

102 *Id.* at § 56(4).

If a party fails to comply with a tribunal's order for security for costs, the tribunal will then be empowered to stay the claim or to dismiss the claim. If the tribunal dismisses the claim, the defaulting party will be barred from reviving the claim by providing security for costs in the future. Choong & Weeramantry, *supra* note 9, at para. 56.20.

103 § 59 of the *Arbitration Ordinance*, *supra* note 5, permits the arbitral tribunal to render an award dismissing a party's claim and/or debarring the party from starting further arbitral proceedings concerning the same subject matter on the basis that this party had unreasonably delayed in making its claim. Choong & Weeramantry, *supra* note 9, at para. 59.05; So & To, *supra* note 18, at para. [59.07].

An arbitral tribunal may make this award and/or order on its own initiative pursuant to § 59(2) or upon a party's application, pursuant to § 59(3). The criteria which an arbitral tribunal should consider in deciding whether to dismiss a claim and/or grant an order to prohibit future proceedings are found in § 59(4). *See also* Choong & Weeramantry, *supra* note 9, at para. 59.12.

104 § 53 of the *Arbitration Ordinance*, incorporating *Model Law* Art. 25(a), *supra* note 5.

105 *Id.*, incorporating *Model Law* Art. 25(b).

- failure by a party to appear at a hearing or to produce documentary evidence[106]

V. Summary

In this chapter, we reviewed the three inter-related topics pertaining to the authority of an arbitral tribunal, that is, the extent of a tribunal's authority or mandate, an arbitrator's obligations or duties as an arbitral tribunal and the power which a tribunal may exercise. Thus, a tribunal's jurisdiction is the extent of its authority as provided in the arbitration agreement or subsequent agreement of the parties. A tribunal's duties may be found in the law of the seat of the arbitration and/or in the applicable institution's rules. The duties set out an arbitrator's obligations. Within the limitations of jurisdiction and duties, the powers of a tribunal may be found—what a tribunal can do in an arbitration.

---

106 *Id.*, incorporating *Model Law* Art. 25(c).

6

Preliminary Meeting and Interlocutories

I. Introduction

With the composition of the arbitral tribunal completed, the next stage of the arbitration process falls between the appointment of the arbitral tribunal and the start of the hearings when the tribunal will hear the parties' presentation of their respective cases.

We begin with a discussion of some of the items which need to be considered at this stage of the arbitration process. In the appendix to this chapter, we present a list of these items, some of which are further discussed in the appendix. Other items are reviewed in greater detail elsewhere in this book.

II. Arbitral Tribunal

Once a dispute arises and a party seeks to commence an administered arbitration, the arbitral institution usually requires a deposit to cover all or part of the costs that will arise in the arbitral proceedings. The total cost is also referred to by the term *costs of the reference*.[1] The costs of the reference include the institution's administration fee, if any; the professional fees of the arbitral tribunal along with the tribunal's expenses for travel and accommodation; and, other expenses that the tribunal may incur in administering the arbitral proceedings. The institution or the arbitral tribunal will make payments from the deposit for administrative costs and other arbitral costs.

Another preliminary matter which overlaps with the appointment of the arbitral tribunal concerns the language to be used for the dispute resolution process. This issue should have been agreed by the time the parties concluded the arbitration agreement, as the language to be used for the arbitration might affect the selection of the arbitral tribunal members. The language might also affect whether translators or interpreters are required. If so, either the parties or the tribunal will need to make

[1] This applies in the instances where the dispute proceeds by way of an institutional arbitration which is also known as an administered arbitration. If the dispute proceeds by way of an *ad hoc* arbitration, it is for the tribunal to require a deposit.

arrangements as early as practicable. If the parties cannot agree on the language of the arbitral proceedings, the tribunal will make a decision as a preliminary matter.

Another matter to be considered by the parties and the tribunal was first raised in Chapter 1, that is, common-law versus civil-law traditions possibly affecting the manner in which an arbitration is conducted. As opined by one source:

> Under the normal [common-law] adversarial system, applicable in Hong Kong, parties are responsible for gathering and presenting the relevant evidence and arguments in support of their respective positions, whilst the judge acts as an umpire, making a decision based on the evidence and arguments tendered by the parties. By way of contrast, under the [civil-law] inquisitorial procedure, the judge may undertake an independent enquiry into the facts by, for example, gathering evidence, examining witnesses, appointing expert witnesses, relying on its own expertise.
>
> In arbitrations, this distinction is blurred. This appears to be the result of arbitration being an internationally adopted method of dispute resolution which takes the best of both systems in order to devise a universally accepted practice. . . . Recognising this, the Arbitration Ordinance (Cap. 609) allows the arbitral tribunal in Hong Kong, who has to conduct an arbitration under the adversarial system, to also act inquisitorially. Having said that, it is rare for an arbitration in Hong Kong to adopt a procedure which is purely or even largely inquisitorial.
>
> The two systems overlap to the extent that no arbitral tribunal can raise issues or advance argument for a party. In other words, the rules of natural justice have to be complied with, and the principle that arbitral tribunals cannot "enter into the arena" remains applicable under both the adversarial and inquisitorial systems.[2]

III. Preliminary Meeting

The intended purpose of a preliminary meeting or a series of preliminary meetings is administrative, that is to organise the upcoming arbitration's procedures and proceedings. This is a type of case management and is also referred to by the term *procedural meeting*.[3] Usually, only one representative from each party will attend. A

---

[2] ARBITRATION IN HONG KONG: A PRACTICAL GUIDE paras. 15.001–15.003 (THE HON CHIEF JUSTICE GEOFFREY MA AND DENIS BROCK, eds., 4th ed. 2017) [hereinafter MA & BROCK]. *See also id.* at paras. 15.105–15.108.

[3] One authority explains further:

> Where rules are not adopted for an arbitration [*e.g.*, an *ad hoc* arbitration], procedural matters have to be laid down by the tribunal. This can be achieved by agreement between the parties, failing which, the tribunal will decide.
>
> The main purpose of a procedural meeting is for the arbitral tribunal to lay down procedures and set a time frame for complying with the same. This is the first meeting between the arbitrator and the parties and the representatives. Parties should be encouraged to state the directions they seek, with reasons for their contentions in advance of the meeting. It is advisable to present a general introduction to the issues and the case at that meeting, as that will help the tribunal in deciding what procedures or time frame should be adopted. The parties must however be assured that such introduction will not bind them.
>
> In international arbitrations involving parties from different jurisdictions, procedural meetings may not always be necessary. Where they are, meetings in persons are not necessary, and these can be

preliminary meeting is usually necessary in arbitral proceedings where a hearing will take place, whereas such meetings may not be necessary in arbitrations being determined on a documents-only basis.[4]

Although each arbitration is unique with its own distinct factual matrix, nonetheless, it is common practice in Hong Kong arbitrations to separate the procedural matters from the substantive disputes. By doing so and by addressing the procedural before the substantive permits the former to be decided in a timeously manner and allows an orderly progress of the procedures without adversely impacting the main hearing.[5]

Decisions of an arbitral tribunal on procedural matters cannot be challenged and are not subject to court review.[6] The orders or directions of an arbitral tribunal may be enforced as if they were court orders. Section 61 of the *Arbitration Ordinance* (Cap. 609) [hereinafter "*Arbitration Ordinance*"] provides:

> 61. Enforcement of orders and directions of arbitral tribunal
>
> (1) An order or direction made, whether in or outside Hong Kong, in relation to arbitral proceedings by an arbitral tribunal is enforceable in the same manner as an order or direction of the Court that has the same effect, but only with the leave of the Court.
>
> (2) Leave to enforce an order or direction made outside Hong Kong is not to be granted, unless the party seeking to enforce it can demonstrate that it belongs to a type or description of order or direction that may be made in Hong Kong in relation to arbitral proceedings by an arbitral tribunal.
>
> (3) If leave is granted under subsection (1), the Court may enter judgment in terms of the order or direction.

> conducted by telephone or video conference.
>
> Where issues are straightforward and simple and the issues in dispute are relatively few, the arbitral tribunal can actually lay down procedures right up to the main hearing at the first procedural meeting. For complex arbitrations, two or more procedural meetings might be necessary so that as the reference progresses, the procedures that have been laid down can be reviewed and if necessary amended.

Id. at paras. 15.017–15.020.

For further discussion of this topic, *see* REDFERN AND HUNTER ON INTERNATIONAL ARBITRATION paras. 6.4–6.42 (NIGEL BLACKABY *et al.*, eds., 6th ed. 2015) [hereinafter REDFERN & HUNTER].

4 MICHAEL J. MOSER AND TERESA Y.W. CHENG, HONG KONG ARBITRATION: A USER'S GUIDE para. 5-060 (3rd ed. 2014) [hereinafter MOSER & CHENG].

5 MA & BROCK, supra note 2, at para. 15.005.

As noted in *id.* at para. 15.004 note 4:

> There are advantages to avoiding the clear separation of the procedural and substantive matters. This is particularly so where the issues are narrow or the amount in dispute is relatively small. Where substantive matters are attended to straightaway, when an oral hearing is held, unnecessary interlocutory proceedings tend to be avoided. The tribunal is more appraised of the issues and merits of the case and thereby able to discourage unnecessary and time or cost wasting interlocutory skirmishes.

6 Decisions or rulings of a tribunal on procedural matters:

> are solely for the decision and/or discretion of the arbitral tribunal. It also limits court intervention whilst retaining the court's supervisory jurisdiction, exercisable only when the conduct complained of is "sufficiently serious or egregious so that once [*sic*] can say a party, [*sic*] has been denied due process."

Id. at para. 15.006 (citation omitted).

(4) A decision of the Court to grant or refuse to grant leave under subsection (1) is not subject to appeal.
(5) An order or direction referred to in this section includes an interim measure.

There are many possible levels of the parties' involvement in preliminary meetings. On one level is the preparation for the arbitral proceedings which can be undertaken by the parties themselves. Either before or after the appointment of the arbitral tribunal, the parties can agree on the arrangements for the arbitral proceedings.[7] This type of arrangement assumes that the tribunal will agree with the parties' arrangements under the concept of party autonomy.

A more common level of parties' involvement in preliminary meetings is the parties acting in consultation with the arbitral tribunal. The usual practice is for the parties and the tribunal to consult about the various procedural issues, the timetable for the arbitral proceedings, and the powers which should be vested in the arbitral tribunal under the *Arbitration Ordinance* where these powers are subject to the contrary agreement of the parties.[8] By conferring with the parties, the tribunal provides the parties an opportunity to present their views. This is to ensure fairness and transparency in the proceedings. This also provides the best possibility of establishing a procedure that suits the parties' needs. Thus, the tribunal can consider the parties' input concerning the management of the proceedings, such as its structure and deadlines. If the arbitral tribunal cannot achieve a consensus, the tribunal will decide and will issue a procedural order informing the parties of its decision.[9] This procedural order is commonly referred to as an *Order for Directions* setting out the timetable of events up to the making of the arbitral tribunal's decision on the merits of the case which is known as an *award*.[10]

---

[7] The preliminary meeting usually takes place after the tribunal has been appointed and before the parties begin to exchange statements setting out the case against each other. *Id.*

[8] *Id.*

[9] *See, e.g.,* UNCITRAL's *Notes on Organizing Arbitral Proceedings* (2016) [hereinafter Notes]; UNCITRAL's Arbitration Rules Art. 17 (2013) [hereinafter Arbitration Rules].

The Notes may be found at this website: http://www.uncitral.org/pdf/english/texts/arbitration/arb-notes/arb-notes-2016-e.pdf (last visited 5 Aug. 2017).

The Arbitration Rules may be found at this website: http://www.uncitral.org/uncitral/en/uncitral_texts/arbitration/2010Arbitration_rules.html (last visited 5 Aug. 2017).

[10] Moser & Cheng, *supra* note 4, at para. 5-060; Notes, *supra* note 9, at paras. 56–64 and paras. 114–136. *See generally* Arbitration Rules, *supra* note 9, at Art. 17.

As one source explained:

> The decisions and directions made by the arbitral tribunal in these procedural meetings must be recorded in writing. It does not matter whether they are in a letter or in a formal document like an Order for Directions. The only important thing is that they must be clear so that the parties know what to follow and more importantly, in light of s.61 of the Arbitration Ordinance (Cap. 609), the court can enforce it if necessary. The directions should set out the acts to be carried out and the time frame by which they should be completed. Where a certain consequence is to follow if such direction is not complied with, this condition should also be carefully and clearly spelt out to enable compliance and enforcement.
>
> It is not necessary to give any reasons for the directions or orders. However, where appropriate, and so the parties know, the arbitral tribunal should indicate very briefly why it has come to the views

A third level of parties' involvement may be where the parties permit the tribunal solely to handle the administrative matters; however, in this situation the parties will not have the ability to adopt or to confer with the arbitral tribunal on the adoption of a procedure which would meet their needs and preferences. As mentioned above, it is common practice for a tribunal to hold a meeting to consult with the parties and to obtain a consensus.[11]

---

it did. Such reasons are particularly important where applications are made with resulting serious implications, eg security for costs or security for the amount in dispute.

MA & BROCK, *supra* note 2, at paras. 15.061–15.062.

[11] Notes, *supra* note 9, at paras 9-14 provides:

(a) General principle of consultation between the parties and the arbitral tribunal

9. It is usual for the arbitral tribunal to involve the parties in making decisions on the organization of the arbitral proceedings and, where possible, to seek their agreement. Such consultations are intrinsic to the consensual nature of arbitration and are normally undertaken with respect to most organizational decisions addressed in the Notes. . . .

10. . . . it is usual for the parties to consult the arbitral tribunal whenever they agree between themselves on any issue that might affect the organization of the arbitral proceedings. When the [parties'] agreement . . . affects the [tribunal's] planning, the parties would usually also seek the agreement of the arbitral tribunal. . . . if the parties agree after the arbitral tribunal has been constituted that an arbitral institution will administer the arbitration, the parties would usually secure the agreement of both the arbitral tribunal and that institution.

(b) Procedural meetings

(i) First procedural meeting

11. It is advisable for the arbitral tribunal to give the parties a timely indication as to the organization of the arbitral proceedings and the manner in which it intends to proceed. In particular, in international arbitrations, parties may be accustomed to differing styles of arbitral proceedings and, without such guidance, they may find certain aspects of the arbitral proceedings unpredictable and difficult to prepare for.

12. . . . the arbitral tribunal may consider holding, at the outset of the arbitral proceedings, a meeting or case management conference at which it determines the organization of the arbitral proceedings and a procedural timetable.

13. A number of issues . . . would usually be addressed at the first procedural meeting, and thus create . . . a common understanding of the procedure among the parties and the arbitral tribunal. If a procedural timetable is established, it may serve . . . to indicate time limits for the communication of written statements, witness statements, expert reports and documentary evidence, so that the parties may plan early in the arbitral proceedings. A procedural timetable may include provisional dates for hearings. In preparing the procedural timetable, the parties and the arbitral tribunal may also wish to consider whether any statutory and/or mandatory time limits on the duration of the arbitral proceedings are provided for in the applicable arbitration law or arbitration rules.

(ii) Subsequent procedural meetings

14. The arbitral tribunal usually holds additional procedural meetings (including what are sometimes referred to as "preparatory conferences" or "pre-hearing conferences") at subsequent stages of the . . . proceedings. Procedural meetings . . . set the stage for the . . . proceedings and aim at ensuring their efficiency. Procedural meetings may be used . . . for the arbitral tribunal to reassess whether further submissions are required or further evidence ought to be presented as well as to discuss matters relating to the organization of a hearing. The procedural timetable can be updated accordingly as the arbitral proceedings progress.

See generally Arbitration Rules, *supra* note 9, at Art. 17.

IV. Tribunal Secretary

Recall that in an *ad hoc* proceeding there is no arbitral institution involved in the arbitration process. The arbitral tribunal and the parties are responsible for the administration or management of the arbitration. In these circumstances, a tribunal may consider the engagement of a *tribunal secretary* to assist with the administration of the arbitration process.[12] Like the arbitral tribunal itself, a tribunal secretary is to be impartial and independent throughout the arbitral proceedings. The responsibility is upon the arbitral tribunal to ensure that its tribunal secretary is and remains impartial and independent. Some tribunals fulfil this requirement by having the tribunal secretary sign a declaration of impartiality and independence.[13]

A tribunal secretary's administrative services may overlap with those of an arbitral institution's services. These services include: booking hearing rooms, arranging translators/interpreters, transcription services, and, booking accommodations and flights for the arbitrators. Other duties more specific to a tribunal secretary may include research, arbitration-related financial transactions, taking informal minutes and, in some cases, performing more substantive functions such as creating first drafts of orders or awards, preparing summaries of facts or the procedural history of the arbitral proceedings, and preparing summaries of case law or published commentaries on legal issues.[14] An arbitral tribunal must be cautious in assigning tasks to its tribunal secretary so as to avoid the delegation of any the arbitral tribunal's legal duties. Doing so could result in a challenge to the arbitral tribunal's award on the ground that the arbitration procedure was not in accordance with the parties' agreement: the tribunal did not perform its mandated decision-making functions.[15]

---

[12] *See* Notes, *supra* note 9, at para. 35 the text of which is set out *infra* note 14.

[13] *Id.* at para. 37 states in full:

> Secretaries are expected to be and remain impartial and independent during the arbitral proceedings. It is the arbitral tribunal's responsibility to ensure this. Some arbitral tribunals do this by requesting the secretary to sign a declaration of independence and impartiality.

[14] *Id.* at para. 35 and para. 36 provide:

> 35. Administrative support might be obtained by engaging a secretary to carry out tasks under the direction of the arbitral tribunal. Such services may also be rendered by a registrar, clerk or administrator. Some arbitral institutions routinely assign secretaries to cases administered by them. Where this is not the case, some arbitrators frequently engage secretaries, particularly in large or complex cases, whereas other arbitrators do not.
>
> 36. Functions and tasks performed by secretaries are broad in range. Secretaries may provide purely organizational support, such as making reservations for hearing and meeting rooms and providing or coordinating administrative services. Some arbitral tribunals wish to have secretaries carry out more substantive functions including legal research and other professional assistance, such as preparing a summary of the facts or the procedural history of the arbitral proceedings, collecting or summarizing case law or published commentaries on legal issues defined by the arbitral tribunal, and preparing draft procedural decisions. However, it is recognized that secretaries are not involved and do not participate in the decision-making of the arbitral tribunal, except in certain rare, specialized types of arbitration (for example, where the specific arbitration rules provide that secretaries are expected to provide legal advice in relation to the decision of the arbitral tribunal if and when the arbitral tribunal is composed only of non-lawyer, subject matter specialists).

[15] In two cases, the losing party challenged the validity of the arbitral award on the basis that the tribunal secretary prepared a substantial portion of the award. *See, e.g.*, the arbitration between Naftogaz of the Ukraine against

If a tribunal secretary is to be appointed, the arbitral tribunal should disclose this intention to the parties, identify the person whom the arbitral tribunal wishes to appoint as the tribunal secretary, the type and the scope of tasks to be performed by the tribunal secretary, and the amount and sources of the proposed remuneration, if any.[16]

Gazprom of Russia conducted under the auspices of the Stockholm Chamber of Commerce, and, OAO Yukos Oil Company's claims against the Russian Federation conducted under the auspices of the Permanent Court of Arbitration.

[16] Notes, *supra* note 9, at paragraph 38 explains:

> If the arbitral tribunal wishes to appoint a secretary, it would normally disclose this fact to the parties, along with the identity of the proposed secretary, the nature of the tasks to be performed by the secretary, and the amount and source of any proposed remuneration. The parties may wish to agree on the role and practices to be adopted in respect of the secretaries, as well as on the financial conditions applicable to their services. Institutional guidelines on secretaries may provide useful information to the parties.

An example of institutional guidelines on the use of a tribunal secretary is the *Notes for Arbitrators* published by the London Court of International Arbitration [hereinafter LCIA] in October 2017 and available at: http://www.lcia.org//adr-services/lcia-notes-for-arbitrators.aspx (last visited 13 Oct. 2017).

The LCIA's website summarized the changes concerning tribunal secretaries:

> [T]he LCIA has adopted changes to its Notes for Arbitrators. These changes maintain the flexibility of LCIA arbitration, clarify the tribunal secretary role, and strengthen the existing elements of the LCIA's approach to tribunal secretaries.
>
> Under the LCIA system, tribunal secretaries are (like arbitrators) required to complete a Statement of Independence and Consent to Appointment, to ensure that the proposed tribunal secretary has no relevant conflicts. The new Notes for Arbitrators now make explicit the LCIA's practice of providing the Statement of Independence to the parties prior to appointment, giving the parties an opportunity to comment on (and if necessary, veto) the proposed individual. The new Notes for Arbitrators also make it explicit that a tribunal secretary's disclosure obligation is ongoing.
>
> The LCIA suggests hourly rate of £50 to £150 per hour for tribunal secretaries if remuneration is appropriate. The new Notes for Arbitrators explicitly requires tribunals to propose a fee rate to the parties, to which the parties must expressly consent.
>
> While previously the parties' written agreement was required for a tribunal secretary to be appointed, arbitrators are now also entitled to set a reasonable time limit for providing approval, at the expiry of which parties are deemed to have approved. This approach retains the primacy of the parties, while ensuring that parties are not able to obstruct the efficient conduct of proceedings through silence.
>
> One of the most contentious issues regarding tribunal secretaries regards the tasks a tribunal secretary should be entitled to carry out. Previously, the LCIA has dealt with this by providing a list of activities that the tribunal secretary should limit themselves to. In light of the broad spectrum of opinions on this matter, the Notes for Arbitrators still provide a list of tribunal secretary tasks, but the list is now a list of tasks that tribunals "may wish to propose". The list is a starting point for the discussion between tribunals and parties – parties must expressly consent to the tasks proposed, ensuring that all arbitrators and parties are comfortable with the tribunal secretary's role at the outset.

http://www.lcia.org/News/lcia-implements-changes-to-tribunal-secretary-processes.aspx (last visited 13 Oct. 2017).

The LCIA *Notes for Arbitrators* emphasized:

> 68. Subject to any applicable law and to paragraphs 69 to 82 below, an Arbitral Tribunal may obtain assistance from a tribunal secretary in relation to an arbitration. However, *in no circumstances may an Arbitral Tribunal delegate its fundamental decision-making function*. (emphasis added)
> 69. *Assistance provided by a tribunal secretary does not relieve any member of an Arbitral Tribunal from their personal responsibility* to ensure that all tasks are performed to the standard required by the LCIA Rules and these notes. All tasks carried out by a tribunal secretary are carried out on behalf of the Arbitral Tribunal, and must be carried out under the supervision of the Arbitral Tribunal. (emphasis added)
> 70. An Arbitral Tribunal must ensure that a tribunal secretary:

Although the topic of *tribunal secretary* has been discussed within the framework of *ad hoc* arbitration, it should be noted that a tribunal secretary may also be utilized in administered arbitrations.

V. Default Proceedings

A party, usually the defending party, might intentionally be absent in an attempt to delay or to thwart the arbitration process. An attempt to delay or to thwart can happen at the stage of appointing the arbitral tribunal. Another attempt to delay or to thwart can happen at the preliminaries stage. A final attempt to delay or to thwart the dispute resolution process might take place at the main arbitral proceedings, *i.e.*, at the hearings stage. What are the consequences if a party defaults, *i.e.*, does not respond to pleadings or does not attend a hearing? These consequences are discussed in the following paragraphs.

(a) only carries out tasks that have been agreed by the parties;
(b) does not provide assistance until approved by the parties in accordance with paragraph 74 below;
(c) does not carry out any tasks that the parties have contracted with the LCIA to provide under the LCIA Rules; and

. . .

If the claimant is the party in default, the arbitral tribunal will dismiss the entire claim.[17] If a respondent is in default, the proceedings continue.[18] If any party fails to appear at a hearing or to produce documentary evidence, the arbitral tribunal may continue with the proceedings and make an award based on the evidence presented and available to the tribunal.[19] Some arbitration rules permit the arbitral tribunal to conduct default proceedings in the absence of one party, that is, on an *ex parte* basis.[20]

---

[17] § 53(1) of the *Arbitration Ordinance* (Cap. 609) [hereinafter *Arbitration Ordinance*], incorporating *Model Law* Art. 25(a). Should a tribunal end the proceedings under *Model Law* Art. 25(a), this does not prevent the claimant from starting arbitral proceedings anew in respect of the same dispute. § 59(2) of the *Arbitration Ordinance* permits the arbitral tribunal to dismiss the claim and to make an order prohibiting the claimant (or the respondent if a counterclaim was made) from bringing further arbitral proceedings in respect of the same dispute if the claimant (or the respondent as the case may be) has unreasonably delayed in pursuing the claim. John Choong and Romesh Weeramantry, The Hong Kong Arbitration Ordinance: Commentary and Annotations para. 53.14 (2nd ed. 2015) [hereinafter Choong & Weeramantry].
The full text of § 53 of the Ordinance follows:

> 53. Article 25 of UNCITRAL Model Law (Default of a party)
> (1) Article 25 of the UNCITRAL Model Law, the text of which is set out below, has effect—
> "*Article 25. Default of a party*
> Unless otherwise agreed by the parties, if, without showing sufficient cause,
> (a) the claimant fails to communicate his statement of claim in accordance with article 23(1), the arbitral tribunal shall terminate the proceedings;
> (b) the respondent fails to communicate his statement of defence in accordance with article 23(1), the arbitral tribunal shall continue the proceedings without treating such failure in itself as an admission of the claimant's allegations;
> (c) any party fails to appear at a hearing or to produce documentary evidence, the arbitral tribunal may continue the proceedings and make the award on the evidence before it."
> (2) Unless otherwise agreed by the parties, subsections (3) and (4) apply except in relation to an application for security for costs.
> (3) If, without showing sufficient cause, a party fails to comply with any order or direction of the arbitral tribunal, the tribunal may make a peremptory order to the same effect, prescribing the time for compliance with it that the arbitral tribunal considers appropriate.
> (4) If a party fails to comply with a peremptory order, then without affecting section 61, the arbitral tribunal may—
> (a) direct that the party is not entitled to rely on any allegation or material which was the subject matter of the peremptory order;
> (b) draw any adverse inferences that the circumstances may justify from the non-compliance;
> (c) make an award on the basis of any materials which have been properly provided to the arbitral tribunal; or
> (d) make any order that the arbitral tribunal thinks fit as to the payment of the costs of the arbitration incurred in consequence of the non-compliance.

Butterworths Hong Kong Arbitration Law Handbook para. [53.02] (Damon YC So, Christopher To *et al.*, eds., 2nd ed. 2018) [hereinafter So & To].

[18] § 53(1) of the *Arbitration Ordinance*, incorporating *Model Law* Art. 25(b), *supra* note 17.
Model Law Art. 25(b) suggests that the failure to submit a defence will not be considered an admission of liability. The arbitration proceedings continue and the claimant still needs to prove its case which might still require an oral hearing. Additionally, the tribunal must fully consider the merits of the case and examine the participating party's submissions before making an award. Choong & Weeramantry, *supra* note 17, at para. 53.16.

[19] § 53(1) of the *Arbitration Ordinance*, incorporating *Model Law* Art. 25(c), *supra* note 17.
Pursuant to *Model Law* Art. 25(c), a tribunal "may" continue the arbitration proceedings and render an award. As such, the tribunal may choose to postpone the hearing or give another opportunity to the party which failed to produce documentary evidence. Choong & Weeramantry, *supra* note 17, at para. 53.19.

[20] *See, e.g.*, Arbitration Rules, *supra* note 9, Art. 30:

To avoid the arbitration being delayed or frustrated by a recalcitrant respondent at the preliminaries stage or at the hearings stage, an arbitral tribunal can proceed without the absent party. The tribunal will continue with the arbitration process; the tribunal cannot make a decision or award simply on the basis that the responding party is absent and thus has defaulted. The claimant nevertheless must present its evidence and prove its claim to the tribunal. The tribunal is to ensure that the absent party has been duly notified of the arbitral proceedings and all documents have been transmitted to the defaulting party. This procedure by a tribunal ensures that the absent party is not prejudiced by its absence.

VI. Interim Measures of Protection and Security for Costs

Sometimes at a preliminary meeting or frequently before the main hearing on the merits of the dispute, an arbitral tribunal will need to make decisions concerning the following requests. One such request involves interlocutory applications. These are termed *interlocutory* because the resulting proceedings are a step or a series of steps taken after the initial stage of the arbitration process but before the main hearing.[21] Therefore, these steps are taken during the arbitration process but are incidental or supplementary to the arbitration's main dispute.

---

1. If, within the period of time fixed by these Rules or the arbitral tribunal, without showing sufficient cause:
    (a) The claimant has failed to communicate its statement of claim, the arbitral tribunal shall issue an order for the termination of the arbitral proceedings, unless there are remaining matters that may need to be decided and the arbitral tribunal considers it appropriate to do so;
    (b) The respondent has failed to communicate its response to the notice of arbitration or its statement of defence, the arbitral tribunal shall order that the proceedings continue, without treating such failure in itself as an admission of the claimant's allegations; the provisions of this subparagraph also apply to a claimant's failure to submit a defence to a counterclaim or to a claim for the purpose of a set-off.
2. If a party, duly notified under these Rules, fails to appear at a hearing, without showing sufficient cause for such failure, the arbitral tribunal may proceed with the arbitration.

In similar language are the provisions of the Hong Kong International Arbitration Centre's Administered Arbitration Rules (2018), Art. 26 which state in full:

26.1 If, within the time limit set by the arbitral tribunal, the Claimant has failed to communicate its written statement without showing sufficient cause for such failure, the arbitral tribunal may terminate the arbitration unless another party has brought a claim and wishes the arbitration to continue, in which case the tribunal may proceed with the arbitration in respect of the other party's claim.

26.2 If, within the time limit set by the arbitral tribunal, the Respondent has failed to communicate its written statement without showing sufficient cause for such failure, the arbitral tribunal may proceed with the arbitration.

26.3 If one of the parties, duly notified under these Rules, fails to present its case in accordance with these Rules including as directed by the arbitral tribunal, without showing sufficient cause for such failure, the arbitral tribunal may proceed with the arbitration and make an award on the basis of the evidence before it.

[21] As explained by one source:

During the course of the proceedings a party may need to restrain another party from disposing of evidence or prevent that party siphoning off assets from a particular country. Such orders are commonly referred to as interim measures of protection, or interim and conservatory measures, or

Interlocutory proceedings would include all actions taken to assist either party with its case; to protect or otherwise address the subject matter of the arbitration; and, to carry out the judgement or award, including orders as to costs and their taxation. Some examples of matters to be handled in interlocutory applications:

- adjournments
- contested amendment of pleadings
- extension of time
- sanctions for a party's default
- security for costs
- security for the amount claimed[22]
- variation of previous arbitral tribunal orders

Interim measures are a type of interlocutory application. Interim measures are temporary orders to prevent or to minimise the disadvantage which might be caused to a party pending the final resolution of the dispute by the tribunal's issuance of an arbitral award and pending the enforcement of that arbitral award.[23] An "interim measure is designed to maintain or restore the status quo until the dispute can be decided by the tribunal."[24] In Hong Kong's *Arbitration Ordinance*:

> Section 35(1)/Article 17 provides a definition of "interim measure" and also provides guidance to the arbitral tribunal as to the interim measures which it may grant. Section 35(2) stipulates that an interim measure includes an injunction, but excludes an order under section 56 of the Arbitration Ordinance . . . [which] deals with the power of the tribunal to make procedural orders such as discovery or preservation of evidence. Section 35(3) empowers a tribunal to make an award to the same effect as the interim measure granted.[25]

Arbitral tribunals sitting outside Hong Kong are authorized under most arbitration laws and arbitral institution rules to order interim measures of protection.[26]

> provisional relief. . . .
>
> However, it is not always the case that a country will permit an arbitral tribunal to order interim measures of protection. In some countries it is considered the preserve of the courts to make these orders. For example, under Italian and Greek law the arbitral tribunal is prohibited . . . from making orders for the interim protection of property. Similarly, under the Thai Arbitration Act 2002 and the Thai Arbitration Institute Rules the power to order interim measures of protection vests exclusively with the national courts.

ANDREW TWEEDDALE & KEREN TWEEDDALE, ARBITRATION OF COMMERCIAL DISPUTES—INTERNATIONAL AND ENGLISH LAW AND PRACTICE paras. 9.37 (2007) [hereinafter TWEEDDALE & TWEEDDALE].

[22] For a more in-depth review of interlocutory applications, *see, e.g.*, MA & BROCK, *supra* note 2, at Chapt. 16.

[23] CHOONG & WEERAMANTRY, *supra* note 17, at para. 35.04.

For further information on interim measures of protection, *see, e.g.*, MA & BROCK, *supra* note 2, at paras. 16.150–16.211; MOSER & CHENG, *supra* note 4, at paras. 5-111–5-114; TWEEDDALE & TWEEDDALE, *supra* note 21, at paras. 9.42–9.52.

[24] CHOONG & WEERAMANTRY, *supra* note 17, at para. 35.11.

[25] *Id.* at para. 35.01.

[26] § 56 of the *Arbitration Ordinance*, *supra* note 17. § 2 of this Ordinance translates "interim measure" as 臨時措施.

BLACK'S LAW DICTIONARY 938 (10th ed. 2014) [hereinafter BLACK'S] defines "interim measures of protection" as

For arbitral tribunals sitting in Hong Kong, as mentioned above, the *Model Law* which was given effect by the *Arbitration Ordinance* contains provisions detailing the authority of tribunals and of courts to make interim orders during the arbitration process.[27] The Arbitration Rules also allow an arbitrator to order and grant various interim measures in the dispute.[28] Examples of interim measures include

---

"an international tribunal's order to prevent a litigant from prejudicing the final outcome of a lawsuit by arbitrary action before a judgement has been reached."

In *Chen Hongqing v Mi Jingtian* [2017] HKCFI 1148, the Hong Kong court granted the request for the appointment of a receiver as an interim measure. This was done to preserve the *status quo*, particularly preventing the transfer of the disputed shares, in support of a CEITAC arbitration being conducted in mainland China. The Hong Kong court acted under the authority granted to it by § 45 of the *Arbitration Ordinance*, *supra*, note 17.

[27] § 35 of the *Arbitration Ordinance*, incorporating *Model Law* Art. 17, *supra* note 17, provides:

(1) Article 17 of the UNCITRAL Model Law, the text of which is set out below, has effect—

"*Article 17. Power of arbitral tribunal to order interim measures*

(1) Unless otherwise agreed by the parties, the arbitral tribunal may, at the request of a party, grant interim measures.

(2) An interim measure is any temporary measure, whether in the form of an award or in another form, by which, at any time prior to the issuance of the award by which the dispute is finally decided, the arbitral tribunal orders a party to:

(a) Maintain or restore the status quo pending determination of the dispute;

(b) Take action that would prevent, or refrain from taking action that is likely to cause, current or imminent harm or prejudice to the arbitral process itself;

(c) Provide a means of preserving assets out of which a subsequent award may be satisfied; or

(d) Preserve evidence that may be relevant and material to the resolution of the dispute."

(2) An interim measure referred to in article 17 of the UNCITRAL Model Law, given effect to by subsection (1), is to be construed as including an injunction but not including an order under section 56.

(3) If an arbitral tribunal has granted an interim measure, the tribunal may, on the application of any party, make an award to the same effect as the interim measure.

Id. at § 37, incorporating *Model Law* Art. 17B provides in part:

(2) The arbitral tribunal may grant a preliminary order provided it considers that prior disclosure of the request for the interim measure to the party against whom it is directed risks frustrating the purpose of the measure.

Id. at § 39, incorporating *Model Law* Art. 17D provides:

The arbitral tribunal may modify, suspend or terminate an interim measure or a preliminary order it has granted, upon application of any party or, in exceptional circumstances and upon prior notice to the parties, on the arbitral tribunal's own initiative.

In relation to court assistance in granting an interim measure, *see, e.g., id.* at § 45 which provides in part:

(2) On the application of any party, the Court may, in relation to any arbitral proceedings which have been or are to be commenced in or outside Hong Kong, grant an interim measure.

(3) The powers conferred by this section may be exercised by the Court irrespective of whether or not similar powers may be exercised by an arbitral tribunal under section 35 in relation to the same dispute.

[28] Art. 26 of the Arbitration Rules, *supra* note 9, provides in full:

(1) The arbitral tribunal may, at the request of a party, grant interim measures.

(2) An interim measure is any temporary measure by which, at any time prior to the issuance of the award by which the dispute is finally decided, the arbitral tribunal orders a party, for example and without limitation, to:

(a) Maintain or restore the status quo pending determination of the dispute;

(b) Take action that would prevent, or refrain from taking action that is likely to cause,

(i) current or imminent harm or

(ii) prejudice to the arbitral process itself;

(c) Provide a means of preserving assets out of which a subsequent award may be satisfied; or

directing the inspection, preservation, custody, detention or sale of relevant property; directing samples to be taken from or observations to be made of the relevant property; directing experiments to be conducted on the relevant property; or, an interim injunction.[29]

A party can apply to the tribunal during the arbitral proceedings for an interim measure of protection over the subject matter in dispute.[30] In exercising the discretion to grant an interim measure, an arbitral tribunal is to decide whether the party requesting an interim measure has met the two requirements under the *Arbitration Ordinance*.[31] These two requirements are:

(d) Preserve evidence that may be relevant and material to the resolution of the dispute.

(3) The party requesting an interim measure under paragraphs 2 (a) to (c) shall satisfy the arbitral tribunal that:

(a) Harm not adequately reparable by an award of damages is likely to result if the measure is not ordered, and such harm substantially outweighs the harm that is likely to result to the party against whom the measure is directed if the measure is granted; and

(b) There is a reasonable possibility that the requesting party will succeed on the merits of the claim. The determination on this possibility shall not affect the discretion of the arbitral tribunal in making any subsequent determination.

(4) With regard to a request for an interim measure under paragraph 2 (d), the requirements in paragraphs 3 (a) and (b) shall apply only to the extent the arbitral tribunal considers appropriate.

(5) The arbitral tribunal may modify, suspend or terminate an interim measure it has granted, upon application of any party or, in exceptional circumstances and upon prior notice to the parties, on the arbitral tribunal's own initiative.

(6) The arbitral tribunal may require the party requesting an interim measure to provide appropriate security in connection with the measure.

(7) The arbitral tribunal may require any party promptly to disclose any material change in the circumstances on the basis of which the interim measure was requested or granted.

(8) The party requesting an interim measure may be liable for any costs and damages caused by the measure to any party if the arbitral tribunal later determines that, in the circumstances then prevailing, the measure should not have been granted. The arbitral tribunal may award such costs and damages at any point during the proceedings.

(9) A request for interim measures addressed by any party to a judicial authority shall not be deemed incompatible with the agreement to arbitrate, or as a waiver of that agreement.

[29] §§ 45, 56, and 60 of the *Arbitration Ordinance*, *supra* note 17.
TWEEDDALE & TWEEDDALE, *supra* note 21, at para. 9.42–9.46 explains:

> Conservatory measures are orders for the protection of goods or evidence. They can take two different forms. The first relates to such measures which are intended to prevent irreparable damage and maintain the status quo. The second relates to measures intended to preserve evidence or assets.
>
> Under certain circumstances an arbitral tribunal or court may order a party to desist acting in a way which will cause irreparable harm to the other. An order may be required to force one party to sell perishable goods or to prevent it trading illegally in competition. . . .
>
> . . .
>
> It is common to find provisions within most modern arbitration legislation or arbitration rules which deal with the preservation of evidence. Under such legislation and rules the arbitral tribunal will have an express power to order the preservation of evidence. . . . (citations omitted)

See MA & BROCK, *supra* note 2, at paras. 16.150–16.211 for further review of interim measures of protection.

[30] SO & TO, *supra* note 17, at para. [21.07].

[31] § 36 of the *Arbitration Ordinance*, incorporating *Model Law* Art. 17A, *supra* note 17, provides:

Article 17A of the UNCITRAL Model Law, the text of which is set out below, has effect—

"Article 17A. Conditions for granting interim measures

(1) The party requesting an interim measure under article 17(2)(a), (b) and (c) shall satisfy the arbitral tribunal that:

(a) Harm not adequately reparable by an award of damages is likely to result if the

- whether a harm not adequately reparable by an award of damages will be likely to result if the measure is not granted and this harm substantially outweighs the harm that is likely to result to the party against whom the measure is directed if such measure is granted
- whether the requesting party has a reasonable possibility of success on the merits of its claim[32]

The party requesting an interim measure may at the same time submit to the arbitral tribunal an *ex parte* application for a preliminary order.[33] The tribunal has the discretion to grant the order if the tribunal considers that the preliminary order is necessary to preserve the subject matter of the dispute. The two conditions required to be satisfied for granting an interim measure of protection also apply to preliminary orders.[34]

A party applying for an interim measure or a preliminary order may be required by the arbitral tribunal to post security for the costs resulting from that

---

measure is not ordered, and such harm substantially outweighs the harm that is likely to result to the party against whom the measure is directed if the measure is granted; and

(b) There is a reasonable possibility that the requesting party will succeed on the merits of the claim. The determination on this possibility shall not affect the discretion of the arbitral tribunal in making any subsequent determination.

(2) With regard to a request for an interim measure under article 17(2)(d), the requirements in paragraphs (1)(a) and (b) of this article shall apply only to the extent the arbitral tribunal considers appropriate."

32 *Id.*; Moser & Cheng, *supra* note 4, at para. 5-111.

33 § 37 of the *Arbitration Ordinance*, incorporating *Model Law* Art. 17B, *supra* note 17.
The purpose of a preliminary order is to prevent the frustration of the interim measure of protection. A preliminary order instructs the party (against whom the order is made) to preserve the status quo until further notice. This prevents that particular party from dissipating its assets or taking any other actions which would cause the interim measure to be ineffective. Choong & Weeramantry, *supra* note 17, at para. 37.09.

34 Moser & Cheng, *supra* note 4, at para. 5-114.
The procedure for preliminary orders is set out in § 38 of the *Arbitration Ordinance*, incorporating *Model Law* Art. 17C, *supra* note 17:

Article 17C of the UNCITRAL Model Law, the text of which is set out below, has effect—

"Article 17C. Specific regime for preliminary orders

(1) Immediately after the arbitral tribunal has made a determination in respect of an application for a preliminary order, the arbitral tribunal shall give notice to all parties of the request for the interim measure, the application for the preliminary order, the preliminary order, if any, and all other communications, including by indicating the content of any oral communication, between any party and the arbitral tribunal in relation thereto.

(2) At the same time, the arbitral tribunal shall give an opportunity to any party against whom a preliminary order is directed to present its case at the earliest practicable time.

(3) The arbitral tribunal shall decide promptly on any objection to the preliminary order.

(4) A preliminary order shall expire after twenty days from the date on which it was issued by the arbitral tribunal. However, the arbitral tribunal may issue an interim measure adopting or modifying the preliminary order, after the party against whom the preliminary order is directed has been given notice and an opportunity to present its case.

(5) A preliminary order shall be binding on the parties but shall not be subject to enforcement by a court. Such a preliminary order does not constitute an award."

party's application. The *Arbitration Ordinance* provides that an arbitral tribunal has the discretion to require the party requesting an interim measure to provide appropriate security in connection with the interim measure. In relation to a preliminary order, however, the Ordinance requires the party applying for a preliminary order to provide security unless the arbitral tribunal considers it unnecessary.[35]

The concept of providing security for the costs incurred also applies in relation to the overall arbitration proceeding. This is also referred to by the term *security for the claim*.[36] In this interlocutory application, the purpose of security for costs is to protect a respondent's successful defence against a losing party's claim and the losing party is unable to pay the respondent's costs.[37] A tribunal is not required to follow the procedures and rules of a court in deciding whether to make an order for security for costs against the claimant as long as the tribunal acts fairly. To obtain an order for security of costs against the losing party, the successful party must show that the losing party would be unable to pay the successful party's costs of defending the claim if the winning party were to succeed. Merely showing that the losing party might not be able to pay such costs is insufficient. Other factors, such as whether the respondent has made a timely application and whether the claimant's claim would be restricted as a result of the order of the security for costs, should also be considered by the tribunal.[38]

---

[35] § 40 of the *Arbitration Ordinance*, incorporating *Model Law* Art. 17E, *supra* note 17, states:

> Article 17E of the UNCITRAL Model Law, the text of which is set out below, has effect—
>
> "Article 17E. Provision of security
>
> (1) The arbitral tribunal may require the party requesting an interim measure to provide appropriate security in connection with the measure.
>
> (2) The arbitral tribunal shall require the party applying for a preliminary order to provide security in connection with the order unless the arbitral tribunal considers it inappropriate or unnecessary to do so."

See also So & To, *supra* note 17, at para. [40.01].

[36] §56(1)(a) of the *Arbitration Ordinance*, *supra* note 17, states in relevant part:

> (1) Unless otherwise agreed by the parties, when conducting arbitral proceedings, an arbitral tribunal may make an order—
>
> (a) requiring a claimant to give security for the costs of the arbitration;
>
> (b) directing the discovery of documents or the delivery of interrogatories;
>
> . . .

[37] *Id.* at Schedule 2, §7(5) translates "security for costs" as 就費用提供保證. § 56 of *id.* translates "security for costs" as 就仲裁費用提供保證.

Black's, *supra* note 26, at 1562, defines "security for costs" as "money, property, or a bond given to a court by a plaintiff or an appellant to secure the payment of costs if that party loses." Although this definition is provided in relation to litigation, the same concept also applies to arbitration.

[38] Moser & Cheng, *supra* note 4, at para. 5-102. As explained in more detail:

> Indisputably, s56(1)(a) of the *Arbitration Ordinance* gives an arbitrator in Hong Kong express power to order that a claimant [is] to provide security for the costs of the respondent (i.e. the respondent's costs of the reference).
>
> The rationale for security for costs is that it provides protection to the respondent who is successful in its defence of a claim in circumstances where the claimant is unable to pay the respondent's costs. The justification is that a claimant takes a risk that the respondent may not be able to meet its costs if it is successful in its claim, but the claimant can weigh that risk when it decides to commence the arbitration. By contrast, a respondent does not choose to start arbitral proceedings and is entitled to be certain that if it is successful in its defence, its costs will be met.

It is also possible to seek security for the claim. Here, the purpose is to ensure that the money in dispute is secured. In other words, any money payable to the claimant under the award is secured pending the determination of the arbitration.[39] Unlike the former *Arbitration Ordinance* (Cap. 341) which expressly permitted both the court and the arbitral tribunal to exercise concurrent powers to require security for the amount in dispute, the present *Arbitration Ordinance* does not provide for such powers. "Since similar powers exist in Hong Kong under s.60(1) of the Arbitration Ordinance and O.29 r.2 of the Rules of the High Court, it is likely that the powers may be used in the same way."[40]

VII. Discovery and Inspection of Documents

Discovery is also known as *disclosure* and is an important interlocutory matter. The adversarial procedure requires the parties to reveal all relevant documents to each other and to the tribunal. Without these documents which relate to the dispute, particularly contemporaneous documents, it would be more difficult for a party to prove its case for the tribunal to decide the dispute. Once the exchange of pleadings is finished, discovery and inspection may take place, assuming that these are agreed by the parties or ordered by the tribunal.

Discovery is a two-stage process. The first stage is eponymously termed *discovery*. This is the stage where each party lists all contemporaneous documents which are or have been in that party's possession, custody or power. One authority has defined "possession, custody or power" as follows:

> . . .
>
> To obtain an order, the respondent must show that the claimant would not be able to pay the respondent's costs of their defence if the respondent is successful. It will be insufficient for the respondent to show that the claimant might be unable to pay such costs. . . . Other factors to be considered include whether it is a *bona fide* claim, the timing of the applications and whether an order will stifle the claimant's claim.
>
> . . .
>
> In practice, it is more difficult to persuade an arbitrator that an order for security for costs is necessary in international arbitral proceedings than in court proceedings. . . . arbitration awards (including an award for costs) are more likely to be enforceable against a claimant's assets outside the place of the arbitration.
>
> . . .
>
> These comments also apply to a claimant's defence to the respondent's counterclaim.

Id. (citations omitted)

See MA & BROCK, *supra* note 2, at paras. 16.124–16.143.

[39] MA & BROCK, *supra* note 2, at paras. 16.151–16.152.

[40] *Id.* at para. 16.146. This authority also suggests an alternative method:

> Further, an arbitral tribunal could achieve security for a claim using the "procedure order *nisi*" approach. This involves an arbitrator refusing to make an order requested by a party unless the party does a particular act. For example, an arbitrator could refuse to make an award unless the respondent secured sums due in respect of disputes between the same parties under different contracts. This is an order which lies within the discretion of the arbitrators, so long as the order does not impede the progress of the arbitration, which would amount to misconduct.

Id. at para. 16.147 (citations omitted).

> The terms 'possession', 'custody' and 'power' broadly mean as follows: (i) 'possession' means physical holding coupled with a proprietary interest, (ii) 'custody' means physical holding but without actual ownership, and (iii) 'power' implies the ownership but without present physical holding, or a legal right to obtain physical possession without the need for anybody's consent thereto.[41]

The situation where all the relevant documents are disclosed is known by the term *general discovery* or *full discovery*. In the situation where a limited class or category of documents or specific documents is to be disclosed is known by the term *limited discovery* or *specific discovery*.[42]

---

[41] So & To, *supra* note 17, at para. [56.07] (citation omitted).
In *Lonrho Ltd v Shell Petroleum* [1980] 1 LR 627, 635 the court explained that:

> the expression '*power*' must, in my view, mean a presently enforceable legal right to obtain from whoever actually holds the document inspection of it without the need to obtain the consent of anyone else. Provided that the right is presently enforceable, the fact that for physical reasons it may not be possible for the person entitled to it to obtain immediate inspection would not prevent the document from being within his power . . .

A law firm explains the application of discovery in Hong Kong:

> 10. A party must disclose all documents that are or have been in his "possession, custody or power" in Hong Kong or anywhere else in the world. This means that documents must be disclosed if a party has physical possession of them (whether or not he has a right to possess them), or if he could obtain them by enforcing some right to possession. For documents to be in the power of a party, the party must have an immediate and enforceable right to them. Thus, the documents of a party's agent (such as an insurance broker) which the agent can be compelled to release must be disclosed. But documents of an associated company may not have to be disclosed and this should be checked with a lawyer before such documents are collected.
> 11. The discovery obligation extends to the disclosure of documents that used to be in a party's possession, custody or power. So, if documents have been lost or have been disposed of in the course of routine destruction of files prior to litigation, those documents must be described and an explanation given of the circumstances in which they were lost or disposed of.

Discovery in Civil Proceedings in Hong Kong, Lovells LLP 2 (2009). Available at: http://www.hoganlovells.ru/files/Publication/f0a64b8b-4869-417f-8932-f9cf973d1859/Presentation/PublicationAttachment/fe4592d9-311f-455c-8e8b-00b236d9a9ab/DiscoveryincivilproceedingsHongKong.pdf (last visited 8 Aug. 2017).
The phrase "possession, custody or power" has also been explained by an Australian law firm with reference to the case of *Norman Stewart Taylor v Santos Ltd* (1998) 71 SASR 434 as follows:

> Possession is defined as the right to possession of the document.
>
> Custody for the purpose of discovery is defined as the actual, physical or corporeal holding of a document regardless of the right of possession.
>
> Power for the purpose of discovery is defined as an enforceable right to inspect the document or obtain possession or control of the document from the person [who] ordinarily has it in fact.
>
> Documents which are in the possession or power of the agent for the party are in possession or power of the party for discovery purposes. A document in the hands of a third person is not within the power of a party if the party can only inspect the document if the third person agrees to permit inspection, or agrees to refrain from so exercising control of the document as to prevent inspection.

Discovery of Documents, Hutchinson Legal (2017) at: http://www.hutchinsonlegal.com.au/discovery-of-documents/ (last visited 8 Aug. 2017).
See also 9 Halsbury's Laws of Hong Kong, para. [90.0576] (2nd ed. 2016); Charles Hollander, Documentary Evidence in Hong Kong paras. 7-039–7-056 (2015).

[42] The following is a more comprehensive description of discovery by one authority:

> Arbitration practice has developed in such a way that the mode of disclosure is more limited than court-style discovery, under which all relevant documents have to be listed and disclosed whether they advance or destroy one's own case or that of their opponent. In arbitration, the practice commonly adopted is that documents to be relied upon by a party are appended to the pleadings/statement of case. This clearly can be unsatisfactory as a party can be selective in its production of

The second stage of the discovery process is known as *inspection*. This is the stage where each party may physically inspect, review, and make copies of documents referred to in those lists, with the exception of privileged documents. Discovery followed by inspection is the complete process although this process is commonly and simply termed *discovery*. This common practice is followed in this book.

The discovery stage may include any documents in the possession, custody or power of a party which are relevant to the dispute. The classic definition of *relevant document* is:

> a document which it is reasonable to suppose contains information which may enable a party either to advance his case or to damage that of his opponent, or which may fairly lead him to a train of enquiry having either of those consequences.[43]

> documents. Arbitral tribunals are vested with the power to order disclosure of specific documents pursuant to requests to produce. These two methods together generally result in disclosure of most if not all the truly relevant and material documents.
>
> This limited mode of discovery accords with international arbitration practice generally. Disclosure starts with documents substantiating the claim or defence and supplemented by specific documents which have not been voluntarily disclosed.
>
> There are, however, instances where court-style discovery may be more suitable, for instance, in insurance arbitrations. In deciding which mode is more suitable, the tribunal usually starts with the practice in arbitration, namely limited discovery, and consider if there are justifications for the imposition of a wider court-style discovery.
>
> It is sometimes said that there is little or no sanction which an arbitral tribunal can adopt in the event of a party failing to comply with an order to disclose. In practice, the tribunal can warn the party that adverse inference may be drawn against them for refusing to comply with the order. Importantly, under s.61 of the Arbitration Ordinance, this order may be enforced and converted to a court order and parties who do not comply with the court order may be cited for contempt of court. The IBA Guidelines on Party Representation in International Arbitration 2013, if adopted, may, in certain cases, render the party representative subject to measures that may be taken by a tribunal for misconduct.

Ma & Brock, *supra* note 2, at paras. 15.041–15.044 (citations omitted). *See also id.* at paras. 16.007–16.022, 16.026–16.049 for further exposition on the topic of discovery.

§ 61 of the *Arbitration Ordinance, supra* note 17, is set out in the beginning of this chapter.

Guidelines on Party Representation in International Arbitration (2013) [hereinafter Guidelines] was introduced in Chapter 3. The Guidelines publication is available at: https://www.ibanet.org/Publications/publications_IBA_guides_and_free_materials.aspx Practice Rules and Guidelines (last visited 26 Aug. 2017).

Of relevance to this chapter are the following sections of the Guidelines:

- §§ 11–17 (and accompanying Comments to Guidelines): concerning Evidence
- §§ 18–25 (and accompanying Comments to Guidelines): concerning Witnesses and Experts
- §§ 26–27 (and accompanying Comments to Guidelines): concerning Remedies for Misconduct

43 *Compagnie Financière et Commerciale du Pacifique v Peruvian Guano Co* (1882) 11 QBD 55.

Rules on the Taking of Evidence in International Arbitration [hereinafter Rules] was first published in 2010 by the International Bar Association and is available at: https://www.ibanet.org/Publications/publications_IBA_guides_and_free_materials.aspx# (last visited 26 Aug. 2017). In Art. 3(3)(b) of these Rules is found the test for production of evidence, relevant and material: "a statement as to how the Documents requested are relevant to the case and material to its outcome."

Inquisitorial Rules on the Taking of Evidence in International Arbitration (hereinafter The Prague Rules) is available at: http://www.praguerules.com/upload/medialibrary/697/697f654d36c0275b310cb3ccc1e0e9f3.pdf (last visited 5 May 2018). Art. 4 of The Prague Rules provide in part:

> 4.1. Generally, the Arbitral Tribunal shall avoid extensive production of documents, including any form of e-discovery.
>
> 4.2. The Party, however, may request the Arbitral Tribunal to order the other Party to produce (a) specific document(s) which:

The discovery stage may be omitted and the inspection stage may be implemented immediately. Inspection may also be omitted. The *Arbitration Ordinance* does not require either stage. An arbitral tribunal is authorized to order discovery.[44] A tribunal is also under the duty to manage the arbitration. Within the parameters of this duty, however, the precise form of discovery to be ordered is within the arbitral tribunal's discretion.[45] Therefore, a tribunal must determine the form of discovery which is appropriate in order to avoid unnecessary delay and expense.[46]

As previously noted, an arbitral tribunal is not required to order discovery. An arbitral tribunal may thus dispense totally with discovery or to limit discovery in an appropriate case, subject to its compliance with the rules of natural justice. The applicable test is whether any substantial injustice is likely to result from a decision to exclude or to limit discovery. For example, discovery should not be ordered when, considering all the circumstances of the case, the tribunal determines that discovery would be unnecessary.[47] Alternatively, a restrictive form of discovery may be more suitable under the appropriate circumstances. Following are some examples of instances where discovery may be restricted or limited, *i.e.*, specific discovery:

- discovery is limited to a particular issue or set of issues
- discovery is limited to relevant documents or categories of document only. In construction disputes in particular, it is common for discovery to be done by *bundle*. Rather than listing individual documents, the parties may list a bundle of documents, *e.g.*, a bundle containing the category of: correspondence between two particular individuals during a specified time period.

Another instance where discovery is limited concerns privileged materials. The term *privileged* applies especially to relevant materials which ought to be disclosed if not for this claim of confidentiality. Privileged materials should be listed as part

---

a. is relevant and material to the outcome of the case;
b. is not in the public domain; and
c. is in the possession of the other Party.

[44] § 56(1)(b) and § 56(1)(d) of the *Arbitration Ordinance*, *supra* note 17. § 56(1) provides in full:

(1) Unless otherwise agreed by the parties, when conducting arbitral proceedings, an arbitral tribunal may make an order—
(a) requiring a claimant to give security for the costs of the arbitration;
(b) directing the discovery of documents or the delivery of interrogatories;
(c) directing evidence to be given by affidavit; or
(d) in relation to any relevant property—
(i) directing the inspection, photographing, preservation, custody, detention or sale of the relevant property by the arbitral tribunal, a party to the arbitral proceedings or an expert; or
(ii) directing samples to be taken from, observations to be made of, or experiments to be conducted on the relevant property.

[45] *J E Taylor & Co Ltd v Paul Brown* [1993] 1 HKLR 285; *Anangel Peace Compania Naviera v Bacchus International Commercial Corpn, The Anangel Peace* [1981] 1 Lloyd's Rep 452.

[46] *See* § 46(3)(c) of the *Arbitration Ordinance*, incorporating *Model Law* Art. 18, *supra* note 17.

[47] *J E Taylor v Brown*, *supra* note 45.

of the first stage of the discovery process, but inspection of these materials can be prohibited. The most common claims of privilege arising in arbitration involve:

- legal professional privilege: is generally exercisable over communications concerning legal advice between a lawyer and client regardless of whether this advice pertains to a particular dispute.
- legal litigation privilege: applies to communications between a party or its legal representatives and a third party, such as an expert.
- without prejudice privilege: concerns materials, generally correspondence, prepared in connection with settlement negotiations. The proposals contained in these settlement negotiations cannot be used against either party.

Regardless whether general discovery or specific discovery is agreed by the parties or ordered by the arbitral tribunal, a list of documents is prepared by each party. This list contains two schedules:

- Schedule A
  Part 1—in this section is the list of documents relevant to the dispute which are in the possession, custody or power of the disclosing party, and to which there is no objection.
  Part 2—in the section is the list of documents relevant to the dispute which are in the possession, custody or power of the disclosing party, over which are claimed privilege.
- Schedule B
  In this section are listed the documents which have been but are no longer in the possession, custody or power of the disclosing party. Generally, the documents which are listed in this section are those which have been lost or destroyed.

"An increasingly common formatting tool for organising and presenting this process of document request, objection and decision is to use a so-called *Redfern* schedule . . ."[48] One source explains:

> The purpose of the *Redfern* schedule is to crystallise the precise issues in dispute, so that the arbitral tribunal knows the position that the parties have reached following the exchanges between them. This makes it possible for the arbitral tribunal to make an informed decision as to whether or not a particular document, or class of documents, should be produced, without having to be involved in the details of the exchanges between the parties' lawyers and, usually, without the need for a meeting.[49]

Recall that the discovery stage is followed by the inspection stage where the physical review and reproduction of the non-privileged documents are undertaken

[48] REDFERN AND HUNTER, *supra* note 3, at para. 6.100.
[49] *Id.* at para. 6.101 (footnote omitted).

by the party to whom these documents have been disclosed. Following inspection, the parties usually prepare what is known as an *agreed bundle of documents*. The parties are prepared to admit this bundle of documents as evidence without the need for proving the authenticity of these documents, although the parties may contest the interpretation of the information contained in the documents.

VIII. Summary

In this chapter, we reviewed the preparatory activities which occur after the appointment of the arbitral tribunal but before the actual hearing of the parties' dispute. Some of these activities to be considered at one or more preliminary meetings might include: the timetable for the exchange of pleadings; appointment of a tribunal secretary; interim measures required, if any; and, whether discovery is required and, if so, what type. The following appendix sets out a list of items which could be considered or acted upon before the main hearing begins.

Appendix: Preliminary Meeting

In this section of the chapter, an outline is presented of some of the items to be reviewed in a preliminary meeting.[50] This outline can also serve as a checklist of items upon which the tribunal and the parties to confer in order to decide such matters as:

1. To see the original arbitration agreement to confirm its existence and the terms which it contains
2. The Arbitral Tribunal's *Terms of Appointment* and *Schedule of Charges* (if not previously agreed)
3. To identify the issues in the parties' dispute:
    a. raised in the claim
    b. raised in the defence
    c. based in the counterclaim, if any
4. Type of arbitration, *e.g.*:
    a. documents-only
    b. full oral hearing
    c. short procedure
    d. adversarial/inquisitorial[51]

---

[50] For a similar list, *see* MA AND BROCK, *supra* note 2, at paras. 15.021–15.022. *See also* Notes, *supra* note 9, especially its chapter on *List of Matters for Possible Consideration in Organizing Arbitral Proceedings*.

[51] In essence, the adversarial system searches for the truth through the contentions and evidence of the disputing parties. The decision-maker is passive, serving as an observer and referee. The inquisitorial system involves searching for the truth through the arbitral tribunal's own investigations. Legal and arbitral proceedings in Hong Kong are conducted adversarially. Unless otherwise agreed by the parties, it is possible for an arbitrator to act inquisitorially. § 56(7) of the *Arbitration Ordinance*, *supra* note 17.

   e. which arbitration rules to apply, if any
5. Preliminary issues, if any
6. Form of case submission to be adopted:
   a. statements of case
   b. formal pleadings
   c. exchange of letters
7. Programme/timetable for submissions of documents and pleadings
8. Scott Schedule[52]
9. Discovery of documents[53]

   A typical order for discovery would generally include the following provisions:
   a. discovery by list of documents, either generally or by reference to specific relevant issues
   b. after close of pleadings, exchange of lists within an agreed or a specified time period
   c. inspection of the documents to take place as agreed or a specified time period thereafter

   A further direction may be made as to the agreed bundle of documents to be produced for the hearing. This direction may be made at a later stage or be tied directly in with the order for discovery.
10. Types of discovery:
    a. limited or full discovery
    b. with submissions
    c. by lists after close of pleadings
    d. no discovery
11. Communications with the arbitral tribunal members
12. Agreement of figures, plans, drawings, photographs, correspondence, etc.
13. Representation by lawyers, other individuals or by the party
14. Hearing
15. Venue:
    a. duration
    b. arrangements
    c. date
16. Expert witnesses:
    a. necessity
    b. number

---

[52] A form of pleading commonly used, where the contentions of the parties appear in tabular form. *See* http://www.feg.com.au/Glossary.htm for an example. Other examples can easily be found on the internet.

[53] Frequently, a Redfern Schedule is used. This schedule is a tabular form with a column for each of the following: Document requested; Relevance and materiality; Responses and objection; Decision of the tribunal. *See* Redfern & Hunter, *supra* note 3, at para. 1.238 and the sample schedule contained therein. For a more detailed explanation of the schedule along with its use and application, *see id.* at paras. 6.100–6.103. Other similar versions of a Redfern Schedule can be found on the internet.

   c. disciplines
   d. exchange of reports
   e. without prejudice meeting of experts either before or after their reports are exchanged
   f. access to the evidence for experts
   g. whether the experts' reports are to serve as evidence in chief
17. Witnesses of fact:
   a. exchange of proofs of evidence
   b. proofs as evidence in chief
   c. whether subpoenas are necessary (this is an exclusive power of the court and cannot be issued by an arbitral tribunal)[54]
18. Bundle of correspondence
19. Transcript of the hearing
20. Examination of witnesses on oath or affirmation
21. Interpreter
22. Legal authorities
23. Determination whether a pre-hearing review is necessary
24. Determination whether opening and closing addresses are to be in writing
25. List of agreed items in dispute
26. Advance limitation of party costs[55]
27. Reasoned award
28. Taxation, *i.e.*, assessment, of costs:
   a. by arbitral tribunal
   b. by Taxing Master
29. Any other business

---

[54] § 55(1) of the *Arbitration Ordinance*, *supra* note 17 provides:

(1) Article 27 of the UNCITRAL Model Law, the text of which is set out below, has effect—

"Article 27. Court assistance in taking evidence

The arbitral tribunal or a party with the approval of the arbitral tribunal may request from a competent court of this State assistance in taking evidence. The court may execute the request within its competence and according to its rules on taking evidence."

Id. at § 56(8)(c) states: "Unless otherwise agreed by the parties, an arbitral tribunal may . . . direct the attendance before the arbitral tribunal of witnesses in order to give evidence or to produce documents or other evidence."

[55] *Id.* at § 57(1) specifies: "Unless otherwise agreed by the parties, an arbitral tribunal may direct that the recoverable costs of arbitral proceedings before it are limited to a specified amount."

7
Pleadings

I. Introduction

After the successful appointment of the arbitral tribunal and completion of the preliminary matters, the next stage of the arbitration process is the preparatory work to be done by the parties to enable the following phase: the main hearings.

At this preparatory stage, the parties provide written submissions. As explained by one authority:

> The immediate purposes of the parties' initial statements are to facilitate the appointment of the arbitral tribunal, to guide the institution or arbitral tribunal in establishing the amount of the deposit to be paid by the parties to secure the costs of the arbitration, to enable the arbitral tribunal to identify the issues that arise for determination, and to make appropriate procedural orders for the next steps. In nearly all cases of any substance, however, the arbitral tribunal orders the exchange of further, fuller written pleadings, as well as an appropriate level of evidence gathering, before the oral stage of proceedings is reached.[1]

Keep in mind that parties frequently conduct arbitration as an adversarial process. In these situations, an arbitral tribunal normally will decide the dispute based upon the arguments and evidence provided by the parties. Generally, the tribunal would not be involved in the parties' development of their case or the parties' manner of presenting their arguments and evidence.[2] Nonetheless, the arbitral

---

[1] Redfern and Hunter on International Arbitration para. 6.66 (Nigel Blackaby *et al.*, eds., 6th ed. 2015) [hereinafter Redfern & Hunter].

[2] Note, however, that the arbitral tribunal may act inquisitorially in relation to the whole or any part of the arbitration proceedings, unless the parties otherwise agree: § 56(7) of the *Arbitration Ordinance* (Cap. 609) [hereinafter *Arbitration Ordinance*] which states:

> Unless otherwise agreed by the parties, an arbitral tribunal may, when conducting arbitral proceedings, decide whether and to what extent it should itself take the initiative in ascertaining the facts and the law relevant to those arbitral proceedings.

In choosing to act inquisitorially pursuant to § 56(7) of this Ordinance, an arbitral tribunal should also fulfil the obligations imposed by § 46 of this Ordinance. These obligations include the obligation to treat the parties equally and fairly, and, to provide each of the parties with a reasonable opportunity to present its case. An arbitral tribunal should not render a decision or award based on facts, law or evidence which was ascertained by the tribunal itself without providing each party an opportunity to address such matters. John Choong and Romesh Weeramantry, The Hong Kong Arbitration Ordinance: Commentary and Annotations para. 56.24

tribunal will have an influence over certain aspects of the parties' case. We will discuss this influence in the following sections of this chapter.

Before continuing with the discussion, we provide the definitions of the terms used in this chapter:

- *traditional pleadings* are the type of pleadings used in courts, such as in Hong Kong and the United Kingdom, and are limited to assertions of fact[3]
- *statements of case* is the term generally used to describe a type of pleading which contains a party's allegations of fact, presentation of legal arguments and possibly evidence[4]
- any other document designed to identify the facts or issues in dispute or otherwise to set out the case

One should note that different authors and organizations occasionally use different terms to refer to the same item. Some arbitration rules use the term *submissions* rather than the term *pleadings*.[5] For example, the German Arbitration Institute (*Deutsche Institution für Schiedsgerichtsbarkeit*) whose Arbitration Rules (2018) provide:

> "Submissions" as used in the Rules refer to all communications in writing exchanged between or among the parties, the arbitral tribunal and the DIS, including the Request for Arbitration, the Answer, any counterclaims, any additional claims, any Request against an Additional Party, any and all pleadings filed in the course of the arbitration, along with the respective attachments thereto.[6]

Many different expressions are used to describe written submissions. Some examples are:

- statement of claim
- statement of case
- memorial
- points of claim

These lead to corresponding expressions such as:

- statement of defence
- statement of reply
- counter-memorial
- reply to points of claim/defence to points of claim

(2nd ed. 2015) [hereinafter CHOONG & WEERAMANTRY].

3 *Traditional pleadings* are presented in detail in Part II of this chapter.

4 *Statement of case* is presented in detail in Part II of this chapter.

5 For some, the use of this term can be confusing. In litigation in the United Kingdom and Hong Kong, the term *submission* refers to the presentation of verbal or written arguments rather than to a document which sets out the issues in dispute.

6 *Deutsche Institution für Schiedsgerichtsbarkeit* [hereinafter DIS] Arbitration Rules (2018), Art. 3.2.

Other terms such as *reply*, *rejoinder*, *replique*, *duplique*, and similar phrases are used for additional rounds of written submissions.[7]

In Hong Kong, the Rules of the High Court (hereinafter "RHC") do not apply to arbitration. Hong Kong's *Arbitration Ordinance* (Cap. 609) does not require pleadings and discovery.[8] Although many jurisdictions' laws or rules do not require traditional pleadings, nevertheless, this type of pleadings is frequently used in arbitration. Where appropriate, parties and/or tribunals may consider adopting the less formal statements of case with limited or no discovery and inspection.[9] In arbitration, the terms *pleadings*, *statement of case* and *submissions* are usually used interchangeably and sometimes the term *pleadings* may also refer to both traditional court-style pleadings and the less formal statements of case. Traditional pleadings, statements of case or submissions serve to identify the issues in dispute and the relief sought.[10]

Recall that an arbitral tribunal is under a duty to manage the arbitration. Should the parties fail to agree as to the form that pre-hearing submissions should take, the arbitral tribunal would then decide upon a procedure appropriate to the dispute,

---

[7] Redfern and Hunter, *supra* note 1, at para. 6.71.
This source continues by stating:

> The different expressions used to describe written submissions are not wholly interchangeable and none are capable of precise definition. In general, it may be said that the term 'points of claim' indicates a relatively short document, the primary purpose of which is to define the issues and state the facts upon which the claimant's claims are founded. By contrast, the expressions 'statement of claim' and 'memorial' imply a more comprehensive documentary submission, intended to include argument relating to the legal issues, as well as incorporating (in annexes or appendices) the documentary evidence relied upon and the written testimony of witnesses, together with any experts' reports on matters of opinion.

Id. at para. 6.72.

[8] § 51 of the *Arbitration Ordinance*, incorporating *Model Law* Art. 23, *supra* note 2, does not require the use of traditional pleadings. This section thus promotes the use of alternatives in order to expedite the dispute resolution process and to minimize costs.

[9] *See* the case of *Imperial Leatherware Co Pty Ltd v Macri & Marcellino Pty Ltd* (1991) 22 NSWLR 653, cited with approval in *Unistress Building Construction Ltd v Humphreys Estate (Forrestdale) Ltd* [1992] 2 HKLR 145; *J E Taylor & Co Ltd v Paul Brown* [1993] 1 HKLR 285.
§ 3(2)(a) of the *Arbitration Ordinance*, *supra* note 2, states:

> (2) This Ordinance is based on the principles—
> (a) that, subject to the observance of the safeguards that are necessary in the public interest, the parties to a dispute should be free to agree on how the dispute should be resolved.

[10] Michael J. Moser and Teresa Y.W. Cheng, Hong Kong Arbitration: A User's Guide para. 5-081 (3rd ed. 2014) [hereinafter Moser & Cheng].

avoiding unnecessary delay and expense.[11] The precise form is within the arbitral tribunal's discretion, while observing and maintaining natural justice.[12]

II. Pleadings

Having provided an introduction, the topics of this chapter are now discussed in more detail. In this section, we discuss the need and the purpose for pleadings. One purpose of pleadings is to set out the issues or matters in dispute. It is through pleadings that the opposing party and the arbitral tribunal are informed of the claims and possibly the evidence being relied upon to support the claims. The functions of pleadings are as follows:

- for a party to develop a better understanding of its own case and its opponent's case by:
    - identifying material facts
    - identifying areas of difference or dispute
    - isolating issues of fact and of law
    - narrowing the issues
    - identifying issues of liability and quantum, *i.e.*, the amount of damages claimed
    - highlighting evidentiary burdens and requirements
- to allow the tribunal to understand the allegations, the remedy or damages that is being claimed, and, the opposing party's defence
- to provide a permanent record of the issues and questions to be decided, generally for the purposes of *res judicata*[13]
- to identify the need for and the extent of discovery[14]

---

[11] § 46(3)(c) of the *Arbitration Ordinance*, incorporating *Model Law* Art. 18, *supra* note 2, states:

> (3) When conducting arbitral proceedings or exercising any of the powers conferred on an arbitral tribunal by this Ordinance or by the parties to any of those arbitral proceedings, the arbitral tribunal is required—
>
> . . .
>
> (c) to use procedures that are appropriate to the particular case, avoiding unnecessary delay or expense, so as to provide a fair means for resolving the dispute to which the arbitral proceedings relate.

The tribunal's obligations under this section may affect decisions on issues such as the extent of discovery, whether to appoint expert witnesses, or whether to hold an oral hearing. The tribunal may need to perform a "balancing exercise" in order to fulfil its obligations under this provision. CHOONG & WEERAMANTRY, *supra* note 2, at para. 46.24.

[12] *See* § 46 of the *Arbitration Ordinance*, *supra* note 2.

[13] BLACK'S LAW DICTIONARY 1504 (10th ed. 2014) [hereinafter BLACK'S] defines *res judicata* as:

> An issue that has been definitively settled by judicial decision. . . . An affirmative defense barring the same parties from litigating a second lawsuit on the same claim, or any other claim arising from the same transaction or series of transactions and that could have been – but was not – raised in the first suit.

[14] *See* Chapter 6 for a more detailed discussion on discovery.

BLACK'S, *supra* note 13, defines the term "discovery" as "[the] compulsory disclosure, at a party's request, of information that relates to the litigation."

The parties generally attempt to agree the form of pleading to be adopted for their particular case and the schedule for submitting the pleadings. These are matters which should be handled at the preliminary meeting(s) and the arbitral tribunal will make appropriate orders through one or more Order for Directions.[15] By adopting a set of institutional arbitration rules, the parties may commit themselves to a particular form of procedure and case presentation, *e.g.*, Hong Kong International Arbitration Centre's Administered Arbitration Rules.[16]

The Honourable Mr. Justice Patrick Chan, The Concise Hong Kong English-Chinese Legal Dictionary 277 (2005) [hereinafter English-Chinese Legal Dictionary] defines "discovery" as "a pre-trial procedure where a party to proceedings makes available for inspection all relevant documents to the other party. Although all relevant documents must be disclosed, not all require production" and translates "discovery" as 文件披露.

[15] An *Order for Directions*, also known as a *Procedural Order*, sets out the timetable of events up to the making of the arbitral tribunal's decision on the merits of the case, which is known as an *award*. *See* Chapter 6 for more details.

[16] The Hong Kong International Arbitration Centre's Administered Arbitration Rules (2018) [hereinafter HKIAC Arbitration Rules] provide in part:

Article 16 – Statement of Claim

16.1 Unless the Statement of Claim was contained in the Notice of Arbitration (or the Claimant elects to treat the Notice of Arbitration as the Statement of Claim), the Claimant shall communicate its Statement of Claim to all other parties and to the arbitral tribunal within a time limit to be determined by the arbitral tribunal.

16.2 The Statement of Claim shall include the following particulars:
(a) a statement of the facts supporting the claim;
(b) the points at issue;
(c) the legal arguments supporting the claim; and
(d) the relief or remedy sought.

16.3 The Claimant shall annex to its Statement of Claim all supporting materials on which it relies.

16.4 The arbitral tribunal may vary any of the requirements referred to in Article 16 as it deems appropriate.

Article 17 – Statement of Defence

17.1 Unless the Statement of Defence was contained in the Answer to the Notice of Arbitration (or the Respondent elects to treat the Answer to the Notice of Arbitration as the Statement of Defence), the Respondent shall communicate its Statement of Defence to all other parties and to the arbitral tribunal within a time limit to be determined by the arbitral tribunal.

17.2 The Statement of Defence shall reply to the particulars of the Statement of Claim (set out in Article 16.2(a) to (c)). If the Respondent has raised an objection to the jurisdiction or to the proper constitution of the arbitral tribunal, the Statement of Defence shall contain the factual and legal basis of such objection.

17.3 Where there is a counterclaim, set-off defence or cross-claim, the Statement of Defence shall also include the following particulars:
(a) a statement of the facts supporting the counterclaim, set-off defence or cross-claim;
(b) the points at issue;
(c) the legal arguments supporting the counterclaim, set-off defence or cross-claim; and
(d) the relief or remedy sought.

17.4 The Respondent shall annex to its Statement of Defence all supporting materials on which it relies.

17.5 The arbitral tribunal may vary any of the requirements in Article 17 as it deems appropriate.

Article 18 – Amendments to the Claim or Defence

18.1 During the course of the arbitration, a party may amend or supplement its claim or defence, unless the arbitral tribunal considers it inappropriate to allow such amendment having regard to the circumstances of the case. However, a claim or defence may not be amended in such a manner that the amended claim or defence falls outside the jurisdiction of the arbitral tribunal.

Pleadings are normally served sequentially by each party on its opponent. An example is as follows:

18.2 HKIAC may adjust its Administrative Fees and the arbitral tribunal's fees (where appropriate) if a party amends its claim or defence.

...

Article 20 – Further Written Statements

The arbitral tribunal shall decide which further written statements, if any, in addition to the Statement of Claim and the Statement of Defence, shall be required from the parties and shall set the time limits for communicating such statements.

The HKIAC Arbitration Rules may be found at the following website: http://www.hkiac.org/arbitration/rules-practice-notes/administered-arbitration-rules/hkiac-administered-2018-1#16 (last visited 1 Nov. 2018).

For *ad hoc* arbitrations, the Hong Kong International Arbitration Centre's Domestic Arbitration Rules (2014) [hereinafter HKIAC Domestic Rules] provide in part:

Article 6 Submission of Parties' Written Statements and Documents

6.1 In default of agreement between the parties or determination of the Arbitrator the written stage of the proceedings shall be as set out in this Article . . .

6.2 Within 28 days of receipt by the Claimant of notification of the Arbitrator's acceptance of the appointment, the Claimant shall send to the Arbitrator a Statement of Claim setting out a full description in narrative form of the nature and circumstances of the dispute specifying all factual matters and, if necessary for the proper understanding of the claim, a summary of any contentions of law relied upon and the relief claimed.

6.3 Within 35 days of receipt of the Statement of Claim, the Respondent shall send to the Arbitrator a Statement of Defence setting out a full description in narrative form of the factual matters and contentions of law in the Statement of Claim which he admits or denies, on what grounds, and specifying any other factual matters and, if necessary for the proper understanding of the defence, a summary of any contentions of law relied upon. Counterclaims, if any, shall be submitted with the Statement of Defence in the same manner as claims set out in the Statement of Claim.

6.4 Within 21 days of receipt of the Statement of Defence the Claimant may send to the Arbitrator a Statement of Reply which, where there are Counterclaims, shall include a Defence to Counterclaims.

6.5 If the Statement of Reply contains a Defence to Counterclaims, the Respondent may within a further 21 days send to the Arbitrator a Statement of Reply regarding Counterclaims.

6.6 All Statements referred to in this Article shall be accompanied by copies . . . of all essential documents on which the party concerned relies and which have not previously been submitted by any party, and . . . by any relevant samples.

6.7 The Arbitrator may, at any stage of the proceedings, if so requested by a party or at the Arbitrator's own discretion, order the parties to produce any additional documents he may specify.

The HKIAC Domestic Rules may be found at the following website:
http://www.hkiac.org/sites/default/files/ck_filebrowser/PDF/arbitration/e_domestic_2014.pdf (last visited 20 Jul. 2017).

The United Nations Commission on International Trade Law [hereinafter UNCITRAL] published its set of Arbitration Rules (2013) [hereinafter Arbitration Rules] which provides for similar procedures:

Art 20 Statement of claim

Art 21 Statement of defence

Art 22 Amendments to the claim or defence

Art 23 Pleas as to the jurisdiction of the arbitral tribunal

Art 24 Further written statements

The Arbitration Rules may be found at the following website: https://www.uncitral.org/pdf/english/texts/arbitration/arb-rules-2013/UNCITRAL-Arbitration-Rules-2013-e.pdf (last visited 20 Jul. 2017).

See also REDFERN & HUNTER, *supra* note 1, at paras. 6.67–6.69 for a brief summary of the related rules of other arbitral institutions.

Statement of case format	*Traditional pleadings format*
Statement of Claim	Points of Claim
Statement of Defence (and Counterclaim, where applicable)	Points of Defence (and Counterclaim)
Statement of Reply (to Defence)	Points of Reply (to Defence)
and Defence to Counterclaim	and Defence to Counterclaim
Statement of Reply to Defence	Points of Reply to Defence
to Counterclaim	to Counterclaim

At any particular time, the following documents, also known as *pleadings*, may be interspersed among the above forms of pleading:

Statement of case format (cont'd)	*Traditional pleadings format (cont'd)*
Clarifications	Further and Better Particulars
Amendments	Amendments

The expressions used in each column are often used interchangeably. It is not the terminology that is important; the importance is that the differences of substance between the two types of pleading are understood. In the following section, the purpose of these documents is briefly set out.

A. General Content and Sequence of Pleadings

As this chapter is rather technical and the details best left for legal professionals, each of the pleadings listed above and its function is only briefly reviewed.

The Statement of Claim or Points of Claim is the first pleading submitted by the claimant.[17] In this document, the claimant states that it is making a claim against the respondent. Included in this document are the specifics, referred to as the *particulars*, of the loss or damage. This pleading usually will provide a background of the dispute, setting out the facts and events relating to the dispute, the legal basis of the claim and the legal arguments supporting the claimant's case.[18]

The Statement of Defence or Points of Defence is the respondent's reply to the claim. This document sets forth the respondent's defence(s) to the claim and may

[17] Redfern & Hunter, *supra* note 1, at para. 6.70 comments:

> Written pleadings are usually exchanged sequentially, so that the claimant fires the first shot, the statement of claim, and the respondent answers with the statement of defence (and counterclaim, if any). Exceptionally, however, the arbitral tribunal may direct that the parties should submit their written pleadings simultaneously, so that each party delivers a written submission of its claims against the other on a set date, and then, on a subsequent date, the parties exchange their written answers and so forth. Whilst simultaneous exchanges can reduce the overall duration of the written phase, they are more likely to lead to the arbitral equivalent of 'ships passing in the night'. For this reason, simultaneous exchange remains less common than sequential exchange for pre-hearing submissions.

[18] Moser & Cheng, *supra* note 10, at para. 5-082.

serve to narrow the dispute. This document will specify whether the respondent admits, does not admit or denies each of the allegations in the Statement of Claim. The Statement of Defence may also set out other facts or legal submissions upon which the respondent seeks to rely to counter the claimant's allegations.[19]

The Statement of Counterclaim or Points of Counterclaim is a claim by the respondent against the claimant. This pleading is sometimes referred to as a *cross-claim* or as a *counter-claim*. This is not a defence but a separate claim against the claimant. This counter-claim usually accompanies the Statement of Defence or Points of Defence, hence the counterclaim is normally presented as separate parts of one document entitled Statement of Defence and Counterclaim or Points of Defence and Counterclaim. The matters addressed in the respondent's Statement of Counterclaim or Points of Counterclaim are the same as those in the claimant's Statement of Claim or Points of Claim.[20]

The Statement of Reply to Defence or Points of Reply to Defence is a response by the claimant to the respondent's Defence pleading. This Reply is only necessary where the Defence raises new claims, allegations or issues. The claimant's Reply should not raise new issues but should only address the arguments made by the respondent in the Defence.[21] Should the claimant wish to raise new issues, that party should seek permission (referred to as *leave*) from the tribunal to amend the Statement of Claim or Points of Claim.[22]

The Statement of Defence to Counterclaim or Points of Defence to Counterclaim is the claimant's defence to the respondent's Counterclaim. The Statement of Defence to Counterclaim or Points of Defence usually accompanies the Reply, and are presented as separate parts of one document, entitled Statement of Reply and Defence to Counterclaim or Points of Reply and Defence to Counterclaim.

Statement of Reply to Defence to Counterclaim is the respondent's reply to the claimant's defence to its counterclaim.[23]

---

19 *Id.*

20 *Id.*

21 *Id.*

22 § 51 of the *Arbitration Ordinance*, incorporating *Model Law* Art. 23(2), *supra* note 2, provides in part:

> Article 23 of the UNCITRAL Model Law, the text of which is set out below, has effect—
>
> "*Article 23. Statements of claim and defence*
>
> ...
>
> (2) Unless otherwise agreed by the parties, either party may amend or supplement his claim or defence during the course of the arbitral proceedings, unless the arbitral tribunal considers it inappropriate to allow such amendment having regard to the delay in making it."

Model Law Art. 23(2) empowers the parties to make amendments to the pleadings. Note that the arbitral proceedings could proceed without making any formal amendments to the initial statements of claim or defence as long as the formal rules of court pleadings do not apply to that arbitration. An arbitral tribunal, in deciding whether to grant leave for a party to amend its pleadings, should also consider the inconvenience and prejudice involved to the opposing party while ensuring that each party would have a reasonable opportunity to present its case after allowing such amendment. Choong & Weeramantry, *supra* note 2, at para. 51.13.

23 Moser & Cheng, *supra* note 10, at para. 5-082.

The parties are obliged to ensure that all pleadings provided to the tribunal are also provided to the opposing party.[24] This procedure is known as *service* or *to serve*. The time limits for submission of pleadings will either be agreed by the parties or fixed by the arbitral tribunal.[25] Though there is no standard time limit in international arbitrations, a period of up to three months between submissions is quite common.[26]

B. Clarifications/Further and Better Particulars

One party may request from the opposing party further information or details in order to clarify points raised in the opposing party's pleadings. This request is known as *Clarifications*[27] or as *Further and Better Particulars* [hereinafter "F&BPs"].[28]

In relation to Clarifications/F&BPs, a party may seek only such details or particulars which ought to have been included in the original pleading; the requesting party cannot use this pleading to request evidence.[29] *Fishing expeditions* are not permitted.[30] An arbitral tribunal which is not acting under the formal rules of pleading has more scope to decide whether or not to order Clarifications/F&BPs.

In the first instance, a party seeking Clarifications/F&BPs must serve this request on the opposing party. If the opposing party refuses to provide the information, the arbitral tribunal will decide whether to order the opposing party to comply with the request to provide the information. Costs might be ordered against a party who unreasonably requested Clarifications/F&BPs or against a party who unjustifiably refused to provide Clarifications/F&BPs.

III. Amendment of Pleadings

A party may request that one or more of its pleadings be revised. This is known as an *amendment*. The purpose of an amendment to pleadings in arbitration may be

---

24 2 Halsbury's Laws Of Hong Kong para. [25.096] (2nd ed. 2016) (citations omitted).
25 *Id.*
26 Redfern & Hunter, *supra* note 1, at para. 6.74.
27 If following the *statement of case* format and method of pleadings.
28 If following the *traditional pleadings* format and method of pleadings.
29 Moser & Cheng, *supra* note 10, at para. 5-082.
30 Black's, *supra* note 13, at 754, defines *fishing expedition* as:

> An attempt, through broad discovery requests or random questions, to elicit information from another party in the hope that something relevant might be found; esp., such an attempt that exceeds the scope of discovery allowed by procedural rules.

In the case of *Regina v Margaret Jean Fitch*, 2005 SKQB 257 the court said at para. 2: "guard against the pursuit of what have been termed 'fishing expeditions'—speculative quests for information without any real expectation about the outcome of the quest or its relevance to the case."

In case of *George William Harris v The Queen*, 2001 DTC 5322, the court stated at para. 45: "The term fishing expedition has been generally used to describe an indiscriminate request for production, in the hope of uncovering helpful information."

stated by comparison to RHC Ord 20 r 8(1), *i.e.*, "determining the real question in controversy between the parties, or . . . correcting any defect or error."

Amendments of pleadings may be sought:

- to correct mistakes in the original submissions
- when relevant facts are discovered after submission of the pleading
- in response to a request for Clarifications/F&BPs
- to raise new issues
- to change a legal argument on the alleged facts
- where additional evidence is disclosed through discovery and inspection[31]

Leave, or permission, to amend a pleading will normally be given, even during a hearing, if there is no unfairness or injustice.[32] However negligent or careless the omission and however late the request, the amendment should be permitted if there is no injustice to the opposing party.[33] There is no injustice if the opposing party can be compensated for the expense relating to the amendment.[34] Where justice cannot be achieved by compensation, the arbitral tribunal may consider the strain placed upon the opposing party, particularly if this party is an individual rather than a business corporation.[35]

Should an arbitral tribunal grant a request for an amendment of pleadings, usually the tribunal also would order the requesting party to pay the costs of and caused by the amendment and grant permission to the opposing party to amend its pleadings consequentially. If a party's request to amend a pleading was granted during the hearing, the opposing party may have an adjournment of the hearing in order to address the amendments.

IV. Memorials

Before proceeding further, another approach or style to exchanging claims and defences ought to be discussed. Recall Chapter 1 where some of the differences between the common-law legal system and the civil-law legal system are discussed. This dichotomy is again apparent in relation to memorials. *Memorials* can be considered as a type of pleadings but with all the supporting evidence included, *e.g.*, witness statements, expert reports, supporting documents, etc., and exchanged

---

[31] The definition and translation of "discovery" has been set out in *supra* note 14. *See* Chapter 6 for an in-depth discussion on discovery.
BLACK'S, *supra* note 13, at 916, defines "inspection" as "a careful examination of something, such as goods (to determine their fitness for purchase) or items produced in response to a discovery request (to determine their relevance to a lawsuit)."
§ 48 of the *Arbitration Ordinance*, *supra* note 2, translates "inspection" as 檢查.

[32] *See* the cases of *Cropper v Smith* (1884) 26 Ch D 700; *Clarapede & Co v Commercial Union Association* (1883) 32 WR 262.

[33] *Clarapede v Commercial Union*, *supra* note 32.

[34] *Cropper v Smith*, *supra* note 32; *Clarapede v Commercial Union*, *supra* note 32.

[35] *Ketteman v Hansel Properties Ltd* [1987] AC 189.

together. With the pleadings approach, the exchange usually is sequential: first the claim and the defence/counterclaim by the respective parties, followed by an exchange of expert reports, then an exchange of evidence and finally an exchange of witness statements.

It is said that the civil-law legal system adherents are inclined to follow the memorial approach, while the common-law legal system adherents are inclined to favour the pleadings approach. A commonly-cited example is the difference in approach between the International Chamber of Commerce (headquartered in France), which favours memorials, and the London Court of International Arbitration (headquartered in England), which favours pleadings.[36] Publications by proponents for both approaches can be found on the internet with relative ease.[37] These publications generally note the difference in the approaches and the advantages and disadvantages of each.

Regardless of one's preference, it should be noted that there is now an apparent trend toward the use of memorials in international commercial arbitration. If, indeed, there is increasing use of memorials, the reader should be aware of these different approaches.

V. Arbitration without Pleadings

Pleadings are not always necessary. The nature of some arbitration cases is such that they can be handled without any pleadings. Examples of such instances are:

- cases where the disputes are relatively simple with limited issues—in these cases, it may possible for the arbitral tribunal at a preliminary meeting to determine the issues between the parties. These issues may then be used as the basis for pleadings, discovery and/or witness statements/reports

---

[36] Perhaps an exception to this generalization is the Singapore International Arbitration Centre's Investment Arbitration Rules (2017). Art. 17 provides for the memorials approach to pleadings. The relevant part of these rules provide:

> 17.2 The Claimant shall, within a period of time to be determined by the Tribunal, send to the Respondent and the Tribunal a Memorial, setting out in full detail:
> a. a statement of facts supporting the claim;
> b. the legal grounds or arguments supporting the claim;
> c. any witness statement and/or expert report supporting the claim; and
> d. the relief claimed together with the amount of all quantifiable claims.
>
> 17.3 The Respondent shall, within a period of time to be determined by the Tribunal, send to the Claimant and the Tribunal a Counter-Memorial, setting out in full detail:
> a. a statement of facts supporting the defence and any counterclaim;
> b. the legal grounds or arguments supporting the defence and any counterclaim;
> c. any witness statement and/or expert report supporting the defence and any counterclaim; and
> d. the relief claimed together with the amount of all quantifiable counterclaims.

[37] *See, e.g.*, Michael Grose and Kristian Cywicki, *Pleadings or Memorials: Which Are More Appropriate for Construction Arbitrations?* 4(1) BCDR International Arbitration Review 43 (2017).

- the same situation as above, but the parties submit an agreed statement of the issues to the arbitral tribunal to be used for the further conduct of the dispute
- cases involving only legal issues and/or where declarations or interim awards[38] are sought on preliminary points of law[39]
- cases involving only simple factual matters and not involving any legal issues, *e.g.*, "look-sniff" commodity arbitrations[40]

VI. Summary

In this brief chapter, we sought to introduce the reader to the documents which the parties use to advance their case before the tribunal. We also discussed the need to serve pleadings upon the opposing party, and, any responses or counter-claims by the opposing party to the initial documents. Also reviewed was the purpose of pleadings which clarified the parties' positions or which provided additional information concerning the dispute. The chapter concluded with a section concerning when and what types of changes or revisions may be made to pleadings, and, instances where pleadings are not required.

[38] BLACK'S, *supra* note 13, at 493, defines "declaration" as "a formal statement, proclamation, or announcement, esp. one embodied in an instrument."
ENGLISH-CHINESE LEGAL DICTIONARY, *supra* note 14, at 239, defines the term "declaration" as "a formal, imperative statement creating or preserving a right" and translates this term as 聲明/宣言/宣佈.
BLACK'S, *supra* note 13, at 164, defines "interim award" as "an arbitral panel's decisions on the applicable law and its jurisdiction made before the panel decides the issues in an arbitration."
In Hong Kong, an interim award is often referred to by the term "preliminary order." *See*, *e.g.*, § 37 and Part 6 of the *Arbitration Ordinance*, *supra* note 2, which translate "preliminary order" as 初步命令.

[39] Lands Tribunal Rules (Cap. 17A) Rule 18 translates "preliminary point of law" as 初步法律論點.

[40] As mentioned in Chapter 2, this type of arbitration is also known as *scratch-sniff*. In mercantile disputes of the past before modern technology, disputes over the size or quality of products, *e.g.*, oranges, would be resolved by the merchants securing the advice or opinion another merchant who would decide the dispute by looking, scratching and sniffing the oranges to determine their grade and quality. After receiving the assessment of the neutral, the disputing merchants can negotiate a price based upon the determined grade and quality of the oranges.

8

Procedure at the Hearing and Evidence

I. Introduction

There are no required procedural rules for a tribunal to follow in conducting an arbitration.[1] Consequently, there is a wide variety of procedures from which an arbitral tribunal and parties can select. At one extreme, the informal arbitration dispenses with pleadings, discovery and witnesses; frequently, there is no hearing. At the other extreme, the formal arbitration is modelled on court litigation which involves pleadings, discovery of documents, witness testimony under oath, cross-examination and arguments by counsel.

The simplest type of informal arbitration is the *scratch-sniff* arbitration. This type of informal arbitration involves a procedure where the arbitrator examines, sometimes by actually scratching or sniffing, the subject of the dispute and makes a decision. For example, merchants may be disputing the clarity of a diamond which would affect its value. These merchants may appoint another diamond merchant as arbitrator to assess the diamond's clarity. The arbitrator proceeds to examine the gemstone and makes a decision after which the merchants can proceed as the market price of diamonds of that particular clarity is already known.

Another type of informal arbitration where there is no hearing is commonly known as a *documents-only* arbitration where the arbitral proceedings are conducted

---

[1] One source commented:

> In general, an arbitral tribunal must conduct the arbitration in accordance with the procedure agreed by the parties. If it fails to do so, the award may be set aside, or refused recognition and enforcement. However, the freedom of the parties to dictate the procedure to be followed in an international arbitration is not unrestricted. The procedure that they establish must comply with any mandatory rules and public policy requirements of the law of the juridical seat of the arbitration. It must also take into account the provisions of the international conventions on arbitration, which aim to ensure that arbitral proceedings are conducted fairly. Accordingly, a balance must be struck between the parties' wishes concerning the procedure to be followed and any overriding requirements of the legal regime that governs the arbitration.

Redfern and Hunter on International Arbitration para. 6.02 (Nigel Blackaby *et al.*, eds., 6th ed. 2015) [hereinafter Redfern & Hunter]. *See also id.* at paras. 6.19–6.25; *Brunswick Bowling & Billiards Corp v Shanghai Zhonglu Industrial Co Ltd* [2011] 1 HKLRD 707 at paras. 84–88. Specifically, the *Brunswick* court noted in para. 87: "in a situation where the arbitrators discern potential problem with the opportunity to a party presenting his case fairly arising from a procedure agreed by the parties, they are obliged to raise it with the parties instead of following blindly what had been agreed."

based only on the parties' submitted documents. To eliminate the hearing stage of the proceedings, parties under most arbitration laws and arbitration rules will have to choose specifically the documents-only form of proceedings in their arbitration agreement.

This chapter, however, focuses upon arbitration proceedings where hearings are held and where evidence is submitted by the parties. In these situations, the parties frequently will have agreed upon the procedure for the arbitration at the time they made the underlying contract, *e.g.*, the parties would specify that the arbitration procedure be in accordance with a particular set of rules, such as the Rules of Arbitration of the International Chamber of Commerce (2017), or, UNCITRAL Arbitration Rules (2013). Alternatively, the parties may agree a set of rules at the time they submit a dispute to the arbitral tribunal. Should the parties fail to agree the procedure to be followed during the arbitration, the arbitral tribunal would determine the procedures that are appropriate to the particular case.[2] The tribunal is not bound to adopt rigid, court-style procedures.[3] The tribunal may even adopt an inquisitorial procedure if the parties do not agree to the contrary. Regardless of the procedure to be adopted, the arbitral tribunal must observe natural justice.[4]

II. Logistical Matters

Before proceeding further to discuss the hearing stage, there are some items concerning the logistics and arrangements necessary in preparation for the hearing.

---

[2] § 46(3) of the *Arbitration Ordinance* (Cap. 609) [hereinafter *Arbitration Ordinance*], adopting the intent of *Model Law* Art. 18, provides:

> (3) When conducting arbitral proceedings or exercising any of the powers conferred on an arbitral tribunal by this Ordinance or by the parties to any of those arbitral proceedings, the arbitral tribunal is required—
> (a) to be independent;
> (b) to act fairly and impartially as between the parties, giving them a reasonable opportunity to present their cases and to deal with the cases of their opponents; and
> (c) to use procedures that are appropriate to the particular case, avoiding unnecessary delay or expense, so as to provide a fair means for resolving the dispute to which the arbitral proceedings relate.

[3] *Imperial Leatherware Co Pty Ltd v Macri & Marcellino Pty Ltd* (1991) 22 NSWLR 653, cited with approval in the Hong Kong case of *Unistress Building Construction Co Ltd v Humphreys Estate (Forrestdale) Ltd* [1992] 2 HKLR 145.

For example, in relation to the evidence to be presented at the hearing, one source stated:

> An arbitral tribunal is not bound by strict rules of evidence and can admit any evidence that it considers relevant to the proceeding. The tribunal may determine the admissibility, relevance, materiality and weight of evidence at its discretion. Such discretion must, however, be exercised "fairly and impartially." (citations omitted)

Arbitration in Hong Kong: A Practical Guide para. 15.081 (The Hon Chief Justice Geoffrey Ma and Denis Brock, eds., 4th ed. 2017) [hereinafter Ma & Brock].

[4] § 56(7) of the *Arbitration Ordinance*, *supra* note 2, which states: "Unless otherwise agreed by the parties, an arbitral tribunal may, when conducting arbitral proceedings, decide whether and to what extent it should itself take the initiative in ascertaining the facts and the law relevant to those arbitral proceedings."

See also id. at § 46, incorporating *Model Law* Art. 18.

In an *ad hoc* arbitration proceeding, the parties and the arbitral tribunal will decide the venue where and the times when the hearings and further meetings will be held. The *ad hoc* arbitration may thus take place in the facilities of an office centre, hotel or arbitration institution. In an administered arbitration proceeding, the institution may assist in the arrangement of such administrative matters. Usually, in two-party disputes, four rooms are booked:

- the hearing room itself
- one room for each party
- one room for the tribunal for private meetings and discussions

In the hearing room, the seating arrangement usually is organized with the arbitral tribunal at one end of the table and the parties on either side of the arbitral tribunal. Seating may be in a conference style or meeting style, whichever is convenient for the arbitral tribunal and the parties, along with their staff and legal representatives.[5]

Another logistical matter to be considered in organizing the hearing concerns record-keeping. During the hearing, the arbitral tribunal will take its own notes. The parties and/or their lawyers will also take their own notes. Where a dispute is complex or of a high value, a transcription service often is retained. Like a court stenographer, also known as a court reporter, a transcription service provides an immediate online record that can be highlighted and searched by the tribunal and by the parties. This service usually also provides a hardcopy at the end of each hearing day.

As part of its record-keeping duties, the arbitral tribunal maintains possession of the documents, evidence or exhibits produced during the proceedings. Having possession of the documents and evidence would be useful to the tribunal for reference during its deliberations. At the conclusion of the arbitral proceedings, these materials would be discarded, unless requested otherwise.

A related matter to be considered in organizing an international commercial arbitration is the need for interpretation or translation services. Where the documents or the language of the arbitral proceedings is unfamiliar to a party or parties or to an arbitrator, translators or interpreters should be considered. The arbitral tribunal should give directions as to which party shall pay the additional cost incurred for the translation or interpretation.[6]

---

[5] *See, e.g.*, the United Nations Commission on International Trade Law's *Notes on Organizing Arbitral Proceedings* paras. 32–34 (2nd ed. 2016) [hereinafter Notes].

[6] § 50 of the *Arbitration Ordinance*, incorporating *Model Law* Art. 22, *supra* note 2, stipulates that:

> Article 22 of the UNCITRAL Model Law, the text of which is set out below, has effect—
>
> "*Article 22. Language*
>
> (1) The parties are free to agree on the language or languages to be used in the arbitral proceedings. Failing such agreement, the arbitral tribunal shall determine the language or languages to be used in the proceedings. This agreement or determination, unless otherwise specified therein, shall apply to any written statement by a party, any hearing and any award, decision or other communication by the arbitral tribunal.

The arbitral tribunal is under a duty to ensure that the parties are aware of the date, time and venue for the hearing. The tribunal should provide formal written notice to both parties in order to avoid the possibility of any misunderstanding or miscommunication. Failure to give notice would be a breach by the arbitral tribunal of its mandatory obligation to observe natural justice.[7] In such an instance, the arbitral tribunal's award could be set aside on the ground that proper notice of the proceedings was not given.[8] In *Sun Tian Gang v Hong Kong & China Gas (Jilin) Ltd*,[9] the winning party commenced arbitration against the losing party while the losing party was imprisoned and did not receive proper notification of the arbitration. The arbitral award was set aside on the basis that the losing party did not have the opportunity to present its case.

III. Hearings

If a party defaults by failing to appear at a hearing, an arbitral tribunal would not be justified to proceed *ex parte* without giving due notice to the absent party. The tribunal should postpone this hearing and provide written notice to both parties that the arbitral tribunal intends, on a specified date at a specified time and place, to proceed with the reference regardless of whether the defaulting party attends. Such a notice is usually marked *Peremptory*.[10]

> (2) The arbitral tribunal may order that any documentary evidence shall be accompanied by a translation into the language or languages agreed upon by the parties or determined by the arbitral tribunal."

See also UNCITRAL Arbitration Rules Art. 19 (2013) concerning *Language* to be used in the arbitration process. *See also* paras. 20–26 of the Notes, *supra* note 5. Paragraph 20 states:

> The parties may agree on the language or languages in which the arbitral proceedings will be conducted. Such agreement ensures that the parties have the capacity to communicate in the language or languages of the arbitral proceedings. In the absence of such agreement, the arbitral tribunal will usually determine the language or languages. Common criteria for that determination are the primary language of the contract(s) or other legal instruments under which the dispute arose, and the language commonly used by the parties in their communication. The parties and the arbitral tribunal usually choose a single language to conduct the arbitral proceedings . . .

7 *See* § 46(3) of the *Arbitration Ordinance*, incorporating *Model Law* Art. 18, *supra* note 2.

8 *See id.* at § 81(1), incorporating *Model Law* Art. 34(2)(a)(ii).

9 [2016] 5 HKLRD 221.

10 Black's Law Dictionary 1318 (10th ed. 2014) [hereinafter Black's] defines "peremptory" as "final; absolute; conclusive; incontrovertible."

§ 53(3) of the *Arbitration Ordinance*, *supra* note 2, translates "peremptory" as 最後.

§ 53 of the *Arbitration Ordinance*, *supra* note 2, provides that should a party fail to comply with any order or direction of the arbitral tribunal, the tribunal has the power to make a *peremptory order* requiring compliance with such order or direction within the prescribed time period and to set out the consequences of non-compliance. John Choong and Romesh Weeramantry, The Hong Kong Arbitration Ordinance: Commentary and Annotations para. 53.02 (2nd ed. 2015) [hereinafter Choong & Weeramantry].

Choong & Weeramantry further elaborates at paras. 53.21 and 53.23:

> A peremptory order repeats an order that has not been complied with, and attaches a time limit for compliance and a clear statement of consequences that will follow if there is a failure to comply.
>
> . . .
>
> The powers that are available to the tribunal include precluding a party from relying upon any allegation or material which was the subject matter of the peremptory order, drawing any adverse inferences

In the event that the claimant is in default, for example, by not continuing with its claim, the arbitral tribunal may dismiss the claim and thereby end the arbitration. If the respondent is in default, for example, by not continuing with its defence against the claim, the arbitral tribunal will continue with the proceedings and make an award in default. Unlike the common law courts, an arbitral tribunal is unable to issue a summary award based upon the claimant's submission being unopposed by the other party.

> Unlike a court, an arbitral tribunal has no authority to issue an award akin to a default judgement. Its task is to make a determination of the disputes submitted to it. Accordingly, even if a party fails to present its case, the arbitral tribunal must consider the merits and make a determination of the substance of the disputes. Where it is clear from the beginning that a party (usually the respondent) does not propose to take part, the arbitral tribunal usually ensures that all notifications of hearings and correspondence continued to be sent to the defaulting party, and that all of the participating party's submissions and evidence are placed before the defaulting party in written form. The tribunal will then be justified in holding only a brief hearing, on an *ex parte* basis, to review the claims and raise any questions.[11]

In the event of the other party's default, the tribunal will require the claimant to prove each element of its case in order to obtain an award.[12]

A. Privacy/Confidentiality

Unlike a court which is opened to the public, an arbitration is private. Only the parties, their legal representatives and witnesses are entitled to attend, together with those who assist the presentation of a party's case, *e.g.*, a stenographer or an interpreter. Others may only attend by agreement of the parties and the arbitral tribunal. If the credibility of a witness is in issue, that witness may be excluded from the hearing until called upon to give evidence. In Hong Kong, there are sections of the *Arbitration Ordinance* (Cap. 609) [hereinafter "*Arbitration Ordinance*"] which pertain to confidentiality in arbitration-related court proceedings and confidentiality requirements upon the parties to an arbitration.[13]

> that the circumstances may justify from the non-compliance, making an award on the basis of any materials which have been properly provided to the arbitral tribunal, and making any order that the arbitral tribunal thinks fit as to the payment of the costs of the arbitration incurred in consequence of the non-compliance. (citation omitted)

11 Redfern & Hunter, *supra* note 1, at para. 6.196.

12 A more detailed discussion of default hearings may be found in *id.* at paras. 6.191–6.199.

13 § 16 of the *Arbitration Ordinance*, *supra* note 2, provides:

> (1) Subject to subsection (2), proceedings under this Ordinance in the court are to be heard otherwise than in open court.
> (2) The court may order those proceedings to be heard in open court—
> (a) on the application of any party; or
> (b) if, in any particular case, the court is satisfied that those proceedings ought to be heard in open court.

B. Representation

A party may choose to present its case at the hearing or the party may choose to be represented by a third party, such as a solicitor or counsel.[14] A party intending to

---

Id. at § 17 states:

(1) This section applies to proceedings under this Ordinance in the court heard otherwise than in open court ("closed court proceedings").

(2) A court in which closed court proceedings are being heard must, on the application of any party, make a direction as to what information, if any, relating to the proceedings may be published.

(3) A court must not make a direction permitting information to be published unless—

(a) all parties agree that the information may be published; or

(b) the court is satisfied that the information, if published, would not reveal any matter (including the identity of any party) that any party reasonably wishes to remain confidential.

(4) Despite subsection (3), if—

(a) a court gives a judgment in respect of closed court proceedings; and

(b) the court considers that judgment to be of major legal interest,

the court must direct that reports of the judgment may be published in law reports and professional publications.

(5) If a court directs under subsection (4) that reports of a judgment may be published, but any party reasonably wishes to conceal any matter in those reports (including the fact that the party was such a party), the court must, on the application of the party—

(a) make a direction as to the action to be taken to conceal that matter in those reports; and

(b) if the court considers that a report published in accordance with the direction made under paragraph (a) would still be likely to reveal that matter, direct that the report may not be published until after the end of a period, not exceeding 10 years, that the court may direct.

(6) A direction of the court under this section is not subject to appeal.

Id. at § 18 provides:

(1) Unless otherwise agreed by the parties, no party may publish, disclose or communicate any information relating to—

(a) the arbitral proceedings under the arbitration agreement; or

(b) an award made in those arbitral proceedings.

(2) Nothing in subsection (1) prevents the publication, disclosure or communication of information referred to in that subsection by a party—

(a) if the publication, disclosure or communication is made—

(i) to protect or pursue a legal right or interest of the party; or

(ii) to enforce or challenge the award referred to in that subsection,

in legal proceedings before a court or other judicial authority in or outside Hong Kong;

(b) if the publication, disclosure or communication is made to any government body, regulatory body, court or tribunal and the party is obliged by law to make the publication, disclosure or communication; or

(c) if the publication, disclosure or communication is made to a professional or any other adviser of any of the parties.

[14] In contrast to local court litigation which only allows parties to be represented by barristers and solicitors admitted in Hong Kong, § 63 of the *Arbitration Ordinance*, *supra* note 2, allows parties to an arbitration to choose their own representatives, advisers and advocates, regardless of their nationalities and qualifications:

63. Representation and preparation work

Section 44 (Penalty for unlawfully practising as a barrister or notary public), section 45 (Unqualified person not to act as solicitor) and section 47 (Unqualified person not to prepare certain instruments, etc.) of the Legal Practitioners Ordinance (Cap. 159) do not apply to—

(a) arbitral proceedings;

(b) the giving of advice and the preparation of documents for the purposes of arbitral proceedings; or

(c) any other thing done in relation to arbitral proceedings, except where it is done in connection with court proceedings—

(i) arising out of an arbitration agreement; or

be represented by a third party is obligated to give notice of such intention to the opposing party so that the latter may be similarly represented. This is particularly important if one party will be legally represented. If this notice has not been given, the arbitral tribunal should enquire of the unrepresented party whether it wishes to have legal representation. If so, the arbitral tribunal should adjourn the proceedings to allow legal services to be obtained and to be adequately prepared.

A refusal by the arbitral tribunal to adjourn the proceedings in such circumstances may amount to misconduct. The unrepresented party may seek to set aside any of the tribunal's awards on the basis that the unrepresented party was unable to present its case.[15]

The matter of representation should be addressed at the first preliminary meeting in order to avoid causing any need for adjournments at a later date.[16]

C. Leave to Amend Pleadings

Here, the term *leave* simply means "permission." As discussed in the previous chapter, a party wishing to amend its case must obtain the tribunal's permission if the opposing party does not agree. The general rule is that permission to amend should be given whenever such amendment does not cause disadvantage or unfairness to the opposing party.[17] Where the disadvantage to the opposing party is additional expenses, the tribunal may order the amending party to pay to the opposing party the costs caused by the amendment, regardless which party succeeds in the

(ii) arising in the course of, or resulting from, arbitral proceedings.

See Michael J. Moser and Teresa Y.W. Cheng, Hong Kong Arbitration: A User's Guide para. 5-024 (3rd ed. 2014) [hereinafter Moser & Cheng]; Ma & Brock, *supra* note 3, at para. 10.222.

[15] *See* § 81(1) of the *Arbitration Ordinance*, incorporating *Model Law* Art. 34(2)(a)(ii), *supra* note 2.

[16] For discussion of preliminary meetings, *see* Chapter 6.

[17] Art. 23(2) of the United Nations Commission on International Trade Law's *Model Law on International Commercial Arbitration* [hereinafter *Model Law*] provides that each party to an arbitration may amend or supplement its claim or defence at any stage of the proceedings unless the arbitral tribunal considers it inappropriate having considered the delay in making such amendments. §51 of the *Arbitration Ordinance*, incorporating the *Model Law* Art. 23, *supra* note 2, provides in full:

Article 23 of the UNCITRAL Model Law, the text of which is set out below, has effect—

"*Article 23. Statements of claim and defence*

(1) Within the period of time agreed by the parties or determined by the arbitral tribunal, the claimant shall state the facts supporting his claim, the points at issue and the relief or remedy sought, and the respondent shall state his defence in respect of these particulars, unless the parties have otherwise agreed as to the required elements of such statements. The parties may submit with their statements all documents they consider to be relevant or may add a reference to the documents or other evidence they will submit.

(2) Unless otherwise agreed by the parties, either party may amend or supplement his claim or defence during the course of the arbitral proceedings, unless the arbitral tribunal considers it inappropriate to allow such amendment having regard to the delay in making it."

See Moser & Cheng, *supra* note 14, at para. 5-083.

arbitration. Where the amendment comes late in the proceedings and may cause delay, the presumption nevertheless should be to allow the amendment.[18]

When deciding whether to grant leave to amend, the arbitral tribunal must consider whether the issue raised by the amendment is within the tribunal's jurisdiction. If the issue is outside of the arbitral tribunal's jurisdiction and the opposing party does not consent to the issue being determined by the arbitral tribunal, leave to amend should be refused.

D. Documents

The amount of photocopying required for a hearing can be large. Therefore, the documents should be limited to those which are relevant to the issues and to which reference will be made during the hearing. In order to save time in the hearing, it is common practice to have the parties agree to the documents to be used, and to place these documents in *agreed bundles of documents* arranged in an appropriate order and numbered for ease of retrieval.[19]

E. Witnesses

An arbitral tribunal may, unless the parties otherwise agree, request the attendance of witnesses in order to give evidence or to produce documents or other items of evidence.[20] Although a tribunal can direct a witness to attend, the tribunal does not possess what is known as *coercive powers*[21] to force a witness to attend. A court, on the other hand, has similar but wider powers. Unlike an arbitral tribunal, a court can issue subpoenas to compel a witness to attend a hearing.[22]

An arbitral tribunal may, unless the parties agree otherwise, examine the parties or their witnesses under oath or affirmation. For this purpose, the tribunal may administer oaths and take affirmations.[23] An arbitral tribunal should administer an

---

[18] *See also* Chapter 7 concerning pleadings and discovery.

[19] The *agreed bundles of documents* should include all of the documents referred to by both parties in their submissions and evidence. In addition, parties may prepare an agreed statement of facts, a list of issues for the arbitral tribunal's determination and a list of key persons in the dispute and their relationships with each other. Moser & Cheng, *supra* note 14, at para. 5-142.

[20] *See* the text of § 56(8)(c) of the *Arbitration Ordinance*, *supra* note 2, which is set out in *infra* note 23.

[21] The case of *HKSAR v Lam Hon Kwok Popy* [2012] HKEC 914 translates "coercive power" as 實施脅迫的權力. *Id.* at para. 30.

[22] Order 32, rule 7 of the Rules of the High Court (Cap. 4A). § 55(2) of the *Arbitration Ordinance*, incorporating *Model Law* Art. 27, *supra* note 2, provides: "The Court may order a person to attend proceedings before an arbitral tribunal to give evidence or to produce documents or other evidence."

[23] § 56(8) of the *Arbitration Ordinance*, *supra* note 2, provides:

> (8) Unless otherwise agreed by the parties, an arbitral tribunal may—
> (a) administer oaths to, or take the affirmations of, witnesses and parties;
> (b) examine witnesses and parties on oath or affirmation; or
> (c) direct the attendance before the arbitral tribunal of witnesses in order to give evidence or to produce documents or other evidence.

oath[24] or an affirmation[25] in accordance with the *Oaths and Declarations Ordinance* (Cap 11). Failing to do so may make more difficult the prosecution difficult of a party or a witness for perjury.[26]

The usual sequence of taking evidence from a witness is as follows:

- examination-in-chief by the party introducing the evidence
- cross-examination by the opposing party
- re-examination by the party introducing the evidence. The witness is again questioned by the original attorney to address the witness' testimony on cross-examination[27]

F. Traditional Sequence of Events at the Hearing

In the following paragraphs, we provide a summary of the usual sequence of events at the hearing stage of an arbitration following traditional procedures. Thereafter each step of this sequence is examined in greater detail.

If the parties choose a litigation-like procedure for their hearing, the proceedings would be much like a traditional court hearing. Recall that the traditional procedures used in Hong Kong courts, and most common-law legal systems, are frequently adversarial. *Adversarial proceedings* generally involve each party presenting its case and attempting to reveal any flaws in the evidence or arguments of the opposing party. Contrast these procedures with inquisitorial proceedings, which are adopted in many countries with a civil-law legal system. *Inquisitorial proceedings* generally involve the judges or arbitrators questioning the witnesses with little or no cross-examination by the opposing party.[28]

The Hong Kong government's *e-Legislation Glossary* [hereinafter *e-legislation glossary*] translates "administer an oath or affirmation" as 監誓. *See* the *Glossary* website at: https://www.elegislation.gov.hk/glossary/en (last visited 21 Jul. 2017).

[24] BLACK'S, *supra* note 10, at 1239 explains "oath" as:

> A solemn declaration, accompanied by a swearing to God or a revered person or thing, that one's statement is true or that one will be bound to a promise. The person making the oath implicitly invites punishment if the statement is untrue or the promise is broken. The legal effect of an oath is to subject the person to penalties for perjury if the testimony is false.

e-legislation glossary, *supra* note 23, translates "oath" as 宗教式宣誓.

[25] BLACK'S, *supra* note 10, at 70 defines "affirmation" as a "solemn pledge equivalent to an oath but without reference to a supreme being or to swearing; a solemn declaration made under penalty of perjury, but without an oath." THE HON MR JUSTICE PATRICK CHAN, THE CONCISE HONG KONG ENGLISH-CHINESE LEGAL DICTIONARY (2005) [hereinafter ENGLISH-CHINESE LEGAL DICTIONARY] 32 translates "affirmation" as 非宗教式誓詞.

[26] § 31 of the *Crimes Ordinance* (Cap. 200) defines "perjury" as:

> any person lawfully sworn as a witness or as an interpreter, either generally or in a particular judicial proceeding, wilfully makes a statement in any judicial proceeding which is material in that proceeding and which he knows to be false or does not believe to be true . . . shall be guilty of perjury.

Id. translates "perjury" as 宣誓下作假證供.

[27] *See, e.g.*, MA & BROCK, *supra* note 3, at para. 15.202. These terms and procedures will be explained in more detail in the following section.

[28] This topic is discussed in greater detail in Chapter 1. *See also*, MA & BROCK, *supra* note 3, at paras. 15.001–15.003.

Again, the parties and the arbitral tribunal will agree on the sequence of oral arguments and the taking of evidence. The usual procedure is summarized as follows. If the respondent raises preliminary or procedural objections, the arbitral tribunal usually will hear these objections and the claimant's reply on these preliminary issues before proceeding to hear the dispute's substantive issues.

For the substantive issues, the claimant, as the party bringing the claim, is usually heard first in an opening speech, sometimes referred to as the *opening statement* or simply as *opening*. The respondent's speech is its reply to the claim. These speeches provide a summary of the disputes, the issues in the disputes, and, what is claimed or denied. In some instances, the parties' opening statements are submitted in writing, and the actual opening remarks at the hearing are limited because each party proceeds on the assumption that the arbitral tribunal has full knowledge of the written submissions and the evidence submitted on the record.[29]

Following each party's opening speech, that party presents its evidence through witnesses. As another time-saving measure, where written witness statements are filed, the parties and the arbitral tribunal may agree that these witness statements would replace the examinations-in-chief.[30] After the examination of witnesses, the parties may make closing speeches. Written post-hearing briefs may or may not be submitted after the end of the hearing. These briefs may be filed consecutively or sequentially. The arbitral tribunal then closes the hearing stage of the proceedings. Generally, no further submissions of evidence are permitted.[31]

Having provided in the above paragraphs a summary of the main procedure of a traditional hearing, each of these stages of the proceedings is now reviewed in more detail in the following sections.

i. Commencing the hearing

At the hearing stage of the arbitration process, it is common practice for the arbitral tribunal to:

- identify the parties involved in the arbitration
- confirm that the parties' contract contains an arbitration agreement
- confirm the manner of each arbitrator's appointment
- provide a summary outline of the dispute
- summarise briefly the events leading to the hearing

29 Redfern & and Hunter, *supra* note 1, at para. 6.172.

30 Moser & Cheng, *supra* note 14, at para. 5-131.

31 As summarized by Ma & Brock, *supra* note 3, at para. 15.197:

The usual order is:

(1) claimant's opening;
(2) claimant's evidence;
(3) respondent's opening;
(4) respondent's evidence;
(5) respondent's closing; and
(6) claimant's closing.

Upon completion of the above introductory matters, the tribunal would declare formally the commencement of the arbitration hearing and invite the claimant to begin the proceedings.

ii. Opening and closing the claimant's case

The claimant, or its representative, *opens* its case with an introduction of the claimant and of the opposing party, followed by an introduction of the other members of the claimant's team. The claimant then outlines the facts of its case and any legal submissions in its support. If the respondent has made a counterclaim, the claimant would also open its defence to the counterclaim at this time. The claimant then presents its oral and written evidence by calling the claimant's witnesses.

The claimant proceeds with its case by calling each of its witnesses for questioning. This is known as the *examination-in-chief*.[32] The respondent then questions each of these witnesses. This is known as *cross-examination*.[33] Subsequently, the claimant has another opportunity to question again each of its witnesses. This is known as *re-examination*.[34] After the claimant completes the presentation of its evidence

---

[32] In some jurisdictions, this is also known as "direct examination." BLACK'S, *supra* note 10, at 556 defines "direct examination" as: "The first questioning of a witness in a trial or other proceeding, conducted by the party who called the witness to testify."

ENGLISH-CHINESE LEGAL DICTIONARY, *supra* note 25, at 337 translates "examination in chief" as 主問 and defines "examination in chief" as:

> A witness is examined in chief by or on behalf of the party for whom he is called to give evidence. Leading questions are not generally permitted at this stage. Examination in chief is a highly skilled exercise, requiring great tact and discretion to unfold the witness's evidence, so far as possible in narrative form and in chronological order, without 'leading' him, that is, asking him questions which suggest the answers desired.

[33] BLACK'S, *supra* note 10, at 458 defines "cross-examination" as:

> The questioning of a witness at trial or hearing by the party opposed to the party in whose favor the witness has testified. The purpose of cross-examination is to discredit a witness before the fact-finder in any of several ways, as by bringing out contradictions and improbabilities in earlier testimony, by suggesting doubts to the witness, and by trapping the witness into admissions that weaken the testimony. The cross-examiner is typically allowed to ask leading questions but is traditionally limited to matters covered on direct examination and to credibility issues.

ENGLISH-CHINESE LEGAL DICTIONARY, *supra* note 25, at 223 translates "cross-examination" as 盤問 and provides that: "Cross-examination takes place after a witness has given his or her evidence in chief. Leading questions are permitted during cross-examination."

[34] In some jurisdictions, this is known as "re-direct examination" or more simply as "re-direct."

BLACK'S, *supra* note 10, at 1468 defines "redirect examination" as: "A second direct examination, after cross-examination, the scope ordinarily being limited to matters covered during cross-examination."

ENGLISH-CHINESE LEGAL DICTIONARY, *supra* note 25, at 337 translates "re-examination" as 覆問 and defines "re-examination" as:

> Further questioning of a witness by the party who called the witness after cross-examination of the witness has been completed. The purposes of re-examination are to question the witness in order to allow the witness to clarify or explain matters arising in cross-examination to remove ambiguities and uncertainties or answers which may lead to a distortion of the account which the witness could give, and to rehabilitate the credibility or character of the witness, and to enable him to explain what he had said in evidence during his cross-examination. No questions may be asked in re-examination which introduce wholly new matters except by leave of the court. Leading questions must not be asked during re-examination. Re-examination must be conducted in like manner as at the trial of a cause or matter.

supporting its claim, the claimant *closes* the opening stage of its case, usually with a summary.

The claimant then waits for the respondent to present its case and its evidence. Once the respondent has done so and following the respondent's closing address, the claimant makes its final submission to the arbitral tribunal in which the claimant summarises and closes its case. Thus, in litigation-style arbitration where the respondent submits evidence to the arbitral tribunal, the claimant is the first party to proceed and the last party to conclude.

iii. Opening and closing the respondent's case

Once the claimant closes its case, the respondent then opens its own case and presents its witnesses. The respondent, or its representative, begins with an introduction of the respondent and the members of its team. This is followed by an outline of the facts of its case and any legal submissions in its support. The respondent then introduces its evidence by calling witnesses. The sequence of presenting evidence by the respondent is the same as above for the claimant: the claimant cross-examines each of the respondent's witnesses after which the respondent re-examines its witnesses.

After presenting its evidence, the respondent makes its final submission to the arbitral tribunal. In this final submission, the respondent summarises and closes its case. If, however, the respondent presents no evidence, the claimant is required to close its case before the respondent, giving the respondent the opportunity to make the final closing or submission to the tribunal.

iv. Intervention by the arbitral tribunal

The *Arbitration Ordinance* authorizes an arbitral tribunal to take the initiative to ascertain facts that are relevant to the proceedings, which includes acting inquisitorially, although this power can be excluded by the parties in their arbitration agreement.[35] Consequently, an arbitral tribunal may ask questions of a witness at any time. Generally, however, a tribunal will wait until the end of re-examination in order to avoid disrupting the flow of evidence. The arbitral tribunal may intervene with questions and requests for clarification much more freely during the final submissions.

Both parties should be given the opportunity to examine and cross-examine a witness if the arbitral tribunal's questioning raises new or potentially misleading points which require clarification. Failure to do so on the part of the tribunal might

[35] § 56(7) of the *Arbitration Ordinance*, *supra* note 2; MOSER & CHENG, *supra* note 14, at para. 5-124.
At present, it is rare to adopt inquisitorial-style procedures in arbitrations in Hong Kong. Inquisitorial-style procedures are more common in arbitrations where the arbitral tribunal comprises both civil-law and common-law arbitrators. CHOONG & WEERAMANTRY, *supra* note 10, at para. 56.26.
See also Chapter 1 for a discussion of adversarial and inquisitorial legal systems; BUTTERWORTHS HONG KONG ARBITRATION LAW HANDBOOK para. [47.09] and para. [56.15] (DAMON YC SO, CHRISTOPHER TO *et al.*, eds., 2nd ed. 2018) [hereinafter SO & TO].

cause the award to be set aside or become unenforceable.[36] In *Apex Tech Investment Ltd v Chuang's Development (China) Ltd*,[37] the Hong Kong court refused to enforce an arbitral award on the basis that the arbitral tribunal had made the award based on its own investigations without providing the parties the opportunity to comment on the matters arising from these investigations.[38] The *Arbitration Ordinance* permits an arbitral tribunal to make its own enquiries if the parties' submissions are insufficient for the tribunal to come to a decision.[39]

v. Closing the hearing

The arbitral tribunal should declare the hearing closed after the final submissions of the parties. Generally, no further evidence will be accepted after the close of the hearing. Whether any post-hearing memoranda would be submitted will be determined by the parties and the arbitral tribunal. Finally, where possible, the tribunal should indicate to the parties when its decision, known as the *final award*, would be made.

IV. Evidence

In the previous section concerning the arbitration hearing, we mentioned the parties giving *evidence*. There are several types of evidence. Generally, in arbitration, an arbitral tribunal will be concerned with the following types of evidence:

- oral evidence, *i.e.*, statements made by the parties and their witnesses, including experts. A witness of fact relates its perception and recollection of the events within its knowledge. As mentioned previously, it is possible that a witness does this in a written witness statement. A common practice in some jurisdictions is for the parties' lawyers to assist in the preparation of these witness statements. There is a cultural difference in this respect. In the civil-law legal system, lawyers do not assist witnesses in preparing their witness statements, as this is considered tampering with a witness. In the common-law legal system, lawyers do assist the witnesses, to varying degrees, with their preparation of witness statements. Different jurisdictions also have differing views on whether a party should be allowed to testify, and

36 Moser & Cheng, *supra* note 14, at para. 5-124.

37 [1996] 2 HKLR 155.

38 Choong & Weeramantry, *supra* note 10, at para. 56.25.

39 *Id.* at para. 56.26 explains:

> In practice, inquisitorial-style procedures are likely to remain rare in arbitrations taking place in Hong Kong. However, a tribunal comprised of civil-law and common-law arbitrators may rely upon section 56(7) and adopt a procedure containing aspects of both traditions. The provision is also useful in enabling a tribunal actively to pursue its enquiries where it feels that the parties' submissions are insufficient to enable it properly to reach a conclusion. But tribunals must avoid using this power as an alternative to encouraging the parties fully to make their cases.

whether witnesses (including parties who testify) should be allowed in the hearing room while other witnesses are presenting their evidence.

- documentary evidence, *i.e.*, documents produced for inspection
- real evidence, *i.e.*, material objects produced for inspection
- hearsay evidence, *i.e.*, evidence of fact not actually perceived by a witness but proved to have been stated by another person[40]
- primary evidence, *i.e.*, evidence which itself suggests that it is the best evidence and which has to be produced if available
- secondary evidence, *i.e.*, evidence which itself suggests the existence of better evidence and which is rejected if primary evidence is available

A. Rules of Evidence

The courts have rules of evidence which must be followed in litigating a court case. As some arbitrations follow traditional court procedure, these rules of evidence are also sometimes followed. Most arbitrations, however, do not observe such strict evidentiary rules, even if the arbitration itself follows a litigation style of procedure.

In Hong Kong, the *Arbitration Ordinance* provides that an arbitral tribunal is not bound by the rules of evidence which are applied in court.[41] Therefore, for arbitrations seated in Hong Kong, it is the arbitral tribunal which determines the

---

40 English-Chinese Legal Dictionary, *supra* note 25, at 425 translates "hearsay evidence" as 傳聞證據.

41 § 47(3) of the *Arbitration Ordinance*, *supra* note 2, provides:

> When conducting arbitral proceedings, an arbitral tribunal is not bound by the rules of evidence and may receive any evidence that it considers relevant to the arbitral proceedings, but it must give the weight that it considers appropriate to the evidence adduced in the arbitral proceedings.

§ 47(3) of the *Arbitration Ordinance* requires an arbitral tribunal to assess the weight to be given to the evidence but does not expressly presume that the evidence being excluded by the tribunal is inadmissible.

The International Bar Association's *Rules on the Taking of Evidence in International Arbitration* (2010) [hereinafter IBA Rules] serves as a useful guide for arbitral tribunals to follow in assessing the weight of evidence. Art. 9(2) of the IBA Rules provides a list of grounds for a tribunal to consider in deciding whether to exclude certain items of evidence:

> The Arbitral Tribunal shall, at the request of a Party or on its own motion, exclude from evidence or production any Document, statement, oral testimony or inspection for any of the following reasons:
> (a) lack of sufficient relevance to the case or materiality to its outcome;
> (b) legal impediment or privilege under the legal or ethical rules determined by the Arbitral Tribunal to be applicable;
> (c) unreasonable burden to produce the requested evidence;
> (d) loss or destruction of the Document that has been shown with reasonable likelihood to have occurred;
> (e) grounds of commercial or technical confidentiality that the Arbitral Tribunal determines to be compelling;
> (f) grounds of special political or institutional sensitivity (including evidence that has been classified as secret by a government or a public international institution) that the Arbitral Tribunal determines to be compelling; or
> (g) considerations of procedural economy, proportionality, fairness or equality of the Parties that the Arbitral Tribunal determines to be compelling.

See Choong & Weeramantry, *supra* note 10, at paras. 47.19–47.20.

admissibility of evidence.[42] The tribunal consequently has the discretion to deal with matters of admissibility, relevance, cogency and weight of evidence.[43] The tribunal may receive any evidence which the tribunal considers relevant to the proceedings, but giving such weight to the evidence as the tribunal considers appropriate.

There are several grounds upon which an arbitral tribunal may reject or deny the admission of evidence. The main grounds for excluding such evidence are that:

- the evidence is privileged, *e.g.*,
    - privilege against self-incrimination
    - legal professional privilege[44]
      Also known as *legal privilege*, this privilege applies to communications between lawyer and client made when seeking or receiving legal advice. Communications between a client or its legal adviser and a third party in contemplation of actual litigation or arbitration are also privileged.
    - without prejudice communications[45]
      Without prejudice evidence arises, when in an attempt to settle a dispute, the parties make certain statements in correspondence, negotiations or mediation. These statements cannot be put in evidence without the consent of both parties – these statements are covered by a joint privilege.[46] No particular form of words is required to render a document privileged; the critical factor is the parties' intention determined by the objective circumstances of the case. The use of the words *without prejudice* in a document is only indicative; the words need not appear at the head of the document but can appear in its text. If the document is one of a series of *without prejudice* communications, this phrase need not be used.
    - public interest privilege
      A party cannot be required to produce privileged evidence in an arbitration.[47] A party simply claiming that particular information is confidential or privileged does not make that information or evidence privileged.

---

[42] If the parties are legally represented, objections will be raised if there appears to be defects in the evidence presented, *e.g.*, relevance. Where one party is not legally represented, the arbitral tribunal should draw that party's attention to the question of admissibility of the evidence and invite an objection from that party if the arbitral tribunal considers the defect to be material.

[43] 2 Halsbury's Laws of Hong Kong para. [25.099] (2nd ed. 2016) (citations omitted).

[44] "Legal professional privilege" is said to apply to "communications between lawyers and their clients for the purpose of obtaining or giving legal advice" and is translated as 法律專業特權. Moser & Cheng, *supra* note 14, at para. 5-090.

[45] Black's, *supra* note 10, at 1837, defines "without prejudice" as: "Without loss of any rights; in a way that does not harm or cancel the legal rights or privileges of a party."

English-Chinese Legal Dictionary, *supra* note 25, at 1055 defines "without prejudice" as a "statement made without an intention to affect the legal rights of any person" and translates "without prejudice" as 無損權利.

[46] *See, e.g.*, Moser & Cheng, *supra* note 14, at para. 72.

[47] § 56(9) of the *Arbitration Ordinance*, *supra* note 2, provides: "A person is not required to produce in arbitral proceedings any document or other evidence that the person could not be required to produce in civil proceedings before a court."

- the evidence is irrelevant to any issue in the arbitration
- the evidence is merely opinion, unless the witness is an expert by qualification and/or experience
- the evidence is hearsay and not limited to facts within the witness' personal knowledge

B. Witnesses: Examination

In this chapter's section on Hearings, we introduced the procedure usually used for witness testimony in a litigation-type arbitration. In this section, we revisit the examination of witnesses of fact in more detail, particularly in terms of evidence rather than procedure.

An examination-in-chief is limited to the matters contained in the witness' statement. While giving evidence, a witness of fact is not allowed to read from or to refer to its witness statement. The party taking the witness through its evidence, either in chief or in cross-examination, may make reference to the statement while examining the witness. A witness whilst giving evidence is, however, permitted to refer to contemporaneous notes, *e.g.*, a diary, in order to refresh its memory.

A *leading question* is one which suggests the answer required of the witness. An example of leading a witness is: "You used Sulfate-Resisting Portland Concrete meeting BS 4027, didn't you?" Leading questions are not allowed to be asked of a witness during examination-in-chief or re-examination, except where necessary to contradict evidence already given by a witness for the opposing party.[48] Leading questions which mislead the witness through false assumptions or actual misstatements are not permitted.[49]

Cross-examination of a witness need not be confined to the facts in dispute. This may result in challenging the witness' character and credibility. The main object of cross-examination is to show that the witness is biased, partial or untruthful; that the evidence is inconsistent; and/or that the witness' knowledge or recollection of events is poor. Leading questions may be asked during cross-examination.

On re-examination of a witness, the questioning must be limited to matters which arise out of cross-examination. The purpose is to give an opportunity to

Generally, in court litigation, issues of privilege are heard by a judge who will not be the judge ultimately deciding the case. On the other hand, an arbitral tribunal needs to deal with both interlocutory disputes and to render the final award on the merits of the case. Parties might not wish to have the tribunal deciding the issues of privilege, and, giving the final award. In such instances, it is possible for the parties to use arbitral rules such as the IBA Rules, *supra* note 41, which permit the arbitral tribunal to appoint an impartial expert to review the allegedly privileged documents. In the event the documents are determined by the expert as privileged, the arbitral tribunal would not have seen the documents. This procedure addresses the possibility that the tribunal will become biased after viewing the privileged documents. CHOONG & WEERAMANTRY, *supra* note 10, at para. 56.29.

Again, pursuant to § 47(3) of the *Arbitration Ordinance*, *supra* note 2, the strict rules of evidence do not apply to arbitration. Nevertheless, the rules of evidence pertaining to privilege and fundamental protections for parties cannot be excluded.

48 *Moor v Moor* [1954] 2 All ER 458, 1 WLR 927 (CA).

49 ENGLISH-CHINESE LEGAL DICTIONARY, *supra* note 25, at 551, translates "leading question" as 引導性詰問.

the witness to explain apparent inconsistencies in its evidence and to explain fully matters that were only partially addressed during cross-examination.

Witness conferencing has eventually become an alternative to traditional cross-examination. *Witness conferencing* refers to placing "two or more witnesses together to answer questions from the tribunal."[50] This method is not usually applied to the examination of factual witnesses. Witness conferencing is more commonly used in examining expert witnesses and is discussed further in the following section.

C. Opinion/Expert Evidence

The term *opinion* refers to an inference from observed facts. The general rule is that a witness can only testify to that which the witness has directly perceived or experienced. The arbitral tribunal is to draw inferences from the *facts* presented by the witness. Therefore, the general rule is that the opinion evidence of a witness is not admissible. The exception to this rule concerns matters requiring specialist knowledge or skill. In such occasions, the tribunal may not possess the specialist knowledge to draw the appropriate conclusion from the facts stated by a witness.

Another type of witness, therefore, is allowed to assist by stating an opinion concerning these matters, provided that this type of witness has expertise in these matters. Expert evidence is opinion evidence provided on a particular issue by an expert in that field. Expert evidence is admissible if the arbitral tribunal gives permission to call an expert, unless the parties have agreed between themselves to call experts. In granting permission to call expert evidence, the arbitral tribunal should specify how many experts are required on each side. The arbitral tribunal's order also should state the date for exchange of the various experts' reports and the date for exchange of any supplemental reports.[51]

An expert generally fulfils a dual role. In one role, the expert advises the party which hired the expert on the technical issues within the expert's field of expertise. The expert may provide advice on the draft pleadings and suggest lines of research to be pursued. When writing the report, however, the expert must be entirely objective and impartial since an expert's primary role is to assist the arbitral tribunal in arriving at a just decision. The expert should not serve as the advocate for its client.[52] In one court case, the House of Lords has said that:

> While some degree of consultation between experts and legal advisers is entirely proper, it is necessary that expert evidence presented to the court should be, and should be seen to be, the independent product of the expert, uninfluenced as to form or content by the exigencies of litigation.[53]

---

[50] Redfern & Hunter, *supra* note 1, at para. 6.180.

[51] *See also* Chapter 7 concerning discovery of evidence.

[52] Moser & Cheng, *supra* note 14, at para. 5-132.

[53] *Stuart Whitehouse (suing by his mother and next friend Eileen Whitehouse) v J A Jordan* [1981] 1 WLR 246 at 256.

In another case, *Arjowiggins HKK2 Ltd v X Co*,[54] the Hong Kong court criticized the expert:

> [Respondent's expert] has failed to address, or to address adequately, the issues of whether or not the parties had reached a supplemental agreement on the arbitration body, and whether HKIAC can be determined as the arbitration body from the agreed HKIAC Rules. I agree that [Respondent's expert] has failed to give his opinion as an independent expert of the Court, and has simply reargued the case of the Respondent as advanced by the Respondent's team, of which [Respondent's expert] formed a part, in the PRC proceedings and in the Arbitration.[55]

As mentioned above, an expert witness may be appointed by the parties or by the arbitral tribunal.[56] Moreover, despite the earlier statement, a party-appointed

---

See also the other guidelines on expert evidence enunciated in *National Justice Compania Naviera SA v Prudential Assurance Co Ltd, The Ikarian Reefer* [1993] 2 Lloyd's Rep 68 which had summarized the duties and responsibilities of expert witnesses:

- An expert witness should provide independent assistance to the court [and the arbitral tribunal] by way of objective, unbiased opinion in relation to matters within his expertise . . . An expert witness in the High Court [and the arbitral tribunal] should never assume the role of an advocate.
- An expert witness should state the facts or assumptions upon which his opinion is based. He should not omit to consider material facts which could detract from his concluded opinion . . .
- An expert witness should make it clear when a particular question or issue falls outside his expertise.
- If an expert's opinion is not properly researched because he considers that insufficient data is available, then this must be stated with an indication that the opinion is no more than a provisional one . . . In cases where an expert witness, who has prepared a report, could not assert that the report contained the truth, the whole truth and nothing but the truth without some qualification, that qualification should be stated in the report . . .
- If, after exchange of reports, an expert witness changes his view on a material matter having read the other side's expert's report or for any other reason, such change of view should be communicated (through legal representatives) to the other side without delay and when appropriate to the court [and the arbitral tribunal].
- Where expert evidence refers to photographs, plans, calculations, analyses, measurements, survey reports or other similar documents, these must be provided to the opposite party at the same time as the exchange of reports.

54 [2016] HKEC 2472. The facts of this case is discussed in more detail in Chapter 10.

55 [2016] HKEC 2472 at para. 26.

56 § 54(1) of the *Arbitration Ordinance*, incorporating *Model Law* Art. 26, *supra* note 2, authorizes an arbitral tribunal to appoint its own experts. Nevertheless, the parties can exclude this authorization in their arbitration agreement or by adopting one of those institutions whose rules require the arbitral tribunal to consult the parties before appointing its own experts. Choong & Weeramantry, *supra* note 10, at para. 54.06. § 54 of the Ordinance provides in full:

(1) Article 26 of the UNCITRAL Model Law, the text of which is set out below, has effect—

"*Article 26. Expert appointed by arbitral tribunal*

(1) Unless otherwise agreed by the parties, the arbitral tribunal
   (a) may appoint one or more experts to report to it on specific issues to be determined by the arbitral tribunal;
   (b) may require a party to give the expert any relevant information or to produce, or to provide access to, any relevant documents, goods or other property for his inspection.

(2) Unless otherwise agreed by the parties, if a party so requests or if the arbitral tribunal considers it necessary, the expert shall, after delivery of his written or oral report, participate in a hearing where the parties have the opportunity to put questions to him and to present expert witnesses in order to testify on the points at issue."

(2) Without affecting article 26 of the UNCITRAL Model Law, given effect to by subsection (1), in

expert witness is viewed as inclined to present a more favourable interpretation of the evidence to support the appointing party. Hence this evidence is challenged and tested by cross-examination of the expert. Where each party appoints its own expert, the arbitral tribunal may require the experts of both parties to meet and jointly report on matters that they agree or disagree, and the tribunal may require that the evidence of both experts be given together by witness conferencing during the hearing.[57]

A tribunal-appointed expert witness is independent of the parties and prepares its evidence on instruction of the arbitral tribunal. Each party will have an opportunity to cross-examine the tribunal-appointed expert.[58] The parties are also entitled to present their own expert witness evidence to challenge the tribunal-appointed expert unless the parties have agreed to the contrary. In the case of *Paklito Investment Ltd v Klockner East Asia Ltd*,[59] the court refused to enforce an award on the basis that the defendant did not have the opportunity to comment on the report produced by the tribunal-appointed expert.[60] The arbitral tribunal may ask questions of this expert witness in order to make clarifications if necessary. Nevertheless, the arbitral tribunal is not bound to accept the evidence of any expert witness. The expert's report serves only to assist the tribunal in understanding or determining the issues in dispute. The parties' liability will be determined by the arbitral tribunal.

While giving evidence, an expert witness may:

- refresh its memory by reference to its notes
- refer to its own report
- refer to previous reports and relevant published material

An expert may also quote other cases and judgments in which it provided evidence that was accepted by the arbitral tribunal.

In the previous section, we introduced witness conferencing. Conferencing is used with expert witnesses since it can effectively identify the different experts' areas of agreement and disagreement. Witness conferencing thus may narrow the expert witnesses' differences in the event of conflicting expert opinions if used with

---

assessing the amount of the costs of arbitral proceedings (other than the fees and expenses of the tribunal) under section 74—

(a) the arbitral tribunal may appoint assessors to assist it on technical matters, and may allow any of those assessors to attend the proceedings; and

(b) the parties must be given a reasonable opportunity to comment on any information, opinion or advice offered by any of those assessors.

Note that the tribunal's appointment of an expert under § 54(1) of the *Arbitration Ordinance* is little used in Hong Kong. Parties usually prefer to call their appointed experts. Moser & Cheng, *supra* note 14, at para. 5-132.

57 Choong & Weeramantry, *supra* note 10, at para. 54.13.

58 § 54(1) of the *Arbitration Ordinance*, incorporating *Model Law* Art. 26(2), *supra* note 2, provides the parties with the right to question the tribunal-appointed expert at a hearing. *See* Choong & Weeramantry, *supra* note 10, at para. 54.16.

59 [1993] 2 HKLR 39.

60 Choong & Weeramantry, *supra* note 10, at para. 54.16.

traditional cross-examination.[61] This procedure also gives the arbitral tribunal an opportunity to make an immediate and direct comparison between the witnesses' earlier testimony, both written and oral.[62]

If witness conferencing is employed, the expert witnesses will be asked to meet and prepare lists of matters on which they agree or disagree and the reasons for such disagreement. This procedure may take place either before or after the experts have compiled their written reports.[63]

The arbitral tribunal will then prepare an agenda comprising matters on which the experts have not agreed and present it to the parties before the hearing. After both the factual witnesses and the expert witnesses have been cross-examined, the expert witnesses of both parties will then come before the arbitral tribunal.[64] The arbitral tribunal will ask the expert witnesses to explain the basis for reaching the opinions in their own expert reports and the main points of their reports. Sometimes, the tribunal may ask experts with conflicting opinions to debate their points of disagreement with each other.[65]

D. Arbitrator's Own Knowledge

In adversarial proceedings, an arbitral tribunal must decide the dispute based upon the evidence submitted by the parties. A tribunal cannot decide the dispute based upon material obtained from other sources, such as through the tribunal's own investigations. An arbitral tribunal cannot use knowledge obtained in a different capacity without disclosing this to the parties. Where an arbitral tribunal is permitted to act in an inquisitorial capacity, the arbitral tribunal must not take the parties by surprise in making the award. In other words, an arbitral tribunal must not make an award based upon the tribunal's own investigation or evidence without submitting these matters to the parties for comment.[66]

The case of *Annie Fox v P G Wellfair Ltd*[67] concerned a defective block of flats. The respondent was the builder who had gone into liquidation and was unrepresented at the arbitration. The claimants sought to prove their claims by calling six expert witnesses. The arbitrator awarded compensation which was considerably

---

61 Redfern & Hunter, *supra* note 1, at para. 6.181.

62 *Id.* at para. 6.180.

63 *Id.* at para. 6.184.

64 *Id.* at para. 6.185.

65 *Id.* at para. 6.186.

66 Parties must have an opportunity to question the evidence of an expert appointed by the tribunal. § 54(1) of the *Arbitration Ordinance*, incorporating *Model Law* Art. 26(2), *supra* note 2, states in relevant part:

> (2) Unless otherwise agreed by the parties, if a party so requests or if the arbitral tribunal considers it necessary, the expert shall, after delivery of his written or oral report, participate in a hearing where the parties have the opportunity to put questions to him and to present expert witnesses in order to testify on the points at issue.

67 [1981] 2 Lloyd's Rep 514 (CA).

For a discussion of this case in relation to the inquisitorial/civil-law legal system, *see* So & To, *supra* note 35, at para. [56.15].

lower than the amount put forward by the six experts. In order to arrive at the compensation amount, the arbitrator must have made a comparison between the experts' estimates of the repairs and the arbitrator's own calculations, based on a repairs scheme devised and estimated by the arbitrator himself. The High Court removed the arbitrator and set aside the award on the ground of misconduct. The Court of Appeal upheld the High Court's finding that the arbitrator had used his own evidence and used his own specialist knowledge in the absence of evidence from the respondent, but failed to give an opportunity to the claimants to address the arbitrator's evidence. This amounted to misconduct.

A distinction is made between a tribunal acting as its own expert, as in the *Fox* case, and, an arbitral tribunal making use of its specialist knowledge and experience to interpret and weigh the submitted evidence. The latter is proper as the parties have employed the arbitral tribunal members because of that specialist knowledge and experience.

V. Time-saving Methods

In previous sections of this chapter were briefly mentioned some procedural options in the hearing stage to save time and, hence, costs. Increasingly, arbitration is seen as being time-consuming and expensive. Techniques have been introduced in an attempt to reduce the costs of adversarial proceedings while ensuring a fair resolution. Some of these techniques have been mentioned above and are listed below along with others. Still others are discussed in Chapter 11, "Cost-saving Techniques in Arbitration."

Examples of established techniques at the hearing stage include the following:

- written opening submissions
- written closing submissions
- proofs of witnesses of fact standing as evidence-in-chief[68]
- proofs of expert witnesses standing as evidence-in-chief
- *chess clock* or *guillotine* procedures, *i.e.*, an equal but strictly limited time allowed for each party to present its case
- written submissions on preliminary points of law
- bifurcation of the arbitration so that liability is determined before quantum of damages, thereby allowing the parties an opportunity to negotiate a settlement sum upon the decision on liability rather than spending more time and costs disputing the amount

---

[68] MOSER & CHENG, *supra* note 14, at para. 5-131.
BLACK'S, *supra* note 10, at 1409 defines "proof" as: "The establishment or refutation of an alleged fact by evidence; the persuasive effect of evidence in the mind of a fact-finder."
ENGLISH-CHINESE LEGAL DICTIONARY, *supra* note 25, at 751 defines "proof" as: "Evidence which establishes the existence or non-existence of an alleged fact," and, at page 751 translates "proof" as 證明.

VI. Summary

In this chapter, the processes usually followed in an arbitration hearing were discussed, starting with preparations for the hearing. Next, we reviewed matters related to the hearing itself: confidentiality, representation, documents and amendments to these documents, witnesses and the sequence of the presentation of each party's case. The penultimate section introduced the role of evidence in a hearing. In the last section, we mentioned some time-saving techniques that are available to shorten the hearing phase.

9

Contents of the Award

I. Introduction

This lengthier chapter is divided into two parts. The first part focuses on the award itself and its decision concerning the merits, *i.e.*, the substantive matters of the dispute. The second part focuses on an important related matter: which of the disputing parties should be accountable for the costs and interest arising out of and resulting from the parties' dispute. Following in the penultimate chapter of this book, we discuss the topic of enforcing an arbitral award against a recalcitrant party and the topic of challenging an award by a losing party.

Part 1. The Award

I. Arbitral Awards: Generally

The arbitral tribunal has a contract with the parties. Each arbitrator, in exchange for a fee, is to make a binding decision on the parties' dispute. The arbitrator's decision, sometimes referred to as *determination*, is contained in a document called an *award*.[1] An award can be analogous to a court decision which contains a determination of matters such as, for example, the issues and the amount of damages one party pays to the opposing party, including possibly the costs of the arbitration or litigation.

The arbitral tribunal makes decisions about various issues, both procedural and substantive. These decisions may be contained in an order, direction or award.

---

1 Redfern and Hunter on International Arbitration para. 9.05 (Nigel Blackaby *et al.*, eds., 6th ed. 2015) [hereinafter Redfern & Hunter] states: "There is no internationally accepted definition of the term 'award'. Indeed, no definition is to be found in the main international conventions dealing with arbitration, including the Geneva treaties, the New York Convention, and the Model Law."

Procedural decisions are orders,[2] rulings[3] or directions[4] made by the arbitral tribunal over matters such as the management and organization of the arbitral process, including the administrative and logistical aspects of the arbitration.[5] The arbitral tribunal may need to issue several procedural orders or directions at various stages of the arbitral proceedings. These orders or directions are intended to move the dispute resolution forward towards a determination.[6]

As previously stated, arbitral tribunals in international commercial arbitration may grant interim measures of protection to varying degrees. The order of the arbitral tribunal may be described as either an *interim order* or an *interim award*. Such orders are not determinative of the issues in dispute between the parties but are to maintain the status quo and to further the arbitral process.[7] This will be discussed in further detail in the following section.

---

[2] Black's Law Dictionary 1270 (10th ed. 2014) [hereinafter Black's] defines "order" as "a written direction or command delivered by a government official, esp. a court or judge."
§ 14(4) of the *Arbitration Ordinance* (Cap. 609) [hereinafter *Arbitration Ordinance*] translates "order" as 命令.

[3] Black's, *supra* note 2, at 1533, defines "ruling" as "the outcome of a court's decision either on some point of law or on the case as a whole."
§ 34(1)(3) of the *Arbitration Ordinance*, incorporating *Model Law* Art. 16(3), *supra* note 2, translates "ruling" as 裁定.

[4] Black's, *supra* note 2, at 557, defines "direction" as "an order; an instruction on how to proceed." Section 45(8) of the *Arbitration Ordinance*, *supra* note 2, translates "direction" as 指示.

[5] John Choong and Romesh Weeramantry, The Hong Kong Arbitration Ordinance: Commentary and Annotations para. 84.09 (2nd ed. 2015) [hereinafter Choong & Weeramantry].

[6] As reiterated by Redfern & Hunter, *supra* note 1, at para. 9.08:

> The term 'award' should generally be reserved for decisions that finally determine the substantive issues with which they deal. This involves distinguishing between awards, which are concerned with substantive issues, and procedural orders and directions, which are concerned with the conduct of the arbitration. Procedural orders and directions help to move the arbitration forward; they deal with such matters as the exchange of written evidence, the production of documents, and the arrangements for the conduct of the hearing. They do not have the status of awards and they may perhaps be called into question after the final award has been made (for example as evidence of 'bias', or 'lack of due process'). (citations omitted)

[7] *See* for example: Art. 17 of UNCITRAL's *Model Law on International Commercial Arbitration* (2006) [hereinafter *Model Law*]; Art. 26 of UNCITRAL's Arbitration Rules (2013) [hereinafter Arbitration Rules].
As will be discussed in further detail in the following footnotes:

> The term 'award' is one that permeates municipal arbitration legislation, arbitration rules, treaties and conventions. However, it is a term that is often not defined. The UNCITRAL Arbitration Rules, for example, refer to final awards, interim, interlocutory, and partial awards without defining such terms. The International Chamber of Commerce (ICC) Rules of Arbitration refer to interim, partial, and final awards again without providing any definition. . . .
>
> The issue of what constitutes an award is relevant for two reasons. First, the courts at the seat of the arbitration will have different powers in relation to challenges to awards to those they have in relation to challenges to orders. In many countries the arbitration laws will not permit a challenge to be made to an arbitral tribunal's procedural order; it is only the award that can be challenged. In other countries the grounds of challenge differ if the decision is an award rather than a procedural order. . . . Second, the New York Convention only applies to awards. Procedural orders cannot be enforced under the New York Convention.
>
> . . . What constitutes an award is a question with little international agreement. On the one extreme, there is a view that an award must give a party damages or other redress; on the other extreme, there is a view that any decision which is final to the issue decided is an award. (citations omitted)

Andrew Tweeddale & Keren Tweeddale, Arbitration of Commercial Disputes–International and English Law and Practice paras. 10.21 –10.23 (2007) [hereinafter Tweeddale & Tweeddale].

Here, *award* refers to a tribunal's decision on the substantive issues, also known as the merits, of the parties' dispute. There are several purposes of such an arbitral award. The principal reasons are as follows:

- To resolve or end the issue in dispute which is addressed in that particular award. This is known as *res judicata*.[8] The legal principle of *res judicata* means that the issue has been decided and cannot be further arbitrated or litigated again.
- To notify the parties and to communicate the arbitrator's decision on a particular issue of the parties' dispute or on the whole dispute.
- To provide the successful party with evidence of the opposing party's liability. This will assist in the award's enforcement if the losing party attempts to avoid its obligations under the award.

II. Types of Award

Recall that there are two categories of decisions which an arbitral tribunal can issue. One category of decisions includes interim or interlocutory orders. An *interim order*, which is also known as an *interlocutory order*, does not finally dispose of the substantive issues in dispute.[9] For example, an interim decision may deal with jurisdiction, a preliminary point of construction or interpretation, or, the law applicable to the merits of the case.[10] In some situations, these decisions are given the

---

[8] Black's, *supra* note 2, at 1504, defines "*res judicata*" as "an issue that has been definitively settled by judicial decision" and can serve as

> An affirmative defense barring the same parties from litigating a second lawsuit on the same claim, or any other claim arising from the same transaction or series of transactions and that could have been – but was not – raised in the first suit.

In summary, the principle of *res judicata* applies where (1) there has been an earlier decision on the issue, (2) a final judgment on the merits of the case had been handed down, and (3) the same parties are involved.
In *陳偉文 訴 入境事務處處長* (HCAL20/2000), "*res judicata*" has been translated as 既判力.

[9] Under § 37 of the *Arbitration Ordinance*, incorporating *Model Law* Art. 17B, *supra* note 2, a party may request an interim measure together with an *ex parte* application for a preliminary order. The arbitral tribunal has the power to grant a preliminary order provided it considers that prior disclosure of the request for the interim measure to the party against whom the interim measure is directed risks frustrating the purpose of the measure. Michael J. Moser and Teresa Y.W. Cheng, Hong Kong Arbitration: A User's Guide para. 5-114 (3rd ed. 2014) [hereinafter Moser & Cheng].
Section 38 of the *Arbitration Ordinance*, incorporating *Model Law* Art. 17C(4), *supra* note 2, provides that: "A preliminary order shall expire after twenty days from the date on which it was issued by the arbitral tribunal." Upon the expiration of twenty days, the preliminary order will need to be converted into an *inter partes* interim measure. The arbitral tribunal may issue an interim measure adopting or modifying the preliminary order after the party against whom the preliminary order is directed has been given notice and the opportunity to present its case. This enables the arbitral tribunal to continue the effect of the preliminary order by way of a more "permanent" interim measure not subject to a 20-day lifespan. Choong & Weeramantry, *supra* note 5, at para. 38.11.

[10] Moser & Cheng, *supra* note 9, at para. 5-161.
Arbitration in Hong Kong: A Practical Guide para. 17.025 (The Hon Chief Justice Geoffrey Ma and Denis Brock, eds., 4th ed. 2017) [hereinafter Ma & Brock] explains:

> Interim or partial awards must also be distinguished from interlocutory or procedural directions, which are not generally considered to be awards and need to be considered separately for the purposes of review and/or enforcement. To avoid confusion and possible argument, the arbitral tribunal should

named *award* in order to assist in the overseas enforcement of the arbitral tribunal decisions.[11] These decisions are not the focus of this chapter but are mentioned here in an attempt to avoid confusion.[12]

The focus of this chapter is on the second category of arbitral decision, a final and binding award, of which we review three types.[13] One type of award is known as a *partial award, interlocutory award* or *interim award*.[14] This type of award is a

---

avoid using the terminology of awards when making interlocutory directions. (citations omitted)

11 Part of this confusion over terminology may be owing to:

- § 35(1) of the *Arbitration Ordinance*, which incorporates *Model Law* Art. 17 *supra* note 7. Section 2 of Art. 17 states:

  > An interim measure is any temporary measure, whether in the form of an award or in another form, by which, at any time prior to the issuance of the award by which the dispute is finally decided, the arbitral tribunal orders a party to . . .

- § 35(3) of the *Arbitration Ordinance* permits an arbitral tribunal to "make an award to the same effect as the interim measure."

CHOONG & WEERAMANTRY, *supra* note 5, at paras. 35.18–35.19 notes:

> An interim measure granted by the arbitral tribunal is as such not enforceable, although in practice an order is usually voluntarily complied with . . . The lack of real "teeth" attaching to an order could potentially lead to a recalcitrant party ignoring the order and dissipating assets, reducing or even potentially destroying the value of the eventual award. In such a situation, the tribunal has discretion to support the order by making an award to the same effect . . .
>
> The rationale for this is that in some jurisdictions, only "awards" are directly enforceable whereas "orders" may not be. Therefore, if the tribunal's interim measure is converted into the form of an "award", this may increase the likelihood of its enforceability overseas. That said, it is important to recognise that in some jurisdictions, even if an "interim measure" is rendered in the form of an "award", this may not be sufficient to ensure that the resulting award is enforceable. This is because in such jurisdictions, only final and binding decisions qualify as "awards", whereas an interim measure (even if made in the form of an "award") will only be regarded as interim or provisional in nature. (citations omitted)

For an analysis of enforcement of interim measures, *see* § 61 of the *Arbitration Ordinance*, *supra* note 2; CHOONG & WEERAMANTRY, *supra* note 5, at paras. 43.03–43.14 and paras. 61.00–61.13.

12 CHOONG & WEERAMANTRY, *supra* note 5, at paras. 71.08–71.09 explains:

> In some instances, the term "interim awards" is used interchangeably with "interlocutory awards" or even "partial awards". In other instances, the term interim awards is used more loosely, to refer to an award that does not dispose finally of a particular claim (unlike a partial award) but which decides a preliminary issue relevant to disposing of such a claim, e.g. choice of law. Although less common, "interim awards" are also sometimes used to refer to decisions granting provisional relief and in this sense, an interim award is subject to revision by the arbitral tribunal on the granting of the final award.
>
> To overcome these ambiguities, some arbitral tribunals use the term "interim final award" or "partial final award" to make it clear that such an award is not subject to further revision. (citation omitted)

13 2 HALSBURY'S LAWS OF HONG KONG'para. [25.121] (2nd ed. 2016) [hereinafter HALSBURY'S] states:

> The Arbitration Ordinance does not generally define the types of award, although it refers to interim and final awards. There is nothing that would preclude an arbitral tribunal from using the universally recognised types of arbitration award, namely (1) a single final award, dealing with all issues referred to the tribunal, including costs; (2) a partial or interim award, clearly so identified, dealing in a final and binding manner with an issue or set of issues referred to the tribunal, leaving other issues and the question of costs for further partial or interim awards and/or a final award; (3) a consent award or award on agreed terms, recording agreed terms of settlement. The Ordinance also makes provision for a further category, the 'additional award'.

14 CHOONG & WEERAMANTRY, *supra* note 5, at para. 71.06 states: "Where a tribunal makes more than one award in the arbitration, the earlier awards are sometimes referred to as interim (or interlocutory) awards, or as partial awards. There is no agreed definition for these terms."

TWEEDDALE & TWEEDDALE, *supra* note 7, at para. 10.36 states: "In England an award which is not a final award will be a partial award. The terms interlocutory award, preliminary award, or interim award are all synonymous

decision on a substantive issue between the parties.[15] A partial award is a final determination of one or more substantive issues in dispute between the parties but is not a decision on all the issues. "The terms interim or partial award are used to denote an award which deals with part of the matters in controversy. The terms are not terms of art."[16] A partial award is useful in determining matters which are susceptible to determination pending the final outcome of the proceedings. Once a partial award is made, a considerable amount of time and money can be saved.[17] Thus, it is possible to have the first partial award deciding only one of four issues, *e.g.*, Issue II. A second partial award might then decide the last issue, *e.g.*, Issue IV. The two remaining issues might be decided in a final award which is discussed below.

The power of a tribunal to make partial awards derives from either the arbitration agreement or the applicable law. If parties choose to incorporate international or institutional arbitration rules in their arbitration agreement, such rules usually empower the tribunal to make partial awards.[18] For example, Hong Kong's *Arbitration Ordinance* provides that "[u]nless otherwise agreed by the parties, an arbitral tribunal may make more than one award at different times on different aspects of the matters to be determined."[19]

A *final award* is the last award that decides all of the remaining substantive issues in dispute between the parties.[20] In the example above, the final award will decide the remaining issues, Issue I and Issue III. It is also possible for a tribunal to issue a partial award deciding all the issues between the parties except for costs. The final award will then incorporate the partial award and the award on costs in a single document for ease of enforcement. As noted by one authority:

> The final award is an award in which the arbitral tribunal deals with all the matters which remain in controversy. It may be the tribunal's only award, in which case it

---

with the term partial award."

HALSBURY'S, *supra* note 13, at para. [25.125] makes this distinction: "The award should finally determine all disputes which the parties referred to arbitration, unless it is a partial award. A partial award is final as to the matters with which it deals and cannot be revisited later."

15 MA & BROCK, *supra* note 10, at para. 17.024 provides:

> An interim award is a final determination of a part of the matters in controversy. Hence, some arbitrators use the term "interim final award" or "partial final award" to make it clear that the award is not subject to further revision. It also follows that a party which is dissatisfied with an interim or partial award must exercise its powers to seek redress against the award, without delay, rather than to await the final outcome of the proceedings.

16 *Id.* at para. 17.022, footnote 18 states:

> The term "partial" is more commonly adopted in the international arena, where the courts of certain jurisdictions will only enforce final awards. To avoid any doubt some arbitrators will go so far as to call an award a "partial final" award.

17 REDFERN AND HUNTER, *supra* note 1, at para. 9.19.

18 *Id.* at para. 9.20; MA & BROCK, *supra* note 10, at para. 17.023.

19 § 71 of the *Arbitration Ordinance*, *supra* note 2.

20 It is noted that in the *Arbitration Ordinance*, *supra* note 2, the terms "award" and "final award" are not defined; only "Macao award" and "Mainland award" are defined. As regards the *Model Law*, *supra* note 7, "nowhere in the Model Law is a 'final award' defined nor does it give any guidance as to the different types of award that are available." CHOONG & WEERAMANTRY, *supra* note 5, at para. 68.06.

> will deal with all the substantive issues and costs. It may be the last in a series of awards, in which case it will deal with all [the] remaining issues including costs. The term "final" is adopted to demonstrate the arbitral tribunal's intent to deal with all matters which remain in controversy.[21]

Both types of awards are final as to the matters with which they deal. Again, the term *final award* can have two meanings. One meaning may refer to one complete document dealing with all the issues referred for determination, such as liability, quantum or amount of compensation to be paid, interest and costs. Another meaning may refer to the last award at the end of a series of interim awards, *e.g.*:

- Interim awards are made on liability and quantum plus interest. A final award is made on costs, *e.g.*, where there has been a payment into court.
- One interim award is made on Issues II. A second interim award is made on Issues I, III, and V. A final award is made on Issue IV and Issue VI, interest, and costs.[22]

Before issuance of the tribunal's final award, the parties may agree to settle their dispute. The terms of the parties' agreement may be adopted as the arbitral tribunal's award. This third type of award thus is not the decision of the arbitral tribunal but of the parties. The arbitral tribunal endorses the parties' settlement agreement in order to give the parties' settlement agreement the same effect as an award decided by the tribunal. In such instances, this award is known as a *consent award* which is also known as an *award on agreed terms*. An arbitrator is not obligated to sign a consent award. Again, if the parties settle their dispute, in whole or in part, the settlement terms can be adopted by the arbitration tribunal in a *consent interim award* or a *consent final award*, as the case may be.[23] Like an award deliberated by the arbitral tribunal, a consent award serves to:

---

[21] Ma & Brock, *supra* note 10, at para. 17.027.
See Choong & Weeramantry, *supra* note 5, at para. 68.06.

[22] In either event:

> Once an arbitral tribunal has published its final award its job is at an end. It is functus officio, subject only to any rights agreed by the parties and limited statutory rights which may lead to the arbitration being revived in part. Any award which the arbitral tribunal purports to issue after publication of its final award which does not fall within the limited rights of redress against an award is ineffective.

Ma & Brock, *supra* note 10, at para. 17.029 (citation omitted).
As for the timing of issuing awards, one needs to refer to the institutional rules or the law of the seat of the arbitration. *See id.* at paras. 17.005–17.013; Choong & Weeramantry, *supra* note 5, at paras. 72.00–72.21.
An interesting case arose in Australia concerning final awards. An arbitrator intentionally omitted a claim, due to insufficient information on which to render a decision, in his Final Award. The court decided that rather than an inadvertent or accidental omission, intentionally omitting to decide a claim meant that the arbitrator's mandate remained. The arbitrator's obligation remained outstanding and was not *functus officio* despite the characterization that the award was "final." *Blanalko Pty Ltd v Lysaght Building Solutions Pty Ltd* [2017] VSC 97.

[23] *See, e.g.*, Ma & Brock, *supra* note 10, at paras. 17.015–17.021; Halsbury's, *supra* note 13, at para. [25.126].
§ 66 of the *Arbitration Ordinance*, incorporating *Model Law* Art. 30, *supra* note 2, provides:

> (1) Article 30 of the UNCITRAL Model Law, the text of which is set out below, has effect—
>
> "*Article 30. Settlement*
>
> (1) If, during arbitral proceedings, the parties settle the dispute, the arbitral tribunal

- dispose of the dispute in an orderly manner
- ensure the dispute is *res judicata*
- make certain that the arbitral tribunal is *functus officio*[24]
- facilitate summary enforcement[25]

An award may be a *reasoned award* or an *award without reasons*. The latter is commonly known as a *non-speaking award*. A reasoned award contains the reasoning used by the arbitral tribunal to come to its conclusion as to liability. A non-speaking award refers to the fact that the award does not address or "speak" of the tribunal's reasoning. Pursuant to the *Arbitration Ordinance*, a reasoned award must be given unless the parties agree otherwise; or, the award is a consent award.[26]

---

shall terminate the proceedings and, if requested by the parties and not objected to by the arbitral tribunal, record the settlement in the form of an arbitral award on agreed terms.

(2) An award on agreed terms shall be made in accordance with the provisions of article 31 and shall state that it is an award. Such an award has the same status and effect as any other award on the merits of the case."

(2) If, in a case other than that referred to in article 30 of the UNCITRAL Model Law, given effect to by subsection (1), the parties to an arbitration agreement settle their dispute and enter into an agreement in writing containing the terms of settlement ("settlement agreement"), the settlement agreement is, for the purposes of its enforcement, to be treated as an arbitral award.

For further discussion of this section of the Ordinance, *see* Choong & Weeramantry, *supra* note 5, at paras. 66.00–66.17.

[24] Black's, *supra* note 2, at 787, defines "*functus officio*" as "(of an officer or official body) without further authority or legal competence because the duties and functions of the original commission have been fully accomplished." Ma & Brock, *supra* note 10, at para. 17.001 states:

> The arbitral process is directed towards achieving a binding determination of the parties' dispute. Once an arbitral tribunal has determined an issue and rendered an award in respect of that issue, its job is done. It is *functus officio*. This means that, subject to limited exceptions . . . the arbitral tribunal is powerless to revisit its award.

Redfern & Hunter, *supra* note 1, at para. 9.18 notes:

> Subject to certain exceptions, the delivery of a final award renders the arbitral tribunal *functus officio*: it ceases to have any further jurisdiction in respect of the dispute, and the special relationship that exists between the arbitral tribunal and the parties during the currency of the arbitration ends.

[25] The mechanics of summary enforcement of awards and settlement agreements are governed by Order 73, rule 10 of the Rules of the High Court (Cap. 4A) [hereinafter High Court Rules]. *See also* § 61 and Part 10 of the *Arbitration Ordinance*, *supra* note 2, in relation to enforcement provisions.

[26] § 67 of the *Arbitration Ordinance*, incorporating *Model Law* Art. 31, *supra* note 2, states:

(1) Article 31 of the UNCITRAL Model Law, the text of which is set out below, has effect—

"*Article 31. Form and contents of award*

(1) The award shall be made in writing and shall be signed by the arbitrator or arbitrators. In arbitral proceedings with more than one arbitrator, the signatures of the majority of all members of the arbitral tribunal shall suffice, provided that the reason for any omitted signature is stated.

(2) The award shall state the reasons upon which it is based, unless the parties have agreed that no reasons are to be given or the award is an award on agreed terms under article 30.

(3) The award shall state its date and the place of arbitration as determined in accordance with article 20(1). The award shall be deemed to have been made at that place.

(4) After the award is made, a copy signed by the arbitrators in accordance with paragraph (1) of this article shall be delivered to each party."

(2) Article 31(4) of the UNCITRAL Model Law, given effect to by subsection (1), has effect subject to section 77.

III. Rules Applicable to the Merits

An arbitral tribunal usually decides the dispute between the parties based on the law that applies to the contract between the disputing parties. An exception is where the parties have authorized the tribunal to decide the dispute on the basis of fairness or without reference to law, as an *amiable compositeur*[27] or *ex aequo et bono*.[28] In an arbitration *amiable compositeur* or *arbitration ex aequo et bono*, there:

As mentioned in Chapter 3, the Ordinance provides for an "opt-in" provision for the parties to have a domestic arbitration. In this regard, the *Arbitration Ordinance* does not appear to permit non-speaking awards for domestic arbitrations. Schedule 2 of the Ordinance, however, implies that non-speaking awards are possible. In Schedule 2, § 5(2) states in part that it is possible to have an "agreement to dispense with the reasons for an arbitral tribunal's award." Likewise, in Schedule 2, § 7(2)(a) states that where an award "does not contain the arbitral tribunal's reasons for the award," the court may order the reasons to be stated. The court is empowered to make a further order in respect of the additional costs of arbitration arising from its order for reasons under Schedule 2, section 7(3) of the *Arbitration Ordinance*. Choong & Weeramantry, *supra* note 5, at para. Sch2.114.

Notwithstanding the absence of a general duty to give reasons in a domestic arbitration, guidance as to when reasons should be given was offered in *Michael Warde v Feedex International Inc* [1984] 1 Lloyd's Rep 310, where the court stated:

- when one party requests reasons, a reasoned award should be given, except in exceptional circumstances
- where both parties request reasons, reasons should be given. Conversely, if both parties state that a reasoned award is not required, their wishes should be respected, though at the same time they may ask the arbitrator to provide reasons in a separate document not forming part of the award.
- if one party asks for no reasons and the other party remains silent, no reasons should be given but the arbitrator should consider asking the silent party's wishes in the event that this party is unaware of its rights.
- if neither party requests reasons, the arbitrator should consider asking the parties. Where, however, the parties are represented by counsel, the arbitrator is justified in assuming that an unreasoned award is required.

27 Black's, *supra* note 2, at 102, defines "*amiable compositeur*" as:

> An arbitrator empowered, by agreement of the parties, to settle a dispute on the basis of what is equitable and good (*ex aequo et bono*), subject to procedural fairness and the terms of the arbitration agreement as opposed to the settled substantive rules of a given legal system.

§ 64 of the *Arbitration Ordinance*, incorporating *Model Law* Art. 28(3), *supra* note 2, translates "*amiable compositeur*" as 友好仲裁員.

Choong & Weeramantry, *supra* note 5, at para. 64.20 defines this term:

> Arbitration *amiable compositeur* also has been described as involving the determination of the dispute on the basis of fairness, reasonableness, equity and good conscience, without having to follow strict legal or contractual requirements. However, the arbitral tribunal deciding as *amiable compositeur* in some jurisdictions:
> (a) Is said to have a mandate primarily to "settle" the dispute rather than to adjudicate upon it;
> (b) May be authorised to fill gaps in the parties' bargain;
> (c) May be required to reach a business solution, even if to do so would conflict with the arbitrator's personal conception of equity. (citation omitted)

28 Black's, *supra* note 2, at 679, defines "*ex aequo et bono*" as "according to what is equitable and good."

§ 64 of the *Arbitration Ordinance*, incorporating *Model Law* Art. 28(3), *supra* note 2, translates "*ex aequo et bono*" as 公平善意原則.

Choong & Weeramantry, *supra* note 5, at para. 64.19 defines this term:

> Arbitration *ex aequo et bono* has been said to entitle the tribunal to decide according to principles of fairness, reasonableness, equity and good conscience, without having to follow strict legal or contractual requirements. This term may have a variety of meanings, including:
> (a) To apply relevant rules of law but to dispense with purely formalistic rules;
> (b) To apply relevant rules of law but to dispense with those which operate unfairly or harshly in the particular case;

is much uncertainty about what these terms mean and what these types of arbitration entail, it is likely that the parties' authorisation will have to spell out the tribunal's remit in detailed terms and the powers it may exercise.[29]

Where the parties have made an express choice in their contract, the arbitral tribunal must apply the law chosen by the parties. If the parties have not made any choice or their choice does not cover all the issues in dispute, the tribunal decides the law or rules of law by which it will decide the dispute. In some jurisdictions, the tribunal is required to use the conflict of law rules of the given jurisdiction. In other jurisdictions, the tribunal can choose the law that the tribunal considers most appropriate.[30] In either instance, the arbitral tribunal decides which law or rules of law should supplement the parties' agreement or their chosen rules. The term *law* refers here to a national law. The term *rules of law* refer to non-national laws, standards or principles. If there is no express choice or a gap in the choice, the arbitral tribunal would then refer to the arbitration rules applicable to the dispute or the national arbitration law of the seat to determine the applicable law.[31]

Under some international contracts, the parties expressly may agree not to apply a set of law or rules in determining their dispute. The parties can authorize the arbitrator to act as an *amicable compositeur*. In this role, the arbitral tribunal decides the dispute based on fairness and on what is just. The arbitral tribunal does not need to justify its decision based on law but solely on a perception of what is a fair resolution between the disputing parties.[32]

(c) To disregard a strict construction of a contract. (citation omitted)

See also Butterworths Hong Kong Arbitration Law Handbook para. [64.16] (Damon YC So, Christopher To *et al.*, eds., 2nd ed. 2018) [hereinafter So & To] for a similar definition and a discussion of this term.

[29] Choong & Weeramantry, *supra* note 5, at para. 64.21. *See also* So & To, *supra* note 28, at para. [64.16].

[30] For example, *see* Art. 21(1) of the International Chamber of Commerce's Rules of Arbitration (2017) [hereinafter ICC Rules]. Art. 21(1) states:

> The parties shall be free to agree upon the rules of law to be applied by the arbitral tribunal to the merits of the dispute. In the absence of any such agreement, the arbitral tribunal shall apply the rules of law which it determines to be appropriate.

These ICC rules are found at this website: https://iccwbo.org/dispute-resolution-services/arbitration/rules-of-arbitration/ (last visited 11 Jul. 2017).

[31] *See, e.g.*, *Model Law*, *supra* note 7, at Art. 28; Arbitration Rules, *supra* note 7, at Art. 33; and, Art. 36 of the Hong Kong International Arbitration Centre's Administered Arbitration Rules (2018) [hereinafter HKIAC Arbitration Rules].

[32] *See, e.g.*, *Model Law*, *supra* note 7, at Art. 28; Arbitration Rules, *supra* note 7, at Art. 33.1; and, HKIAC Arbitration Rules, *supra* note 31, at Art. 36.2.

However, an arbitral tribunal acting as amiable compositeur is still subject to the following restrictions:

(a) Article 28(4) states that in all cases, the arbitral tribunal shall take into account trade usage applicable to the transaction;

(b) Section 46 provides that the parties shall be treated with equality and shall be given reasonable opportunity of presenting their cases;

(c) Article 34(2)(b)(ii) provides that an award may be set aside if it is in conflict with the public policy of the State of the place of arbitration.

Choong & Weeramantry, *supra* note 5, at para. 64.24.

See also So & To, *supra* note 28, at para. [64.16] for a definition and a discussion of this term.

Recall that an arbitral tribunal is appointed to decide a dispute and this tribunal may be comprised of a single arbitrator or several arbitrators. A sole arbitrator does not need to deliberate with anyone in making a decision. In an arbitral tribunal with more than one arbitrator, the arbitrators will meet after the closure of the proceedings in order to deliberate the issues in order to arrive at a decision. In either situation, each arbitrator's decision is personal and cannot be delegated to another arbitrator or another individual. During these deliberations, the party-appointed arbitrator might assist the other tribunal members to understand and to appreciate the case presented by its appointing party.

If an arbitral tribunal consists of several members, there is the possibility that the tribunal cannot come to a unanimous decision. In such situations, a majority decision constitutes the decision of the whole arbitral tribunal. The advantage of an odd-numbered arbitral tribunal is that tie votes are avoided. Under some arbitration rules, if there is a tie vote, the presiding arbitrator casts the deciding vote. Such a vote automatically creates a majority decision for the arbitral tribunal's award. Under the ICC rules, where there is no majority, the tribunal president's vote will decide the issues.[33]

There is no fixed rule concerning drafting the tribunal's award in a tribunal with multiple members. It is possible for the presiding arbitrator to prepare a first draft for discussion. Alternatively, the tribunal may agree that each arbitrator draft the tribunal's decision on one or more issues for inclusion into the award's final draft. Another possibility is that the tribunal may assign the member whose native language is the language of the arbitration to prepare the final draft of the award.[34]

A dissenting arbitrator may write a dissent which, depending upon the jurisdiction, may be attached to the majority opinion. Most laws and arbitration rules, however, do not permit attachment of dissenting opinions.

IV. Remedies

An arbitral tribunal may award any remedy which would be available to a court to grant an injured party in a civil case. Thus, the following remedies would be

[33] *See, e.g.*, ICC Rules, *supra* note 30, at Art. 31; Arbitration Rules, *supra* note 7, at Art. 31.1; and, HKIAC Arbitration Rules, *supra* note 31, at Art. 33.1.

[34] *See, e.g.*, *Model Law*, *supra* note 7, at Art. 29.

available to the parties in arbitration: damages,[35] declaration,[36] specific performance,[37] indemnity,[38] or rectification[39] of a contract.

Section 70 of the *Arbitration Ordinance* provides:

> Subject to subsection (2) and section 103D(6), an arbitral tribunal may, in deciding a dispute, award any remedy or relief that could have been ordered by the Court if the dispute had been the subject of civil proceedings in the Court.
>
> Unless otherwise agreed by the parties, the arbitral tribunal has the same power as the Court to order specific performance of any contract, other than a contract relating to land or any interest in land.

V. Essentials of a Valid and Enforceable Award

It is important to determine what law governs the validity of the award to ensure its enforceability. In this section, we use the Ordinance and the *Convention on the Recognition and Enforcement of Foreign Arbitral Awards* (done in New York, 1958) [hereinafter "*New York Convention*"] for guidance. With the *New York Convention* currently having 157 signatory states, a final award in an international arbitration will likely be a Convention Award. Therefore, the Convention's requirements for an award would provide us with a guide.

---

[35] § 42 of the *Arbitration Ordinance*, *supra* note 2, translates "damages" as 損害賠償.
BLACK'S, *supra* note 2, at 472, defines "damages" as "money claimed by, or ordered to be paid to, a person as compensation for loss or injury."

[36] UNCITRAL's website translates "declaration" as 聲明. *See* the Chinese version of the website at: http://www.uncitral.org/uncitral/zh/uncitral_texts/sale_goods/1980CISG.html (last visited 31 Jan. 2018).
The English version of this website may be found at: http://www.uncitral.org/uncitral/en/uncitral_texts/sale_goods/1980CISG.html (last visited 31 Jan. 2018).
BLACK'S, *supra* note 2, at 492 defines "declaration" as "a formal statement, proclamation, or announcement, esp. one embodied in an instrument."

[37] Order 86, rule 1(a) of the High Court Rules, *supra* note 25, translates "specific performance" as 強制履行.
BLACK'S, *supra* note 2, at 1617, defines "specific performance" as

> The rendering, as nearly as practicable, of a promised performance through a judgment or decree; specif., a court-ordered remedy that requires precise fulfillment of a legal or contractual obligation when monetary damages are inappropriate or inadequate, as when the sale of real estate or a rare article is involved.

[38] The HKIAC's website translates "indemnity" as 彌償. *See* the Chinese version of the website at: http://www.hkiac.org/zh-hant/arbitration/why-hong-kong (last visited 31 Jan. 2018). The English version of this website may be found at: http://www.hkiac.org/arbitration/why-hong-kong (last visited 31 Jan. 2018).
BLACK'S, *supra* note 2, at 886, defines "indemnity" as

> (1) A duty to make good any loss, damage, or liability incurred by another. (2) The right of an injured party to claim reimbursement for its loss, damage, or liability from a person who has such a duty. (3) Reimbursement or compensation for loss, damage, or liability in tort; esp., the right of a party who is secondarily liable to recover from the party who is primarily liable for reimbursement of expenditures paid to a third party for injuries resulting from a violation of a common-law duty.

[39] § 23A of the *Wills Ordinance* (Cap. 30) translates "rectification" as 更正. BLACK'S, *supra* note 2, at 1467, defines "rectification" as:

> (1) A court's equitable correction of a contractual term that is misstated; the judicial alteration of a written contract to make it conform to the true intention of the parties when, in its original form, it did not reflect this intention. (2) A court's slight modification of words of a statute as a means of carrying out what the court is convinced must have been the legislative intent.

Recall that a final award determines all substantive issues in dispute between the parties which has not already been decided previously in a partial award. Recall, too, that a partial award is final as to its decisions or contents. Unless the parties have agreed to dispense with reasons, the award must be reasoned and determine all the issues submitted to the tribunal.

A. Requirements as to Form

The following legal requirements apply to an arbitration conducted under the *Arbitration Ordinance*. Firstly, the award is to be in writing: The parties need a record of:

- the decision of the arbitral tribunal
- the obligations which the tribunal have ordered the parties to undertake
- the remedies and/or damages which the arbitral tribunal has awarded to the parties

Where the losing party does not comply with the award, the successful party can seek enforcement of the award before a national court. For this court, the contents of the award will serve as a record of the tribunal's decision and the reasons for this decision. Where the award is challenged by one of the parties before a national court, this court will need a written award to review in order to determine whether one of the conditions for challenging the award has been met and in what manner this court should exercise its discretion.[40]

Another requirement is the tribunal's signature. The award is the arbitrators' decision and their signatures confirm that the award is theirs. The signatures also conclude the tribunal's mandate from the parties and the arbitrators' entitlement to any fees owed. On rare occasions, an arbitrator may disagree with the majority of arbitrators on the tribunal and refuse to sign an award.[41] In such a situation, the remaining arbitrators will sign and explain the reasons for the missing signature.[42]

---

[40] § 67 of the *Arbitration Ordinance*, incorporating *Model Law* Art. 31, *supra* note 2. The text of § 67 is set out in *supra* note 26.

[41] In such an instance, the majority of arbitrators will prevail. MA & BROCK, *supra* note 10, at para. 17.072.
§ 65 of the *Arbitration Ordinance*, incorporating *Model Law* Art. 29, *supra* note 2, provides for this situation:

> Article 29 of the UNCITRAL Model Law, the text of which is set out below, has effect—
>
> "*Article 29. Decision-making by panel of arbitrators*
>
> In arbitral proceedings with more than one arbitrator, any decision of the arbitral tribunal shall be made, unless otherwise agreed by the parties, by a majority of all its members. However, questions of procedure may be decided by a presiding arbitrator, if so authorized by the parties or all members of the arbitral tribunal."

[42] § 67 of the *Arbitration Ordinance*, incorporating *Model Law* Art. 31, *supra* note 2. The text of § 67 is set out in *supra* note 26.
MA & BROCK, *supra* note 10, at paras. 17.073–17.074 states:

> Where an arbitrator refuses to sign an award, the arbitration agreement and procedural rules may provide for this. However it is rare for this to be addressed in the arbitration provision, and is not addressed in many rules, in such circumstances, the Arbitration Ordinance assists. The Ordinance

As previously mentioned, the award needs to be a reasoned award.[43] The purposes for this requirement include the following:

- An arbitral award can be set aside on the basis of inadequate reasons.[44]
- Unless the parties have expressly dispensed with such requirement in the arbitration agreement, most international or institutional rules of arbitration require the tribunal to give reasons for the award. For example, the ICDR Rules 2014 require arbitrators to give reasons for the award unless parties have agreed to the contrary.[45] Another example is the Hong Kong International Arbitration Centre's Administered Arbitration Rules (2018) which require the arbitral tribunal to provide reasons for the award unless parties have agreed to dispense with such requirement.[46]

The award is to be dated. The operative part of the award takes effect from the date written on the award. Therefore, if any deadline (known as a limitation period) applies to enforcement, setting aside, or nullification of the award, the limitation period is calculated from the date of the award.[47]

The final requirement is that the place of arbitration is stated. The arbitration's venue indicates the origin of the award. From where the award originates determines whether it is a Convention Award, subject to Article 1 of the *New York Convention*.[48]

By virtue of the Ordinance, the above requirements also apply to:[49]

- a correction to an award[50]

> provides that signatures by the majority of the arbitral tribunal shall suffice, provided reason for the omitted signature is stated. (citation omitted)
>
> The relevant procedural rules may determine whether the views of the dissenting arbitrator should be set out in a dissenting opinion. In the absence of such guidance it is suggested that the dissenter's opinion should not be set out in a separate opinion, but should be canvassed in the majority award. (citation omitted)

In the Canadian case of *D Frampton & Co Ltd v Sylvio Thibeault and Navigation Harvey & Freres Inc* [1988] FCJ No. 305, the court determined that an award can be rendered by two arbitrators as long as they have stated the reason for the omitted signature (if any) under Art. 31 of the *Model Law*. CHOONG & WEERAMANTRY, *supra* note 5, at para. 67.07.

43 § 67 of the *Arbitration Ordinance*, incorporating *Model Law* Art. 31(2), *supra* note 2.
See, e.g., *Westpoint Insurance Corp v Gordon Runoff Ltd* [2010] NSWCA 57, an Australian case which discussed the adequacy of reasons provided in an arbitral award. *See also* the case of *Oil Basins v BHP Billiton* [2007] VSCA 255 which decided that the nature of the dispute should dictate the standard of reasoning in an award.

44 *See Oil Basins v BHP Billiton*, *supra* note 43.

45 ICDR is the acronym for the International Centre for Dispute Resolution which has published its International Dispute Resolution Procedures (Including Mediation and Arbitration Rules) (2014) [hereinafter ICDR Rules]. Art. 30 of these rules provides: "The tribunal shall state the reasons upon which an award is based, unless the parties have agreed that no reasons need be given."
The organization's website: www.adr.org/sites/default/files/ICDR%20Rules_0.pdf (last visited 28 Aug. 2017).

46 CHOONG & WEERAMANTRY, *supra* note 5, at para. 67.15. *See* HKIAC Arbitration Rules, *supra* note 31, at Art. 35.4.

47 § 67 of the *Arbitration Ordinance*, incorporating *Model Law* Art. 31(3), *supra* note 2.

48 *Id.*

49 *Id.* at § 69.

50 *Id.* For an example of Hong Kong courts' approach to this matter, see *Hong Kong Institute of Education v Aoki Corporation* [2004] 2 HKLRD 760. In that case, the court considered the presence and effect of foreign (Japanese

- an interpretation of an award
- an additional award

B. Substantive Requirements

Five basic substantive legal requirements must be fulfilled in order to ensure the enforceability of the award:

(i) compliance with the parties' submission to arbitration:
  (a) made within jurisdiction
  (b) dealing only with disputes submitted to arbitration
  (c) all disputes dealt with (but note the exception for interim awards)[51]
(ii) cogency: an unambiguous adjudication by the arbitrator[52]
(iii) certainty:
  (a) no contradictions, illogicalities or ambiguities
  (b) completeness of all elements in calculations
  (c) clarity of findings of fact, holdings of law and orders
  (d) consistency between findings of fact and holdings of law
  (e) reasons must be adequate and intelligible
(iv) finality:
  (a) no delegation
  (b) no reserving decisions for later determination (but note the exception for interim awards)
  (c) award is final and binding unless the parties otherwise agree[53]
(v) capability of performance:
  (a) depends on the type of remedy awarded

---

in that case) insolvency proceedings, and whether recognizing such proceedings would be "just and equitable." CHOONG & WEERAMANTRY, *supra* note 5, at para. 84.12, note 15.

51 The *Model Law* does not prohibit the making of interim awards (also known as *partial awards*) in international cases. Likewise, under the *Arbitration Ordinance, supra* note 2, interim awards are permitted. *See, e.g.*, § 71 of the *Arbitration Ordinance, supra* note 2.

52 HALSBURY'S, *supra* note 13, at para. [25.125] states: "The award should be cogent, in the sense that there is an unambiguous adjudication of the matters in dispute."

53 § 73 of the *Arbitration Ordinance, supra* note 2 provides:

(1) Unless otherwise agreed by the parties, an award made by an arbitral tribunal pursuant to an arbitration agreement is final and binding both on—
  (a) the parties; and
  (b) any person claiming through or under any of the parties.
(2) Subsection (1) does not affect the right of a person to challenge the award—
  (a) as provided for in section 26 or 81, section 4 or 5 of Schedule 2, or any other provision of this Ordinance; or
  (b) otherwise by any available arbitral process of appeal or review.

A similar approach is implicit from the *Model Law*. In the English case of *Shell Egypt West Manzala GmbH v Dana Gas Egypt Ltd* [2009] 2 CLC 481, the High Court held that the three words of "final, conclusive and binding" were not sufficient to exclude the parties' right of appeal against an arbitral award pursuant to the English *Arbitration Act*. CHOONG & WEERAMANTRY, *supra* note 5, at para. 73.17.

(b) what action must be taken by the unsuccessful party—precise obligations to be met
(c) timeframe (this item is also relevant to certainty)

These requirements apply as much to the arbitrator's orders on interest and costs as they do to the award on the substantive dispute referred.[54]

C. Effects of Non-compliance with Substantive Requirements

Failure by a Hong Kong arbitral tribunal to observe the substantive requirements might result in the following consequences. In relation to arbitrations conducted under the Ordinance:

- enforcement in Hong Kong of an award made in Hong Kong under the *Model Law* may be denied, either under a summary procedure[55] or on an action on the award
- a *Model Law* award made in Hong Kong but exceeding jurisdiction may be set aside in Hong Kong, in whole or in part[56]
- an award made in Hong Kong but in excess of jurisdiction may not be enforced overseas under art V(1)(c) of the *New York Convention*

For China arbitrations, an award made in Hong Kong but in excess of jurisdiction may not be enforced in the People's Republic of China under the Hong Kong/PRC *Arrangement between the Mainland and the Hong Kong Special Administrative Region on the Mutual Enforcement of Arbitration Awards* of 20 June 1999. This agreement was enacted into law as part of the *Arbitration Ordinance*.

D. Delivery to Parties/Publication of the Arbitral Award

After writing, signing and dating the award, it must be published and delivered to the parties. Certain obligations begin to run from the date of the award rather than the time the award is delivered to the parties. Therefore, the award should be delivered to the parties as soon as possible.[57]

Under some institutional arbitration rules, the draft award must be reviewed (the term for this review process is *scrutinized* or *scrutiny*) by the arbitral institution and approved before signature by the tribunal and publication to the parties.[58]

---

54 For a further list of essential elements of an award, *see* Ma & Brock, *supra* note 10, at paras. 17.043–17.052.

55 § 61 of the *Arbitration Ordinance*, *supra* note 2.

56 *Id.* at § 81, incorporating *Model Law* Art. 34(2)(a)(iii).

57 So & To, *supra* note 28, at para. [67.19].

58 For example:
- The ICC Rules, *supra* note 30, at Art. 33 requires the arbitral tribunal to submit the draft award to the ICC's Court for scrutiny.
- The New Zealand International Arbitration Centre's Standard Arbitration Rules, § 34.9–§ 34.11

Under some arbitration laws, the award needs to be registered with the local courts before becoming effective and ready for delivery to the parties. The arbitral tribunal is to comply with all preconditions required for the delivery of its award.

E. Correction, Interpretation, and Addition to the Award

In theory, once an arbitral tribunal has published its final award to the parties, it is *functus officio* and has no further power to deal with the dispute. In reality, there are certain actions which can be taken by the parties and the tribunal after publication of the tribunal's award.[59] We discuss some of these actions in this section.

One of these actions is that the arbitral tribunal is entitled to correct any errors in computation or errors of a clerical or typographical nature upon the request of the parties to the arbitration.[60] Alternatively, a tribunal may do this on its own initiative and authority.[61] Alternatively, a party to the arbitral proceedings may apply, within the time limit set out in the applicable rules or law, to the arbitral tribunal

likewise provides for scrutiny of an arbitral tribunal's draft award.

- The Arbitration Rules of the Singapore International Arbitration Centre in Rule 32.3 requires the tribunal to submit a draft of its award to the Registrar for review as to form.

[59] As noted by Halsbury's, *supra* note 13, at para. [25.131]:

> Arbitration proceedings terminate automatically on the making of a final award and the mandate of the tribunal terminates . . . Where an award on agreed terms is made by the arbitral tribunal, the proceedings and the mandate of the tribunal may either terminate automatically . . . or following an order of the tribunal terminating the proceedings . . . In any event, *the mandate of the tribunal terminates subject to the right of the parties to request a correction to or interpretation of the original award or the making of an additional award and to the power of the High Court to suspend proceedings to set aside an award so that the tribunal may resume the arbitration proceedings or otherwise deal with the objection that has given rise to the application to set aside.* (citations omitted; emphasis added)

[60] § 69(1) of the *Arbitration Ordinance*, incorporating *Model Law* Art. 33(1), *supra* note 2.

Choong & Weeramantry, *supra* note 5, at para. 69.04 explains:

> Article 33 concerns the correction and interpretation of an arbitral award after it has been issued. The need for this provision stems from the fact that under article 32(3) of the Model Law, the mandate of the arbitral tribunal terminates after the final award has been issued. However, after an arbitral award has been made, the parties may identify errors, ambiguities, or omissions in the award. It is therefore necessary to have a provision that specifically deals with the correction of computational, clerical, and typographical errors, notwithstanding the *functus officio* doctrine. Article 33 also contemplates the giving of interpretations on specific points in the award and empowers the arbitral tribunal to make additional awards. (citations omitted)

See also So & To, *supra* note 28, at para. [69.09]; Halsbury's, *supra* note 13, at para. [25.127].

[61] For example, § 69(1) of the *Arbitration Ordinance*, incorporating *Model Law* Art. 33(2), *supra* note 2, empowers the tribunal to correct errors on its own initiative within 30 days from the date of award in the absence of any request from parties. Choong & Weeramantry, *supra* note 5, at para. 69.23.

Another example is provided by Choong & Weeramantry, *supra* note 5, at para. 69.32:

> Section 69(3) empowers an arbitral tribunal to review an award of costs within 30 days of the date of the award if, when making the award, the tribunal was not aware of any information relating to costs (including any offer for settlement) which it should have taken into account. Section 69(4) provides the arbitral tribunal may confirm, vary or correct the award of costs on a review under section 69(3) of the Arbitration Ordinance.

for a correction.[62] Needless to say, the other party is required to be notified of this request.[63]

A party may, within the time allowed by the relevant rules or laws and with notice to the other party, request the tribunal to give an interpretation of all or part of the award.[64] The interpretation shall be given in writing and forms a part of the award. Most arbitrators are sceptical about requests for correction or interpretation, which are often viewed by the tribunal as requests for a different decision.[65]

A party to the arbitral proceedings may request the arbitral tribunal to make an additional award on claims raised and presented in the arbitral proceedings but not included in the award.[66] This request should be made within the time limit allowed

---

[62] Depending upon the situation and the applicable rules, a party might make its application for a correction to the institution in an administered arbitration.

[63] As summarized by one authority:

> Section 69(1) provides that upon the application of a party the arbitral tribunal may make an additional award upon a claim presented in the arbitration proceedings but omitted from the award. In addition, under s.69(1) the arbitral tribunal may correct any errors in computation, any clerical or typographical errors or any errors of a similar nature. . . . a distinction was drawn between an additional award and a side letter, purporting to clarify the award. The latter did not form part of the award.
>
> Under the Opt In provisions of Sch.2, the Court may under ss.4 and 5 remit an award in whole or in part to an arbitral tribunal. If an award is remitted the arbitral tribunal shall make a fresh award in respect of the matters remitted within three months unless the Court sets a different period.
>
> The courts have given a generous interpretation to these provisions. Relief has been given where there was an accidental slip or omission of one of the parties or their counsel. It has also permitted an arbitral tribunal to remedy its failure to award interest . . . The section does not, however, permit the arbitral tribunal to reopen the award generally. However, s.69(3) permits an arbitral tribunal to review its costs award, if, when making the award, the tribunal was not aware of any information relating to costs. This provision is particularly directed towards any offers for settlement which may have been made.

Ma & Brock, *supra* note 10, at paras. 17.040–17.042 (citations omitted).

See also, Choong & Weeramantry, *supra* note 5, at paras. 69.13 and 69.24.

[64] Halsbury's, *supra* note 13, at para. [25.128] explains:

> A party may . . . request the arbitral tribunal to give an interpretation of a specific point or part of the award. There is no power for the tribunal to take the initiative in this regard. A party requesting an interpretation must do so within 30 days of receipt of the award, unless the parties have otherwise agreed. The tribunal must . . . hear the parties . . . The tribunal must, if it considers the request to be justified, give the interpretation within 30 days . . . of the request, unless the tribunal considers it necessary to extend the time limit . . . The interpretation forms part of the award and must be made in accordance with the requirements of the Arbitration Ordinance as to form, content and delivery of awards generally. (citations omitted)

[65] Choong & Weeramantry, *supra* note 5, at para. 69.31 notes:

> Corrections and interpretations have the same status of an award. Accordingly there may be other changes to an award necessitated or consequential to the corrections and interpretations. . . . This does not empower the tribunal to make extensive revisions. The provisions are not intended to allow the arbitral tribunal to change their mind on an issue which has been decided and published in the award. . . . In order to protect the finality of awards, the prevailing approach to corrections and interpretations . . . is to interpret the arbitral tribunal's scope to correct and interpret an award narrowly. Courts have refused to permit corrections based upon a reassessment of a party's evidence or the parties' arguments, and it is rare for interpretations to be sought or granted. Arbitral tribunals should reject any request which goes beyond the interpretation of the award, as the interpretation is not meant to empower the tribunal to change the substance of their ruling. The parties cannot effectively reopen the case after the award has been made through the correction and interpretation mechanism.

[66] Halsbury's, *supra* note 13, at para. [25.129] states:

by the relevant rules and law and on providing the other party with notice of this request. The party cannot use this request to present new issues not raised during the arbitral proceedings. Any such additional award must comply with all formal requirements for a valid award.[67]

Part 2. Costs and Interest

I. Introduction to Costs

In conducting an arbitration, there are expenses. These include:

- fees and reimbursable expenses of the arbitral tribunal
- administrative costs of the arbitral proceedings
- fees paid to the arbitration institution or appointing authority
- cost of expert advice or assistance required by the arbitral tribunal
- legal costs of the winning party if claimed during the arbitral proceedings[68]

The main provisions governing the award of costs are set out in the *Arbitration Ordinance*.[69] The allocation of costs is in the arbitral tribunal's discretion.[70] This discretion must be exercised judicially, fairly and impartially.[71]

There are two main categories of costs in an arbitration.[72] One category is known as *costs of the reference*. These are the costs related to bringing the dispute

---

> A party may . . . request the arbitral tribunal to make an additional award as to claims presented at the proceedings but omitted from the original award or awards. There is no power for the tribunal to take the initiative in this regard. A party requesting an additional award must do so within 30 days of receipt of the original award. The parties may agree to exclude the power to request an additional award or to fix an alternative time limit for the request. The tribunal must first hear the parties on the matter . . . If the tribunal considers the request to be justified, it must make an additional award within 60 days . . . unless the tribunal considers it necessary to extend the time limit within which to make the additional award. (citations omitted)

67 *See* for example: *Model Law*, *supra* note 7, at Art. 33; Arbitration Rules, *supra* note 7, at Art. 35 to Art. 37; HKIAC Arbitration Rules, *supra* note 31, at Art. 40.

68 *See* Arbitration Rules, *supra* note 7, at Arts. 40 and 42.1; HKIAC Arbitration Rules, *supra* note 31, at Art. 34.1(d).

69 § 74 to § 78 of the *Arbitration Ordinance*, *supra* note 2.

70 Choong & Weeramantry, *supra* note 5, at para. 74.16 states:

> In allocating costs, the tribunal may take into account factors such as the parties' relative success in their claims, the conduct of the parties such as non-compliance with directions made, and the law of the place of enforcement of the award. The tribunal may also direct that the recoverable costs of arbitral proceedings before it are limited to a specified amount. (citations omitted)

71 § 46 of the *Arbitration Ordinance*, incorporating *Model Law* Art. 18, *supra* note 2. In the case of *Kin Shing (Leung's) General Contractors Ltd v Chinese University of Hong Kong* [2011] HKEC 1049, the Hong Kong Court of Appeal held that an arbitrator's exercise of discretion as to costs may include considering all offers of settlement. *See also* the case of *Lewis v Haverfordwest Rural District Council* [1953] 1 WLR 1486.

72 Choong & Weeramantry, *supra* note 5, at paras. 74.08–74.09 explains:

> In England and Hong Kong, a distinction has traditionally been drawn between the "costs of the reference" and "costs of the arbitral award," the former generally covering the costs incurred by the parties in putting their respective cases in the arbitration whereas the latter covers the administrative costs of the reference, including the fees of the arbitral tribunal. In England, this has been replaced by

to arbitration: *e.g.* the parties' legal costs, the costs of their expert witnesses and witnesses of fact and the costs of the hearing room, but not the costs of the parties' own management time in dealing with the dispute.[73]

The second category of costs is known as *costs of the award*. These are the costs relating to producing the decision: the arbitral tribunal's fees and expenses for time spent on preliminary meetings, dealing with interlocutory matters, attending any visit or view, the hearing, and the preparation of the award.[74] The arbitral tribunal is entitled to payment of its fees and costs before releasing the award to the parties.

Some examples of a costs order in an award may include the following:[75]

- "I make no order as to costs."—The arbitral tribunal may add the following phrase: "save that the arbitrator's fees and disbursements, *i.e.*, the costs of the award, shall be shared equally between the parties."
- In the event the claimant is the successful party and the respondent is the losing party: "The respondent shall bear the claimant's costs of the reference and shall pay the costs of the award."

An award of costs creates a debt for that amount. A party may either sue for payment of an award of costs or seek to enforce it summarily.[76]

A. Deposits

Parties in both *ad hoc* and institutional arbitration proceedings are usually required to make deposits towards the cost of the arbitration. Depending upon the situation, the deposits are made either after the commencement of the arbitral proceedings but before the arbitral tribunal is constituted, or upon constitution of the arbitral tribunal.

Under an institutional arbitration proceeding, each institution maintains a scale of fees or a formula for calculating the amount of fees. The parties pay the fee to the arbitration institution, which then uses a portion of these fees to pay the arbitral tribunal. Some institutions do not permit arbitrators to discuss fees with the parties. Other institutions may permit the arbitral tribunal to negotiate its fee

---

the term, "costs of the arbitration," whereas in Hong Kong, this has been replaced by the term, "costs of arbitral proceedings."

In Hong Kong, the term "costs of arbitral proceedings" is used and has the same effect as the combined costs of the reference and the costs of the arbitral award. (citations omitted)

See also HALSBURY'S, *supra* note 13, at para. [25.136].

73 *See, e.g.*, CHOONG & WEERAMANTRY, *supra* note 5, at para. 74.08.

74 *Id.*

75 We adopt the suggestion in MA & BROCK, *supra* note 10, at para. 17.036:

> Arbitral tribunals may make costs awards, which deal with liability for the costs of the reference or award. The terminology "costs award", however, should be avoided; instead reference should be made to an interim or final award to avoid any confusion regarding the nature of the award.

76 § 61 of the *Arbitration Ordinance, supra* note 2.

directly with the parties. In other situations, arbitrators include their fees in their award.

Under *ad hoc* proceedings, the parties and arbitrators agree on the fees or how the fees will be calculated. The parties and the tribunal also agree on the amount and the time when the deposits will be paid into the arbitral tribunal's account (usually into the presiding arbitrator's bank account if more than one arbitrator is appointed), which is maintained for purposes of the arbitration.[77] In an *ad hoc* arbitration, the tribunal may include its fee in the award.

B. General Rules in Awarding Costs

> There is the settled practice of the courts that in the absence of special circumstances a successful litigant should receive his costs and that it is necessary to show some grounds for exercising the discretion of refusing an order which would give them to him, and the discretion must be judicially exercised . . . [These words] mean that the arbitrator must not act capriciously and must, if he is going to exercise his discretion, show a reason connected with the case and one which the court can see is a proper reason.[78]

If a claimant recovers all or part of its claim, the claimant has succeeded in winning its case. If a claim does not meet with success, the party bringing the claim has lost. Where the *costs follow the event* rule applies, the *event* is a claimant succeeding in its claim. Where the claimant wins the case, the claimant's costs are generally recoverable. If the claimant loses its case, the claimant pays the respondent's costs, *i.e.*, the costs of the reference. The same rule applies to the costs of the award.[79]

In some situations, the winning claimant might be denied all or part of its costs. For example, if the claimant:

- acted in the arbitration in such a manner as to cause unnecessary dispute and expense
- did something wrongful in the events out of which the dispute arises
- acted unreasonably and oppressively

---

77 Arbitration Rules, *supra* note 7, at Art. 41; UNCITRAL *Notes on Organizing Arbitral Proceedings* (2016) [hereinafter Notes] paras. 28 to 30; ICC Rules, *supra* note 30, at Art. 37.
Similarly, Art. 24 of the London Court of International Arbitration's Arbitration Rules (2014) pertains to deposits. These LCIA rules are found at this website: http://www.lcia.org/dispute_resolution_services/lcia-arbitration-rules-2014.aspx (last visited 12 Jul. 2017).
Paras. 43 to 49 of UNCITRAL's Notes set out guidance concerning deposit of costs; and, fixing and allocating costs.
Further information may be found at this website: http://www.uncitral.org/pdf/english/texts/arbitration/arb-notes/arb-notes-2016-e.pdf (last visited 12 Jul. 2017).

78 *Lewis v Haverfordwest Rural District Council*, *supra* note 71, at 1487.

79 *Matheson & Co Ltd v A Tabah & Sons* [1963] 2 Lloyd's Rep 270.

A successful claimant may also be required to pay its own costs by virtue of an agreement to that effect, if this agreement is made after a dispute has arisen. If such an agreement is made before a dispute has arisen, it is void.[80]

A claimant who wins all or part of its claim will normally be awarded its costs and the costs of the award. In such an instance, the respondent will need to pay the claimant's costs and the costs of the award. Even if the claimant succeeds only in a small part of its claim, the *costs follow the event* rule is still observed.

There are exceptions to this rule. If one or more of the following applies, the arbitral tribunal may exercise its discretion in favour of reducing the costs awarded to the winning party:

- the costs would have been significantly less if the claim had only been for the amount awarded
- the claimant lost on a substantial issue or issues within the arbitration
- the claimant won a small amount on a basis quite different from that argued by it at the arbitration
- the claimant won a small amount in respect of a grossly exaggerated claim
- the claimant lied in the arbitration[81]

This list of exceptions to the *costs follow the event* rule is not exhaustive.

---

[80] § 74 of the *Arbitration Ordinance, supra* note 7, which state in relevant part:

(1) An arbitral tribunal may include in an award directions with respect to the costs of arbitral proceedings (including the fees and expenses of the tribunal).

(2) The arbitral tribunal may, having regard to all relevant circumstances (including the fact, if appropriate, that a written offer of settlement of the dispute concerned has been made), direct in the award under subsection (1) to whom and by whom and in what manner the costs are to be paid

(3) The arbitral tribunal may also, in its discretion, order costs (including the fees and expenses of the tribunal) to be paid by a party in respect of a request made by any of the parties for an order or direction (including an interim measure).

(4) The arbitral tribunal may direct that the costs ordered under subsection (3) are to be paid forthwith or at the time that the tribunal may otherwise specify.

(5) Subject to section 75, the arbitral tribunal must—

(a) assess the amount of costs to be awarded or ordered to be paid under this section (other than the fees and expenses of the tribunal); and

(b) award or order those costs (including the fees and expenses of the tribunal).

(6) Subject to subsection (7), the arbitral tribunal is not obliged to follow the scales and practices adopted by the court on taxation when assessing the amount of costs (other than the fees and expenses of the tribunal) under subsection (5).

(7) The arbitral tribunal—

(a) must only allow costs that are reasonable having regard to all the circumstances; and

(b) unless otherwise agreed by the parties, may allow costs incurred in the preparation of the arbitral proceedings prior to the commencement of the arbitration.

(8) A provision of an arbitration agreement to the effect that the parties, or any of the parties, must pay their own costs in respect of arbitral proceedings arising under the agreement is void.

(9) A provision referred to in subsection (8) is not void if it is part of an agreement to submit to arbitration a dispute that had arisen before the agreement was made.

That is, if the agreement as to costs is concluded after the dispute has arisen, it is presumed that the parties had made the agreement at arm's length and thus such an agreement is legally enforceable. CHOONG & WEERAMANTRY, *supra* note 5, at para. 74.44.

See also HALSBURY'S, *supra* note 13, at para. [25.137].

[81] Note, however, that misconduct by a witness in the arbitration is not a reason for denying a party its costs.

If the respondent brings a successful counterclaim, the costs may be divided between the parties. The basis will vary depending on the situation. If the counterclaim is an issue wholly independent of the claim, in which case the arbitral tribunal may award costs in respect of each element, or if the counterclaim is a set-off in defence to the claim, in which case the costs award may be a combined award. In this situation, the costs award might use wording similar to the following: "The Respondent shall pay ___ % of the Claimant's costs and a like amount of the costs of the award."[82]

A court will not disturb an arbitral tribunal's award of costs merely because the court might have come to a different conclusion:

> In reviewing an arbitrator's decision on costs it is of the greatest importance to remember that the decision is within his discretion and not that of the courts. It is nothing to the point that I might have reached a different decision and that some other judge or arbitrator might have differed from both of us. I would neither wish, nor be entitled, to intervene, unless I was satisfied that the arbitrator has misdirected himself.[83]

The courts may, however, intervene under the following circumstances:

- if the tribunal's discretion has been based on an incorrect principle, *e.g.*, total disregard of the *costs follow the event* rule
- if the principle cannot be determined from the award and the award is one which no reasonable tribunal would make, by inference the tribunal applied a wrong principle in making the costs award
- if the arbitral tribunal did not exercise any discretion at all, *e.g.*, a mechanistic application of the *costs follow the event* rule in circumstances which justified a departure from this usual order

C. Offers to Settle and Their Effect

There are a number of ways in which a respondent can minimize its risk of paying costs. Here, we examine three common methods used in attempting to reduce the risk of being ordered to pay costs in an award.

One way is by *payment into court*. In litigation, a respondent can protect itself against the costs involved in defending a money claim. This is done by making a payment into court of an amount the respondent is prepared to offer to pay to the claimant. If the respondent does so, the issue becomes whether the claimant obtains a larger amount by continuing the litigation than by accepting the amount which the respondent paid into the court.

---

82 A counterclaim is an independent claim which may be made by a respondent against a claimant. A set-off is a defence to the claim which, if successful, extinguishes the claim.

83 *Tramountana Armadora SA v Atlantic Shipping Co SA* [1978] 2 All ER 870, 875.

If the claimant continues the litigation after the respondent's payment into court and obtains a larger award than the amount paid in, the claimant "wins" its case. If, however, the claimant continues with the litigation but obtains an amount equal to or lesser than the amount paid into court, the claimant is considered to have "lost" its case. Continuing the action after the time of payment into court has resulted in wasted expenditure and the claimant must pay the respondent's costs from the date of the payment into court.

> If the claimant in the end has achieved no more than he would have achieved by accepting the offer, the continuance of the arbitration after that date has been a waste of time and money. *Prima facie*, the claimant should recover his costs up to the date of the offer and should be ordered to pay the respondent's costs after that date. If he has achieved more by going on, the respondent should pay the costs throughout.[84]

One authority states:

> that the concept of payment into court is not familiar to parties from other jurisdictions. Further, it seems that the payment into court procedure, in connection with arbitration proceedings, is not widely used. Upon the Committee's recommendation, the procedure for payment into court in arbitrations has now been removed and the matter is left to the arbitral tribunal to decide as a matter of discretion, whether an offer put forward is genuine. Section 74(2) now makes it clear that a "written offer of settlement" can be taken into account by the tribunal when considering issues of costs. This removes the need for arbitration counsel to be familiar with the Hong Kong Court rules governing payment into court.[85]

Another method for a respondent to minimize the risk of being required to pay costs is through a *sealed offer*. The respondent may make an offer to the claimant, before or during the hearing. The offer is to settle for a specific amount. The respondent advises the claimant that if the offer is rejected, the respondent will place the offer with the tribunal. The respondent then hands a sealed envelope to the arbitral tribunal, requesting the tribunal not to open the envelope until the arbitral tribunal has decided as to liability and quantum. After determining liability and quantum, the tribunal then considers the sealed offer in determining the liability for costs.

The sealed offer method suffers from a disadvantage. The difficulty is that the arbitral tribunal may infer from the sealed envelope and the instructions that the respondent has made an offer to the claimant to settle the dispute. This may prejudice the arbitral tribunal's views on liability. Despite this difficulty, a sealed offer operates on the same principle as payments into court: that of wasted time and costs

---

[84] *Id.* at 877–878.

[85] CHOONG & WEERAMANTRY, *supra* note 5, at para. 74.21.

if the claimant achieves a decision less than or equal to the amount contained in the sealed offer.[86]

Another method of minimizing costs is through the use of a *Calderbank* offer.[87] The respondent makes an offer to the claimant. This offer is of a without-prejudice-except-as-to-costs nature. In its closing speech, the respondent would request the arbitral tribunal to make an interim award dealing with substantive liability and quantum followed by a further hearing to deal with the question of costs. The existence of the *Calderbank* offer is then drawn to the arbitral tribunal's attention. This procedure has fewer drawbacks for the respondent than the sealed offer procedure. A *Calderbank* offer operates on the same principle as payments into court and sealed offers: that the claimant wasted time and costs if the claimant achieves an award less than or equal to the amount contained in the *Calderbank* offer.

D. Limiting Recoverable Costs

This section applies only to orders limiting recoverable costs made during the arbitration. This section does not apply to an award. The making of such orders, however, will have an effect upon the award's recoverable costs.

Unless the parties have agreed to the contrary, the arbitral tribunal may direct that the recoverable costs of arbitration proceedings or any part thereof shall be limited to a specified amount.[88] Such a direction may be varied, *i.e.*, changed.[89] Note

---

86 For further details on offers, *see* CHOONG & WEERAMANTRY, *supra* note 5, at paras. 74.22–74.23.

87 Named after the case of *Jacqueline Anne Calderbank v John Thomas Calderbank* [1975] 3 All ER 333, where Jacqueline sought to divorce her husband John. The procedure for minimizing costs used in this case was approved for general use by the English Court of Appeal in *Oliver Cutts v Albert Head and George Head* [1984] 1 All ER 597. Note that in relation to *Calderbank* offers, the Hong Kong Court of Appeal has held that an arbitrator may consider all offers of settlement in exercising its discretion in relation to costs, regardless whether the offer was a proper *Calderbank* offer. *Kin Shing (Leung's) General Contractors Ltd v Chinese University of Hong Kong*, *supra* note 71. For more details on *Calderbank* offers, *see* CHOONG & WEERAMANTRY, *supra* note 5, at paras. 74.23–74.26.

88 § 57 of the *Arbitration Ordinance*, *supra* note 2, provides in relevant part:

> (1) Unless otherwise agreed by the parties, an arbitral tribunal may direct that the recoverable costs of arbitral proceedings before it are limited to a specified amount.
>
> . . .
>
> (4) In this section—
>
> . . .
>
> (b) a reference to arbitral proceedings includes any part of those arbitral proceedings.

The tribunal's direction made under § 57(1) only limits the amount of costs which may be recovered by the parties. However, the actual amount to be recovered by the winning party will be determined through the process of assessment or taxation. CHOONG & WEERAMANTRY, *supra* note 5, at para. 57.08.

Allowing the cap to be applicable to a particular part of the proceedings is flexible because the concerns about excessive costs may sometimes arise for certain aspects of the proceedings. CHOONG & WEERAMANTRY, *supra* note 5, at para. 57.16.

89 § 57(3) of the *Arbitration Ordinance*, *supra* note 2, states:

> (3) A direction may be made or varied at any stage of the arbitral proceedings but, for the limit of the recoverable costs to be taken into account, this must be done sufficiently in advance of—
>
> (a) the incurring of the costs to which the direction or the variation relates; or
>
> (b) the taking of the steps in the arbitral proceedings which may be affected by the direction or the variation.

that this provision limits not what a party may spend but what it may recover. The purpose of this direction is to:

- promote cost-effective arbitration
- prevent one party from threatening the other party with possible insolvency or a prohibitively high bill of costs

In making such an order, the arbitral tribunal must exercise discretion judicially and in accordance with fairness and impartiality.[90] This is particularly true if the tribunal intends to act on its own volition. Each party will be entitled to be heard before the order is made and to submit arguments and evidence as to the necessity or reasonableness of particular heads of costs and as to the amount of such costs.

The parties may agree between themselves on an allocation of the arbitration costs. In some jurisdictions, such agreement is valid only if made after the dispute arises.[91] Winning parties usually will claim the cost of the arbitration as well as legal costs. If the parties have not agreed on the costs (in some cases, even when the parties have reached a settlement) the tribunal may need to apportion the costs. Although the tribunal has discretion in the apportionment of costs, the usual practice in international arbitration is to apportion on the basis that costs will follow the event.

Exceptions to this custom may include reprehensible conduct by a winning party, acting in bad faith, or unreasonably lengthening or complicating the proceedings. The award of costs is within the discretion of the arbitral tribunal which will justify its decision as part of its reasoned award.[92]

E. The Bases of Costs

An arbitral tribunal has the authority and the discretion to award costs on different bases.[93] These bases follow along with a brief description of each.

The first basis we review is known as *party and party*. Under this basis, the costs payable are those which are "necessary or proper for the attainment of justice

In the United Kingdom case *Home of Homes Ltd v Hammersmith and Fulham London BC* [2003] EWHC 807 (TCC), a cap imposed less than 10 working days before the substantive hearing commenced was held to be too late and unjustified. Choong & Weeramantry, *supra* note 5, at para. 57.13.

90 § 46 of the *Arbitration Ordinance*, incorporating *Model Law* Art. 18, *supra* note 2.

91 Choong & Weeramantry, *supra* note 5, at paras. 74.41–74.44.

92 *See, e.g.*, Arbitration Rules, *supra* note 7, at Art. 40.

93 § 75 of the *Arbitration Ordinance, supra* note 2, stipulates in part:

(1) Without affecting section 74(1) and (2), if the parties have agreed that the costs of arbitral proceedings are to be taxed by the court, then unless the arbitral tribunal otherwise directs in an award, the award is deemed to have included the tribunal's directions that the costs (other than the fees and expenses of the tribunal) are to be taxed by the court on the party and party basis in accordance with rule 28(2) of Order 62 of the Rules of the High Court . . .

(2) On taxation by the court, the arbitral tribunal must make an additional award of costs reflecting the result of such taxation.

(3) A decision of the court on taxation is not subject to appeal.

or for enforcing or defending the rights of the party whose costs are being taxed."[94] Uncertainties over whether an item is payable is resolved in favour of the paying party. If the arbitral tribunal makes no order as to the basis for determining costs, *party and party* will be inferred.[95]

Another basis is known as *common fund*. This is a more generous basis than *party and party* as there will be allowed a reasonable amount in respect of all costs reasonably incurred, including the ordinary rules applicable on a taxation as between solicitor and client.[96] Taxation as between solicitor and client refers to all the costs incurred with the express or implied approval of the client and these costs shall be conclusively presumed to have been reasonably incurred and to have been reasonable in amount.[97] It should be noted, however, that costs which in the circumstances of the case are of an unusual nature and which would not be allowed in a taxation situation where the *party and party* basis applies, shall, unless the solicitor firm expressly informed its client before these costs were incurred that they might not be so allowed, be presumed to have been unreasonably incurred.[98] The *common fund* basis has been described as little more than the *party and party* basis on a more generous scale.[99]

---

[94] Order 62, rule 28(2) of the High Court Rules, *supra* note 25.

[95] Choong & Weeramantry, *supra* note 5, at para. 75.08.

[96] Order 62, rule 28(4) of the High Court Rules, *supra* note 25.

[97] *Id.* at rule 29(2).

[98] *Id.* at rule 29(3).

[99] In the case of *Ngan Wun Yeung v The Lok Sin Tong Benevolent Society Kowloon* [2000] 2 HKC 404 paras. 15–16, the court provided the following in comparing *party and party* to *common fund* bases:

15. Their distinguishing features, together with those of other bases of taxation, are admirably summarized by Megarry V.C. in *EMI Records Ltd. v. Cameron Wallace Ltd. & Another* [1982] 2 All ER 982 at 983:

    "(1) The party and party basis. . . . The essence of this head is thus what is 'necessary or proper'; and this, of course, is the strictest of the normal heads of taxation.
    (2) The common fund basis. . . . The common fund basis seems to have been intended to replace the old 'solicitor and client' basis (in one of the four meanings of the phrase 'solicitor and client': see *Gibbs v. Gibbs* [1952] 1 All ER 942 at 949, [1952] P 332 at 347), though in doing so it not very happily uses the very phrase itself. In the end, the practical result seems to be that taxation on the common fund basis is little more than a party and party taxation conducted 'on a more generous scale': see *Giles v Randall* [1915] 1 KB 290 at 295, [1914-15] All ER Rep 285 at 286, per Buckley LJ. It is sometimes said that on average a common fund taxation produces a figure some 5 to 10 % higher than a party and party taxation; and that may be so."

16. In Halsbury's Laws of England, Vol. 37, para.746 at p.576, the learned editors deal with the common fund basis as follows:

    "The practice of awarding costs on this more generous basis originated in the Court of Chancery, which had a much wider discretion than had the common law courts, but the power now extends throughout the Supreme Court. While it does not offer a complete indemnity, there should be allowed what is fair and proper, taking a liberal view, for this basis is intended to cover all the costs which are properly paid. Thus the taxing officer may not only allow, at an enhanced figure, items which could properly be allowed on a party and party taxation, but may also allow items which would not be allowed on such a taxation."

The last basis to be reviewed is known as *indemnity*. Under this basis, "all costs shall be allowed except insofar as they are of an unreasonable amount or have been unreasonably incurred."[100] Any doubt as to what can be reimbursed is decided in the receiving party's favour. One court has noted, "Orders of indemnity costs are particularly fact sensitive and issue sensitive."[101] An arbitral tribunal would likewise consider all the circumstances, including the facts and issues, before issuing an award on costs.

The *Arbitration Ordinance* gives the arbitral tribunal discretion as to which basis is to be adopted. Nonetheless, the *party and party* basis is usually adopted. The *indemnity* basis is unusual in arbitration. Questions of fraud, gross delay or inexcusable fault are necessary to justify the adoption of the *indemnity* basis.

F. Taxation of Costs

Under administered proceedings, the arbitral institution will determine the costs of the arbitration and collect the funds due from the parties for disbursement. In *ad hoc* arbitration proceedings, the arbitral tribunal fixes the cost of the arbitration (in some cases, in consultation with the appointing authority where necessary), sets up an account, makes demands for deposits and further payments by the parties, and makes disbursements from the account. At the conclusion of the arbitral proceedings, the arbitral tribunal produces a statement of account to both parties, refunding any excess monies paid or demanding any shortfalls. Where a party disputes the rate of fees or charges of the arbitrators, such sums may in some jurisdictions be assessed or taxed by an officer of the court.[102]

An award may refer to taxation, *i.e.*, assessment of the cost of the reference and the cost of the award. The following is a sample:

> The Respondent shall pay the Claimant's costs of the reference to be taxed if not agreed and shall pay the costs of this, my award which I tax and settle in the sum of ________________.

Taxation is the process of determining the amount of costs to be paid if the parties cannot agree the costs. In Hong Kong, taxation of the costs of the reference

[100] Order 62, rule 28 of the High Court Rules, *supra* note 25.

[101] *Wang Din Shin v Nina Kung* [2005] HKCA 133 para. 66. The court also stated at para. 65:

> 65. I accept and it is not in dispute that the Courts in modern times are far more ready to award costs on indemnity basis than previously. As pointed out in *Sung Foo Kee Ltd. V [sic] Pak Lik Co.* [1996] HKCA 653; [1996] 3 HKC 570 and in *The Town Planning Board v Society for the Protection of the Harbour (No. 2)* [2004] HKCFA 22; (2004) 7 HKCFAR 114, the Court should award indemnity costs when appropriate. The dispute, as always is, when is it appropriate and what makes it appropriate. But there must exist fundamentally some "special and unusual features" which justify the Court in departing from the usual order of costs on a party and party basis (see *Wang Din Shin v Nina Wang* CACV 275 of 2004 at paragraph 25).

[102] *See* Arbitration Rules, *supra* note 7, at Art. 39 and Art. 41.5.

usually is performed by a Taxing Master of the High Court.[103] The arbitral tribunal may also tax these costs if the parties have not excluded the tribunal's power to do so.[104]

A different provision applies to the taxation of the costs of the award. Where the arbitral tribunal's fees have not previously been agreed with the parties, they are jointly and severally liable for payment of the arbitral tribunal's reasonable fees on a *quantum meruit* basis and expenses.[105] If a party disagrees with those fees and expenses, that party may apply to the Court of First Instance to have the fees and expenses taxed. The court will then determine the arbitral tribunal's reasonable fees. This may become necessary in the following situations:

- an appointing body appoints a sole arbitrator and the parties cannot agree this arbitrator's fees
- each party appoints an arbitrator and, as is usual, a party is not consulted about the fees payable to the opposing party's appointee

Where fees are agreed, the parties are obligated to pay the arbitrator's fees.

In relation to interlocutory applications, the *costs follow the event* rule also applies. Entitlement to costs may depend upon whether the party seeking costs is ultimately successful in the arbitration. Where the interlocutory application concerned was a normal part of the preliminaries in the arbitration, *e.g.*, a directions hearing, the normal order would be *costs in the cause* or *costs in the arbitration*. These two expressions have similar meanings.

This order allows the party who eventually wins the arbitration to obtain also the costs of the interlocutory application. If the applicant should not have made the application and lost, the general rule as to costs would apply. The order would be that the other party should be reimbursed for its costs of the interlocutory application regardless whether this party wins or loses in the arbitration.

II. Introduction to Interest

An arbitral tribunal's authority to award interest is usually granted expressly by the parties in a contract or arbitration agreement, or, by applicable arbitration laws and rules.[106] Tribunals may award interest on a claim or counterclaim arising from con-

---

103 § 75 of the *Arbitration Ordinance, supra* note 2.

104 *Id.* at § 74(5) provides:

(5) Subject to section 75, the arbitral tribunal must—

(a) assess the amount of costs to be awarded or ordered to be paid under this section (other than the fees and expenses of the tribunal); and

(b) award or order those costs (including the fees and expenses of the tribunal).

105 *Id.* at § 78(1) states:

The parties to proceedings before an arbitral tribunal are jointly and severally liable to pay to the tribunal reasonable fees and expenses, if any, of the tribunal that are appropriate in the circumstance.

106 § 79 of the *Arbitration Ordinance, supra* note 2, provides:

(1) Unless otherwise agreed by the parties, an arbitral tribunal may, in the arbitral proceedings before

tract or on any claim for compensation or restitution. The parties can agree on the rate and the basis of interest to be awarded as part of their contract. In some jurisdictions, the award of interest is treated as a procedural issue. In other jurisdictions, the award of interest is a substantive issue.

The law applicable to the arbitration (the law of the seat of arbitration) will determine whether the arbitration tribunal can award interest and the rate of interest as a substantive issue. The law applicable to the merits of the dispute (the law of the contract) will determine the issue. The rate of interest, start date, end date, and the type of interest payment are at the tribunal's discretion under most laws. A tribunal may award interest from the date on which the cause of action arose until the date of the award, if this has been claimed, or only from the date of the award to the date of payment of the award. The award of interest is not a penalty imposed upon the unsuccessful party.

It might be misconduct for an arbitral tribunal not to award interest where it is claimed and no reason against awarding interest has been made.[107] In an arbitration conducted under the *Model Law*, there is no court review of a failure to make an award of interest. Nonetheless, a party may request the arbitral tribunal to make an additional award dealing with interest.[108]

As previously mentioned, the basis of ordering interest be paid on the award is to compensate the winning party for the loss of the use of the money owed. It is probable that a party will receive pre-award interest if the amount awarded to that party was a specific amount due at a precise date. Interest may be awarded as a general right accruing against the party in breach. Post-judgement interest encourages the unsuccessful party to pay the award promptly so as to avoid increasing the amount of money owed to the winning party.

---

it, award simple or compound interest from the dates, at the rates, and with the rests that the tribunal considers appropriate, subject to section 80, for any period ending not later than the date of payment—

(a) on money awarded by the tribunal in the arbitral proceedings;
(b) on money claimed in, and outstanding at the commencement of, the arbitral proceedings but paid before the award is made; or
(c) on costs awarded or ordered by the tribunal in the arbitral proceedings.

(2) Subsection (1) does not affect any other power of an arbitral tribunal to award interest.
(3) A reference in subsection (1)(a) to money awarded by the tribunal includes an amount payable in consequence of a declaratory award by the tribunal.

Id. at § 80 notes:

(1) Interest is payable on money awarded by an arbitral tribunal from the date of the award at the judgment rate, except when the award otherwise provides.
(2) Interest is payable on costs awarded or ordered by an arbitral tribunal from—
(a) the date of the award or order on costs; or
(b) the date on which costs ordered are directed to be paid forthwith,
at the judgment rate, except when the award or order on costs otherwise provides.
(3) In this section, "judgment rate" (判定利率) means the rate of interest determined by the Chief Justice under section 49(1)(b) (Interest on judgments) of the High Court Ordinance (Cap. 4).

[107] *Panchaud Frères SA v R Pagnan & Fratelli* [1974] 1 Lloyd's Rep 394; *P J van der Zijden Wildhandel NV v Tucker & Cross Ltd* [1976] 1 Lloyd's Rep 341.

[108] § 69 of the *Arbitration Ordinance*, incorporating *Model Law* Art. 33(3), *supra* note 2.

An arbitral tribunal may award simple or compound interest.[109] *Simple interest* refers to the percentage rate calculated on the principal sum while *compound interest* is the capitalization of interest and further interest accrued on the capitalized interest. Generally, in civil law jurisdictions, arbitrators award a statutory, legal or simple rate of interest. In common law jurisdictions, the usual practice is that the tribunal awards compound interest. There is no uniform established practice. A tribunal will exercise its discretion subject to the mandatory provisions of the law of the place of arbitration. This decision is based either upon the parties' agreement or upon the particular facts of the case.

At common law, debts do not carry interest except:

- where there is an express agreement, *e.g.*, in the parties' main contract in which the arbitration clause is a part
- where the applicable arbitration rules provide for an award of interest
- where an implied agreement to pay interest can be found based upon the parties' prior business dealings, or from the nature of the transaction, or from the usual practice of that particular trade or profession
- where it is possible to claim interest for breach of contract, *i.e.*, where the loss of interest was within the reasonable contemplation of the parties when they made the contract[110]

In Hong Kong, the *Arbitration Ordinance* permits a tribunal to order the payment of interest on:

- money claimed in, and outstanding at the commencement of, the arbitral proceedings but paid before the award is made
- money awarded by the tribunal in the arbitral proceedings
- costs awarded or ordered by the tribunal in the arbitral proceedings[111]

Unless otherwise agreed by the parties, an arbitral tribunal has discretion, which must be exercised judicially, to consider the following aspects in relation to its award of interest:

- whether simple interest or compound interest is to be awarded
- the dates the tribunal considers as being appropriate, for any period ending not later than the date of payment
- such rates as the tribunal considers as appropriate
- such rests as the tribunal considers as appropriate (A *rest* is the time period over which interest is compounded.)

---

109 *Id.* at § 79.

110 *President of India v La Pintada Compania Navegaçion SA, The La Pintada* [1985] AC 104. *See also Wadsworth v Lydall* [1981] 1 WLR 598.

111 § 79(1) and § 80 of the *Arbitration Ordinance, supra* note 2.

When is interest paid on the funds awarded by the tribunal? First, the arbitral tribunal should determine when the debtor should have paid the amount owed to the claimant, because a debtor is obligated to find and pay its creditor. The tribunal next should review the contract provision, if any, concerning time of payment. If the contract does not provide for late payment, the tribunal needs to determine the reasonable period. Custom or usage of the particular trade may be of assistance to the arbitral tribunal. If the debtor shows a reason against awarding interest, such as the claimant's extreme delay pursuing payment, the arbitral tribunal has the discretion not to award interest or to award a lesser rate.

Having discussed briefly when interest is to be paid, we now review the amount of interest to be awarded by the arbitral tribunal. The interest rate may be:

- agreed by the parties
- imposed by the relevant arbitration statute
- determined by the tribunal based on the circumstances of the case

A tribunal may specify different interest rates for different time periods of the dispute. The rate of post-award interest is sometimes the same as the rate that applies to court judgements at the place where the award was made. The tribunal should consider the interest rate that is suitable to the currency in which the award is made. The arbitral tribunal must justify the rate of interest awarded in its reasoned award.

An arbitral tribunal should consider the following factors in determining the interest rate(s):

- the normal rate that the creditor would have had to pay its bankers to borrow the amount the tribunal awarded. This would usually be approximately 1% above base commercial lending rates.[112] In Hong Kong, 2% has been suggested.[113]
- any other relevant circumstances that may determine an appropriate rate of interest to award
- foreign currency may have different rates. The general principle is that the successful party should be compensated for not receiving the claimed foreign currency amount/payment when due.

In order for the arbitral tribunal to award compound interest, a party must show that the loss suffered is compensable only by such an award, *e.g.*, where business is conducted through a bank overdraft. In Hong Kong, an award of interest is generally for simple interest at the court's judgment debt rate.[114] This interest is

---

[112] *Tate & Lyle Food and Distribution Ltd v Greater London Council* [1982] 1 WLR 149.

[113] Choong & Weeramantry, *supra* note 5, at para. 79.25 citing to Kaplan, Spruce & Cheng, Hong Kong Arbitration Cases And Materials 109 (1991).

[114] This is the rate of interest on court judgments determined by the Chief Justice as authorized by § 49(1)(b) of the *High Court Ordinance* (Cap. 4). The current rate of interest on court judgments is 8%.

payable on the amount awarded with effect from the date of the award.[115] Note, however, that:

- the arbitral tribunal may order that no interest is payable from the date of the award[116]
- where no payment has been made before the date of the award, interest on this sum is payable up to the date of the award.[117] Interest at the judgment rate is then paid from the date of the award.[118]

III. Summary

This chapter discussed matters related to the arbitral award. We began with the award in general, then reviewed the different types of awards that are possible. Next, we analysed the merits of the award along with the remedies available under an award. For the remainder of Part 1, we examined the requirements for a valid and enforceable award and the steps possible after the last award is issued by the tribunal before it becomes, in theory, *functus officio*.

In Part 2, we considered matters related to the payment of costs of the arbitration and the interest to be paid to the winning party. We presented some methods by which one party's liability for costs can be limited and the bases available for the taxation of costs. We concluded this chapter with a more detailed explanation of interest.

---

[115] § 80 of the *Arbitration Ordinance*, *supra* note 2.

[116] *London and Overseas Freighters Ltd v Timber Shipping Co SA* [1972] AC 1.

[117] § 79(1)(a) of the *Arbitration Ordinance*, *supra* note 2, provides:

> Unless otherwise agreed by the parties, an arbitral tribunal may, in the arbitral proceedings before it, award simple or compound interest from the dates, at the rates, and with the rests that the tribunal considers appropriate, subject to section 80, for any period ending not later than the date of payment—
>
> (a) on money awarded by the tribunal in the arbitral proceedings

[118] *Rocco Giuseppe & Figli v Tradax Export SA* [1984] 1 WLR 742. In Hong Kong, for exceptional instances, a tribunal has discretion to award simple or compound interest under § 79(1)(a) of the *Arbitration Ordinance*, *supra* note 2, from the date of the award until the date of payment, at such interest rates and for such time periods as the tribunal considers appropriate. Doing so would exclude the application of interest under § 80 of the Ordinance.

10

Recognition and Enforcement of the Award

I. Introduction

At the conclusion of an arbitral proceeding, a final award is made by the tribunal. There is usually voluntary compliance by the losing party with the award.[1] This voluntary compliance is also known as *spontaneous execution*. If there is no voluntary compliance by the losing party with the final award, the winning party will need the assistance of a national court to recognise and enforce the arbitral award. The losing party also may approach a national court to invalidate the arbitral award. In this chapter, we discuss each of these possibilities in turn.

II. Recognition and Enforcement

As stated above, a losing party usually will comply with the award. According to informal studies, losing parties comply with the award in the majority of cases. This may be due in part to most arbitral rules, under which the disputing parties have contractually bound themselves to fulfil the terms of the award.[2] Moreover, where the losing party fails, neglects or refuses to fulfil the award's provisions, the losing party can be compelled to do so. In the following section, we discuss the process where a losing party does not honour an award.

A. Recognition

A party may seek only recognition of the award, rather than both recognition and enforcement. "Recognition indicates that the award is accepted by the courts of a

---

[1] In 2008, a survey by a London university examined enforcement. The survey found that "84% of the participating counsel indicated that, in more than 76% of their arbitration proceedings, the non-prevailing party voluntarily complies with the arbitral award . . . according to the interviews, compliance reaches 90%." *International Arbitration: Corporate Attitudes and Practices*, Queen Mary University of London 2 (2008).
See also Redfern and Hunter on International Arbitration paras. 11.01–11.02 (Nigel Blackaby *et al.*, eds., 6th ed. 2015) [hereinafter Redfern & Hunter].

[2] For example, ICC Rules of Arbitration (2017) Art. 22(5) states: "The parties undertake to comply with any order made by the arbitral tribunal."
Redfern & Hunter, *supra* note 1, at para. 11.01.

country as having been validly made."[3] *Recognition* is defined as a process where a court is requested to grant a remedy in respect of a dispute which has been the subject of previous arbitral proceedings and the winning party asks the court to confirm that the arbitral award is valid and binding on the parties to the arbitration by producing the award to the court.[4] As one authority explains:

> 'Recognition', by contrast with enforcement, means that a court before which proceedings are brought between the same parties and in relation to the same subject-matter will recognise the binding effect of an award on the issues before it and so treat those issues as res judicata. The same conditions that govern enforcement of a Convention award govern its recognition.[5]

Recognition of an award may be a declaratory award determining the issues in dispute between the parties. A party may thus only seek recognition of such an award for its finality regarding the issues which the arbitral tribunal has decided

---

[3] Andrew Tweeddale & Keren Tweeddale, Arbitration of Commercial Disputes—International and English Law and Practice para. 13.03 (2007).

[4] Redfern & Hunter, *supra* note 1, at para. 11.20. These authors proceed to explain:

> Recognition . . . is generally a defensive process. It will usually arise when a court is asked to grant a remedy in respect of a dispute that has been the subject of a previous arbitral proceedings. The party in whose favour of the award is made will object that the dispute has already been determined. To prove this, it will seek to produce the award to the court, and will ask the court to recognise it as valid and binding upon the parties in respect of the issues with which it dealt. The award may have disposed of *all* of the issues raised in the new court proceedings and so put an end to those new proceedings as *res judicata* – that is, as matters in issue between the parties that in fact have already been decided. If the award does not dispose of all of the issues raised in the new proceedings, but only some of them, it will need to be recognised for the purposes of issue estoppel, so as to prevent those issues with which it does deal from being raised again. *Id.* at para. 11.20 (emphasis in original).
>
> The use of recognition . . . may be illustrated by considering the example of a company that is made a defendant in legal proceedings by a foreign supplier for goods sold and delivered, but allegedly not paid for. Suppose that the dispute between the company and a foreign supplier has already been submitted to arbitration, and that an award has been made, in which the foreign supplier's claim was dismissed. In these circumstances, the company will ask the court to *recognise* the award as a valid defence to the foreign supplier's new claim. If the court is prepared to do this, the claim is dismissed. The legal force and effect of the foreign award will have been recognised, but the award itself has not been enforced. *Id.* at para. 11.21.
>
> By contrast, where a court is asked to enforce an award, it is asked not merely to recognise the legal force and effect of the award, but also to ensure that it is carried out, by using such legal sanctions as are available. Enforcement goes a step further than recognition. A court that is prepared to grant enforcement of an award will do so because it recognises the award as validly made and binding upon the parties to it, and therefore suitable for enforcement. . . . *Id.* at para. 11.22.
>
> . . .
>
> A party who simply seeks *recognition* of an award will generally do so because he or she needs to rely on the award by way of defence or set-off, or in some other way in court proceedings. For this purpose, the party asks the court concerned to recognise the award as binding on the parties between whom it was made. But the choice of court is not made by the party seeking recognition; it must be a court of the place where the proceedings against him or her are brought – and this fact, of itself, emphasises how important it is that international awards should be accepted as truly 'international' in their validity and effect. *Id.* at para. 11.24.

The *Arbitration Ordinance* (Cap. 609) translates "recognition" as 承認.

[5] Butterworths Hong Kong Arbitration Law Handbook para. [87.04] (Damon YC So, Christopher To *et al.*, eds., 2012) (citations omitted).

between the parties. As alluded to in the above quotation, this is the legal principle known as *res judicata*.[6]

B. Enforcement

As its name implies, *enforcement* means the court is requested to ensure that the award is honoured through the use of appropriate legal sanctions once the court has recognised the validity or legal force of that award.[7] In domestic arbitration, the assets of the losing party are usually located in the country where the arbitral proceedings were conducted. In an international arbitration, the losing party's assets might be located outside the arbitral seat. This is particularly so in situations where the parties are from different countries and had chosen a neutral venue with which

---

[6] "*Res judicata*" is defined by BLACK'S LAW DICTIONARY 1504 (10th ed. 2014) [hereinafter BLACK'S] as "an issue that has been definitively settled by judicial decision" and which serves as

> an affirmative defense barring the same parties from litigating a second lawsuit on the same claim, or any other claim arising from the same transaction or series of transactions and that could have been — but was not — raised in the first suit.

In summary, the principle of *res judicata* applies where (1) there has been an earlier decision on the issue, (2) a final judgment on the merits of the case had been made, and (3) the same parties are involved.

In the case of *陳偉文訴入境事務處處長* (HCAL20/2000), the court translated "*res judicata*" as 既判力.

[7] REDFERN & HUNTER, *supra* note 1, at para. 11.22.

For example, court enforcement in Hong Kong is described thus in 2 HALBURY'S LAWS OF HONG KONG paras. [25.176]–[25.177] (2nd ed. 2016) [hereinafter HALSBURY'S]:

> There is an implied promise at common law in every arbitration agreement that the parties will perform the award. If a party to an arbitration agreement acts in breach of this implied promise by failing to comply with the award, the successful party may bring an action to enforce the award in any court of competent jurisdiction. This remedy is available to a successful party whether the award arises out of a written or an oral arbitration agreement. The plaintiff in an action on the award may claim the following relief: (1) judgment for the amount of the award; (2) a declaration that the award is binding; (3) in appropriate cases, specific performance of the award; (4) damages for failure to perform the award; (5) an injunction restraining the unsuccessful party from failing to comply with the award. (citations omitted)
>
> An award, order or direction made or given in or in relation to arbitration proceedings by an arbitral tribunal is enforceable in the same way as a judgment, of the High Court that has the same effect, but only with the leave of the court or a judge of the court. If that leave is given, the court or judge may enter judgment in terms of the award, award, or permit the enforcement of an order or direction in the same manner as an order direction of the Court that has the same effect. These remedies are only available to a successful party where the award arises out of a written arbitration agreement. The court will grant leave to enforce the award as a judgment. (citations omitted)

For more information on the enforcement of foreign awards, *see, e.g.*, ARBITRATION IN HONG KONG: A PRACTICAL GUIDE paras. 19.025–19.038 (THE HON CHIEF JUSTICE GEOFFREY MA AND DENIS BROCK, eds., 4th ed. 2017) [hereinafter MA & BROCK]; JOHN CHOONG AND ROMESH WEERAMANTRY, THE HONG KONG ARBITRATION ORDINANCE: COMMENTARY AND ANNOTATIONS Chapt. 13 (2nd ed. 2015) [hereinafter CHOONG & WEERAMANTRY], HALSBURY'S, *supra* note 7, at paras. [25.180]–[25.187].

For further details on the enforcement of mainland PRC awards, *see, e.g.*, MA & BROCK, *supra* note 7, at paras. 19.039–19.059 and paras. 22.059–22.072; CHOONG & WEERAMANTRY, *supra* note 7, at paras. 92.00–98.02, HALSBURY'S, *supra* note 7, at paras. [25.188]–[25.191].

For more particulars on the enforcement of Macao awards, *see, e.g.*, MA & BROCK, *supra* note 7, at paras. 19.060–19.062; CHOONG & WEERAMANTRY *supra* note 7, at paras. 98A.00–98A.02; 98B.00–98D.07, HALSBURY'S, *supra* note 7, at paras. [25.192]–[25.195].

the parties have no connection.[8] Therefore, in the latter case, it is important that arbitral awards can be recognized and enforced in foreign countries, not only in the place where the award was rendered.[9] *Enforcement of foreign judgment* is defined as "a court's enforcement of a judgment by a court outside the court's territory after determining that the judgment should be recognised."[10] There are certain requirements to be met before enforcement of a foreign arbitral award can be implemented.[11] These requirements are now discussed.

i. Formal requirements

In some jurisdictions, such as Brazil, an award must firstly be recognized by one court and secondly have enforcement granted by possibly another court.[12] In most jurisdictions, both orders are granted at the same time by the same court. We proceed as if one court will grant both recognition (in some jurisdictions this grant of recognition is referred to by the phrase *leave to enforce an arbitral award*) and enforcement, as is the case in Hong Kong.[13]

---

[8] Redfern & Hunter, *supra* note 1, at para. 11.28.

[9] *Id.*

[10] Black's, *supra* note 6, at 1580.
As explained by one source:

> [W]here a court is asked to enforce an award, it is asked not merely to recognise the legal force and effect of the award, but also to ensure that it is carried out, by using such legal sanctions as are available. Enforcement goes a step further than recognition. A court that is prepared to grant enforcement of an award will do so because it recognises the award as validly made and binding upon the parties to it, and therefore suitable for enforcement. In this context, the terms 'recognition' and 'enforcement' do run together: one is a necessary part of the other.

Redfern & Hunter, *supra* note 1, at para. 11.22.

[11] For arbitrations conducted under §§ 99–103 and Schedule 2 of the *Arbitration Ordinance*, *supra* note 4, the procedures are slightly different. For a discussion of these procedures, *see* Halsbury's, *supra* note 7, at paras. [25.157]–[25.159] and [25.162]–[25.175]. *See also* Ma & Brock, *supra* note 7, at paras. 1.016–1.019 and paras. 8.001–8.018; and for a fuller discussion of Schedule 2, Choong & Weeramantry, *supra* note 7, at Chapt. 16.

[12] Prior to being enforced in Brazil, foreign awards (those awards which are rendered outside the Brazilian territory) must be recognized by the Brazilian Superior Court of Justice (*Superior Tribunal de Justiça*). At this time, the award might be challenged under very limited grounds which are essentially linked to the grounds provided in the *Convention on the Recognition and Enforcement of Foreign Arbitral Awards* (done in New York, 1958) [hereinafter *New York Convention*]. Once the Brazilian Superior Court of Justice has granted the request for recognition (*homologação*) of the foreign award, the interested party may seek enforcement (*execução*) of that award before the competent Brazilian courts, under standard procedures for enforcement of judicial orders. Andre Abbud, Homologação de sentenças arbitrais estrangeiras 263-265 (2008).
See also Renata Brazil-David, *An Examination of the Law and Practice of International Commercial Arbitration in Brazil*, 27(1) Arbitration International 57, 61 (2011).

[13] § 82 and § 83 of the *Arbitration Ordinance*, *supra* note 4, specifically provides that Arts. 35 and 36 of UNCITRAL's *Model Law on International Commercial Arbitration* (regarding the recognition and enforcement of arbitral awards) do not apply to Hong Kong. Hong Kong has taken an independent approach in respect of the recognition and enforcement of arbitral awards which is governed by § 84 of the Ordinance. Choong & Weeramantry, *supra* note 7, at para. 43.13.
Under § 84(1) of the *Arbitration Ordinance*, *supra* note 4, Hong Kong courts would not "recognise" any arbitral award. Rather, they have the discretion to "grant leave" to enforce an arbitral award. In practice, leave to enforce an arbitral award would only be refused in unusual cases. Choong & Weeramantry, *supra* note 7, at para. 84.11 and para. 84.30.

The winning party makes a written application for recognition and enforcement before the appropriate court.[14] This party provides the required items in support of its application:

- original arbitration agreement or a duly certified copy[15]
- authenticated original award or a duly certified copy[16]
- certified translations if either the award and/or the arbitration agreement is not in the official language of the country where recognition and enforcement is sought[17]
- any necessary court fees[18]

UNCITRAL's *Model Law on International Commercial Arbitration* [hereinafter "*Model Law*"] does not provide a time limit by which the winning party must apply for recognition and enforcement. The award represents a debt and is regulated by the limitation period of the jurisdiction where enforcement is sought. These periods vary from jurisdiction to jurisdiction. These periods can be as short as three months and can extend up to an unlimited time, again, according to the statute of limitation in the country where enforcement is sought.[19] Parties anticipating enforcement proceedings must complete their application process within the stated time.

---

[14] Different states or territories have different formalities regarding the written application for recognition and enforcement of an arbitral award. For example, in Hong Kong, every application for recognition and enforcement of arbitral award shall be made *ex parte* supported by an affidavit or affirmation under Order 73, rule 10 of the Rules of the High Court (Cap. 4A) [hereinafter High Court Rules]. All of the items in support of such application as referred to in Order 73, rule 3(a) of the High Court Rules must be attached to the affidavit or affirmation. Furthermore, under Order 73, rule 3(b) of these Rules, the application must include the name and the usual or last known place of abode or business of the applicant and the person against whom it is sought to enforce the award. CHOONG & WEERAMANTRY, *supra* note 7, at para. 84.24.

In Hong Kong, an application for leave to enforce an arbitral award is also known as an action for a "declaratory judgment or order" under Order 15, rule 16 of the High Court Rules which can be started either by way of issuing a Writ of Summons or an Originating Summons under Order 5, rule 4 of these rules.

[15] § 85(b) and § 88(b) of the *Arbitration Ordinance*, *supra* note 4.

[16] *Id.* at § 85(a) and § 88(a). The Hong Kong courts have provided a broad interpretation of the terms "authenticated" and "duly certified." In the case of *Guangdong New Technology Import and Export Corp Jiangmen Branch v Chiu Shing* [1991] 2 HKC 460, the court determined that an affidavit by the winning party's solicitors that the attached copy of the award was a true copy of the duly authenticated award and thus would be sufficient.

[17] For example, in Hong Kong, § 85(c) of the *Arbitration Ordinance*, *supra* note 4, provides that:

> if the award . . . is not in either or both of the official languages [of Hong Kong, *i.e.* Chinese and English], a translation of it in either official language certified by an official or sworn translator or by a diplomatic or consular agent [must be produced].

[18] In Hong Kong, the current court fee for filing an *ex parte* application for leave to enforce an award or a "declaration of enforceability" of an award by way of issuing writ of summons or originating summons is HK$1,045 under Section 1 of Schedule 1 of the High Court Fees Rules (Cap. 4D).

Once the applicant succeeds in obtaining a declaratory judgment or order of enforceability from the court, the foreign award becomes enforceable as if it were a judgment of the local court. The enforcement procedure for a local judgment such as issuing writ of execution, writ of possession, *etc.*, will then apply to that arbitral award. The current court fee for sealing each document used for execution such as a writ of execution, a writ of possession, *etc.* is HK$1,045 under Section 16 of Schedule 1 of the High Court Fees Rules.

[19] In Hong Kong, enforcement proceedings of arbitral awards cannot be brought after six years from the date of the award. Section 4(1)(c) of the *Limitation Ordinance* (Cap. 347) provides that:

> (1) The following actions shall not be brought after the expiration of 6 years from the date on which the cause of action accrued, that is to say—

ii. Grounds for refusing recognition and enforcement

Having discussed the ways in which a winning party may enforce its arbitration award, we now consider the ways in which a losing party may seek to avoid an award's obligations. The bases are very limited for challenging the validity of an award in order to avoid the award's obligations.

A losing party can challenge the recognition and enforcement of an award by opposing the application for enforcement.[20] A losing party needs to demonstrate a real risk of prejudice and that its rights have been substantially violated.[21] An award will be recognized and enforced unless the losing party can prove the existence of one or more of the grounds for refusing recognition and enforcement. Nonetheless, should the losing party prove one or more of these grounds, the enforcing court will have discretion in deciding whether to enforce or invalidate the award.

The *Convention on the Recognition and Enforcement of Foreign Arbitral Awards* (done in New York, 1958) [hereinafter "*New York Convention*" or "Convention"] regulates the recognition and enforcement of arbitration awards made in one Convention state and sought to be enforced in another Convention state.[22] These arbitral awards are referred to as *Convention awards*. Courts have enforced foreign awards, international awards and domestic awards made in another Convention state. The requirements to be satisfied for recognition and enforcement or challenge of an award under the *New York Convention* are the same as those discussed in Chapter 3.

These requirements and conditions are the only grounds and represent maximum standards. A final award made in any of the 157 Convention states can be recognized and enforced on satisfying the same requirements in any of the other Convention states. This makes enforcement of Convention awards easier while creating harmonization of the enforcement regime of foreign arbitral awards. The

---

. . .

(c) actions to enforce an award, where the submission is not by an instrument under seal;

[20] *See* § 86 of the *Arbitration Ordinance*, *supra* note 4.

[21] *Grand Pacific Holdings Ltd v Pacific China Holdings Ltd* [2012] 4 HKLRD 1 (CA).

[22] The *Convention on the Recognition and Enforcement of Foreign Arbitral Awards* [hereinafter *New York Convention*] was *done*, otherwise known as being *signed*, in New York in 1958.

For more information on the enforcement of *New York Convention* awards, *see*, *e.g.*, Ma & Brock, *supra* note 7, at paras. 19.025–19.038; Choong & Weeramantry, *supra* note 7, at Chapt. 13, Halsbury's, *supra* note 7, at paras. [25.180]–[25.187]; Redfern & Hunter, *supra* note 1, at paras. 11.40–11.124; and, Albert Jan van den Berg, The New York Arbitration Convention of 1958 (1981).

For a brief overview of some other international or regional enforcement treaties, see Redfern & Hunter, *supra* note 1, at paras. 11.125–11.130 for ICSID; paras. 11.131–133 for the *Convention on the Settlement by Arbitration of Civil Law Disputes Resulting from Relations of Economic and Scientific-Technical Cooperation* (done in Moscow, 1972); paras. 11.134–11.137 for the *OAS Inter-American Convention on International Commercial Arbitration* (done in Panama, 1975); paras. 11.138–11.139 for the *Riyadh Arab Agreement for Judicial Cooperation* (done in Riyadh, 1983) commonly known as the *Riyadh Convention 1985* and the *Agreement on the Execution of Rulings, Request of Legal Assistance and Judicial Notices*, (done in Oman, 1995) commonly known as the *GCC Convention 1995*.

New York Convention has given arbitration one of its important advantages: the portability of the award.

The grounds allowing a party to nullify an award are found in the *Model Law* and in the *New York Convention*.[23] The grounds in the former can be found in Art. 36.[24] In similar language are the grounds for challenging an award as set out in the *New York Convention* which states at Art. V:

1. Recognition and enforcement of the award may be refused, at the request of the party against whom it is invoked, only if that party furnishes to the competent authority where the recognition and enforcement is sought, proof that:
   (a) The parties to the agreement referred to in article II were, under the law applicable to them, under some incapacity, or the said agreement is not valid under the law to which the parties have subjected it or, failing any indication thereon, under the law of the country where the award was made; or
   (b) The party against whom the award is invoked was not given proper notice of the appointment of the arbitrator or of the arbitration proceedings or was otherwise unable to present his case; or
   (c) The award deals with a difference not contemplated by or not falling within the terms of the submission to arbitration, or it contains decisions on

---

[23] Rule 66(1) of the Hong Kong Court of Final Appeal Rules (Cap. 484A) translates "nullify" as 令 . . . 變為無效.

[24] Hong Kong did not enact all the provisions found in the United Nations Commission on International Trade Law's *Model Law on International Commercial Arbitration* [hereinafter *Model Law*]. One example is *Model Law* Art. 36. As the language of *Model Law* Art. 36 is nearly identical to Art. V of the *New York Convention*, *supra* note 22, Art. 36 is set out in relevant part below:

(1) Recognition or enforcement of an arbitral award, irrespective of the country in which it was made, may be refused only:
  (a) at the request of the party against whom it is invoked, if that party furnishes to the competent court where recognition or enforcement is sought proof that:
    (i) a party to the arbitration agreement referred to in article 7 was under some incapacity; or the said agreement is not valid under the law to which the parties have subjected it or, failing any indication thereon, under the law of the country where the award was made; or
    (ii) the party against whom the award is invoked was not given proper notice of the appointment of an arbitrator or of the arbitral proceedings or was otherwise unable to present his case; or
    (iii) the award deals with a dispute not contemplated by or not falling within the terms of the submission to arbitration, or it contains decisions on matters beyond the scope of the submission to arbitration, provided that, if the decisions on matters submitted to arbitration can be separated from those not so submitted, that part of the award which contains decisions on matters submitted to arbitration may be recognized and enforced; or
    (iv) the composition of the arbitral tribunal or the arbitral procedure was not in accordance with the agreement of the parties or, failing such agreement, was not in accordance with the law of the country where the arbitration took place; or
    (v) the award has not yet become binding on the parties or has been set aside or suspended by a court of the country in which, or under the law of which, that award was made; or
  (b) if the court finds that:
    (i) the subject-matter of the dispute is not capable of settlement by arbitration under the law of this State; or
    (ii) the recognition or enforcement of the award would be contrary to the public policy of this State.

matters beyond the scope of the submission to arbitration, provided that, if the decisions on matters submitted to arbitration can be separated from those not so submitted, that part of the award which contains decisions on matters submitted to arbitration may be recognized and enforced; or

(d) The composition of the arbitral authority or the arbitral procedure was not in accordance with the agreement of the parties, or, failing such agreement, was not in accordance with the law of the country where the arbitration took place; or

(e) The award has not yet become binding on the parties, or has been set aside or suspended by a competent authority of the country in which, or under the law of which, that award was made.

2. Recognition and enforcement of an arbitral award may also be refused if the competent authority in the country where recognition and enforcement is sought finds that:

(a) The subject matter of the difference is not capable of settlement by arbitration under the law of that country; or

(b) The recognition or enforcement of the award would be contrary to the public policy of that country.

We now review each of these grounds. It should be noted again that should a losing party successfully prove the application of one or more of these grounds, the enforcing court may nonetheless exercise its discretion to enforce the award.[25]

Pursuant to Art. V(1)(a), parties to a contract must have the capacity to enter into that contract. The same principle applies to arbitration agreements. If a party is incapable of entering into an arbitration agreement, this agreement would be invalid.[26] Incapacity can be raised at the very beginning of the arbitration or at the time of challenging the award. For an individual, the applicable law to determine capacity is his or her personal law. For a corporation, the applicable law is the law of its place of incorporation. States and state entities may be restricted by their national law from entering into arbitration agreements.[27]

In *State of Ukraine v Norsk Hydro ASA*, a Norwegian party and a Ukrainian party concluded a contract. The law under which this contract was governed was Swedish law. Although the contract had been validly signed under Swedish law,

---

[25] *Model Law, supra* note 24, at Art. 36 states that recognition or enforcement "may be refused" which is permissive language. Compare this with *Model Law* Art. 35 which states that an arbitral award "shall be recognized as binding" and "shall be enforced." Under Art. 35, a court has no discretion; the court must recognise and enforce an award.

The *New York Convention, supra* note 22, at Art. V likewise uses the permissive language "may" rather than the mandatory language "shall."

Should sufficient grounds be made out either to refuse enforcement or to set aside an arbitral award, the court has a residual discretion and may nevertheless enforce the award despite the proven existence of a valid ground. *See Hebei Import & Export Corp v Polytek Engineering Co Ltd* (1999) 2 HKCFAR 111, 136A-B.

[26] *See, e.g.*, Redfern & Hunter, *supra* note 1, at paras. 11.66–11.70.

[27] *Model Law, supra* note 24, at Art. 7 offers two options for defining the arbitration agreement. The first contains a very liberal definition of "writing" while the second does not require any writing at all. Hong Kong has adopted the very liberal definition of "writing."

the way in which the Ukrainian party signed the contract failed to comply with the requirements of Ukrainian law. A dispute arose. The Ukrainian party alleged that no contract existed as this party had not signed properly according to Ukrainian law. The arbitral tribunal considered that there was a valid contract between these parties under Swedish law and made an award based on Swedish law. The Ukrainian party challenged the award in Sweden, the seat of the arbitration. The Swedish court determined that the legal capacity of a party to enter into a contract is not subject to the governing law chosen by the parties in the contract. Rather, the court decided that the applicable law is to be the law of the parties' respective countries of origin. Accordingly, the Swedish court set aside the award on the basis that the Ukrainian party's non-compliance with Ukrainian law regarding the conclusion of contracts resulted in the party's lack of capacity to enter into a contract.[28]

In the case of *Dallah Real Estate v Ministry of Religious Affairs*,[29] the winning party sought to enforce an arbitral award rendered in France against the losing party in England but was refused on the basis that the losing party was the Pakistan Government which was not a party to the arbitration agreement. Indeed, the arbitration agreement was signed by a state-owned enterprise in Pakistan which later ceased to exist. Therefore, the Supreme Court of England and Wales held that the state-owned enterprise was no longer an organ of the Pakistan Government.[30]

Related to Art. V(1)(a), another manner in which an arbitration agreement may be invalid is when the agreement does not meet formal legal requirements, including those requirements imposed by Art. II of the *New York Convention*.[31] The agreement shall be in writing, clearly stating the parties' intention to have a final resolution of part or all of their commercial contract's disputes by arbitration. Modern arbitration laws have recognized various forms of communication which meet this requirement that the arbitration clause is *written*. For example, for an arbitration clause to be *in writing* may include exchanges of business correspondence such as letters, faxes or emails; or, reference to documents containing an arbitration clause other than the contract document in dispute.[32]

---

[28] GIUDITTA CORDERO-MOSS, *Limits to Party Autonomy in International Commercial Arbitration*, 1 OSLO LAW REVIEW 47, 49 (2014) citing to the Swedish Court of Appeal (*Svea Hovrätt*) case of *State of Ukraine v Norsk Hydro ASA*, 17 December 2007, T 3108-06.

[29] [2010] UKSC 46.

[30] REDFERN & HUNTER, *supra* note 1, at para. 11.68.

[31] Article II of the *New York Convention*, *supra* note 22, provides in part:

1. Each Contracting State shall recognize an agreement in writing under which the parties undertake to submit to arbitration all or any differences which have arisen or which may arise between them in respect of a defined legal relationship, whether contractual or not, concerning a subject matter capable of settlement by arbitration.
2. The term "agreement in writing" shall include an arbitral clause in a contract or an arbitration agreement, signed by the parties or contained in an exchange of letters or telegrams.

[32] For information concerning the *in writing* requirement, *see*, *e.g.*, Chapter 2; CHOONG & WEERAMANTRY, *supra* note 7, at paras. 19.17–19.47; HALSBURY'S, *supra* note 7, at para. [25.012]; REDFERN AND HUNTER, *supra* note 1, at paras. 1.44–1.48 and paras. 2.13–2.24.

Art. V(1)(b) pertains to the concept of fairness.[33] The phrases *due process* or *natural justice* are different terms representing the same concept: the minimum standards for the fair and proper conduct of arbitral proceedings. If a party justifiably is unable to present its case, there would be a violation of due process or natural justice. Due process ensures that parties are given a fair hearing by the arbitral tribunal. The term *fair hearing* means that each party is given the opportunity to present its case and to respond to the other party's case. Additionally, due process gives both parties the same opportunity to:

- attend any hearings or sittings of the arbitral tribunal
- be present at the taking of evidence
- be represented or assisted by a representative of its choice, such as lawyers or experts
- see and comment on all materials placed before the arbitral tribunal

The tribunal must not base its decision on any evidence or argument that the parties have not had an opportunity to address.

In the case of *Sun Tian Gang v Hong Kong & China Gas (Jilin) Ltd*,[34] the claimant commenced arbitration against the respondent while the latter was facing criminal charges and was detained in mainland China. Although the respondent was imprisoned and thus did not have proper notice of the arbitration, an award was made in favour of the claimant. The arbitral award was set aside on the basis that the losing party did not have the opportunity to present its case.

In *Ajay Kanoria v Tony Francis Guinness*,[35] the United Kingdom's Court of Appeal refused to enforce an arbitral award on the grounds that the losing party, *i.e.*, the respondent who had failed to attend the hearing because of serious illness, had not been given the opportunity to present its case in response to the legal arguments made by the claimant.[36]

Under Art. V(1)(c), an arbitral tribunal's authority is comparable to a court's jurisdiction.[37] For example, a Hong Kong court has no jurisdiction to decide a case being conducted in Australia, even if the parties are from Hong Kong. Within the territory, a Coroner's Court would have no jurisdiction in a criminal case.

Likewise, an arbitral tribunal cannot act beyond the scope of the parties' agreement. For example, if the parties retain the tribunal to resolve the parties' first dispute, the tribunal cannot also resolve the parties' second dispute. Where an arbitral tribunal does act beyond its authority, the tribunal is said to have exceeded its authority. Thus, the tribunal acts without power or authorization. This excess of

[33] For an analysis of this provision, *see* Redfern & Hunter, *supra* note 1, at paras. 11.71–11.77.
[34] [2016] 5 HKLRD 221.
[35] [2006] EWCA Civ 222, [2006] Arb LR 513.
[36] [2006] 2 All ER (Comm) 413; Redfern & Hunter, *supra* note 1, at para. 11.75.
[37] For an analysis of this section, *see* Redfern & Hunter, *supra* note 1, at paras. 11.78–11.81.

authority may result in the tribunal's award being set aside to the extent that the tribunal was acting beyond its authority, except where it affects the whole award.

An arbitration administered by the Hong Kong International Arbitration Centre has been refused recognition and enforcement by the Beijing Fourth Intermediate People's Court based on a comparable ground. Article 7(3) of the *Arrangements of the Supreme People's Court on the Mutual Enforcement of Arbitral Awards between the Mainland and the Hong Kong Special Administrative Region*[38] is essentially identical to the New York Convention's Art. V(1)(c) and the *Arbitration Ordinance* (Cap. 609) § 95(2)(d)(i), § 95(2)(d)(ii) and § 95(4). The case of *IP Cathay II, LP v Jiting Zhou* involved Cathay seeking the enforcement of an arbitral award against the respondents who claimed that Article 7 applied such that the award could not be enforced against them.[39] The Beijing court decided that because the award found liability on the part of all 21 respondents rather than liability of only the seven parties sought by Cathay, the award dealt with a difference not contemplated by the parties or not falling within the terms of the submission to arbitration. Furthermore, as the liability of the respondents was not apportioned, the decisions on matters and liabilities submitted to arbitration could not be separated from those not so submitted. Consequently, the whole award could not be enforced.

In *General Organization of Commerce and Industrialisation of Cereals of the Arab Republic of Syria v SpA SIMER (Società delle Industrie Meccaniche di Rovereto) (Italy)*,[40] the arbitral tribunal had exceeded its jurisdiction in some but not all respects. Nevertheless, the Italian court allowed partial enforcement of the arbitral award to the extent that the award dealt with matters within the arbitral tribunal's authority.[41]

Art. V(1)(d) pertains to an irregular composition of the tribunal or irregular procedure.[42] The composition of the arbitral tribunal and the procedure adopted by the tribunal must meet the requirements of the parties' arbitration agreement. Alternatively, if the arbitration agreement does not address these matters, the

---

[38] No. 3 [2000], SPC Interpretation, adopted at the 1069th meeting of the Judicial Committee of the Supreme People's Court on June 18, 1999.
Article 7(3) of this document provides:

> 7. The party against whom an application is filed may, after receiving notice of an arbitral award, whether made in the Mainland or in the HKSAR, adduce evidence to show any of the situations set out below. Upon such evidence being examined and any of the said situations being found proved, the relevant court may refuse to enforce the arbitral award:
>
> ...
>
> (3) The award deals with a difference not contemplated by or not falling within the terms of the submission to arbitration, or the award contains decisions on matters beyond the scope of the submission to arbitration. However, if the award contains decisions on matters submitted to arbitration that can be separated from those not so submitted, that part of the award which contains decisions on matters submitted to arbitration shall be enforced;
>
> ...

[39] No. A13027.

[40] (1983) VIII YBCA 386.

[41] REDFERN & HUNTER, *supra* note 1, at para. 11.81.

[42] For a review of this provision, *see id.* at paras.11.82–11.86.

appointment, composition and procedure of the arbitration should comply with the *lex arbitri*.[43] Some examples of irregularity are where:

- the arbitrator does not possess the qualifications required by the parties in their arbitration agreement
- the arbitral tribunal renders an award without giving any reasons or bases for that decision[44]
- the arbitral tribunal consciously disregards the governing law agreed by the parties in the arbitration agreement
- the arbitral authority appointed is not in accordance with the arbitration agreement[45]

In *Encyclopaedia Universalis SA (Luxembourg) v Encyclopaedia Britannica Inc. (US)*,[46] the parties had agreed in their arbitration clause that the two party-appointed arbitrators should choose the third arbitrator, failing which the English Commercial Court would appoint the third arbitrator. The US Court of Appeals for the Second Circuit refused to enforce the award on the grounds that the premature appointment of the third arbitrator by the English Commercial Court upon only the appellant's request had irremediably spoiled the arbitration process.[47]

In *Noble Resources International Pte Ltd v Shanghai Good Credit International Trade Co, Ltd*,[48] the Shanghai court refused to enforce a Singapore International Arbitration Centre [hereinafter "SIAC"] award. The parties had agreed to a dispute

---

43 BLACK'S, *supra* note 6, at 1048, defines "*lex arbitri*" as "the law governing how an arbitration is to be conducted and the relationship between the arbitration and the courts."
The *lex arbitri*:

> governs such largely procedural matters as the steps that the tribunal must follow to ensure that its award is valid and enforceable (such as service of notice of the arbitration on the parties) and the extent to which the parties may resort to national courts to review or appeal an award. The lex arbitri is not the substantive law.

AARON X. FELLMETH AND MAURICE HORWITZ, GUIDE TO LATIN IN INTERNATIONAL LAW (2009) [Online access].

44 Under *Model Law*, *supra* note 24, at Art. 33(2), the award should state the reasons on which it was based. It was a serious irregularity and a denial of due process which caused substantial injustice and unfairness to the parties if an important issue was not addressed. *A v B* [2015] 3 HKLRD 586, 587.

45 The "composition of the arbitral authority not in accordance with the agreement of the parties" is one of the grounds of refusal of recognition and enforcement of an award. If successfully proved that the arbitral tribunal was wrongly constituted, the court nevertheless has the discretion to enforce the award. In the case of *China Nanhai Oil Joint Service Corporation Shenzhen Branch v Gee Tai Holdings Co Ltd* [1995] 2 HKLR 215, the claimant sought to enforce an arbitral award made under the Shenzhen Sub Commission of the China International Economic and Trade Arbitration Commission [hereinafter CIETAC]. The respondent objected on the basis that the composition of the arbitral authority was not in accordance with the parties' arbitration agreement which provided that disputes shall be submitted to CIETAC in Beijing. However, the respondent had fully participated in the arbitral proceedings without raising any objection to the tribunal and had never communicated its objection to CIETAC in Beijing. The court decided that the respondent had a duty of good faith to notify the tribunal or CIETAC Commission in Beijing of its objections to the formation of the tribunal. The respondent's failure to do so was inconsistent with the obligation of good faith and the notion of justice. Accordingly, the court exercised its residual discretion to enforce the award disregarding the fact that the arbitral tribunal was technically wrongly constituted.

46 (2005) XXX YBCA 1136.

47 REDFERN & HUNTER, *supra* note 1, at para. 11.86.

48 (2016) Hu 01 Xie Wai Ren No. 1.

resolution clause providing for three arbitrators under the SIAC Arbitration Rules 2013. An expedited procedure for this dispute eventuated over the Respondent's objection. Under the expedited procedure rules, SIAC normally would appoint one arbitrator, although there was the possibility of appointing three arbitrators. The Shanghai court decided not to recognise or enforce the award on the basis that the composition of the arbitral tribunal and/or the arbitral procedure was not in accordance with the agreement of the parties. Additionally, the court determined that the SIAC Arbitration Rules permitted the appointment of more than one arbitrator under the expedited procedure and SIAC should have given consideration to the parties' agreement concerning the number of arbitrators in order to preserve party autonomy.[49]

Although deference is given to party autonomy, the parties' agreement nonetheless is limited by the mandatory provisions of the law of the seat of arbitration. This implies that an arbitral tribunal may disregard the parties' agreement in order to comply with a mandatory legal provision.

Art. V(1)(e) pertains to final awards which are not yet binding or which have been set aside.[50] If the period for recourse against an award has not yet run, or the award has been set aside or nullified by the competent court at the place of arbitration, a foreign court may refuse to enforce it. For example, in the 2015 case of *EDF International S/A v YPF S/A and Endesa Latinoamérica S/A*,[51] the Brazilian Superior Court of Justice declined to enforce an International Chamber of Commerce [hereinafter "ICC"] arbitration award which was vacated by a court in Argentina, the seat of the arbitration. The Brazilian court has exclusive jurisdiction to decide on applications for recognition of awards and decided that "due to the fact that the award was annulled in Argentina by a court decision issued in that country, it is not possible to have it recognized in Brazil."[52] The Brazilian court decided that the award cannot be recognized in Brazil unless it has become *res judicata* at its country of origin. Therefore, an award that has been nullified at its seat must be null in Brazil, because the award has no effect in its country of origin, Argentina.[53]

---

[49] The SIAC has since amended its expedited procedure rules in 2016 in order to avoid further occurrences of this issue.

[50] Black's, *supra* note 6, at 1580, defines "set aside" as "to annul or vacate (a judgment, order, *etc.*)."

For further details on this section of the *New York Convention*, *see* Redfern & Hunter, *supra* note 1, at paras. 11.87–11.100.

[51] Challenge of Enforcement of Foreign Award n. 5.782-EX; SEC 5.782.

[52] Leonardo de Campos Melo and Fabiano Robalinho Cavalcanti, *Brazil Refuses Recognition of an ICC Award Set Aside in Argentina*, Kluwer Arbitration Blog, (8 Mar. 2016). Link at: http://arbitrationblog.kluwerarbitration.com/2016/03/08/brazil-refuses-recognition-of-an-icc-award-set-aside-in-argentina/ (last visited 8 Aug. 2017).

These lawyers, who work for the firm which represented one of the parties before the Superior Court, stated:

> Although not expressly stated in the judgment handed down by the Reporting Justice, the SCJ´s Special Chamber made it clear during the hearing that recognition proceedings are designed to allow a foreign award to take legal effects in Brazilian territory. According to the SCJ, therefore, recognition is a means of extending the efficacy of the award to another jurisdiction. Thus, if the award no longer has legal effect at the arbitration, there is no efficacy to be extended to the Brazilian territory.

[53] EDF International had sought recognition of the award in France, the United States, Chile, Spain and Brazil.

There have been cases where a foreign court permitted enforcement of an arbitral award despite this award having been set aside by the courts of the country where the award was made.[54] For example, in *Société PT Putrabali Adyamulia v Société Rena Holding et Société Mnogutia Est Epices*,[55] the French court enforced an arbitral award which was set aside by the English court. The French court decided that an international arbitral award was an international decision of justice which did not belong to any specific national legal system; the award's validity should be determined by the laws of the place where recognition and enforcement are sought.[56] Similarly, in *Antilles Cement Corporation (Puerto Rico) v Transficem (Spain)*,[57] the Supreme Court of Spain held that an arbitral award's enforceability is not to be determined by the law of the State where the award was made.[58]

Some courts might enforce arbitral awards that have been set aside by the courts of the countries where the awards were made. The trend, however, is that courts tend to decline enforcement of annulled awards.[59] The case of *L v B*[60] involved a slightly different situation. Here, the unsuccessful party in an arbitration, B, sought to challenge the award at the seat of the arbitration. Shortly thereafter, the

---

The French granted recognition of the award; the American court stayed the proceedings pending the outcome of the parties' applications to have the award set aside; the Chilean and Spanish courts refused recognition of the award as it had been set aside by the Argentinian court. 1 *ICC Dispute Resolution Bulletin* 24 (2017).

54 As more fully explained:

> courts in France, Belgium, Austria, and the United States have shown themselves prepared, on occasion, to recognise and enforce arbitral awards even though they have been set aside by the courts at the seat of arbitration. The justification for this is twofold. First, the language of Article V of the New York Convention . . . is permissive, not mandatory. Specifically, the English language version of the Convention says that the enforcing court *may* refuse recognition and enforcement – not that it *must* do so. Secondly, the New York Convention recognises that there may be more favourable provisions under which an award may be recognised and enforced. . . . In this way, the New York Convention recognises explicitly that, in any given country, there may be a local law that, whether by treaty or otherwise, is more favourable to the recognition and enforcement of arbitral awards than the convention itself. The Convention gives its blessing, so to speak, to any party who wishes to take advantage of this more favourable local law.

Redfern & Hunter, *supra* note 1, at para. 11.93 (emphasis in original).

55 [2007] Rev Arb 507.

56 Redfern & Hunter, *supra* note 1, at para. 11.96.

57 (2006) XXXI YBCA 846.

58 Redfern & Hunter, *supra* note 1, at para. 11.87.

59 *Id.* at para. 11.97.

60 [2016] HKCFI 830; [2016] 4 HKC 254. The court explained that:

> the ground that the Award has not yet become binding on the parties, the mere existence of some challenge made in the supervisory court does not automatically mean that the Award has not become binding. . . . An appeal to set aside an award is to be distinguished from an appeal on the merits. An arbitral award is not binding only if it is open to appeal on the merits before a judge or an appeal tribunal . . .
>
> Under Article III of the New York Convention . . . each contracting state shall recognize arbitral awards as "binding" and enforce them in accordance with the rules of procedure of the territory where the award is relied upon, under the conditions laid down in the Convention. "Binding" is used, rather than "final", the intention being that a party is entitled to apply for recognition and enforcement of an award once it was issued by the arbitral tribunal. The fact that there are proceedings . . . to set aside the Award on the grounds of irregularities, and not on the merits, does not render the Award invalid or not binding.

Id. at paras. 12–13.

successful party, L, sought to enforce the award in Hong Kong. B sought to suspend the enforcement proceedings pending the challenge of the award. The court deciding that it had unfettered discretion, adjourned the enforcement proceedings for four months but ordered B, within 21 days, to deposit as security the outstanding amount of the award and L's costs. It should be noted that the court was of the opinion that the amount of the award could have been paid immediately to L, and if B were ultimately successful in its challenge, the amount would be returned to B.

In *Astro Nusantara International B.V. v PT First Media TBK*[61] there was an arbitration agreement between the parties, according to which an arbitration was being conducted. During the arbitral process, Astro had additional parties joined to the arbitration (Joinder Decision). First Media objected to this Joinder Decision and brought the arbitral award before the Singapore courts to be set aside.

The Singapore Court of Appeal decided that the Joinder Decision was invalid as the arbitral tribunal was not entitled to join entities that were not parties to the agreement. Thus, the arbitral tribunal lacked the jurisdiction to make the awards in favour of these additional parties, and that the Singapore enforcement orders in favour of these additional parties should be set aside.[62]

Art. V(2)(a) applies to non-arbitrable subject matters.[63] The dispute must be of the type which is capable of resolution by arbitration. Whether a dispute can be arbitrated is determined under the law of the seat of arbitration. All states reserve certain disputes for determination by its national courts. Examples of non-arbitrable matters are:

- disputes regarding the validity of patents and trademarks[64]
- tax disputes between citizens and government
- changes to personal status such as divorce and adoption
- criminal matters

One example is *Nikolay Victorovich Maximov v Novolipetsky Metallurgichesky Kombinat*[65] where a dispute had arisen between the seller and the buyer over the

[61] [2018] HKCFA 12.

[62] This case will be discussed in further detail in Section 5 of this chapter.

[63] For a more detailed discussion of this topic, *see* Redfern & Hunter, *supra* note 1, at paras. 11.101–11.104.

[64] Depending upon the jurisdiction, intellectual property disputes may be arbitrated. Following the passing of the Arbitration (Amendment) Bill 2016 by Hong Kong's Legislative Council in June 2017, Hong Kong will permit the arbitration of intellectual property disputes. As noted by the government's Intellectual Property Department:

> The Arbitration (Amendment) Ordinance 2017 ("Amendment Ordinance") was passed by the Legislative Council on 14 June 2017 and published in the Gazette on 23 June 2017. The Amendment Ordinance amends the Arbitration Ordinance (Cap. 609) to, among other things, clarify that all disputes over intellectual property rights ("IPRs") may be resolved by arbitration and that it is not contrary to the public policy of Hong Kong to enforce arbitral awards involving IPRs. Such amendments relating to IPRs arbitration come into effect on 1 January 2018 (except for section 103J which will come into operation upon commencement of section 123 of the Patents (Amendment) Ordinance 2016).

Link: https://www.ipd.gov.hk/eng/IP_Arbitration.htm (last visited 8 Aug. 2018).

[65] Case No. N VAS-15384/11, Ruling of the Supreme Commercial Arbitrazh Court, 30 January 2012.

purchase price of shares in a Russian-incorporated company and the matter had been submitted to arbitration in Russia. The arbitral award was set aside by the Russian court on the grounds that corporate governance disputes are non-arbitrable under Art. 225(1) of the *Arbitration Procedural Code* of Russia.[66]

The number of categories of non-arbitrable matters is declining. An increasing number of courts have recognized an arbitral tribunal's authority to decide disputes which parties could have settled by negotiation. Nonetheless, arbitrating these non-arbitrable matters would be a breach of a state's public policy.

Art. V(2)(b) is applicable to violations to public policy.[67] *Public policy* is a vague phrase referring to the fundamental legal and socio-economic principles of a nation state. A breach of such a principle is a violation of that enforcement state's public policy.[68] An act breaching one nation's public policy, however, might not be a breach in another country.[69]

The recent United States case of *Hardy Exploration & Production (India), Inc. v Government of India, Ministry of Petroleum & Natural Gas*[70] addressed the application of public policy in the US. This case involved Hardy being awarded a contract for the exploration of gas and oil by the Government of India in a designated "Block." A dispute arose over whether there was gas or oil in the Block which would determine the duration of the exploration contract: two years for gas or five years for oil.

The award was in favour of Hardy, ordering India to perform specifically its obligations for an additional three years, for a total of five years. The award further ordered India to pay pre-award interest along with post-award interest at a higher interest rate. Lastly, the tribunal also awarded interest from the date of the award until compliance with or the performance of the award. Hardy brought the award to the US court for enforcement. India raised several objections, two of which are discussed here. On one of the objections, the federal district court decided that

---

66 REDFERN & HUNTER, *supra* note 1, at para. 11.103.

67 An analysis of this topic may be found in *id.* at paras. 11.105–11.122.

68 *Id.* at para. 11.109.

69 *See, e.g.*, *U v A* [2017] HKCFI 398, [2017] HKEC 468 where the court decided upon enforcement of an award made in Hong Kong in a contract dispute between parties from Luxembourg, Hong Kong, Singapore and the PRC. The Hong Kong party and one of the PRC parties challenged the award, claiming a violation of PRC public policy. The violation was the arbitrator's finding that one of the contracts in their transaction was valid despite not receiving the required PRC authorities' approval. The court stated:

> 62. In *Hebei Import & Export Corp v Polytek Engineering Co Ltd* [1999] HKCFA 40; (1999) 2 HKCFAR 111, the Court of Final Appeal explained that "contrary to public policy" means contrary to the fundamental conceptions of morality and justice of the forum, and that in an application to resist enforcement of an award in Hong Kong, the public policy to be considered is that of Hong Kong.
>
> . . .
>
> 71. . . . Considering the public policy interests in favor of enforcing arbitration agreements and arbitral awards in Hong Kong, and the fact that resisting enforcement of the Award on the Mainland is an option open to the Respondents, I cannot agree that it would be just to refuse enforcement of the Award in Hong Kong, on the Respondents' assertion that enforcement of the Award on the Mainland would be against the public policy on the Mainland or against PRC law . . .

70 United States District Court for the District of Columbia, Civil Action No.: 16-140 (RC), decided June 7, 2018.

the enforcement of an arbitral award providing for specific performance against a foreign government would be contrary to American public policy.[71] On the other objection, the court decided that the post-award interest also contravened public policy as the post-award interest was coercive.[72]

Different countries or territories have different concepts of public policy. Another example is *Wicor Holding A.G. v Taizhou Haopu Investments Ltd.*[73] Wicor and Taizhou entered into a joint venture agreement which provided for the ICC Rules of Arbitration to apply. In another instance of poor draftsmanship, the arbitration clause also provided: "if one party initiates the arbitration, the other party shall choose the seat of arbitration." A dispute arose. In July 2011, Taizhou began court proceedings. In December 2012, the court declared the arbitration clause

---

[71] The court stated that:

> courts should rely on the public policy exception only in clear-cut cases where enforcement would violate the forum state's most basic notions of morality and justice. . . . The public policy defense under Article V(2)(b) of the New York Convention is to be construed narrowly and is available only where an arbitration award tends clearly to undermine the public interest, the public confidence in the administration of the law, or security for individual rights of personal liberty or of private property. . . . Such a public policy must be explicit and well defined and dominant, and is to be ascertained by reference to the laws and legal precedents. . . . The provision was not meant to enshrine the vagaries of international politics under the rubric of public policy, and it does not provide that awards that might contravene U.S. interests may be resisted on such grounds. . . . The public policy exception cannot be used to simply question the merits of the underlying award. *Id.* at 19–20 (quotations marks and citations omitted).
>
> . . .
>
> —the Court nevertheless finds that this infringement on India's national sovereignty would contravene the United States' public policy interest in respecting the territorial integrity of other nations for several reasons.
>
> . . .
>
> that forced interference with India's complete control over its territory violates public policy to the extent necessary to overcome the United States' policy preference for the speedy confirmation of arbitral awards. *Id.* at 26.

[72] On this issue, the court in *Hardy Exploration & Production* stated:

> The Court finds that even if the interest awarded by the Tribunal was meant to be compensatory rather than punitive, because this Court cannot enforce the primary component of the award (return of the Block to HEPI), and because the two components of the award are inextricably intertwined, the Court also cannot award interest predicated on compliance with that component of the award. To order otherwise would be to impermissibly coerce India into complying with an order that this Court has determined it cannot issue. The Court cannot coerce through an interest award an action that it cannot order directly. *Id.* at 29.
>
> . . . the practical effect of confirming the Tribunal's award of interest would be to coerce a foreign state into complying with a non-existent order from this Court, a non-existent order which, as explained above, would be a severe affront to India's sovereignty and would violate U.S. public policy. Even if the Tribunal did not intend its award of interest to be punitive, confirmation of this award would leave India in a Catch-22 of either halting the accrual of interest by allowing HEPI back onto the Block—and thereby, effectively, complying with the arbitration award at the behest of this Court—or allowing the sum of money it owes to continue to grow. Indeed, due to the way the arbitration award was composed, there is no way for India to halt the accrual of interest against it, or indeed to even satisfy the award definitively, until it allows HEPI back onto the Block. This portion of the award is so inseparable from the specific performance portion of the award, the confirmation of which would violate U.S. public policy, that the confirmation of the interest portion of the award must also be found, necessarily, the [*sic*] violate U.S. public policy. *Id.* at 30–31.

[73] Civil Action (2015) Tai Zhong Shang Zhong Shen Zi No. 00004.

invalid for failing to specify an arbitral commission as required under PRC law.[74] Before the court's decision, Wicor, in November 2011, initiated arbitration on a different dispute arising from the joint venture agreement. The arbitral tribunal decided the seat to be Hong Kong and rendered an award in 2014 in favour of Wicor which sought enforcement. Enforcement of the award was refused by the Taizhou Intermediate People's Court based on public policy. The reasoning was that the 2012 court decision from Taizhou's litigation proceedings had determined the arbitration clause to be invalid. Therefore, no arbitration clause existed at the time the award was made, 19 months after the court decision. As the arbitral award was premised on a valid arbitration clause, to enforce an invalid arbitration award would be contrary to the social and public interest of the People's Republic of China.

There is a reported instance where an arbitral tribunal seated in New York ordered the respondent to pay the claimant its actual loss along with punitive fines.[75] The fines were 526 times more than the actual loss suffered by the claimant. The claimant sought the enforcement of the arbitral award in Russia. As opposed to the applicable law of New York which allowed the award of punitive damages, the corresponding law of Russia did not. Russian civil law emphasized proportionality between the losses suffered by the injured party and the damages payable by the wrongdoer; the civil law did not allow for fines of a punitive nature. Therefore, the arbitral award which had imposed punitive fines on the respondent was considered by the Russian court as contrary to the main principles of Russian civil law which formed part of the public policy of that country. Accordingly, the arbitral award could not be enforced in Russia.[76]

Public policy will not allow the enforcement of arbitral awards which seek to enforce illegal contracts between the parties to the arbitration. One example is *Abner Soleimany v Sion Soleimany*[77] where an English court refused to enforce an arbitral award which gave effect to a contract between a father and his son involving the smuggling of goods out of Iran in violation of Iranian laws.[78]

Some commentators have suggested a very restricted harmonized definition of international public policy principles for international commercial arbitration. This narrow interpretation of international public policy would include "universal" principles of fundamental rules of natural law and justice, such as fair and equal treatment of parties, and the right of a party to present its case before a neutral judge.[79] As one authority explained:

---

74 [2012] Su Shang Wai Xia Zhong Zi, No, 0012, 11 Dec. 2012.

75 Diana V. Tapola, *Enforcement of Foreign Arbitral Awards: Application of the Public Policy Rule in Russia*, 22(1) Arbitration International 151, 159 (2006) (citation omitted) [hereinafter Tapola].

76 Similarly, Brazil traditionally did not award punitive damages on the basis that indemnification should be compensation to the injured party rather than to penalize the offender. Brazil is now moving towards allowing punitive damages.

77 [1999] QB 785.

78 Redfern & Hunter, *supra* note 1, at para. 11.106.

79 For example, in the USA, "public policy" is interpreted as "the most basic understanding by courts of morals and justice." In Canada, "public policy" commonly refers to the basic principles of public morals. Tapola, *supra*

for example, a dispute over the division of gaming profits from a casino. The dispute may be taken to arbitration and an award made. In many states, the underlying transaction that led to the award would be regarded as a normal commercial transaction and the award would be regarded as valid. However, in states that do not tolerate gambling, the award might well be set aside on the basis that it offends public policy by upholding and interpreting an illegal contract.

Most developed arbitral jurisdictions have similar conceptions of public policy. According to the Swiss Federal Supreme Court, public policy denotes fundamental legal principles, a departure from which would be incompatible with the Swiss legal and economic system. Similarly, German courts have held that an award will violate public policy if it conflicts with fundamental notions of justice, *bonos mores*, or conflicts with principles that are fundamental national or economic values. . . .
. . . there is inevitably a risk that one state may set aside an award that other states would regard as valid. Even though many states take a restrictive approach to the application of public policy, the nebulous nature of the concept may be used by courts in some jurisdictions as a licence to review the merits of a dispute inappropriately. With this in mind, the concept of 'international public policy' (*ordre public international*) has been developed by some jurists and is embodied in the French Code of Civil Procedure. As such, an international arbitral award may be set aside in France 'if the recognition or enforcement of the award is contrary to *international* public policy'. In this way, French law recognises the existence of two levels of public policy: the national level, which may be affected by purely domestic considerations; and the international level, which is less restrictive in its approach.[80]

iii. Suspension of enforcement proceedings and order of security for costs

A party may apply to the court to suspend setting-aside proceedings for a period of time. The purpose for this application is to allow time for the award to be remitted or returned to the arbitral tribunal to correct the defects giving rise to the setting-aside application.[81] If the ground for setting aside the award alleges lack of jurisdiction, invalidity of the award, lack of due process, non-arbitrability or public policy, the defect may not be curable. If the ground is excess of authority and the issues are

---

note 76, at 151-152 (citations omitted).

[80] Redfern & Hunter, *supra* note 1, at paras. 10.82–10.84 (citations omitted).

[81] In *A v B*, *supra* note 44, B commenced arbitration proceedings against A alleging breach of an agreement for the joint development, manufacture, distribution and marketing of a product. A argued that B's claims were time-barred under a clause of the agreement which provided that: "Any action by [B] hereunder must be commenced within one (1) year of the date of delivery of the Product giving rise to the claim or the date the cause of action arose, whichever is earlier." The Arbitrator made an award in favour of B on the basis that A had failed to deliver the products in compliance with the technical standards and contractual requirements. A sought to set aside the award on the time-bar issue. The court held that the time-bar defence raised by A was a material issue which could have substantially affected the award. The arbitrator's failure to consider this defence or to explain the dismissal of A's defence was unfair to A and had exposed A to a real risk of injustice and prejudice. Accordingly, the award was in conflict with public policy. The award was returned to the arbitrator for reconsideration of A's defence so as to eliminate this basis for setting aside the award.
See Redfern & Hunter, *supra* note 1, at paras. 10.21–10.23 for further discussion.

separable, the setting-aside proceedings can be suspended during which time the defects can be fixed.

The party applying for remission of the award to the tribunal may be required by the court to post security for the award whose enforcement has been suspended during the remission of the award. This order of security for costs preserves the award, discourages frivolous proceedings designed to delay compliance with the award, and compensates the winning party for the lack of the award's immediate benefit.

iv. Recourse against an award

A losing party does not need to wait for the winning party to seek recognition and enforcement before challenging the award. A losing party can challenge the award in an attempt to nullify the award or to set aside the award in whole or in part.[82] In an application to set aside, a court may suspend its own proceedings to allow a tribunal to cure the defect and thus eliminate the grounds for setting the award aside,[83] as discussed in the above section.

Most arbitration rules provide that an arbitral award will be final. This means that the parties have given up their right to appeal the award. Many national arbitration laws, however, provide some limited grounds for challenging the validity of awards made in international proceedings. There also may be the possibility of an internal review mechanism in the arbitration rules (for example, ICSID rules or LCIA rules) or a challenge brought to a competent court. The purpose of challenging the award is to render it unrecognized and unenforced.[84]

---

[82] For detailed discussion, *see, e.g.*, MA & BROCK, *supra* note 7, at paras. 20.006–20.025; CHOONG & WEERAMANTRY, *supra* note 7, at Chapt. 12 and Chapt. 13; HALSBURY'S, *supra* note 7, at paras. [25.142]–[25.153].

REDFERN & HUNTER, *supra* note 1, at para. 10.05 explains:

> It is worth clarifying at the outset the distinction between actions to challenge, or set aside, an award and those opposing the enforcement of an award. A challenge to an award (usually) takes place in the courts of the seat of the arbitration and it is an attempt by the losing party to invalidate the award on the basis of the statutory grounds available under the law of the seat. In contrast, actions opposing enforcement . . . may take place in any jurisdiction in which the winning party seeks to enforce an award. . . . [A] party who is dissatisfied with the outcome of an arbitration will have at least two available methods to prevent an award from being given effect: it can affirmatively challenge the validity of the award in the courts of the seat; and/or it can attempt to thwart a party seeking to enforce the award under the New York Convention. . . .

This is more succinctly put by REDFERN & HUNTER, *supra* note 1, at para. 11.17:

> The challenge of an arbitral award . . . is concerned with attacking an award at its source, in the hope of having it modified or set aside in whole or in part. Recognition and enforcement, by contrast, are concerned with giving effect to the award, either in the state in which it was made or in some other state(s).

[83] *Model Law*, *supra* note 24, at Art. 34(4).

For further review of remission of awards, *see* HALSBURY'S, *supra* note 7, at para. [25.152]; REDFERN & HUNTER, *supra* note 1, at paras. 10.21–10.23.

[84] As explained by REDFERN & HUNTER, *supra* note 1, at para. 10.06:

> The purpose of challenging an award before a national court at the seat of arbitration is to have that court declare all, or part, of the award null and void. If an award is set aside or annulled by the relevant court, it will usually be treated as invalid, and accordingly unenforceable, not only by the courts of the

By setting aside an award, the court at the seat of arbitration declares that the award in whole or in part is a nullity and is to be disregarded in whole or in part. The expectation is that other courts also will treat the award as invalid and unenforceable.[85] Despite this expectation, courts of other countries may recognise and enforce an award even after it was set aside by a court in the jurisdiction where the award was made. This situation is due to the permissive language of the *New York Convention*: a court which finds that grounds exist *may*, but is not required to, refuse recognition and enforcement. A court in one country may find that a court in another country had wrongly set aside the award and may thus enforce the award.

Each nation's law provides the time period within which a challenge is to be made. It is the applying party's responsibility to ensure that its application is within the time limit. Time usually begins to accrue when the award has become *final*, in the sense that there is no internal appeal system or remission by a court.[86]

v. Grounds for setting aside

The grounds for setting aside an award are similar to the grounds for refusing recognition and enforcement under both the *Model Law* and *New York Convention*. The grounds for setting aside an award under *Model Law* Article 34 and the *Convention* Art. V can be grouped into two broad categories of jurisdictional issues and procedural issues.[87]

Jurisdictional Issues

- incapacity of a party to the arbitration agreement[88]

> seat of arbitration, but also by national courts elsewhere. This is because, under both the New York Convention and the Model Law, a competent court may refuse to grant recognition and enforcement of an award that has been set aside by a court of the seat of arbitration. . . . The reviewing court cannot alter the terms of an award nor can it decide the dispute based on its own vision of the merits. Unless the reviewing court has a power to remit the fault to the original tribunal, any new submission of the dispute to arbitration after annulment has to be undertaken by commencement of a new arbitration with a new arbitral tribunal. (footnotes omitted)

The effects of a successful challenge of an arbitral award are discussed in *id.* at paras. 10.89–10.92.

[85] But see the earlier discussion in *supra* notes 25 and 53 revealing some courts will nonetheless enforce an award set aside at the seat.

[86] § 81 of the *Arbitration Ordinance*, incorporating *Model Law* Article 34(3), *supra* note 4, states that the aggrieved party should file the petition to set aside the award within three months after it received the award.

[87] Redfern & Hunter, *supra* note 1, at para. 10.41 has a slightly different grouping:

> the grounds for challenge may be broadly categorised as:
> - grounds that relate to the adjudicability of the claim in question (including issues of incapacity, invalid agreements to arbitrate, a tribunal's excess of powers, or the arbitrability of the subject matter of the dispute);
> - procedural grounds (including issues relating to the composition of the arbitral tribunal); and
> - substantive grounds (including mistakes of law, mistakes of fact, and public policy).

[88] *See* Redfern & Hunter, *supra* note 1, at Chapter 2 for an analysis of this topic.

- the arbitration agreement was invalid under the law which the parties have chosen, or if no such choice was made, under the law of the state where the award was made[89]
- the decision was on a dispute outside the scope of the arbitration agreement or fails to deal with all issues submitted by the parties to the tribunal[90]
- composition of the arbitral tribunal or arbitral procedure was not in accordance with the parties' agreement, or was in breach of a mandatory provision of law
- lack of objective arbitrability
- the award is in conflict with public policy of the state[91]

Procedural Issues

- lack of proper notice of the appointment of the arbitrator[92]
- lack of notice of the arbitral proceedings[93]
- a party was otherwise unable to present its case[94]

The case of *Astro Nusantara International B.V. v PT First Media TBK*[95] involved enforcement of arbitral awards against First Media. Under Hong Kong law, an award debtor has 14 days to apply to set aside the enforcement orders.[96] First Media did not make such an application within the time limit and the Court of First Instance entered judgement against First Media. It appealed but the Court of Appeal agreed with the Court of First Instance.

---

89 *Id.*

90 For a review of this subject, *see id.* at paras. 10.45–10.49.

91 *See id.* at paras. 10.81–10.87.

92 *Id.* at paras. 10.53–10.59.

93 In the case of *CEEG (Shanghai) Solar Science & Technology Co, Ltd v LUMOS LLC*, 829 F.3d 1201 (10th Cir. 2016), the United States federal appeals court held that the notice of arbitration was inadequate. In this case, the two parties entered into an agreement. Part of this agreement included the requirement that all communications be in English and arbitration would be under CIETAC. A dispute arose and the notice of arbitration was in the Chinese language with no translation or explanation of the document as the Shanghai company did not inform CIETAC of the English language requirement. By the time LUMOS translated the document, the arbitral tribunal had been appointed. The court stated:

> We conclude that the Chinese-language notice was not reasonably calculated to apprise LUMOS of the proceedings. All previous communications between CEEG and LUMOS had been in English, the Contract reinforced that English would govern the relationship by requiring that the English language version of the Contract would control, and the Agreement memorialized the parties' understanding that all interactions and dispute resolution proceedings would be in English. *Id.* at 1207.
>
> . . .
>
> Hindering the right to participate in the panel-selection process is not a minor procedural misstep. The arbitral tribunal determines the parties' rights with virtually no possibility of appeal or review. . . . We agree . . . that depriving LUMOS of the right to participate in appointing the arbitral tribunal itself evidences substantial prejudice. *Id.* at 1208 (citation omitted).

94 § 86 of the *Arbitration Ordinance*, *supra* note 4; *Model Law*, *supra* note 23, at Art. 34(1) and Art. 34(2); *New York Convention*, *supra* note 10, at Art. V(1) and Art. V(2).

95 [2018] HKCFA 12.

96 Order 73, Rule 10(6) of the High Court Rules, *supra* note 14.

First Media further appealed to the Court of Final Appeal, raising the following issues:

1. What is the test for determining whether an extension of time should be granted for an application to resist enforcement of an arbitral award?
2. In determining whether to extend time for the purposes of an application to resist enforcement on an arbitral award, is it relevant that the award has not been set aside by the courts of the seat of arbitration?

The Court of Final Appeal decided that the previous courts' decision not to extend time was incorrect. The lower courts had failed to give proper consideration to the absence of a valid arbitration agreement. With regard to the second question, the Court of Final Appeal decided that the lower courts should not have taken into account First Media's decision not to set aside the awards at the seat of arbitration. The lower courts had misapplied their discretion in refusing a time extension. This misapplication arose by giving too much weight to the fact that First Media did not apply to have the arbitral awards set aside. The Court of Final Appeal decided that First Media was entitled to choose between the active remedy of setting aside an award at the seat where the award was made, or, the passive remedy of resisting enforcement of an award.[97]

In another recent Hong Kong case, *Arjowiggins HKK2 Ltd v X Co*,[98] two parties formed a joint venture company for the manufacturing of paper products. Arjowiggins was the successful party in a Hong Kong International Arbitration Centre [hereinafter "HKIAC"] administered arbitration. X Co sought to set aside the award on the following grounds:

> (under Article 34 (2) (a) (i)) the arbitration agreement between the parties was invalid under PRC law; that the Award deals with a dispute not contemplated by or falling within the terms of the submission to arbitration or contains decisions on matters beyond the scope of the submission (under Article 34 (2) (a) (iii)); and that (under Article 34 (2) (a) (iv)) the composition of the Tribunal was not in accordance with the agreement of the parties.[99]

In relation to the first point, the court determined that, although no arbitration institution was specified in the arbitration clause, the parties' specification of the HKIAC Arbitration Rules indicated that the HKIAC would be the institution.

---

97 The lower courts' decisions to treat the fact that the awards have not been set aside in Singapore as a major factor in refusing a time extension come into conflict with the choice of remedies principle.
As recently summarized by the court in *Paloma Co Ltd v Capxon Electronic Industrial Co Ltd* [2018] HKCFI 1147:

> On the principles applicable where a party seeks leave to resist enforcement of a Convention award out of time, the Court of Final Appeal in the recent case of *Astro Nusantara* . . . held that the proper test involves looking at all relevant matters and considering the overall justice of the case, eschewing a rigid mechanistic approach (section E.2 of the Judgment).

98 [2016] HKEC 2472.

99 *Id.* at para. 11.

Moreover, these Arbitration Rules referred to the HKIAC. By thus participating in the arbitration proceedings, X Co waived any right to object. As the court noted:

> The Hong Kong courts have made it clear that a party to an arbitration who wishes to rely on any non-compliance with the rules governing the arbitration should do so promptly, and should not proceed with the arbitration as if there had been compliance, keeping the point up its sleeve for later use . . . There is a duty of good faith which required the Respondent in this case to bring to the notice of the Tribunal any objections it may have to the validity of the arbitration agreement. Not having done so, choosing instead not only to fully participate in the Arbitration, but also to make a counterclaim against the Claimant, to adduce factual and expert evidence and to make full submissions on the merits, the Respondent had deprived the Tribunal of the opportunity to rectify any alleged invalidity or defect in the arbitral process, and is estopped and precluded now from raising this complaint and objection as to alleged invalidity and lack of arbitration agreement.[100]
>
> . . .
>
> The question of whether the arbitration agreement is valid is governed by the law of the arbitration agreement, in this case PRC law. However, whether or not the Award should be set aside, and whether enforcement of the Award should be allowed in Hong Kong is a question governed by Hong Kong law.[101]

The second point was decided upon a similar basis: X Co did not object; rather, X Co participated fully in the arbitration proceedings. Furthermore, the court proceedings involving the joint venture company and one of the parties did not affect the scope of arbitration agreement between Argowiggins and X Co. The court pronounced:

> It is clear . . . the claims . . . are made by the Claimant, a separate legal entity to the JV Company . . . These rights and obligations are separate and distinct from the rights of and obligations owed to the JV Company under the Steam Supply Contract. Any submission by the JV Company to the jurisdiction of the PRC courts, and any assumption of jurisdiction by the PRC courts over the JV Company in respect of the Steam Supply Contract, cannot affect the rights of the Claimant to pursue the Arbitration in Hong Kong in respect of the alleged breaches of the Respondent under the JV Contract.[102]
>
> The dispute as to the Respondent's alleged breach of its obligations owed to the Claimant under the JV Contract is clearly a dispute "arising out of or in connection with" the JV Contract, to fall squarely within the scope of the arbitration clause . . . The issues for determination, and decided by the Tribunal, in the Arbitration were whether the Respondent was in breach . . . of the JV Contract by failing to supply steam to the JV Company, and in breach . . . of the JV Contract by seeking the dissolution of the JV Company without the unanimous vote of all directors.[103]

---

[100] *Id.* at para. 32 (citations omitted).
[101] *Id.* at para. 34.
[102] *Id.* at para. 37.
[103] *Id.* at para. 38.

> . . . any adjudication by the PRC courts as to the rights and obligations of the parties to the Steam Supply Contract cannot give rise to any issue of *res judicata* between the Claimant and the Respondent, since the parties to the JV Contract and the Steam Supply Contract are different, and the agreements adjudicated upon are different.[104]

The third basis proposed by X Co for setting aside the award concerned the appointment either of a party's arbitrator or of the third arbitrator. Under the agreement, the default provision stipulated that the Chairman of the HKIAC would make the appointment. In this instance, it was the Council of the HKIAC which appointed the arbitrator when X Co failed to do so. The court decided:

> The Chairman of the HKIAC is part of the Council which made the appointment of [the arbitrator] in this case. I do not accept that the Respondent has furnished proof (as it is required under Article 34 (2) (a) to do) that the ground under Article 34 (2) (a) (iv) has been made out.[105]
>
> Opposition to enforcement and recognition of awards based on unmeritorious technical points or minor procedural complaints have always been viewed with disfavor by the Hong Kong courts. . . . the Court of Appeal made it clear (in the context of inability to present a party's case as a ground of opposition) that "the conduct complained of must be serious, even egregious", before a court could find that a ground has been made out. . . .[106]
>
> Even if a ground can be made out that [the arbitrator] was not appointed by the Chairman, but by the Council only, I fail to see how it can be said that the Respondent suffered any prejudice as a result of the appointment by the Council, and how due process can be said to have been undermined as a result. I am not prepared to exercise my discretion to set aside the Award on the ground that there has been a serious or egregious error in the appointment of [the arbitrator], to constitute a denial of due process.[107]
>
> The points made in the earlier parts of this Decision, as to the Respondent's failure to raise its objections to the Tribunal, apply to this ground of complaint. The Respondent agreed to and confirmed the validity of the composition of the Tribunal by signing the Amended Terms of Appointment, and participated in the Arbitration notwithstanding the alleged irregularity in the appointment, without raising these objections and depriving the Tribunal of the opportunity to rectify any such defect. The Court will not permit the Respondent to raise these alleged irregularities now.[108]

In conclusion, the court considered the motion to set aside the award to be frivolous and "totally without merit" and ordered costs on an indemnity basis.[109]

---

104 *Id.* at para. 39.
105 *Id.* at para. 49.
106 *Id.* at para. 50 (citation omitted).
107 *Id.* at para. 51.
108 *Id.* at para. 52 (citations omitted).
109 *Id.* at para. 53.
See Chapter 9 for the different bases available for the imposition of costs.

vi. Remission of the Award

As mentioned above, arbitral awards may be remitted back to the arbitral tribunal to correct or to cure a defect which might otherwise cause a court to set aside the award.[110]

See the Australian case of *Sino Dragon Trading Ltd v Noble Resources International Pte Ltd* [2016] FCA 1131, a case similar to *Arjowiggins* in that the losing party did not complain until it lost in the arbitration. Here, Australia's federal court addressed Sino Dragon's contended violations of *Model Law* Art. 18 and Art. 34:

> At the time of the arbitration hearing, Sino Dragon took no objection to the procedure which had been adopted, nor did it seek an adjournment or to deal with the evidence of its witnesses in any other way. It acquiesced in the procedure that was adopted. Indeed, its acts and omissions were principally its cause. *Id.* at para. 150.
>
> . . .
>
> Stripping away this multi-dimensional conceptual framework, there are two principal but related questions to consider. Was there a failure to give Sino Dragon a reasonable opportunity to present its case? Was there a lack of equality of treatment? I do not think so. *Id.* at para. 160.
>
> First, the mode used for the evidence of Sino Dragon's witnesses was that chosen by Sino Dragon. Indeed, this was over the objection to some extent of Noble Resources. *Id.* at para. 161.
>
> Second, if there were technical difficulties in the mode used, this was partly caused by Sino Dragon's acts or omissions. Moreover, when technical difficulties occurred, Sino Dragon was nevertheless prepared to continue with the hearing. *Id.* at para. 162.
>
> . . .
>
> Fifth, Mr King [on behalf of Sino Dragon] did not perceive at the time of closing address in the arbitration hearing any lack of reasonable opportunity to present Sino Dragon's case. His statement to the arbitral tribunal is at odds with such a suggestion. Moreover, no issue was raised with the arbitral tribunal then or thereafter about such a lack of opportunity, although Sino Dragon's witnesses appeared to have misgivings after the event. I am entitled to infer from such conduct and the absence of complaint that those charged with running the case for Sino Dragon did not perceive any lack of reasonable opportunity. Such an inference does, together with the other evidence, assist in assessing whether, objectively, there was a lack of reasonable opportunity or a lack of equal treatment. *Id.* at para. 165.

110 *Model Law*, *supra* note 24, at Art. 34(4).

As explained by HALSBURY'S, *supra* note 7, at para. [25.152]:

> The High Court, where it considers it to be appropriate and where a party has so requested, may suspend the setting aside proceedings for a period of time . . . to give the arbitral tribunal an opportunity to resume the arbitral proceedings or to take such other action as, in the opinion of the tribunal, will eliminate the ground for setting aside upon which the application is based. . . . it is submitted that the circumstances in which the court would exercise this power, which are limited and would (at least) embrace those matters formerly considered to be 'technical misconduct', including the following: (1) to permit a rehearing of the case in accordance with any agreement as to procedure made by the parties or directions made by the tribunal at the outset of the arbitral proceedings; (2) to permit a fuller presentation by a party of its case or any part thereof where a sufficient opportunity to do so has been denied, for example, where the tribunal has proceeded *ex parte* on an erroneous basis or where the tribunal has failed to implement a request by one party for an oral hearing; (3) to give the parties an opportunity to comment on evidence given by the tribunal to itself or on the report of a tribunal-appointed expert; (4) to give a party the opportunity of submitting evidence which the tribunal has previously refused to hear. Although this provision gives the tribunal a wide discretion as to the action it should take to eliminate the ground for setting aside the award, the High Court may give guidance as to how this discretion should be exercised. It would still be possible for the arbitral tribunal to reach the same decision, having taken into consideration the views expressed by the court. Having done so, however, resumption of the application to set aside would be unlikely to succeed if the tribunal's discretion has been properly exercised.

III. Summary

It may be appropriate at this stage of the chapter and towards the conclusion of this book to provide a summary of Hong Kong's approach to arbitration. This can be done by quoting the decision in the local case of *KB v S*[111] where the court began its judgement with these observations:

> 1. The attitude of the Hong Kong Court towards enforcement of arbitration awards and parties' agreements to submit their disputes to arbitration has been made demonstrably clear in the authorities. In summary:
>
> (1) The primary aim of the court is to facilitate the arbitral process and to assist with enforcement of arbitral awards.
>
> (2) Under the Arbitration Ordinance ("Ordinance"), the court should interfere in the arbitration of the dispute only as expressly provided for in the Ordinance.
>
> (3) Subject to the observance of the safeguards that are necessary in the public interest, the parties to a dispute should be free to agree on how their dispute should be resolved.
>
> (4) Enforcement of arbitral awards should be "almost a matter of administrative procedure" and the courts should be "as mechanistic as possible" (*Re PetroChina International (Hong Kong) Corp Ltd* [2011] HKCA 168; [2011] 4 HKLRD 604).
>
> (5) The courts are prepared to enforce awards except where complaints of substance can be made good. The party opposing enforcement has to show a real risk of prejudice and that its rights are shown to have been violated in a material way (*Grand Pacific Holdings Ltd v Pacific China Holdings Ltd* [2012] HKCA 200; [2012] 4 HKLRD 1 (CA)).
>
> (6) In dealing with applications to set aside an arbitral award, or to refuse enforcement of an award, whether on the ground of not having been given notice of the arbitral proceedings, inability to present one's case, or that the composition of the tribunal or the arbitral procedure was not in accordance with the parties' agreement, the court is concerned with the structural integrity of the arbitration proceedings. In this regard, the conduct complained of "must be serious, even egregious", before the court would find that there was an error sufficiently serious so as to have undermined due process (*Grand Pacific Holdings Ltd v Pacific China Holdings Ltd* [2012] HKCA 200; [2012] 4 HKLRD 1 (CA)).
>
> (7) In considering whether or not to refuse the enforcement of the award, the court does not look into the merits or at the underlying transaction (*Xiamen Xingjingdi Group Ltd v Eton Properties Limited* [2009] HKCA 223; [2009] 4 HKLRD 353 (CA)).
>
> (8) Failure to make prompt objection to the Tribunal or the supervisory court may constitute estoppel or want of bona fide (*Hebei Import & Export Corp v Polytek Engineering Co Ltd* [1999] HKCFA 40; (1999) 2 HKCFAR 111).

---

[111] [2015] HKCFI 1787; [2016] 2 HKC 325.

(9) Even if sufficient grounds are made out either to refuse enforcement or to set aside an arbitral award, the court has a residual discretion and may nevertheless enforce the award despite the proven existence of a valid ground (*Hebei Import & Export Corp v Polytek Engineering Co Ltd* [1999] HKCFA 40; (1999) 2 HKCFAR 111, 136A-B).

(10) The Court of Final Appeal clearly recognized in *Hebei Import & Export Corp v Polytek Engineering Co Ltd* that parties to the arbitration have a duty of good faith, or to act bona fide (p 120I and p 137B of the judgment).

In conclusion, there are grounds available to a losing party to avoid enforcement of an arbitral award. Despite the existence of such grounds, the general judicial attitude internationally, and particularly of Hong Kong courts, is to recognize the validity of awards and to enforce their provisions.

11

Cost-saving Techniques in Arbitration

I. Introduction

Time is money. In the past few years, techniques have been introduced in an attempt to reduce the costs of adversarial proceedings while ensuring a fair resolution. Some of these time and cost-saving techniques have been mentioned previously in relation to the hearing stage. In this chapter, we look into yet other techniques, in no particular order. These assorted techniques have one common goal: to reduce the time and cost of arbitration. Some techniques reviewed in this book have become accepted and established as common practice without much controversy. Some others are more recent innovations which are less readily accepted by stakeholders due to the techniques' novelty and/or controversial procedure.

II. Requirement for Efficiency

Some institutional rules require the parties and the arbitral tribunal to conduct the arbitration in an expeditious manner. For example, the International Chamber of Commerce [hereinafter "ICC"] requires every effort by the parties and the tribunal to "conduct the arbitration in an expeditious and cost-effective manner," including a mandatory case management conference.[1]

---

[1] ICC Rules of Arbitration (2017) [hereinafter ICC Rules], Art. 22(2) provides:

> In order to ensure effective case management, the arbitral tribunal, after consulting the parties, may adopt such procedural measures as it considers appropriate, provided that they are not contrary to any agreement of the parties.

Appendix VI of these Rules provides in relevant part:

> Article 1: Application of the Expedited Procedure Rules
>
> 1) Insofar as Article 30 of the Rules of Arbitration of the ICC (the "Rules") and this Appendix VI do not provide otherwise, the Rules shall apply to an arbitration under the Expedited Procedure Rules.
> 2) The amount referred to in Article 30(2), subparagraph a), of the Rules is US$ 2,000,000.
>
> . . .
>
> Article 2: Constitution of the Arbitral Tribunal
>
> 1) The Court may, notwithstanding any contrary provision of the arbitration agreement, appoint a sole arbitrator.
> 2) The parties may nominate the sole arbitrator within a time limit to be fixed by the Secretariat. In the absence of such nomination, the sole arbitrator shall be appointed by the Court within as short

In Hong Kong, there are several provisions aimed at achieving efficiency. One example is § 3(1) of the *Arbitration Ordinance* (Cap. 609) which mandates: "The object of this Ordinance is to facilitate the fair and speedy resolution of disputes by arbitration without unnecessary expense." Another example is the Hong Kong International Arbitration Centre [hereinafter "HKIAC"] which has rules which contain provisions implementing the Ordinance's object. For instance, the HKIAC's Administered Arbitration Rules (2018) provide:

> Article 13—General Provisions
>
> 13.1 Subject to these Rules, the arbitral tribunal shall adopt suitable procedures for the conduct of the arbitration in order to avoid unnecessary delay or expense, having regard to the complexity of the issues, the amount in dispute and the effective use of technology . . .
>
> . . . 13.5 The arbitral tribunal and the parties shall do everything necessary to ensure the fair and efficient conduct of the arbitration.

The HKIAC's Domestic Arbitration Rules (2014) provide in Art. 5(2):

> The Arbitrator shall have the power to adopt wherever possible a simplified or expedited procedure and in any case shall have the widest discretion allowed by law to conduct the proceedings so as to ensure the just, expeditious, economical, and final determination of the dispute.

Art. 17.1 of the UNCITRAL Arbitration Rules (2013) contains similar language:

---

a time as possible.

Article 3: Proceedings

1) Article 23 of the Rules shall not apply to an arbitration under the Expedited Procedure Rules.
2) After the arbitral tribunal has been constituted, no party shall make new claims, unless it has been authorized to do so by the arbitral tribunal, which shall consider the nature of such new claims, the stage of the arbitration, any cost implications and any other relevant circumstances.
3) The case management conference convened pursuant to Article 24 of the Rules shall take place no later than 15 days after the date on which the file was transmitted to the arbitral tribunal.

. . .

4) The arbitral tribunal shall have discretion to adopt such procedural measures as it considers appropriate. . . . the arbitral tribunal may . . . decide not to allow . . . document production or to limit the number, length and scope of written submissions and written witness evidence (both fact witnesses and experts).
5) The arbitral tribunal may . . . decide the dispute solely on the basis of the documents submitted by the parties, with no hearing and no examination of witnesses or experts. When a hearing is to be held, the arbitral tribunal may conduct it by videoconference, telephone or similar means of communication.

Article 4: Award

1) The time limit within which the arbitral tribunal must render its final award is six months from the date of the case management conference. The Court may extend the time limit pursuant to Article 31(2) of the Rules.

. . .

Further details on the expedited procedure provisions may be found here: https://iccwbo.org/dispute-resolution-services/arbitration/expedited-procedure-provisions/ (last visited 17 Aug. 2017).

> The arbitral tribunal, in exercising its discretion, shall conduct the proceedings so as to avoid unnecessary delay and expense and to provide a fair and efficient process for resolving the parties' dispute.

Similarly, the Vienna International Arbitral Centre's Rules of Arbitration and Mediation (2018) provide:

> The arbitral tribunal shall conduct the arbitration in accordance with the Vienna Rules and the agreement of the parties in an efficient and cost-effective manner, but otherwise according to its own discretion.[2]

A tribunal's failure to observe this rule may result in the: "conduct of any or all arbitrators . . . may be taken into consideration by the General Secretary in determining the arbitrators' fees."[3] There is a similar obligation and potential penalty for the parties:

> The conduct of any or all parties as well as their representatives . . . and in particular their contribution to the conduct of efficient and cost-effective proceedings, may be taken into consideration by the arbitral tribunal in its decision on costs.[4]

III. Submissions

Here, we discuss procedures during the actual hearing which might result in saved time and hence costs. These procedures involve the parties submitting written documentation and the arbitral tribunal accepting these documents in place of the traditional verbal presentations made by the parties or their representatives. For example:

- written opening submissions in place of the parties delivering the same information verbally at the beginning of the arbitral hearing process
- written closing submissions in lieu of the parties delivering a verbal summary of the case at the conclusion of the arbitral hearing procedures
- written submissions on preliminary points of law which would permit the arbitral tribunal to read the parties' arguments and to be prepared to question

---

2 Vienna International Arbitral Centre's Rules of Arbitration and Mediation (2018), Art. 28(1).

3 *Id.* at Art. 16(6).

There is a similar provision in the German Arbitration Institute (*Deutsche Institution für Schiedsgerichtsbarkeit*) [hereinafter DIS] Arbitration Rules (2018):

> Article 37 Time Limit for the Final Award
>
> The arbitral tribunal shall send the final award to the DIS for review pursuant to Article 39.3, in principle within three months after the last hearing or the last authorized Submission, whichever is later. The Arbitration Council, in its discretion, may reduce the fee of one or more arbitrators based upon the time taken by the arbitral tribunal to issue its final award. In deciding whether to reduce the fee, the Arbitration Council shall consult the arbitral tribunal and take into consideration the circumstances of the case.

4 *Id.* at Art. 38(2).

the parties during the hearing process rather than the parties taking the time to make oral arguments

Similarly, the evidence of factual witnesses and expert witnesses can be submitted in writing, thus allowing the hearing process to proceed directly to the cross-examination of the witnesses:

- proofs of witnesses of fact standing as evidence-in-chief[5]
- proofs of expert witnesses standing as evidence-in-chief
- *chess clock* or *guillotine* procedures, *i.e.*, an equal but strictly limited time allowed for each party to present its case

IV. Emergency Arbitrators

Emergency arbitrator procedures [hereinafter "EAP"] are intended to assist in the expedition of the arbitral process by eliminating the need for recourse to local courts. Prior to the introduction of EAP, parties requiring urgent or emergency measures before the arbitral tribunal is constituted would require resort to the courts, the very situation that parties to an arbitration wish to avoid.[6]

Instances where EAP would be an appropriate recourse include:

- preservation of confidentiality
- unconventional relief
- expedited relief
- relief required before the referral to arbitration
- relief needed before the appointment of the arbitral tribunal
- statutory limitations upon courts to offer interim relief
- need for a specialist emergency arbitrator[7]

The foregoing is premised on the assumption that the EAP is being sought against the opposing party. The EAP would not be useful where a third party is involved, such as a bank, because the emergency arbitrator might not have jurisdiction over a third party not directly related to the arbitration.[8] It is noted, however, that it would be possible for an emergency arbitrator to order a party to the arbitration

---

[5] Michael J. Moser and Teresa Y. W. Cheng, Hong Kong Arbitration: A User's Guide para. 5-131 (3rd ed. 2014).
Black's Law Dictionary 60 (10th ed. 2014) [hereinafter Black's] defines "proof" as "the establishment or refutation of an alleged fact by evidence; the persuasive effect of evidence in the mind of a fact-finder."
The Honourable Mr. Justice Patrick Chan, The Concise Hong Kong English-Chinese Legal Dictionary 751 (2005) [hereinafter English-Chinese Legal Dictionary], defines "proof" as "evidence which establishes the existence or non-existence of an alleged fact" and, at page 751, translates "proof" as 證明.

[6] For an analysis of the territory's approach to EAP, *see* John Choong and Romesh Weeramantry, The Hong Kong Arbitration Ordinance – Commentary and Annotations, paras. 22A–22B.08 (2nd ed. 2015).

[7] Arbitration in Hong Kong: A Practical Guide paras. 12.004–12.014 (The Hon Chief Justice Geoffrey Ma and Denis Brock, eds., 4th ed. 2017) [hereinafter Ma & Brock].

[8] *Id.* at para. 12.017.

to give instructions to a third party. Returning to the example of a bank which is not a party to the arbitration, an emergency arbitrator may order the party in whose name the bank is holding the assets to instruct the bank not to transfer the assets.[9]

An emergency arbitrator procedure would also not be suitable in some other situations. One such situation concerns applications or requests for *ex parte* relief. *Ex parte* refers to something done without notifying the opposing party.[10] As explained by one authority:

> it is often important to obtain relief on an *ex parte* basis to not give notice to the opposing party. Otherwise, the respondent may transfer the funds before a binding decision is handed down. The reason why emergency . . . [arbitrators] are not appointed within this context is because the rules providing for EAPs usually require that the claimant provide copies of the application to the other parties . . . and both parties also must circulate their submissions to the other parties . . . As such, EAPs are generally awarded on an *inter partes* basis.[11]

Another situation involves the seat of the arbitration and whether the laws of the seat of the arbitration would enforce an emergency arbitrator's decision either as an order or as an award.

> This is often a real concern because many jurisdictions have taken no steps to recognise the enforceability of emergency arbitrator's awards/orders. Notable exceptions are Hong Kong and Singapore, which have introduced legislation recognizing the enforceability of such relief. In Hong Kong, the Arbitration Ordinance provides that any relief granted by an emergency arbitrator . . . is enforceable in the same manner as an order or direction of the court with leave of the court. . . .[12]
>
> In addition, as interim relief handed down by the arbitration tribunal can be enforced by the courts in certain jurisdictions, this may in turn give courts the discretion to exercise a similar approach in relation to emergency arbitrator's awards/orders.[13]

EAP is an example of new developments outpacing the existing law. Enforcement of an emergency arbitrator's decision, be it in the form of an award or an order, is

---

9 *Id.* at para. 12.018.

10 As more properly defined, *ex parte* refers to an act:

> Done or made at the instance and for the benefit of one party only, and without notice to, or argument by, anyone having an adverse interest; of, relating to, or involving court action taken or received by one party without notice to the other, usually for temporary or emergency relief.

BLACK'S, *supra* note 5, at 697.

11 MA & BROCK, *supra* note 7, at para. 12.019 (footnote omitted).

The authors further note in *id.* that the Swiss International Arbitration Rules (2012) in "art. 26(3) provides that in exceptional circumstances, the emergency arbitrator may determine a request for interim measures before it has been communicated to the respondent."

12 *Id.* at para. 12.027 (citations omitted).

13 *Id.* at para. 12.028.

For a discussion whether an emergency arbitrator's decision can be enforced as a *final award*, *see id.* at paras. 12.029–12.033.

unclear.[14] The traditional international norms pre-date this development and hence are of varying assistance. As noted by one international law firm, the *Convention on the Enforcement of Foreign Arbitral Awards* (done in New York, 1958) [hereinafter "*New York Convention*"] is silent on this new development.[15] The UNCITRAL *Model Law on International Commercial Arbitration* was last amended more than 10 years ago and does not include the term *emergency arbitrator* in its definition of *arbitral tribunal*.[16]

In conclusion in relation to the EAP:

> Given the current patchwork approach globally, enforcement of interim measures issued by arbitral tribunals remains uncertain and uneven. . . . The uncertainties associated with enforcement is an important issue for users to take into consideration when deciding whether to seek relief from an emergency arbitrator or from a court.[17]

V. Third Party Funding

In the past, some jurisdictions did not permit funding of a claim by a disinterested or non-related party to an arbitration. This prohibition originated from the common-law doctrine known as *maintenance*[18] and *champerty*.[19] In Hong Kong, an exception to this doctrine was made with the *Arbitration and Mediation Legislation (Third Party Funding) (Amendment) Ordinance* in 2017. Part 2 of this Ordinance amends the *Arbitration Ordinance* (Cap. 609) by inserting in it a Part 10A, comprised of sections 98E to 98X.[20] Section 98E provides that "third party funding of arbitration is not prohibited by particular common law doctrines," *i.e.*, maintenance and champerty.[21] Through this amendment to the *Arbitration Ordinance*, Hong

---

14 For further discussion on the enforcement of emergency relief granted under the EAP, *see* 2 HALSBURY'S LAWS OF HONG KONG para. [25.114] (2nd ed. 2016).

15 *Enforceability of interim measures and emergency arbitrator decisions*, Norton Rose International Arbitration Report 2018 – Issue 10, p. 18.

16 *Id.*

17 *Id.* at 19.

18 The term *maintenance* is defined as "the giving of assistance or encouragement to one of the parties to an action by a person who has neither an interest in the action nor any other motive recognized by the law as justifying his interference." *Winnie Lo v HKSAR* (2012) 15 HKCFAR 16, para. 10 (citation omitted).

19 *Id.* at paras. 10–11 defines the term *champerty* as:

> a particular kind of maintenance, namely maintenance of an action in consideration of a promise to give to the maintainer a share of the subject matter or proceeds thereof, if the action succeeds.
> . . . Champerty is maintenance for a share in the proceeds of litigation. (citations omitted)

20 For historical interest, the case of *Cannonway Consultants Ltd v Kenworth Engineering Ltd* [1995] 1 HKC 179 held that maintenance and champerty did not apply to arbitrations. This decision was questioned by the Court of Final Appeal in the case of *Siegfried Adalbert Unruh v Hans-Joerg Seeberger* (2007) 10 HKCFAR 31. The changes made to the *Arbitration Ordinance* (Cap. 609) [hereinafter *Arbitration Ordinance*] by the *Arbitration and Mediation Legislation (Third Party Funding) (Amendment) Ordinance* has now settled the matter.

21 *Arbitration Ordinance*, *supra* note 20, at § 98E states in full:

> The purposes of this Part are to—
> (a) ensure that third party funding of arbitration is not prohibited by particular common law doctrines; and

Kong now permits a third party to provide funding for an arbitration seated in Hong Kong or to fund services provided in the territory for arbitrations seated elsewhere.[22] Additionally, the funding can be provided for arbitration-related matters such as Emergency Arbitrators or securing Hong Kong court assistance in aid of the arbitration.[23]

VI. Expedited Procedure

In an attempt to minimize the time and cost involved in arbitration, some arbitral institutions provide for an expedited process in instances where a dispute does not exceed a certain amount.[24] For example, Art. 9A of the Arbitration Rules of the London Court of International Arbitration (2014) [hereinafter "LCIA Arbitration Rules"] provide for the expedited formation of the arbitral tribunal:

> 9.1 In the case of exceptional urgency, any party may apply to the LCIA Court for the expedited formation of the Arbitral Tribunal under Article 5.
> 9.2 Such an application shall be made to the Registrar in writing (preferably by electronic means), together with a copy of the Request (if made by a Claimant)

(b) provide for measures and safeguards in relation to third party funding of arbitration.

[22] *Id.* at § 98J defines the term "third party funder" to be:
(1) A third party funder is a person—
(a) who is a party to a funding agreement for the provision of arbitration funding for an arbitration to a funded party by the person; and
(b) who does not have an interest recognized by law in the arbitration other than under the funding agreement.
(2) In subsection (1)(b), the reference to a person who does not have an interest in an arbitration includes—
(a) a person who does not have an interest in the matter about which an arbitration is yet to commence; and
(b) a person who did not have an interest in an arbitration that has ended.

[23] *Id.* at § 98F provides:
arbitration (仲裁) includes the following proceedings under this Ordinance—
(a) court proceedings;
(b) proceedings before an emergency arbitrator; and
(c) . . .
arbitration body (仲裁機構)—
(a) in relation to an arbitration (other than the proceedings mentioned in paragraphs (b) and (c))—means the arbitral tribunal or court, as the case may be;
(b) in relation to proceedings before an emergency arbitrator—means the emergency arbitrator; or
(c) . . .

[24] For further discussion, *see* REDFERN AND HUNTER ON INTERNATIONAL ARBITRATION paras. 6.26–6.40 (NIGEL BLACKABY *et al*, eds., 6th ed. 2015) [hereinafter REDFERN & HUNTER].
An Australian law firm, Corrs Chambers Westgarth, has prepared an article reviewing the expedited procedure in the Asia Pacific region. Link: http://www.corrs.com.au/thinking/insights/expedited-arbitration-asia-pacific-institutional-rules-overview-and-comparative-table-guide/ (last visited 13 Sep. 2018). This article also contains a link to the firm's summary table of the Expedited Procedure provisions of five regional institutions and the ICC. Link: http://www.corrs.com.au/assets/thinking/downloads/International-Arbitration-Expedited-Procedure-Provisions-2018-19.pdf (last visited 13 Sep. 2018). As noted by the law firm, the China International Economic and Trade Arbitration Commission has adopted the term *Summary Procedure* in place of the more commonly used term *Expedited Procedure* while the Australian Centre for International Commercial Arbitration refers to its expedited procedure provisions as *Fast Track Arbitration Rules*.

or a copy of the Response (if made by a Respondent), delivered or notified to all other parties to the arbitration. The application shall set out the specific grounds for exceptional urgency requiring the expedited formation of the Arbitral Tribunal.

9.3 The LCIA Court shall determine the application as expeditiously as possible in the circumstances. If the application is granted, for the purpose of forming the Arbitral Tribunal the LCIA Court may abridge any period of time under the Arbitration Agreement or other agreement of the parties (pursuant to Article 22.5).

Under the LCIA Arbitration Rules, it would be possible to expedite the appointment of the arbitral tribunal. The Dubai International Arbitration Centre has similar rules in effect.[25] In Germany, the *Deutsche Institution für Schiedsgerichtsbarkeit* Arbitration Rules (2018) [hereinafter "DIS Arbitration Rules"] provides for expedited proceedings in Annex 4. The Arbitration Institute of the Stockholm Chamber of Commerce [hereinafter "SCC"] has provided for this process in its Rules for Expedited Arbitrations (2017) [hereinafter "Expedited Rules"]. The Hong Kong International Arbitration Centre implemented new rules on 1 November 2018 which contain provisions for the expedited procedure.[26]

Another procedure to expedite the arbitration process involves using simplified procedures and/or shortened time frames. This can be achieved by the tribunal exercising its discretion, by the parties' agreeing to the expedited process, or by using the appropriate institution's rules.[27] An example of an institution's expedited

---

[25] Article 12 of the Dubai International Arbitration Centre Arbitration Rules (2007) [hereinafter DIAC Arbitration Rules] states:

12.1 On or after the commencement of the arbitration, any party may apply to the Centre for the expedited formation of the Tribunal, including the appointment of any replacement arbitrator where appropriate.

12.2 Any such application shall be made to the Centre in writing, copied to all other parties to the arbitration and shall set out the specific grounds for exceptional urgency in establishing the Tribunal.

12.3 The Centre may, in its complete discretion, adjust any time-limit under these Rules for formation of the Tribunal, including service of the Answer and of any matters or documents adjudged to be missing from the Request.

The DIAC Arbitration Rules may be found at this link: http://www.diac.ae/idias/rules/Arb.Rules%202007/3THE%20TRIBUNAL/ (last visited 17 Aug. 2017).

[26] The HKIAC Administered Arbitration Rules (2013) provided for expedited procedures in Art. 41 and for Emergency Arbitrator Procedures in Schedule 4.

The new version of these rules came into effect in 1 November 2018 [hereinafter HKIAC Arbitration Rules]. Article 42 of the new version contains provisions for expedited procedure.

[27] Redfern & Hunter, *supra* note 24, at para. 6.32.

This source noted:

> Several arbitral institutions have developed rules for the faster resolution of disputes by means of a simplified procedure. As might be expected, the rules differ from one institution to another, but the Swiss Rules serve as a good example of how the procedure can work significantly to reduce the duration of an average arbitration. Under these Rules:
>
> - a sole arbitrator is appointed, unless the arbitration agreement otherwise provides and the parties are unable to agree to the appointment of a sole arbitrator;

rules is the various arbitration rules of the New Zealand International Arbitration Centre [hereinafter "NZIAC"]. One set of NZIAC's Expedited Arbitration Rules provides for an award to be issued within 60 working days.[28] Another set of rules provides for a hearing not exceeding three days and an award to be issued within 90 working days.[29] A third and final set of expedited rules provides for a hearing not exceeding five days and an award to issue within 120 days.[30] All three set of expedited rules do not allow amendments to claims, defences and counterclaims, or defences to counterclaims. Additionally, all three sets of rules permit summary procedures.

Another example is the DIS Arbitration Rules which provide for:

- Art. 27—Efficient Conduct of the Proceedings[31]

- written pleadings are limited to a statement of case, a defence, and "if applicable" a counterclaim and reply;
- unless the parties agree to a documents-only arbitration, a single hearing is held for the examination of witnesses and experts, and for oral argument; and
- the award is made within six months of the date of the transmittal of the file to the arbitral tribunal, which states the arbitrator's reasons in summary form (or does not give reasons at all if the parties so agree).

It is noteworthy that, while this procedure is mandatory for cases in which the total amount in dispute does not exceed CHF1 million, it is available for disputes of a greater amount if the parties so agree. Such processes offer hope for parties who wish to avoid the delay and cost involved in a traditional international arbitration process.

Id. at para. 6.33 (citations omitted).

See also the HKIAC Small Claims Procedures, for arbitral disputes under US$50,000, and the HKIAC's 'Documents' Only Procedures.

[28] The NZIAC EIA60 Arbitration Rules are intended for disputes where the "amount claimed by the claimant is less than NZ$250,000, or the claimant is seeking declaratory relief only, these EIA60 Arbitration Rules will apply unless otherwise agreed by the parties." Furthermore, "[w]hile these Rules are particularly suitable for disputes where the amount claimed is less than NZ$250,000, they may be adopted for larger disputes by agreement of the parties." Link: https://www.nziac.com/arbitration/arbitration-rules/eia60-expedited-rules/ (last visited 1 Apr. 2018).

[29] The NZIAC EIA90 Arbitration Rules are intended for disputes where the disputed amount is equal to or greater than NZ$250,000 to less than NZ one million dollars. These rules, however, may be adopted for smaller or larger disputes by the parties. Link: https://www.nziac.com/arbitration/arbitration-rules/eia90-expedited-rules/ (last visited 1 Apr. 2018).

[30] The NZIAC EIA120 Arbitration Rules are intended for disputes where the disputed amount is equal to or greater than NZ$1,000,000 to less than NZ$2,500,000. These rules, however, may be adopted for smaller or larger disputes by the parties. Link: https://www.nziac.com/arbitration/arbitration-rules/eia120-expedited-rules/ (last visited 1 Apr., 2018).

[31] Art. 27 provides:

27.1: The arbitral tribunal and the parties shall conduct the proceedings in a time- and cost-efficient manner taking into account the complexity and economic importance of the dispute.

27.2: The arbitral tribunal shall hold a case management conference as soon as possible after its constitution, in principle within 21 days.

...

27.4: During the case management conference, the arbitral tribunal shall discuss with the parties the procedural rules to be applied in the proceedings pursuant to Article 21 as well as the procedural timetable.

With a view to increasing procedural efficiency, the arbitral tribunal shall specifically discuss the following with the parties:

(i) each of the measures set forth in Annex 3 (Measures for Increasing Procedural Efficiency) in order to determine whether any of them should be applied;

- Measures for Increasing Procedural Efficiency in relation to case management by the tribunal—Annex 3[32]
- Expedited Proceedings which include a six-month time limit for the arbitral panel to issue its final award—Annex 4[33]

In essence, an expedited procedure is intended to shorten the time frame involved in an arbitration, thereby reducing the time and hence the cost. As one law firm noted:

> expedited procedure rules do not limit the scope of the arbitration. . . . expedited procedures can sometimes involve imposing compressed timelines on a full-blown arbitration which has all the usual stages of proceedings.[34]

One consequence of adopting new techniques is the concern by an arbitral tribunal that its award might be challenged. Two cases demonstrate the different approaches taken by the courts arising from expedited procedures. The first case arose in Singapore where the unsuccessful party in an arbitration challenged the award on the grounds that the arbitral procedure was not in accordance with the parties' agreement. The parties' arbitration clause did not specify which version of the Singapore International Arbitration Centre [hereinafter "SIAC"] rules were to apply. The court determined that the version of the rules in existence at the time the arbitration commenced should apply rather than the version at the time of concluding the contract. The SIAC rules at the time the arbitration commenced contained provisions for an expedited procedure (including the provision for one arbitrator while the arbitration agreement provided for three) whereas the previous rules existing at the time of contract creation did not. Thus, the court concluded that the expedited procedure was in accordance with the parties' arbitration agreement.[35]

> (ii) the provisions of Annex 4 (Expedited Proceedings) in order to determine whether they should be applied;
>
> (iii) the possibility of using mediation or any other method of amicable dispute resolution to seek the amicable settlement of the dispute or of individual disputed issues.
>
> . . .
>
> 27.6: The arbitral tribunal may hold additional case management conferences as needed and may issue additional procedural orders or amend the procedural timetable as needed.

Link: http://www.disarb.org/upload/varia/180119_DIS_NewRules_EN.PDF (last visited 17 Apr. 2018).

[32] The English text of Annex 3 may be found here: http://www.disarb.org/en/16/rules/-id38 (last visited 17 Apr. 2018).

[33] The English text of Annex 4 may be found here: http://www.disarb.org/en/16/rules/-id38 (last visited 17 Apr. 2018).

The Arbitration Rules of the Arbitration Institute of the Stockholm Chamber of Commerce (2017) [hereinafter SCC Rules] at Art. 43 also provides for a six-month time limit for the final award. Link: http://sccinstitute.com/media/169838/arbitration_rules_eng_17_web.pdf (last visited 1 Apr. 2018).

[34] *Summary awards and expedited procedures: Strike out or home run?*, Norton Rose International Arbitration Report 2018 – Issue 10, p. 14.

[35] *AQZ v ARA* [2015] SGHC 49.

As stated in the court's decision on the matter:

> 123 The Supplier's arguments under this ground are in the alternative to its primary position that there was no valid arbitration agreement between the parties. Assuming that there was such an agreement, the Supplier first contends that the arbitral procedure was not in accordance with the

The second case involved similar facts.[36] An SIAC award was refused enforcement by a Shanghai court under the *New York Convention*. In this dispute, the parties' arbitration clause provided for a three-member tribunal. The parties arbitrated under the 2013 SIAC rules which provided for an expedited procedure with only one arbitrator.[37] The claimant applied to the SIAC for arbitration of the parties' dispute under the expedited process. The respondent objected to the appointment of only one arbitrator and allegedly also objected to the expedited procedure. The respondent did not further participate in the arbitration. The claimant, being successful in its claim, sought recognition and enforcement of the award in mainland China. The respondent resisted enforcement on the basis that the composition of the tribunal was not in accordance with the parties' agreement.

---

agreement of the parties because it was erroneously conducted under the Expedited Procedure . . . of the SIAC Rules 2010, and that there is no provision for such a procedure in the Arbitration Rules of the SIAC (3rd Ed, 1 July 2007) ("SIAC Rules 2007") which . . . are the applicable rules. Second, the Supplier argues that even if the SIAC Rules 2010 are applicable, the composition of the arbitral tribunal . . . was not in accordance with the parties' agreement since they had expressly agreed to arbitration before three arbitrators.

. . .

125 There is a presumption that reference to rules of a particular tribunal in an arbitration clause refers to such rules as are applicable at the date of commencement of arbitration and not at the date of contract, provided that the rules contain mainly procedural provisions. If the rules contain mainly substantive provisions, then those in force as at the date the contract was entered into would apply . . .

. . .

132 . . . the SIAC Rules 2010 have been incorporated into the Parties' contract and therefore . . . the rules together with the rest of the contract must be interpreted purposively. I am of the view that "express assent" . . . is not necessary for the Expedited Procedure provision to override the parties' agreement for arbitration before three arbitrators . . . A commercially sensible approach to interpreting the parties' arbitration agreement would be to recognise that the SIAC President does have the discretion to appoint a sole arbitrator. Otherwise, regardless of the complexity of the dispute or the quantum involved, a sole arbitrator can never be appointed to hear the dispute notwithstanding the incorporation of the SIAC Rules 2010 which provide for the tribunal to be constituted by a sole arbitrator when the Expedited Procedure is invoked. That would be an odd outcome, especially since the Supplier appears to accept that the Expedited Procedure provision is no different from any other procedural rule contained in the SIAC Rules 2010.

133 Furthermore, due regard can be given to the fact that the agreement had been signed before the Expedited Procedure provision came into force. . . . when making the decision whether to displace the default provision and appoint a greater number of arbitrators instead, the SIAC President can and should take into account not just the complexity of the dispute, the quantum involved and the parties' agreement on the number of arbitrators . . . but also whether the contract concerned was signed before the Expedited Procedure provision came into force.

134 . . . the Supplier objected to the arbitration being heard pursuant to the Expedited Procedure provision. However, it only objected on the grounds that the parties had not agreed to the application of this procedure . . . The Supplier did not expressly rely on the fact that the contract had been entered into before the Expedited Procedure provision came into force as a reason why that provision should not apply. Nonetheless there is nothing that suggests that the SIAC President had not taken that fact into consideration when he decided to allow the Buyer's application for the arbitration to be conducted under the Expedited Procedure provision.

[36] *Noble Resources International Pte Ltd v Shanghai Good Credit International Trade Co, Ltd* (2016) Hu 01 Xie Wai Ren No. 1 (Shanghai No. 1 Intermediate People's Court).

[37] Art. 5 of the *Arbitration Rules of the Singapore International Arbitration Centre* (2013) may be found here: http://www.siac.org.sg/our-rules/rules/siac-rules-2013 (last visited 21 Sep. 2017). It should be noted that the SIAC has since amended its rules in 2016 to address the concerns raised in the *AQZ* and *Noble Resource* cases.

The Shanghai court agreed with the respondent and declined recognition and enforcement of the award because the parties' autonomy as expressed in their arbitration clause requiring three arbitrators was violated by the appointment of a sole arbitrator. The parties did not agree to change this requirement for the expedited process; the court reasoned, therefore, that the SIAC should have proceeded with the expedited process with a panel of three arbitrators. Failing to do so resulted in the tribunal not being composed pursuant to the parties' arbitration agreement.

VII. Summary Procedures

Different from expedited procedure, summary procedures are nonetheless an innovation intended to provide a speedy arbitral process. Under this procedure a party may apply to the arbitral tribunal for the early dismissal of a claim or a defence on the basis that a claim or a defence is manifestly without legal merit, or, that a claim or defence is manifestly outside the jurisdiction of the tribunal.[38] One arbitral institution provides:

> (1) A party may request that the Arbitral Tribunal decide one or more issues of fact or law by way of summary procedure, without necessarily undertaking every procedural step that might otherwise be adopted for the arbitration.
> (2) A request for summary procedure may concern issues of jurisdiction, admissibility or the merits. It may include, for example, an assertion that:
> (i) an allegation of fact or law material to the outcome of the case is manifestly unsustainable;
> (ii) even if the facts alleged by the other party are assumed to be true, no award could be rendered in favour of that party under the applicable law; or
> (iii) any issue of fact or law material to the outcome of the case is, for any other reason, suitable to determination by way of summary procedure.[39]

[38] The Arbitration Rules of the Singapore International Arbitration Centre, Rule 29.1 (6th ed. 2016). *See* Redfern & Hunter, *supra* note 24, at paras. 6.38–6.40 for further discussion of summary or early determination.

[39] Article 39 of the SCC Rules, *supra* note 33, provides in full:

Article 39 Summary procedure

(1) A party may request that the Arbitral Tribunal decide one or more issues of fact or law by way of summary procedure, without necessarily undertaking every procedural step that might otherwise be adopted for the arbitration.

(2) A request for summary procedure may concern issues of jurisdiction, admissibility or the merits. It may include, for example, an assertion that:

(i) an allegation of fact or law material to the outcome of the case is manifestly unsustainable;

(ii) even if the facts alleged by the other party are assumed to be true, no award could be rendered in favour of that party under the applicable law; or

(iii) any issue of fact or law material to the outcome of the case is, for any other reason, suitable to determination by way of summary procedure.

(3) The request shall specify the grounds relied on and the form of summary procedure proposed, and demonstrate that such procedure is efficient and appropriate in all the circumstances of the case.

(4) After providing the other party an opportunity to submit comments, the Arbitral Tribunal shall issue an order either dismissing the request or fixing the summary procedure in the form it deems appropriate.

The *Note to Parties and Arbitral Tribunals on the Conduct of the Arbitration Under the ICC Rules of Arbitration* [hereinafter "ICC Note"] issued in October 2017 by the ICC contain similar language and procedures.[40] The new HKIAC Arbitration Rules (2018) also contains similar language. Art. 43 "Early Determination Procedure" provides in part:

> 43.1 The arbitral tribunal shall have the power, at the request of any party and after consulting with all other parties, to decide one or more points of law or fact by way of early determination procedure, on the basis that:
> (a) such points of law or fact are manifestly without merit; or
> (b) such points of law or fact are manifestly outside the arbitral tribunal's jurisdiction; or
> (c) even if such points of law or fact are submitted by another party and are assumed to be correct, no award could be rendered in favour of that party.

The intended purpose of a summary procedure is to expedite the arbitral process by the early elimination of baseless claims, counterclaims or defences. The

(5) In determining whether to grant a request for summary procedure, the Arbitral Tribunal shall have regard to all relevant circumstances, including the extent to which the summary procedure contributes to a more efficient and expeditious resolution of the dispute.

(6) If the request for summary procedure is granted, the Arbitral Tribunal shall seek to make its order or award on the issues under consideration in an efficient and expeditious manner having regard to the circumstances of the case, while giving each party an equal and reasonable opportunity to present its case pursuant to Article 23 (2).

[40] The ICC Note provides:

B – Expeditious and Efficient Conduct of the Arbitration

57. The Rules require the arbitral tribunal and the parties to make every effort to conduct the arbitration in an expeditious and cost-effective manner, having regard to the complexity and value of the dispute (Article 22(1)).

. . .

C – Expeditious Determination of Manifestly Unmeritorious Claims or Defenses

59. This section includes guidance as to how an application for the expeditious determination of manifestly unmeritorious claims or defenses may be dealt with, within the broad scope of Article 22.

60. Any party may apply to the arbitral tribunal for the expeditious determination of one or more claims or defenses, on grounds that such claims or defenses are manifestly devoid of merit or fall manifestly outside the arbitral tribunal's jurisdiction ("application"). The application must be made as promptly as possible after the filing of the relevant claims or defenses.

61. The arbitral tribunal has full discretion to decide whether to allow the application to proceed. In so doing, it shall take into consideration any circumstances it considers to be relevant, including . . . the need to ensure time and cost efficiency.

62. If the arbitral tribunal allows the application to proceed it shall promptly adopt the procedural measures it considers appropriate, after consulting the parties. The responding party or parties shall be given a fair opportunity to answer the application. Further presentation of evidence will be allowed only exceptionally. When the arbitral tribunal determines that a hearing is appropriate, such hearing may be conducted by videoconference, telephone or similar means of communication.

63. . . . the arbitral tribunal shall decide the application as promptly as possible and state the reasons for its decision in as concise a fashion as possible. The decision may be in the form of an order or award. . . . the arbitral tribunal may decide on the costs of the application pursuant to Article 38 or reserve this decision to a later stage.

. . .

standard to be achieved for a successful summary procedure is high. The commonly used language is "manifestly devoid of merit" or "manifestly outside of the arbitral tribunal's jurisdiction." Nonetheless, if brought in good faith and if successful, a summary procedure would save both time and expense. On the other hand, abuse of this procedure would result in increased time and expense being wasted on a frivolous proposal to undertake an early determination procedure. One final note concerning summary procedure is an arbitral tribunal may decline to consider adopting such a process due to what is termed *due process paranoia*.[41]

VIII. Consolidation

Consolidation is the bringing together of several cases into one arbitration. This procedure has been available for some time.[42] However, consolidation is usually possible only where the cases are within the same institution's jurisdiction, as the generally accepted interpretation of "arbitration agreements to be compatible" is

---

[41] As defined by one source:

> Due process paranoia is defined by the [2015 Queen Mary International Arbitration Survey entitled "Improvements and Innovations in International Arbitration"] as "a perceived reluctance by [arbitral] tribunals to act decisively in certain situations for fear of the award being challenged on the basis of a party not having had the chance to present its case fully".

Due Process Paranoia, Kluwer Arbitration Blog (June 16, 2016). Link: http://arbitrationblog.kluwerarbitration.com/2016/06/06/due-process-paranoia/ [last visited 8 Aug. 2017].

In a subsequent blog on this topic, the authors stated:

> In that first blog, due process paranoia was defined as the perceived reluctance by arbitral tribunals to act decisively (for example by rejecting applications for extensions of time, refusing amendments to submissions, rejecting new evidence or declining to reschedule a hearing) for fear of the award being challenged on the basis of a party not having had the chance to present its case fully.

Due Process Paranoia (Part 2): Assessing the Enforcement Risk under the English Arbitration Act, Kluwer Arbitration Blog (Feb 20, 2017). Link: http://arbitrationblog.kluwerarbitration.com/2017/02/20/due-process-paranoia-part-2-assessing-the-enforcement-risk-under-the-english-arbitration-act/ [last visited Aug. 8, 2017].

For further discussion, *see also* Klaus Peter Berger, J. Ole Jensen, *Due process paranoia and the procedural judgment rule: a safe harbor for procedural management decisions by international arbitrators, 32(3)* Arbitration International 415 (2017).

[42] For example, Art 10 of the ICC Rules, *supra* note 1, provides:

> Consolidation of Arbitrations
>
> The Court may, at the request of a party, consolidate two or more arbitrations pending under the Rules into a single arbitration, where:
>
> a) the parties have agreed to consolidation; or
>
> b) all of the claims in the arbitrations are made under the same arbitration agreement; or
>
> c) where the claims in the arbitrations are made under more than one arbitration agreement, the arbitrations are between the same parties, the disputes in the arbitrations arise in connection with the same legal relationship, and the Court finds the arbitration agreements to be compatible.
>
> . . .

See also:

- the DIS Arbitration Rules (2018), Art. 17: Multi-Contract Arbitration, and, Art. 18: Multi-Party Arbitration
- the SCC's Rules for Expedited Arbitrations (2017), Art. 15: Multiple contracts in a single arbitration, and, Art. 16: Consolidation of arbitrations
- Asian International Arbitration Centre [hereinafter "AIAC"] Arbitration Rules (2018), Rule 10: Consolidation of Proceedings and Concurrent Hearings.

that the same institutional rules apply to the two arbitrations to be consolidated.[43] For example, pursuant to the HKIAC Administered Arbitration Rules, the:

> HKIAC shall have the power, at the request of a party and after consulting with the parties and any confirmed or appointed arbitrators, to consolidate two or more arbitrations pending under these Rules where:
> (a) the parties agree to consolidate; or
> (b) all of the claims in the arbitrations are made under the same arbitration agreement; or
> (c) the claims are made under more than one arbitration agreement, a common question of law or fact arises in all of the arbitrations, the rights to relief claimed are in respect of, or arise out of, the same transaction or a series of related transactions and the arbitration agreements are compatible.[44]

Recently, SIAC proposed cross-institutional consolidations in order to avoid fragmentation of disputes involving similar or identical factual or legal issues arising from one complex project such as a large construction project involving many sub-contractors, suppliers, guarantor banks, insurance companies, and the like.[45] SIAC's proposal is for:

---

43 As explained in a press release:

> Rules on consolidation, joinder and intervention in international arbitration play an important role in the international arbitral process. By allowing related issues to be resolved in a single proceeding, consolidation permits more efficient and cost-effective dispute resolution, whilst minimising the risk of inconsistent decisions in related disputes.
>
> These benefits have led a number of arbitral institutions to adopt provisions in their institutional rules that allow the consolidation of related disputes and/or the joinder of additional parties. The 2016 SIAC Arbitration Rules contain a state-of-the art set of provisions for consolidation, as do the rules of other leading arbitral institutions, including the International Chamber of Commerce Court of Arbitration (ICC).
>
> Importantly, however, the consolidation provisions of existing institutional rules of leading arbitral institutions do not permit the consolidation of arbitrations that are subject to different sets of institutional arbitration rules (for example, SIAC and ICC arbitrations), even if they satisfy the other criteria for consolidation. Instead, existing institutional rules provide for the consolidation of arbitral proceedings only where the parties' various arbitration agreements are compatible, including by incorporating the same institutional arbitration rules. Thus, a SIAC arbitration can be consolidated with another SIAC arbitration, but not with an ICC arbitration; likewise, an ICC arbitration can be consolidated with another ICC arbitration, but an ICC arbitration cannot be consolidated with a SIAC arbitration.

Singapore International Arbitration Centre, *Proposal on Cross-Institution Consolidation Protocol*, Press Release (December 19, 2017) [hereinafter SIAC Proposal]. Link:
http://www.siac.org.sg/images/stories/press_release/2017/%5bPress%20Release%5d%20PROPOSAL%20ON%20CROSS-INSTITUTION%20CONSOLIDATION%20%20PROTOCOL.pdf (Last visited: Dec 29, 2017).

44 Art. 28.1 of the HKIAC Administered Arbitration Rules, *supra* note 26.

45 A recent example of this fragmentation is the dispute involving *Autoridad del Canal de Panama v Sacyr SA* which resulted in two cases: [2017] EWHC 2228 (Comm) and [2017] EWHC 2337 (Comm). The dispute involved the widening of the Panama Canal, a project awarded to a consortium by the Panama Canal Authority. The consortium obtained financial guarantees in favour of the Panama Canal Authority. These guarantees provided for ICC arbitration in Miami with Panamanian law being the substantive law. Later guarantees provided for resort to the English courts, applying UK law to these guarantee contracts. In the first court case, the judge declined to stay the court proceedings in favour of the arbitration being started in Miami, as the "matter" before the court was not the same, albeit related, "matter" being referred to arbitration. Therefore, the English court had exclusive jurisdiction. In the second of the litigation cases, the consortium argued for a delay in the trial court proceedings

a cross-institution consolidation protocol, which leading arbitral institutions could adopt and incorporate into their institutional arbitration rules and utilise for administering consolidated arbitrations:

a. The consolidation protocol would set out a new, standalone mechanism for addressing the timing of consolidation applications, the appropriate decision-maker (*i.e.* the institution(s) or the tribunal) and the applicable criteria to determine when arbitral proceedings are sufficiently related to warrant cross-institution consolidation. A joint committee appointed from members of the Courts or Boards of the concerned arbitral institutions would be mandated to decide the applications, with a specific committee being appointed for each application.
b. Once consolidated, the proceedings should be administered only by one institution applying its own arbitration rules. The institutions can agree on objective criteria to determine which institution should administer the consolidated dispute, such as the number of disputes subject to the different rules or the time of commencement of the first proceeding.

The arbitral institutions' rules would be amended to incorporate the consolidation protocol. By adopting the institutional rules in their arbitration agreements, parties would in turn give the protocol the same contractual force as other provisions of the institutional rules. The consolidation protocol would not change the current requirement that the arbitration agreements designate the same seat.

The consolidation of arbitral proceedings offers important benefits to parties that help reduce the complexity, cost and time of proceedings. The cross-institution consolidation of arbitrations under different institutional rules takes these benefits further, making arbitration an even more effective system of dispute resolution.[46]

IX. Joinder

Like the concept of consolidation, joinder is intended to address disputes arising from multiple parties and/or multiple contracts. *Joinder* is "the uniting of parties or claims in a single lawsuit."[47] For example, the DIS Arbitration Rules in Art. 19 provide for "Joinder of Additional Parties." Likewise, the SCC's Expedited Rules in Art. 14 provide for "Joinder of additional parties" and the SCC's Arbitration Rules (2017) in Art. 13 provides for the same. The latest set of arbitration rules by the Kuala Lumpur Regional Arbitration Centre[48] in Rule 9 provides for "Joinder of

while the consortium sought leave to appeal from the Court of Appeal. The consortium further argued that by further participating in the litigation, the consortium would be deemed to have waived its right to arbitrate. The trial court rejected both of the consortium's arguments.

46 SIAC Proposal, *supra* note 41.

The SIAC proposal itself, titled *Memorandum Regarding Proposal on Cross-Institution Consolidation Protocol*, is available online: http://www.siac.org.sg/images/stories/press_release/2017/Memorandum%20on%20Cross-Institutional%20Consolidation%20(with%20%20annexes).pdf (last visited: 29 Dec. 2017).

47 Black's, *supra* note 5, at 965.

48 Officially renamed in February 2018 as the "Asian International Arbitration Centre." *See* the AIAC Arbitration Rules (2018), Rule 9.

Parties." The latest version of arbitration rules by the HKIAC provides in Art. 27 for "Joinder of Additional Parties."

X. Hybrid Processes

The DIS issued a new set of arbitration rules in 2018. Art. 26 of these rules provides in full: "Unless any party objects thereto, the arbitral tribunal shall, at every stage of the arbitration, seek to encourage an amicable settlement of the dispute or of individual disputed issues." This provision seems to expand the role of the tribunal in permitting the tribunal to participate in assisting amicable settlement.

Other jurisdictions such Hong Kong,[49] New Zealand[50] and Australia[51] permit an arbitration/mediation/arbitration procedure before the same neutral. Singapore provides for a similar process; however, the arbitration procedure is conducted at the Singapore International Arbitration Centre while the mediation process is conducted at the Singapore International Mediation Centre, before different neutrals at each centre.[52]

Proponents posit that the purpose of these hybrid processes is to save time and costs, as there is no duplication of time to convey the case to different neutrals: the mediator and the arbitral tribunal. Additionally, having one neutral familiar with the details of the case would assist in the neutral's evaluation of the parties'

---

[49] *Arbitration Ordinance*, *supra* note 20, at § 33 states:

33. Power of arbitrator to act as mediator

(1) If all parties consent in writing, and for so long as no party withdraws the party's consent in writing, an arbitrator may act as a mediator after the arbitral proceedings have commenced.

(2) If an arbitrator acts as a mediator, the arbitral proceedings must be stayed to facilitate the conduct of the mediation proceedings.

(3) An arbitrator who is acting as a mediator—
   (a) may communicate with the parties collectively or separately; and
   (b) must treat the information obtained by the arbitrator from a party as confidential, unless otherwise agreed by that party or unless subsection (4) applies.

(4) If—
   (a) confidential information is obtained by an arbitrator from a party during the mediation proceedings conducted by the arbitrator as a mediator; and
   (b) those mediation proceedings terminate without reaching a settlement acceptable to the parties,

   the arbitrator must, before resuming the arbitral proceedings, disclose to all other parties as much of that information as the arbitrator considers is material to the arbitral proceedings.

(5) No objection may be made against the conduct of the arbitral proceedings by an arbitrator solely on the ground that the arbitrator had acted previously as a mediator in accordance with this section.

[50] The New Zealand International Arbitration Centre refers to this process as *Arb – Med*. *See* the Centre's Arb – Med Rules available at: https://www.nziac.com/arb-med/arb-med-rules/ (Last visited 3 May 2018).

[51] For domestic arbitrations only. *See, e.g.*, § 27D of the *Commercial Arbitration Act 2017* for the Australian Capital Territory. Link: http://www.legislation.act.gov.au/a/2017-7/current/pdf/2017-7.pdf (last visited 3 May 2018). New South Wales' *Commercial Arbitration Act 2010* contains identical provision as does South Australia's *Commercial Arbitration Act 2011*.

[52] *See, e.g.*, Christopher Boog, *The New SIAC/SIMC AMA-Protocol: A Seamless Multi-tiered Dispute Resolution Process Tailored to the User's Needs*, Asian Dispute Review 91 (2015).

positions which in the mediation phase might encourage the parties to reconsider their positions.

Another advantage of these hybrid processes is that any settlement agreement reached during the mediation phase can be incorporated into a final award which would be easily enforceable internationally through the *New York Convention*. While this procedure remains an advantage, its effect is anticipated to be diminished with the impending implementation of the *Convention on International Settlement Agreements Resulting from Mediation* (to be known as the *Singapore Convention* 2019) which would permit the international enforcement of mediation settlements in a similar manner to the international enforcement of arbitration awards under the *New York Convention*.[53]

Opponents posit that there is a reluctance to adopt these hybrid processes, especially by practitioners trained in the common-law legal system due to the perception of a conflict of interest when a single neutral assumes both an arbitrator's role and a mediator's role.[54] This conflict is most obvious in the treatment of confidential and privileged information obtained during the mediation phase when in private caucus sessions, where each party is encouraged to make full and frank disclosure. Should this phase be unsuccessful, there is a perception that the information obtained might influence the neutral's adjudication of the resumed arbitration.

This tension is further exacerbated by the requirement that confidential information obtained during the private caucus during the mediation phase is to be disclosed to the other party. For example, the *Arbitration Ordinance* at § 33(4) provides:

> If confidential information is obtained by an arbitrator from a party during the mediation proceedings conducted by the arbitrator as a mediator; and those mediation proceedings terminate without reaching a settlement acceptable to the parties, *the arbitrator must*, before resuming the arbitral proceedings, *disclose to all other parties as much of that information as the arbitrator considers is material* to the arbitral proceedings. (emphasis added)

There is also a tension in a blended mediation and arbitration procedure on a theoretical basis. Mediation, particularly facilitative mediation, is seen as a process where a neutral facilitates the parties to negotiate an acceptable settlement based on the parties' true needs rather than perceived legal rights. Arbitration, on the other hand, is seen more as private litigation where the neutral serves as the decision-maker determining each party's legal rights rather than as facilitator.

The traditional stepped-process contained in a multi-tiered dispute resolution clause, also known as an *escalation clause*, seems less controversial. Here, for example, the parties may require friendly negotiation between them to be concluded within a contract-specified time, failing which the parties would proceed to

---

[53] Also discussed in Chapter 1 along with the *Singapore Convention* is the UNICTRAL *Model Law on International Commercial Mediation and International Settlement Agreements Resulting from Mediation* (2018).

[54] Those practitioners from other legal systems, particularly the PRC and Germany, seem to have less reluctance to adopt these hybrid procedures.

mediation with one neutral with settlement before a contract-specified time, failing which the parties would proceed to arbitration before a different neutral. This type of dispute resolution clause has been held to be a valid arbitration clause.[55] Further, each step in the dispute resolution process is considered to be a pre-requisite before escalation to the next step.[56]

XI. Summary

In this chapter, we gathered a variety of time-saving and cost-saving measures which are intended to lower the costs of an arbitration. Some of these diverse and unrelated measures are already in use and accepted as a standard or routine choice for the parties or the tribunal. Other measures are more innovative and not as readily accepted due to the measure's untested nature. An example of this reluctance to adopt new measures can be seen as a result of the cases of *AQZ v ARA* and *Noble Resources v Shanghai Good Credit*, where in each case the validity of the award was challenged. As the principal purpose of an arbitral tribunal is to produce a valid and thus enforceable award, due process paranoia might limit the inclination to adopt innovative approaches to expedite proceedings. A uniform interpretation and application of the rules and certainty of enforcement should eliminate inconsistencies and uncertainty, which are an anathema for business and for arbitration.

---

[55] *Ling Kong Henry v Tanglin Club* [2018] SGHC 153; *Westco Airconditioning Ltd v Siu Chong Construction & Engineering* [1998] 1 HKC 254; and, *Channel Tunnel Group v Balfour Beatty Ltd* [1993] 1 All ER 664. *See also Lim Choon Hock (also known as William Lim) v Hung Ka Hai Clement* [2016] HKCFI 1439; *Emirates Trading Agency LLC v Prime Mineral Exports Private Limited* [2014] EWHC 2104 (Comm); and, Ewelina Kajkowska, Enforceability of Multi-Tiered Dispute Resolution Clauses (2017).

[56] *See, e.g., Peterborough City Council v Enterprise Managed Services Ltd* [2014] EWHC 3193; *DGT Steel and Cladding Ltd v Cubitt Building and Interiors Ltd* [2007] EWHC 1584 (TCC).

Table of Cases

Table of Legislation (Institutional Rules and Other Publications)

Arbitral Institutions' Rules (alphabetized by institutions' acronym: AIAC, ICC, HKIAC, LCIA, SIAC)

Other Publications

Table of Legislation (Laws and Subsidiary Legislation)

Miscellaneous Conventions

Index

www.ingramcontent.com/pod-product-compliance
Ingram Content Group UK Ltd.
Pitfield, Milton Keynes, MK11 3LW, UK
UKHW021836100926
8556IPUK00004B/380

9 789888 528226